By Shotaro Ishinomori

The Legend of Zelda™
A Link to the Past

Story & Art by Shotaro Ishinomori

The Legend of Zelda: A Link to the Past
TM & © 2015 Nintendo. All Rights Reserved.

THE LEGEND OF ZELDA: A LINK TO THE PAST
by Shotaro ISHINOMORI
Book planning and editing: APE/Shigesato ITOI
©1993 ISHIMORI PRO
All rights reserved.
Original Japanese edition published by SHOGAKUKAN.
English translation rights in the United State of America, Canada,
the United Kingdom, Ireland, Australia and New Zealand arranged
with SHOGAKUKAN.
Previously published as a comic series in Volumes 32-43 of Nintendo
Power Magazine. Copyright © 1992. All Rights Reserved.
All characters featured in this issue and the distinctive likenesses thereof
are trademarks of Nintendo of America Inc.

Translation / Dan Owsen
Cover & Interior Design / Yukiko Whitley
Design Assistant / Justin Brillo
Editor / Elizabeth Kawasaki

Printed in the U.S.A.

Published by VIZ Media, LLC
1355 Market St., Suite 200
San Francisco, CA 94103

10 9 8 7 6 5 4 3 2 1
First printing, May 2015

www.viz.com

www.perfectsquare.com

THE LEGEND OF
ZELDA
A LINK TO THE PAST

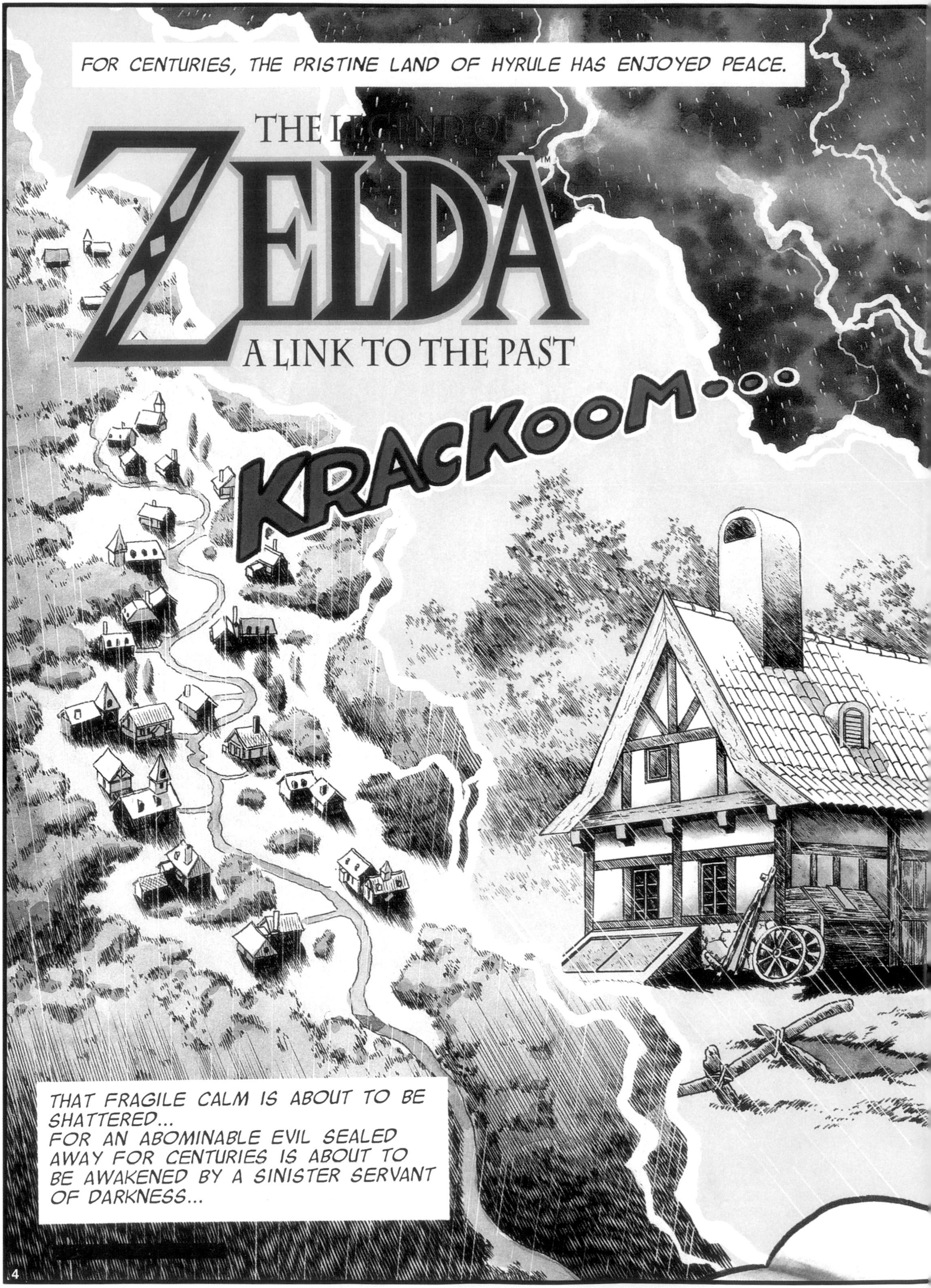
FOR CENTURIES, THE PRISTINE LAND OF HYRULE HAS ENJOYED PEACE.
THE LEGEND OF ZELDA™ A LINK TO THE PAST
KRACKOOM...
THAT FRAGILE CALM IS ABOUT TO BE SHATTERED... FOR AN ABOMINABLE EVIL SEALED AWAY FOR CENTURIES IS ABOUT TO BE AWAKENED BY A SINISTER SERVANT OF DARKNESS...

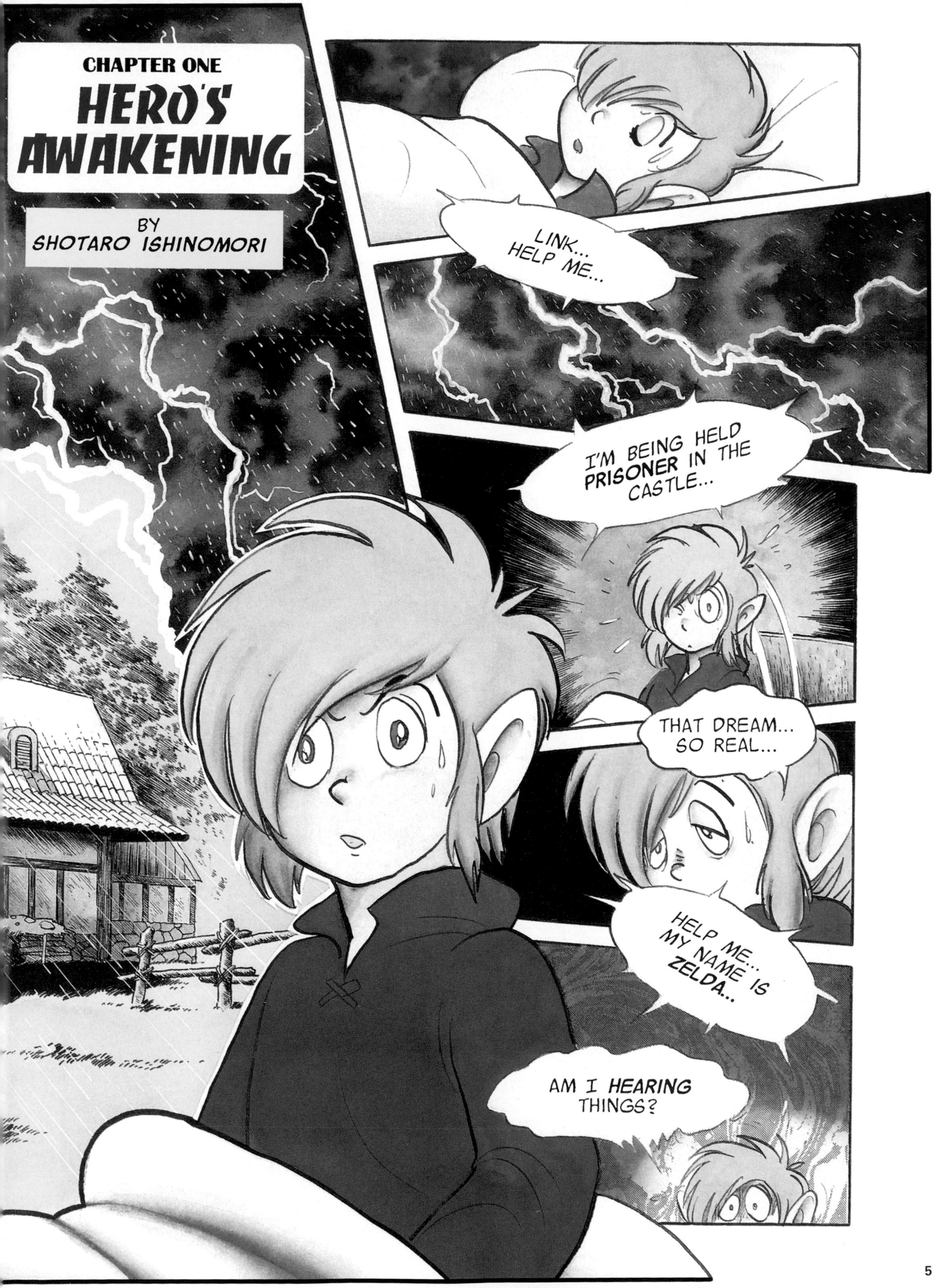
CHAPTER ONE
HERO'S AWAKENING
BY SHOTARO ISHINOMORI
LINK... HELP ME...
I'M BEING HELD PRISONER IN THE CASTLE...
THAT DREAM... SO REAL...
HELP ME... MY NAME IS ZELDA...
AM I HEARING THINGS?

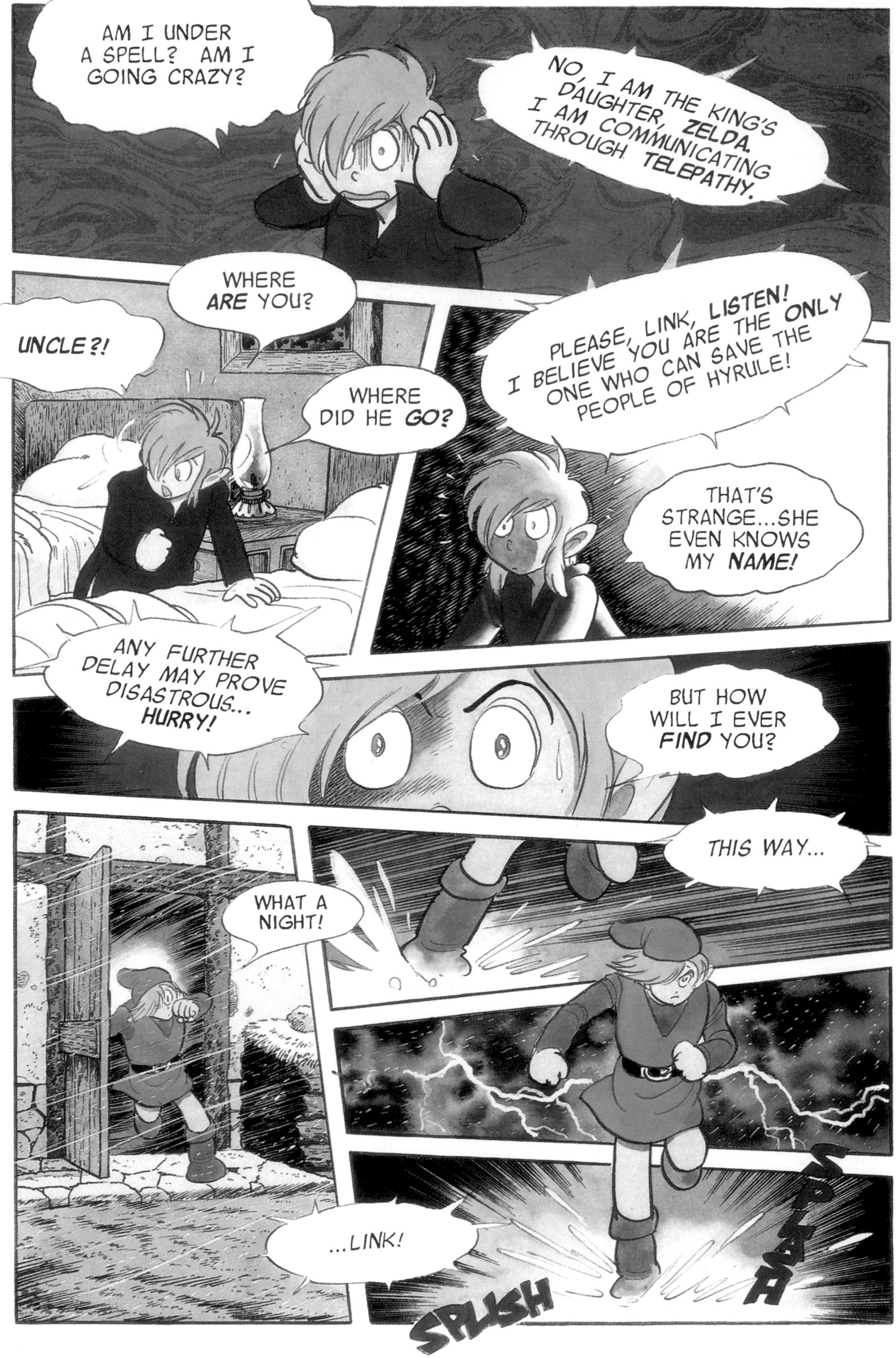
AM I UNDER A SPELL? AM I GOING CRAZY?
NO, I AM THE KING'S DAUGHTER, ZELDA. I AM COMMUNICATING THROUGH TELEPATHY.
UNCLE?!
WHERE ARE YOU?
WHERE DID HE GO?
PLEASE, LINK, LISTEN! I BELIEVE YOU ARE THE ONLY ONE WHO CAN SAVE THE PEOPLE OF HYRULE!
THAT'S STRANGE...SHE EVEN KNOWS MY NAME!
ANY FURTHER DELAY MAY PROVE DISASTROUS... HURRY!
BUT HOW WILL I EVER FIND YOU?
WHAT A NIGHT!
...LINK!
THIS WAY...
SPLISH
SPLASH

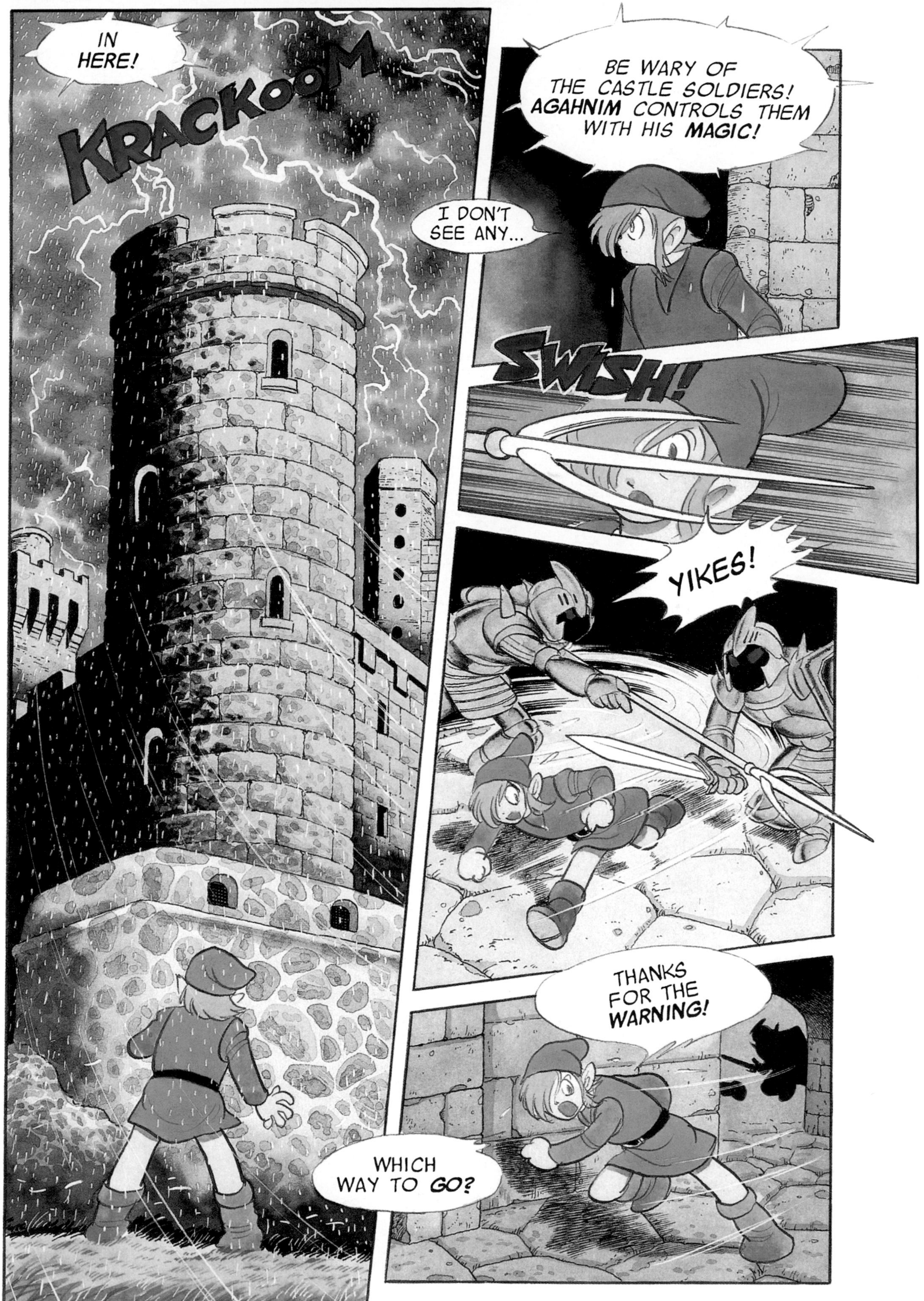

IN HERE!
KRACKOOM
BE WARY OF THE CASTLE SOLDIERS! AGAHNIM CONTROLS THEM WITH HIS MAGIC!
I DON'T SEE ANY...
SWISH!
YIKES!
WHICH WAY TO GO?
THANKS FOR THE WARNING!

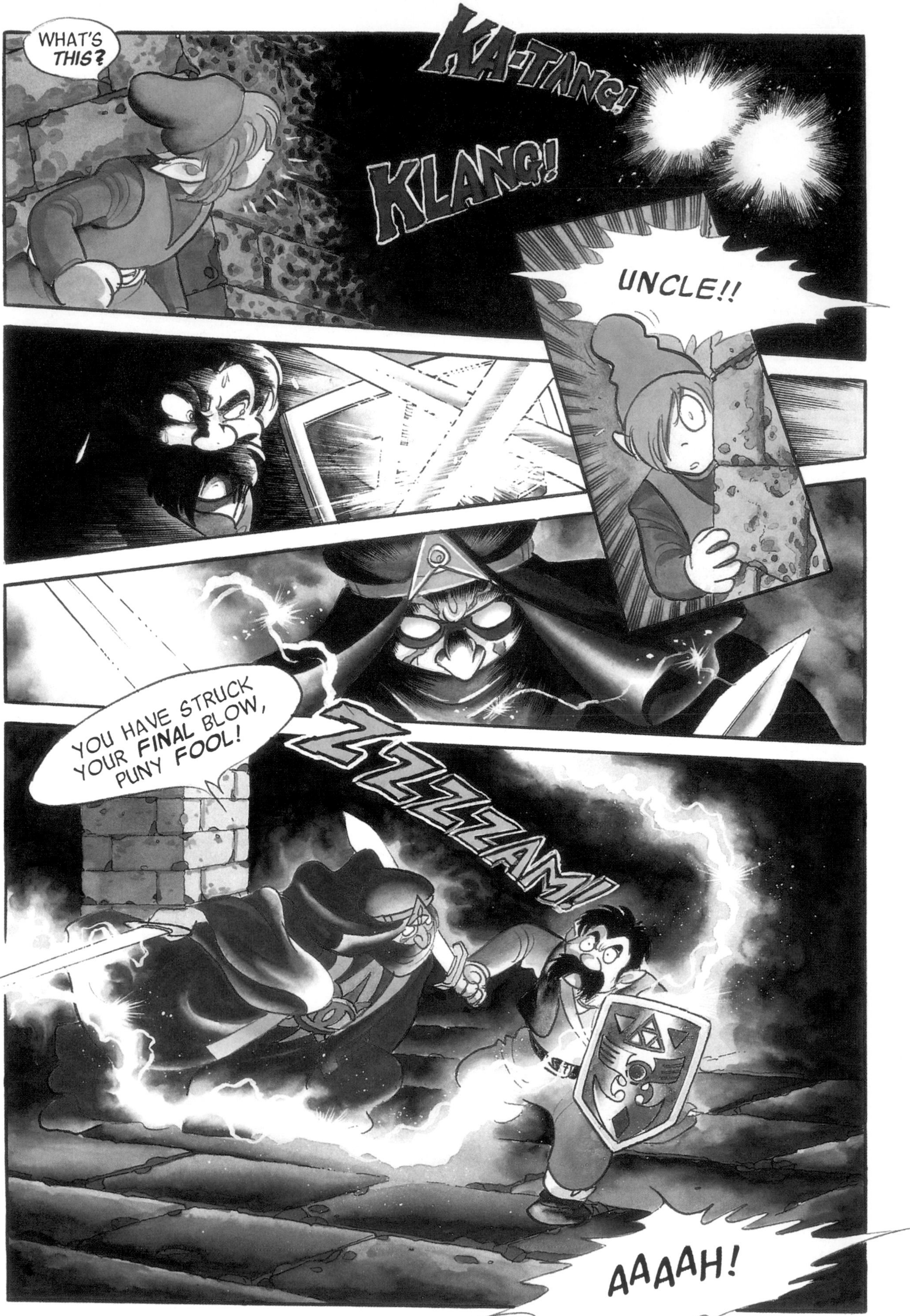
WHAT'S THIS?
KA-TANG!
KLANG!
UNCLE!!
YOU HAVE STRUCK YOUR FINAL BLOW, PUNY FOOL!
ZZZZZAM!!
AAAAH!

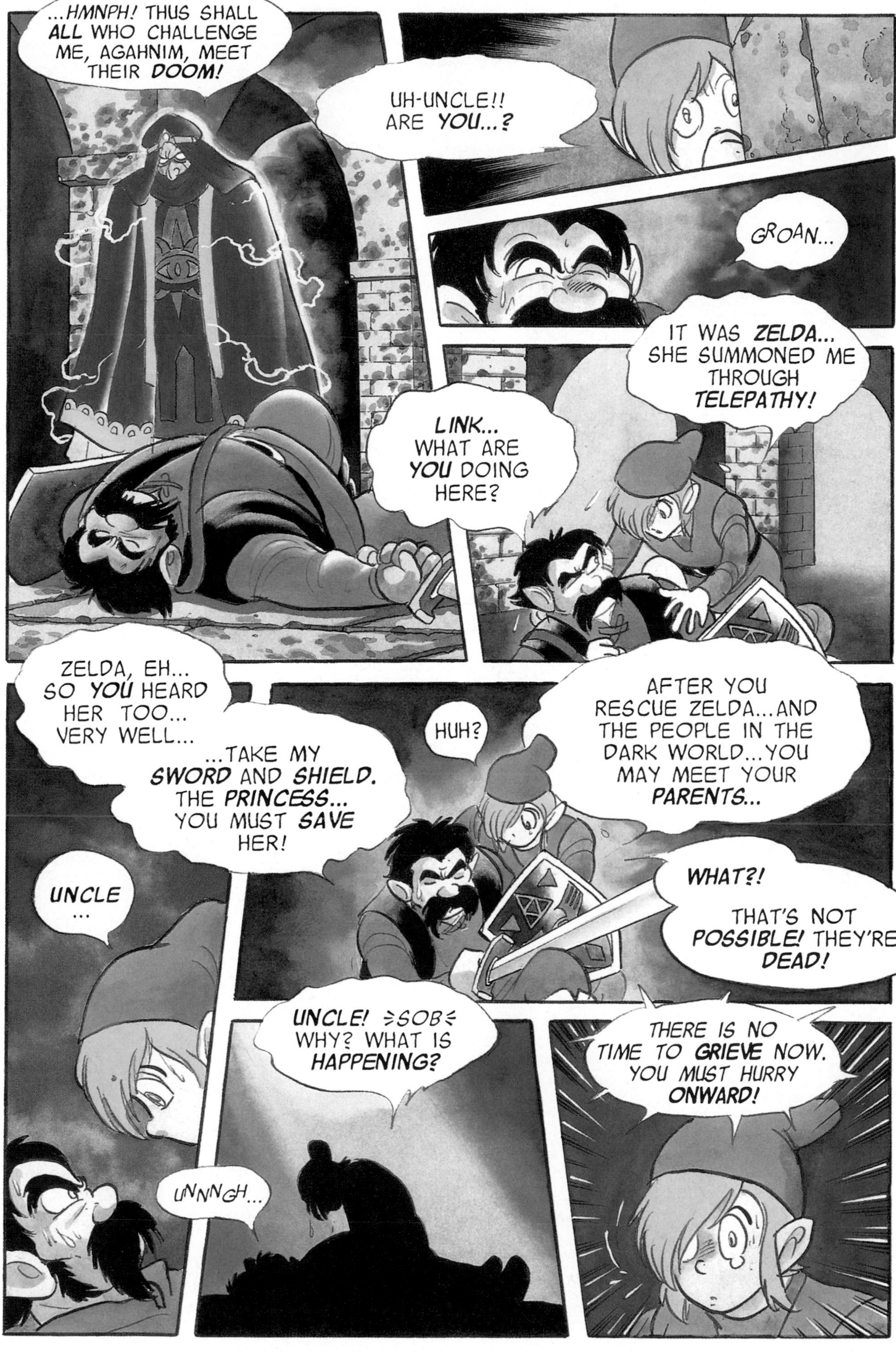
...HMNPH! THUS SHALL ALL WHO CHALLENGE ME, AGAHNIM, MEET THEIR DOOM!
UH-UNCLE!! ARE YOU...?
GROAN...
LINK... WHAT ARE YOU DOING HERE?
IT WAS ZELDA... SHE SUMMONED ME THROUGH TELEPATHY!
ZELDA, EH... SO YOU HEARD HER TOO... VERY WELL...
...TAKE MY SWORD AND SHIELD. THE PRINCESS... YOU MUST SAVE HER!
HUH?
AFTER YOU RESCUE ZELDA...AND THE PEOPLE IN THE DARK WORLD...YOU MAY MEET YOUR PARENTS...
UNCLE ...
WHAT?!
THAT'S NOT POSSIBLE! THEY'RE DEAD!
UNNNGH...
UNCLE! ≶SOB≶ WHY? WHAT IS HAPPENING?
THERE IS NO TIME TO GRIEVE NOW. YOU MUST HURRY ONWARD!

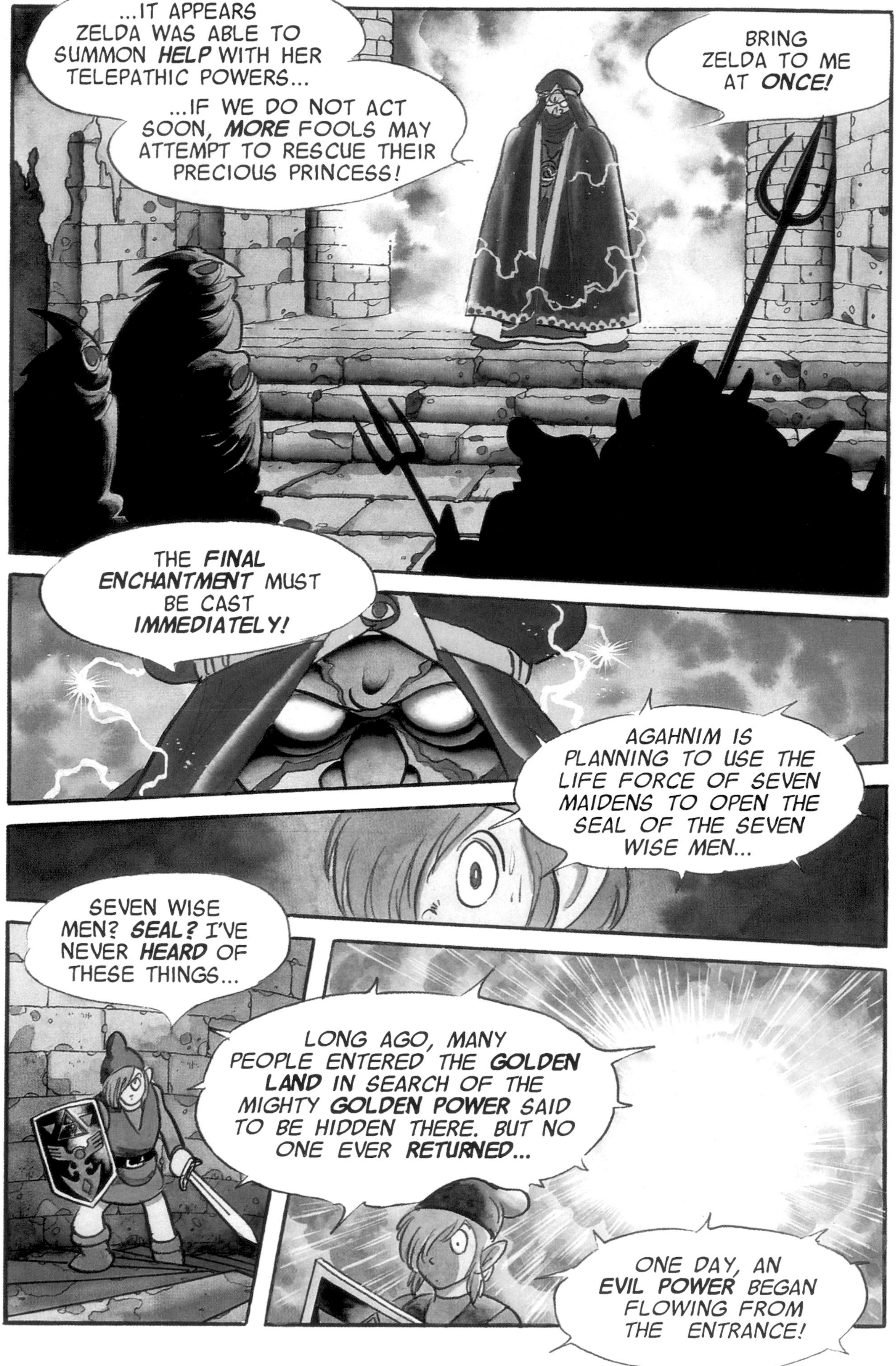
...IT APPEARS ZELDA WAS ABLE TO SUMMON HELP WITH HER TELEPATHIC POWERS...
...IF WE DO NOT ACT SOON, MORE FOOLS MAY ATTEMPT TO RESCUE THEIR PRECIOUS PRINCESS!
BRING ZELDA TO ME AT ONCE!
THE FINAL ENCHANTMENT MUST BE CAST IMMEDIATELY!
AGAHNIM IS PLANNING TO USE THE LIFE FORCE OF SEVEN MAIDENS TO OPEN THE SEAL OF THE SEVEN WISE MEN...
SEVEN WISE MEN? SEAL? I'VE NEVER HEARD OF THESE THINGS...
LONG AGO, MANY PEOPLE ENTERED THE GOLDEN LAND IN SEARCH OF THE MIGHTY GOLDEN POWER SAID TO BE HIDDEN THERE. BUT NO ONE EVER RETURNED...
ONE DAY, AN EVIL POWER BEGAN FLOWING FROM THE ENTRANCE!

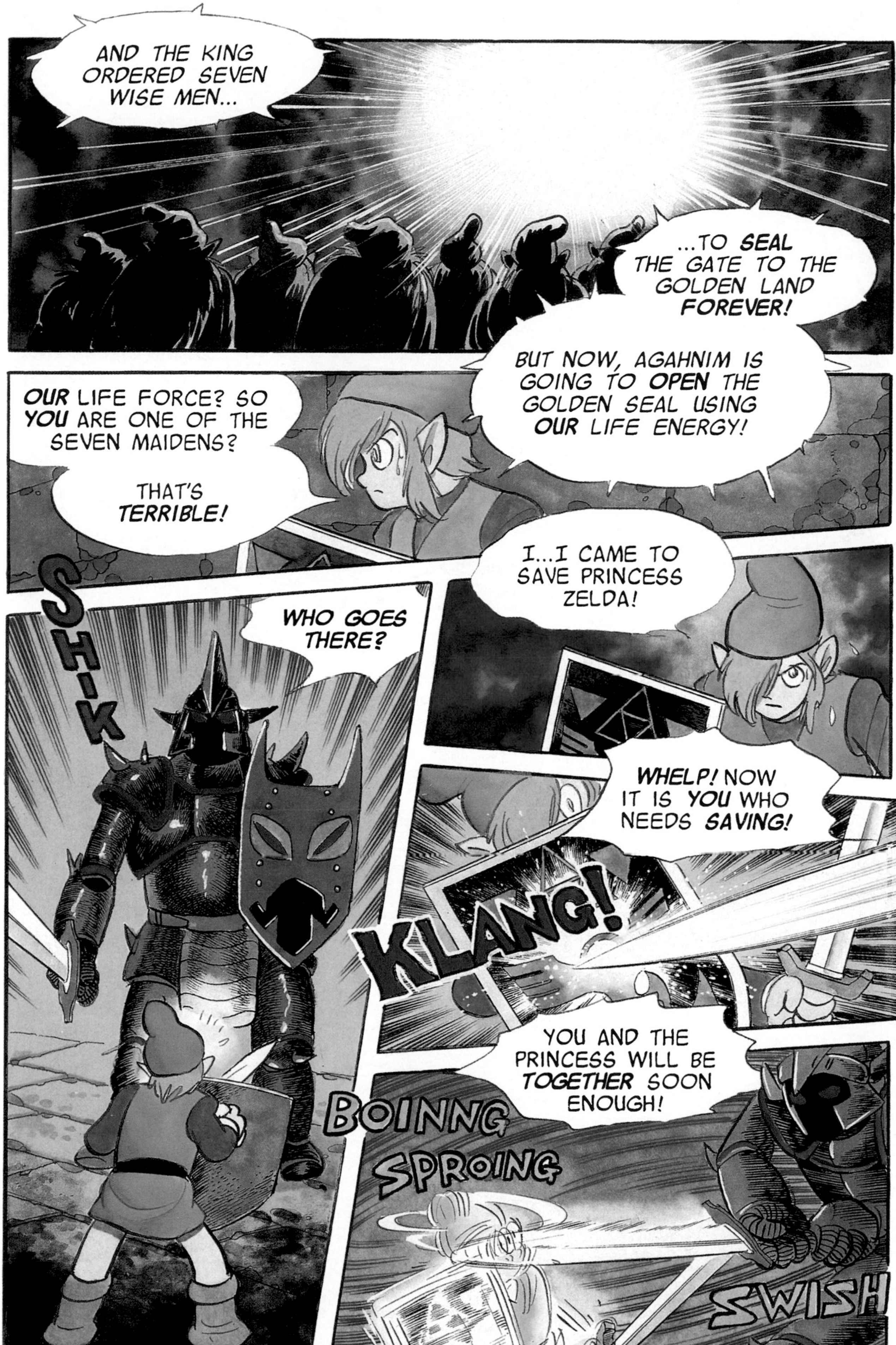
AND THE KING ORDERED SEVEN WISE MEN...
...TO SEAL THE GATE TO THE GOLDEN LAND FOREVER!
OUR LIFE FORCE? SO YOU ARE ONE OF THE SEVEN MAIDENS?
THAT'S TERRIBLE!
BUT NOW, AGAHNIM IS GOING TO OPEN THE GOLDEN SEAL USING OUR LIFE ENERGY!
SHIK
WHO GOES THERE?
I...I CAME TO SAVE PRINCESS ZELDA!
WHELP! NOW IT IS YOU WHO NEEDS SAVING!
KLANG!
YOU AND THE PRINCESS WILL BE TOGETHER SOON ENOUGH!
BOINNG
SPROING
SWISH

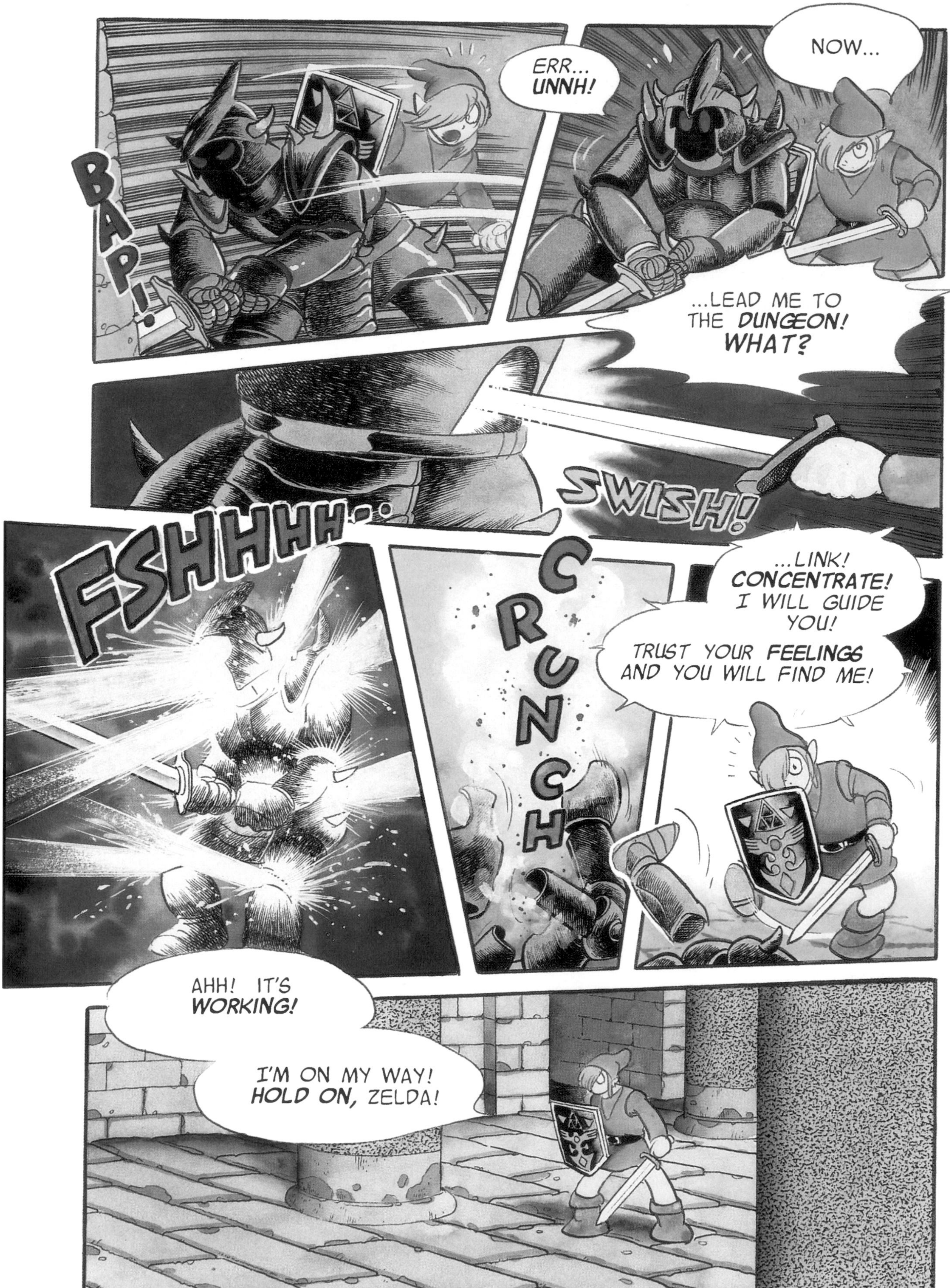
BAP!
ERR... UNNH!
NOW...
...LEAD ME TO THE DUNGEON! WHAT?
SWISH!
FSHHHH...
CRUNCH
...LINK! CONCENTRATE! I WILL GUIDE YOU!
TRUST YOUR FEELINGS AND YOU WILL FIND ME!
AHH! IT'S WORKING!
I'M ON MY WAY! HOLD ON, ZELDA!

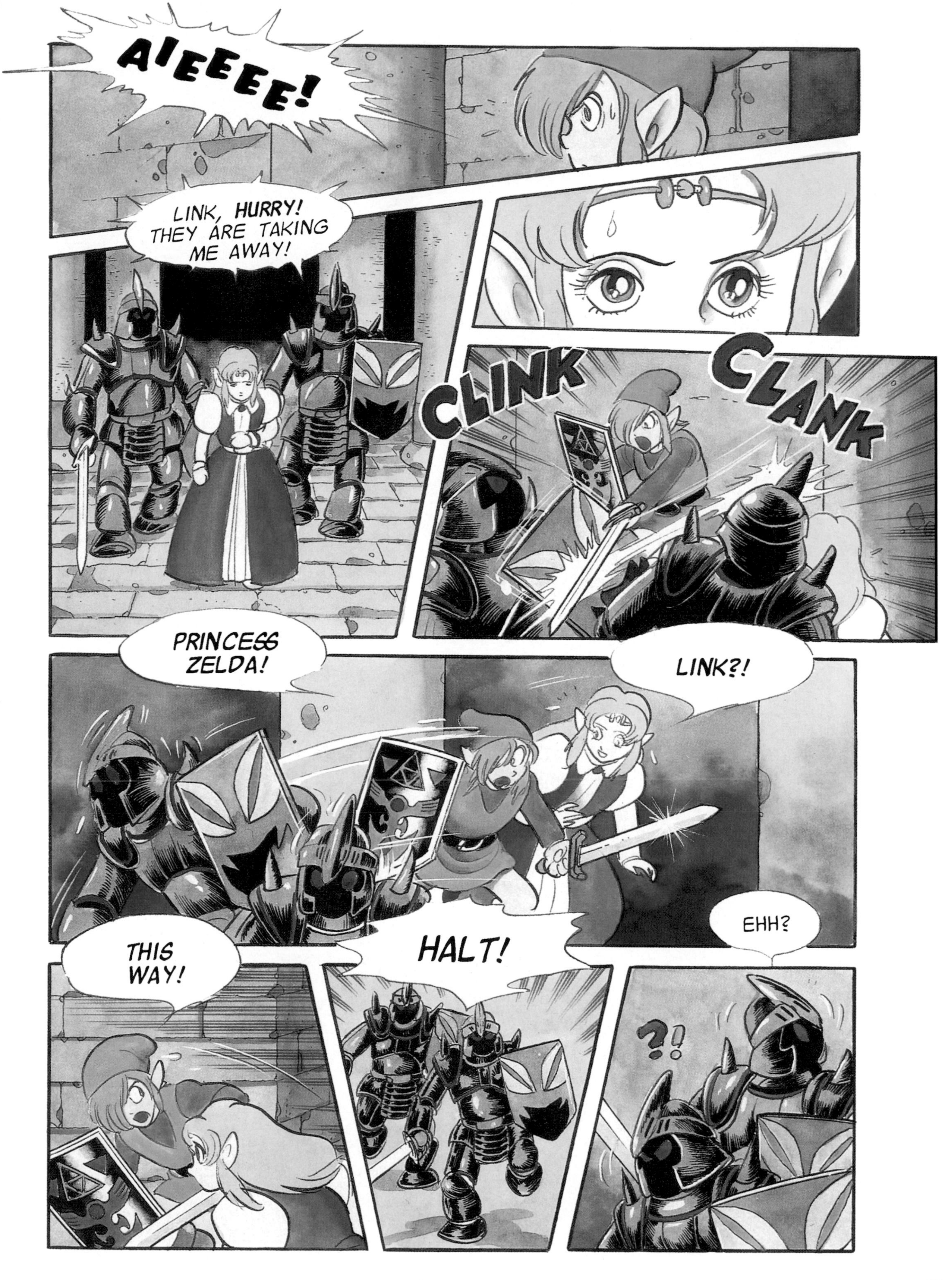
AIEEEEE!
LINK, HURRY! THEY ARE TAKING ME AWAY!
CLINK
CLANK
PRINCESS ZELDA!
LINK?!
THIS WAY!
HALT!
EHH?
?!

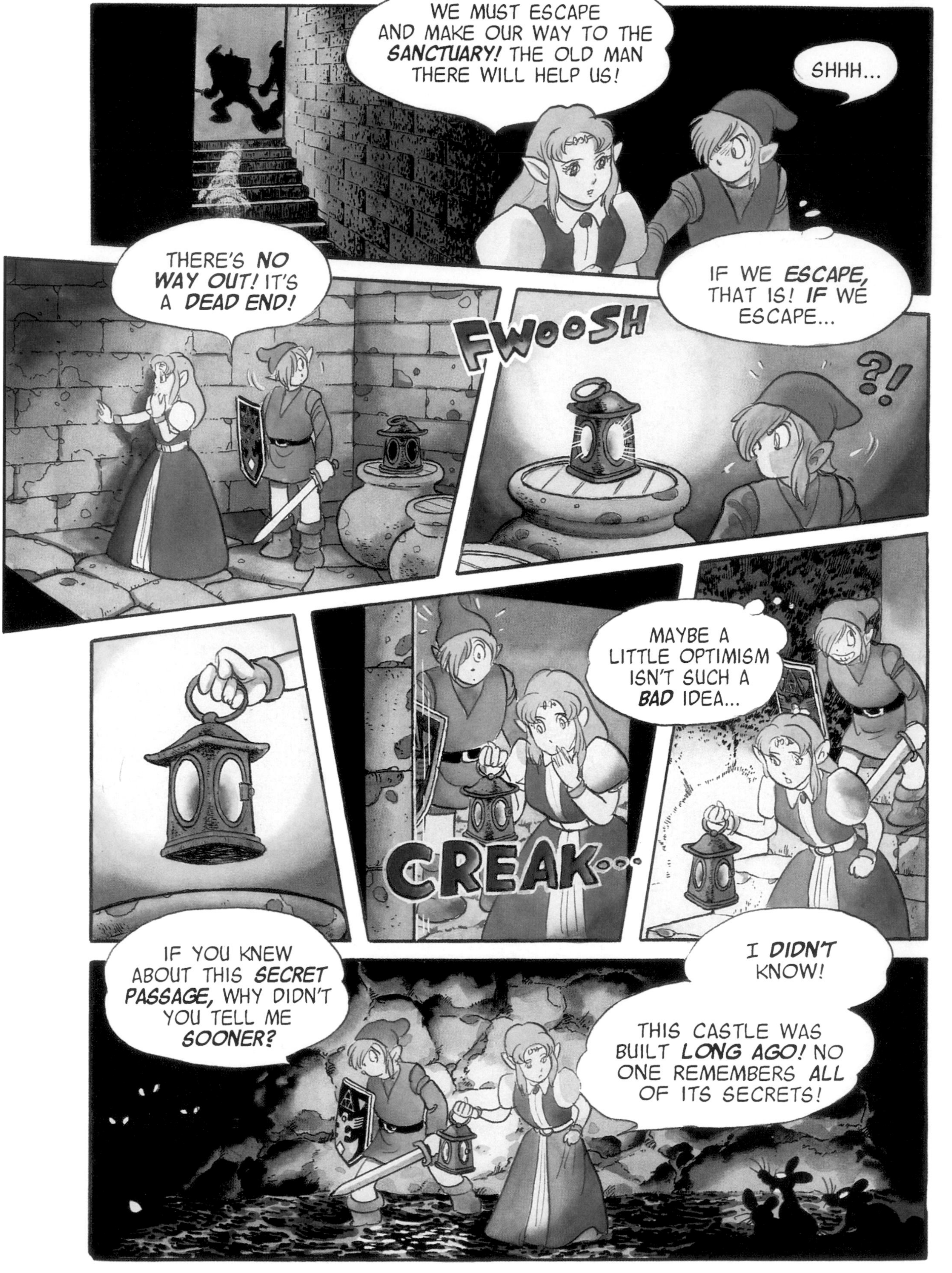
WE MUST ESCAPE AND MAKE OUR WAY TO THE SANCTUARY! THE OLD MAN THERE WILL HELP US!
SHHH...
THERE'S NO WAY OUT! IT'S A DEAD END!
IF WE ESCAPE, THAT IS! IF WE ESCAPE...
FWOOSH
?!
MAYBE A LITTLE OPTIMISM ISN'T SUCH A BAD IDEA...
CREAK...
IF YOU KNEW ABOUT THIS SECRET PASSAGE, WHY DIDN'T YOU TELL ME SOONER?
I DIDN'T KNOW!
THIS CASTLE WAS BUILT LONG AGO! NO ONE REMEMBERS ALL OF ITS SECRETS!

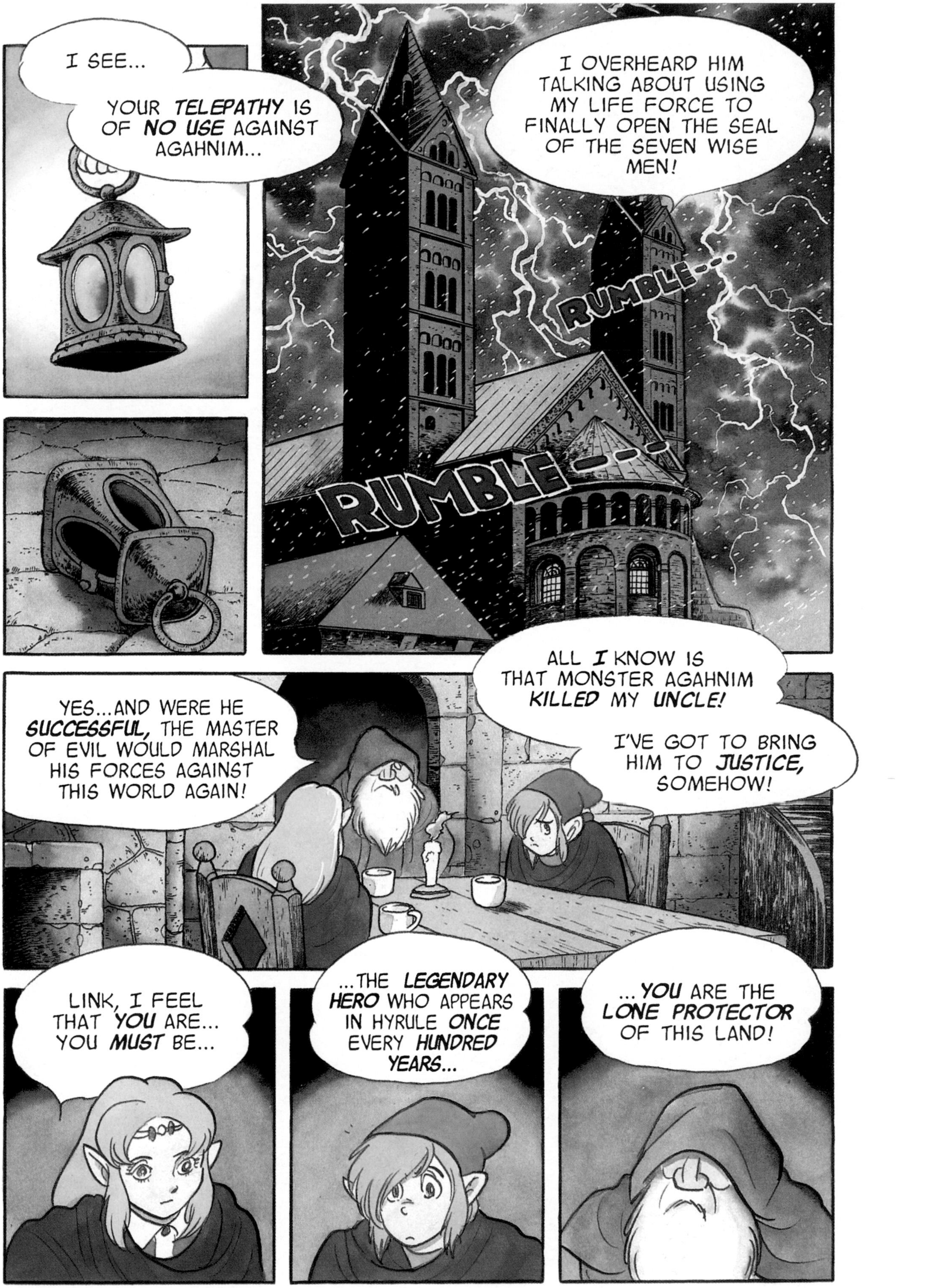
I SEE...
YOUR TELEPATHY IS OF NO USE AGAINST AGAHNIM...
I OVERHEARD HIM TALKING ABOUT USING MY LIFE FORCE TO FINALLY OPEN THE SEAL OF THE SEVEN WISE MEN!
RUMBLE...
RUMBLE...
YES...AND WERE HE SUCCESSFUL, THE MASTER OF EVIL WOULD MARSHAL HIS FORCES AGAINST THIS WORLD AGAIN!
ALL I KNOW IS THAT MONSTER AGAHNIM KILLED MY UNCLE!
I'VE GOT TO BRING HIM TO JUSTICE, SOMEHOW!
LINK, I FEEL THAT YOU ARE... YOU MUST BE...
...THE LEGENDARY HERO WHO APPEARS IN HYRULE ONCE EVERY HUNDRED YEARS...
...YOU ARE THE LONE PROTECTOR OF THIS LAND!

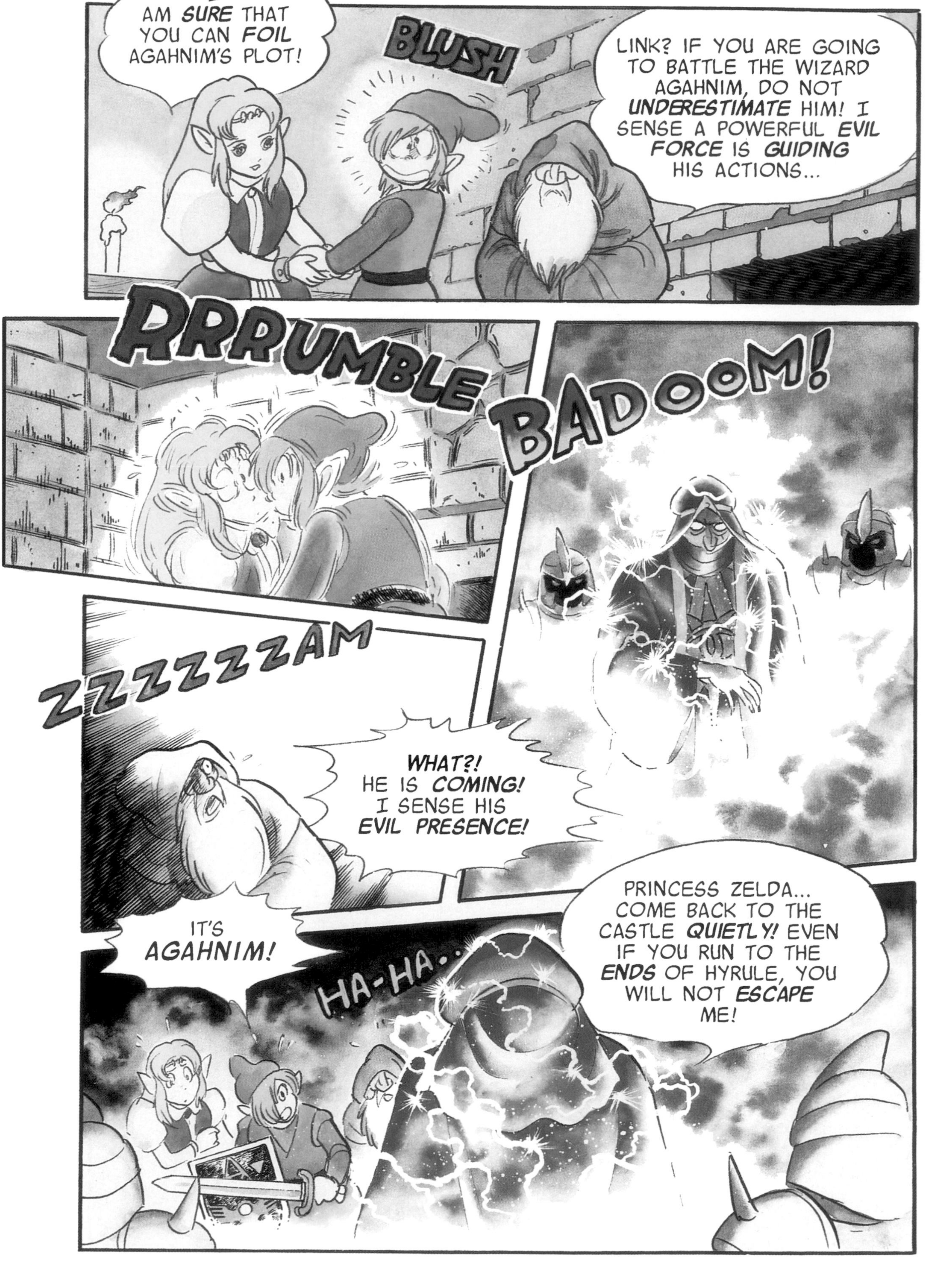
I AM SURE THAT YOU CAN FOIL AGAHNIM'S PLOT!
BLUSH
LINK? IF YOU ARE GOING TO BATTLE THE WIZARD AGAHNIM, DO NOT UNDERESTIMATE HIM! I SENSE A POWERFUL EVIL FORCE IS GUIDING HIS ACTIONS...
RRRUMBLE
ZZZZZZZAM
WHAT?! HE IS COMING! I SENSE HIS EVIL PRESENCE!
BADOOM!
IT'S AGAHNIM!
HA-HA...
PRINCESS ZELDA... COME BACK TO THE CASTLE QUIETLY! EVEN IF YOU RUN TO THE ENDS OF HYRULE, YOU WILL NOT ESCAPE ME!

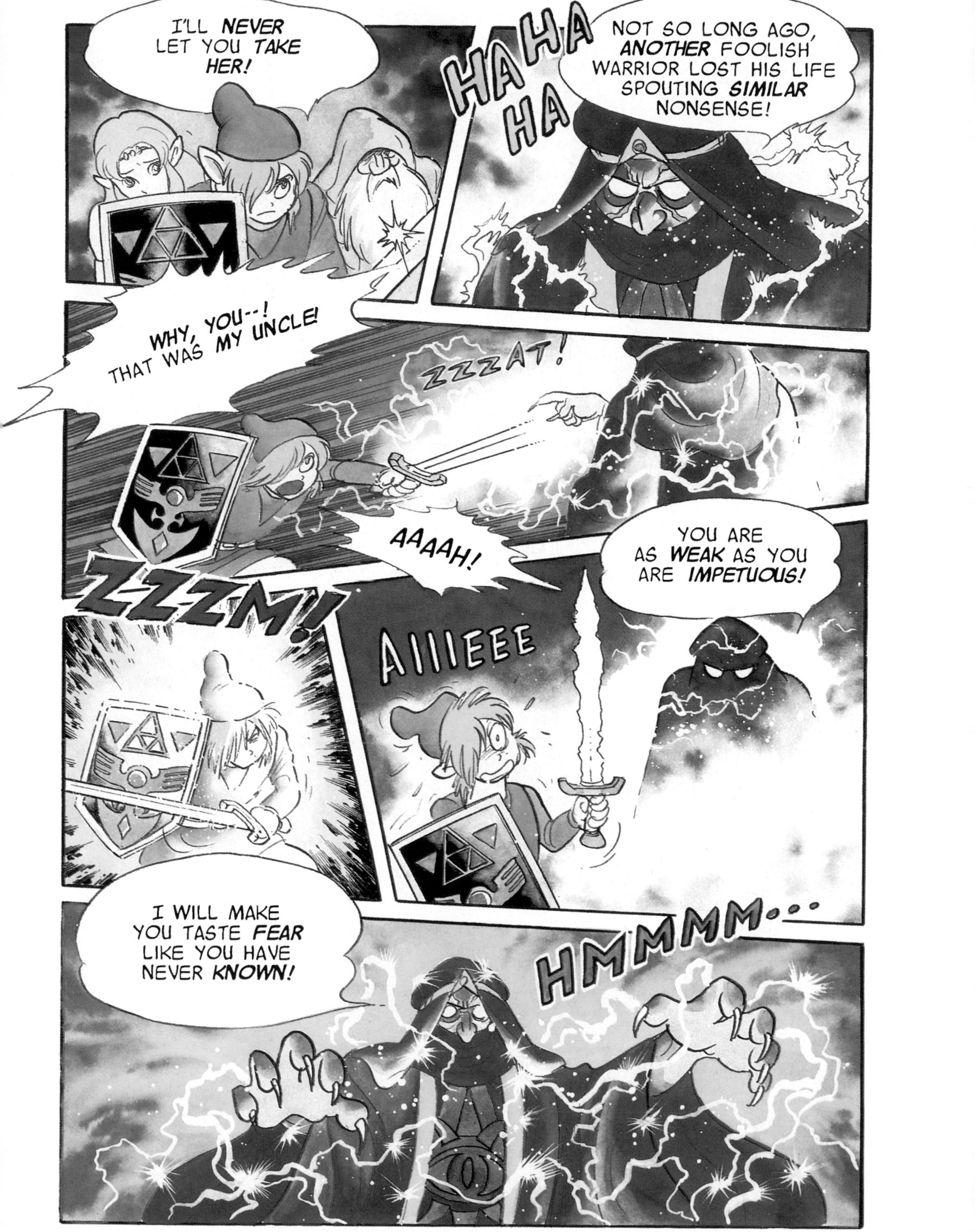
I'LL NEVER LET YOU TAKE HER!
HA HA HA
NOT SO LONG AGO, ANOTHER FOOLISH WARRIOR LOST HIS LIFE SPOUTING SIMILAR NONSENSE!
WHY, YOU--! THAT WAS MY UNCLE!
ZZZAT!
AAAAH!
ZZZM!
YOU ARE AS WEAK AS YOU ARE IMPETUOUS!
AIIIEEE
I WILL MAKE YOU TASTE FEAR LIKE YOU HAVE NEVER KNOWN!
HMMMM...

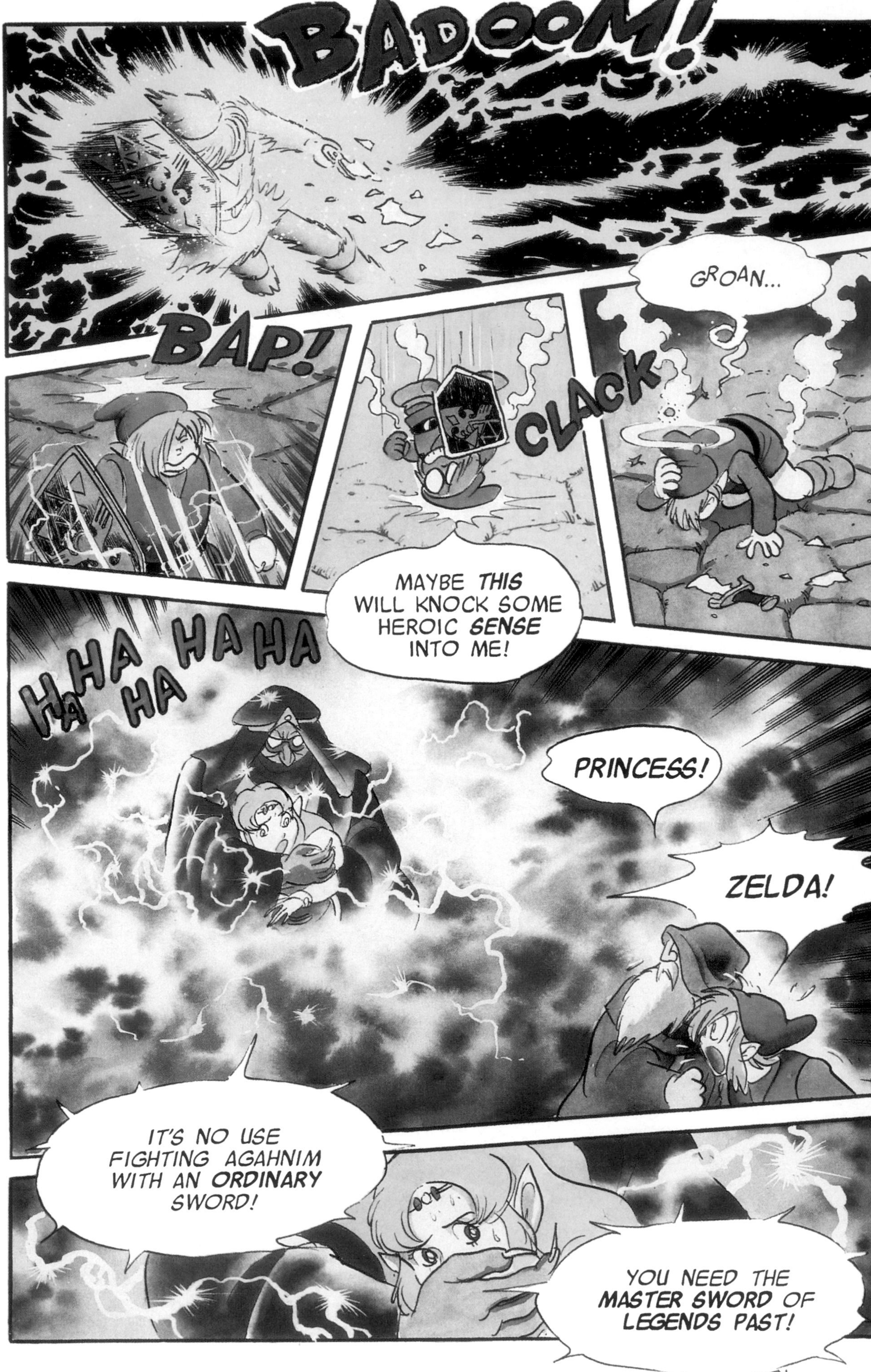
BADOOM!
BAP!
CLACK
GROAN...
MAYBE THIS WILL KNOCK SOME HEROIC SENSE INTO ME!
HAHA HAHA HA HA
PRINCESS!
ZELDA!
IT'S NO USE FIGHTING AGAHNIM WITH AN ORDINARY SWORD!
YOU NEED THE MASTER SWORD OF LEGENDS PAST!

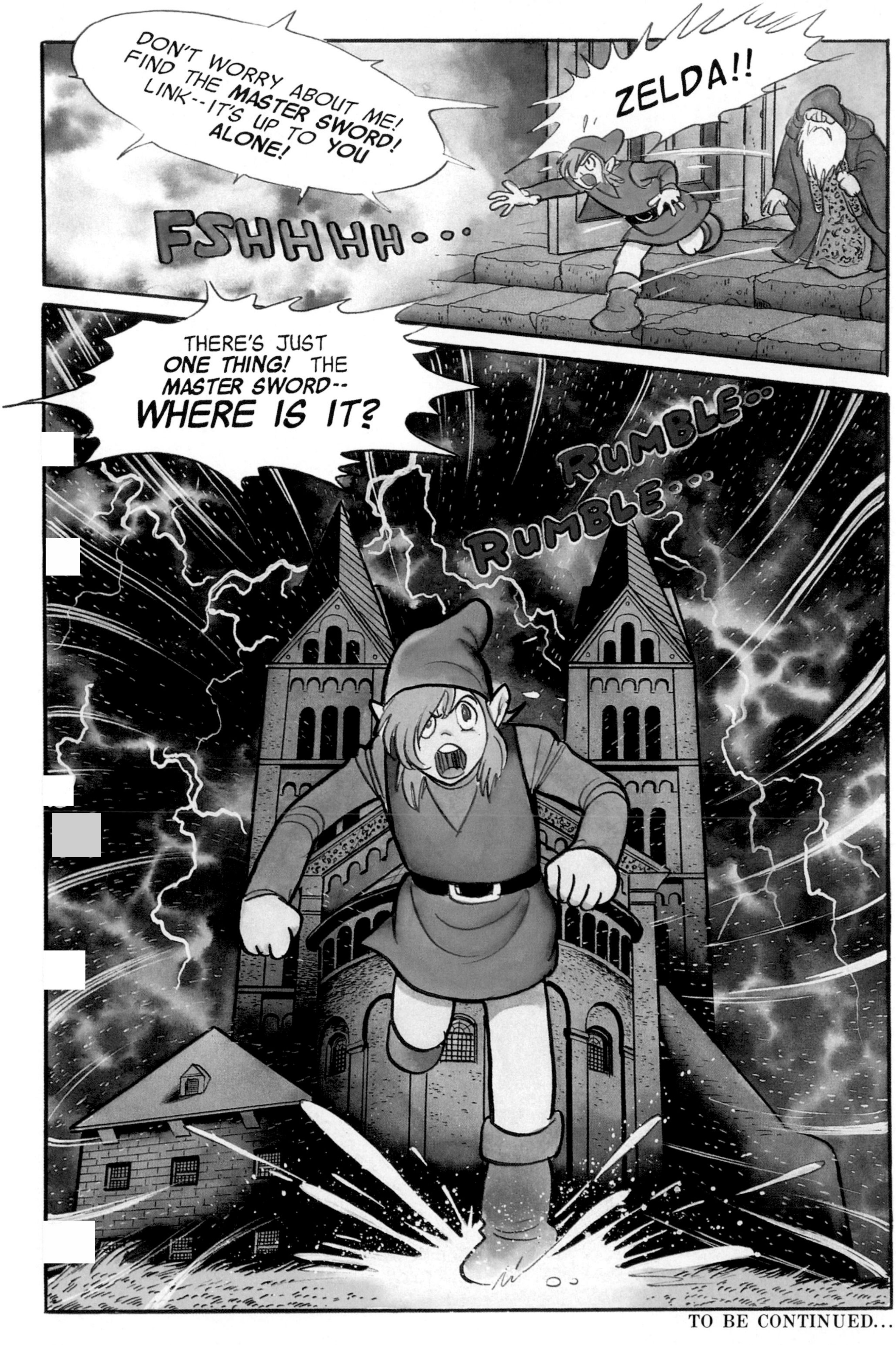
DON'T WORRY ABOUT ME! FIND THE MASTER SWORD! LINK--IT'S UP TO YOU ALONE!
ZELDA!!
FSHHHH...
THERE'S JUST ONE THING! THE MASTER SWORD-- WHERE IS IT?
RUMBLE..
RUMBLE...

TO BE CONTINUED...

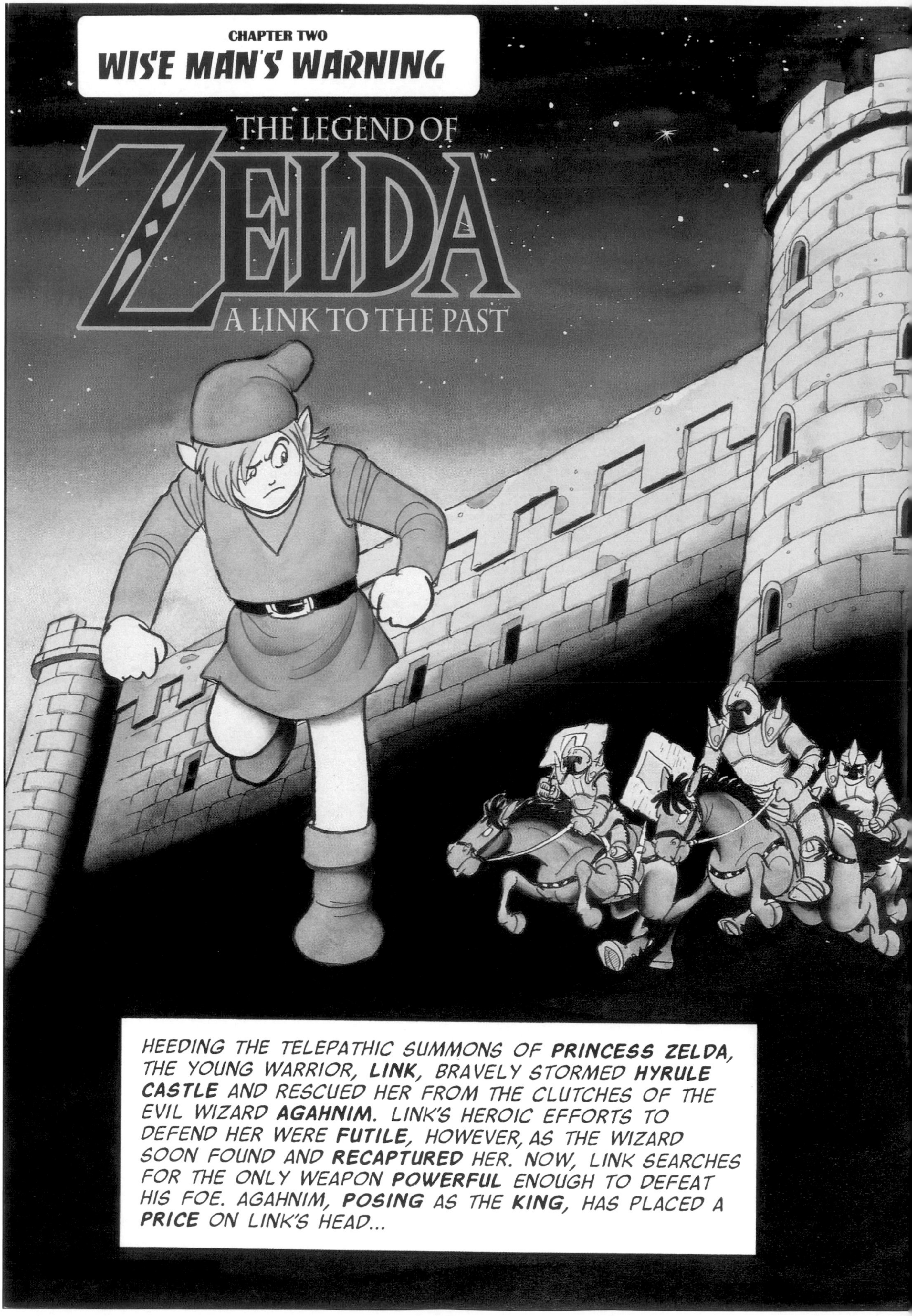
CHAPTER TWO
WISE MAN'S WARNING
THE LEGEND OF ZELDA A LINK TO THE PAST
HEEDING THE TELEPATHIC SUMMONS OF PRINCESS ZELDA, THE YOUNG WARRIOR, LINK, BRAVELY STORMED HYRULE CASTLE AND RESCUED HER FROM THE CLUTCHES OF THE EVIL WIZARD AGAHNIM. LINK'S HEROIC EFFORTS TO DEFEND HER WERE FUTILE, HOWEVER, AS THE WIZARD SOON FOUND AND RECAPTURED HER. NOW, LINK SEARCHES FOR THE ONLY WEAPON POWERFUL ENOUGH TO DEFEAT HIS FOE. AGAHNIM, POSING AS THE KING, HAS PLACED A PRICE ON LINK'S HEAD...

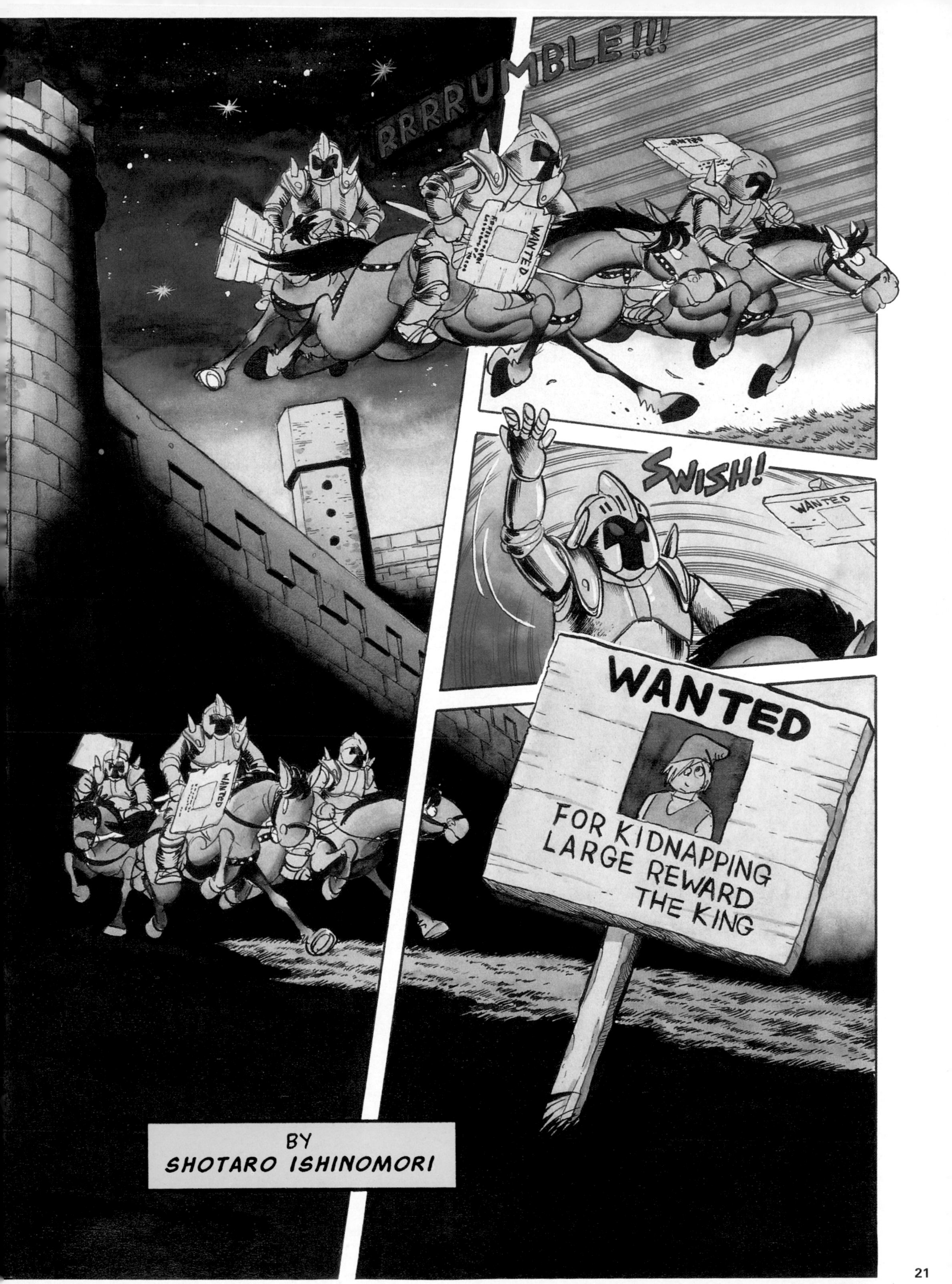
RRRRUMBLE!!!
SWISH!
WANTED
FOR KIDNAPPING
LARGE REWARD
THE KING
BY
SHOTARO ISHINOMORI

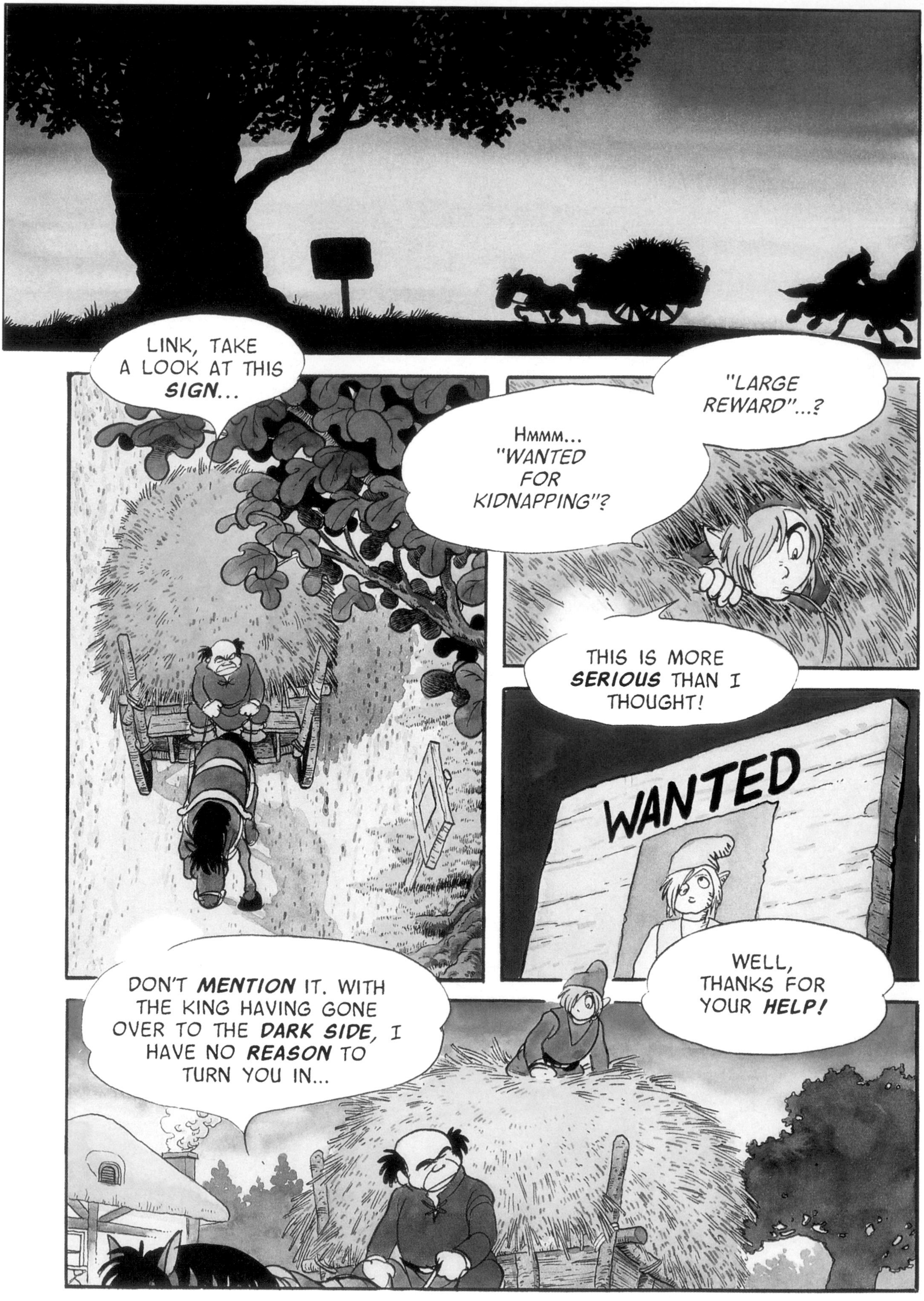
LINK, TAKE A LOOK AT THIS SIGN...
HMMM... "WANTED FOR KIDNAPPING"?
"LARGE REWARD"...?
THIS IS MORE SERIOUS THAN I THOUGHT!
WANTED
DON'T MENTION IT. WITH THE KING HAVING GONE OVER TO THE DARK SIDE, I HAVE NO REASON TO TURN YOU IN...
WELL, THANKS FOR YOUR HELP!

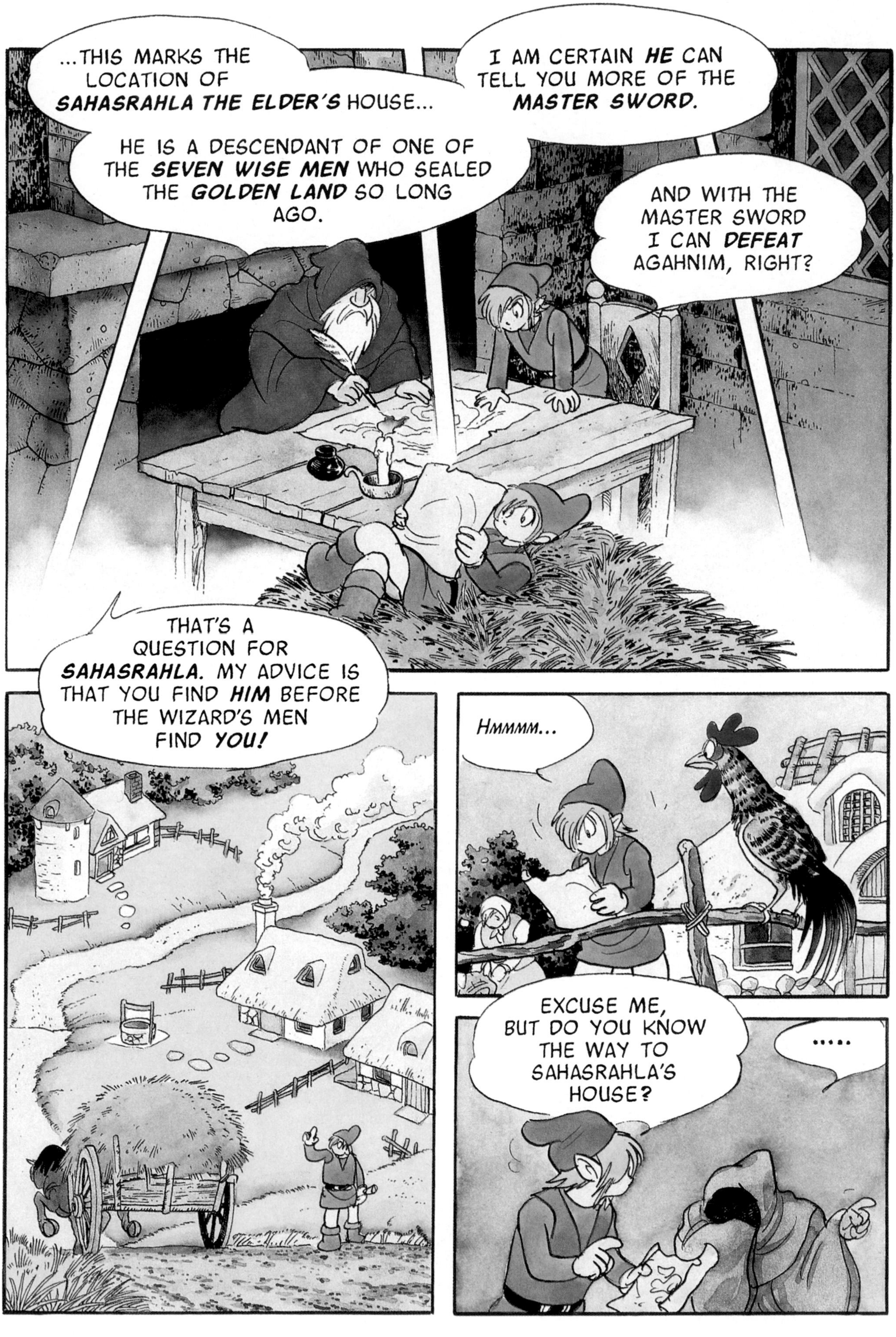
...THIS MARKS THE LOCATION OF SAHASRAHLA THE ELDER'S HOUSE...
HE IS A DESCENDANT OF ONE OF THE SEVEN WISE MEN WHO SEALED THE GOLDEN LAND SO LONG AGO.
I AM CERTAIN HE CAN TELL YOU MORE OF THE MASTER SWORD.
AND WITH THE MASTER SWORD I CAN DEFEAT AGAHNIM, RIGHT?
THAT'S A QUESTION FOR SAHASRAHLA. MY ADVICE IS THAT YOU FIND HIM BEFORE THE WIZARD'S MEN FIND YOU!
HMMMM...
EXCUSE ME, BUT DO YOU KNOW THE WAY TO SAHASRAHLA'S HOUSE?
.....

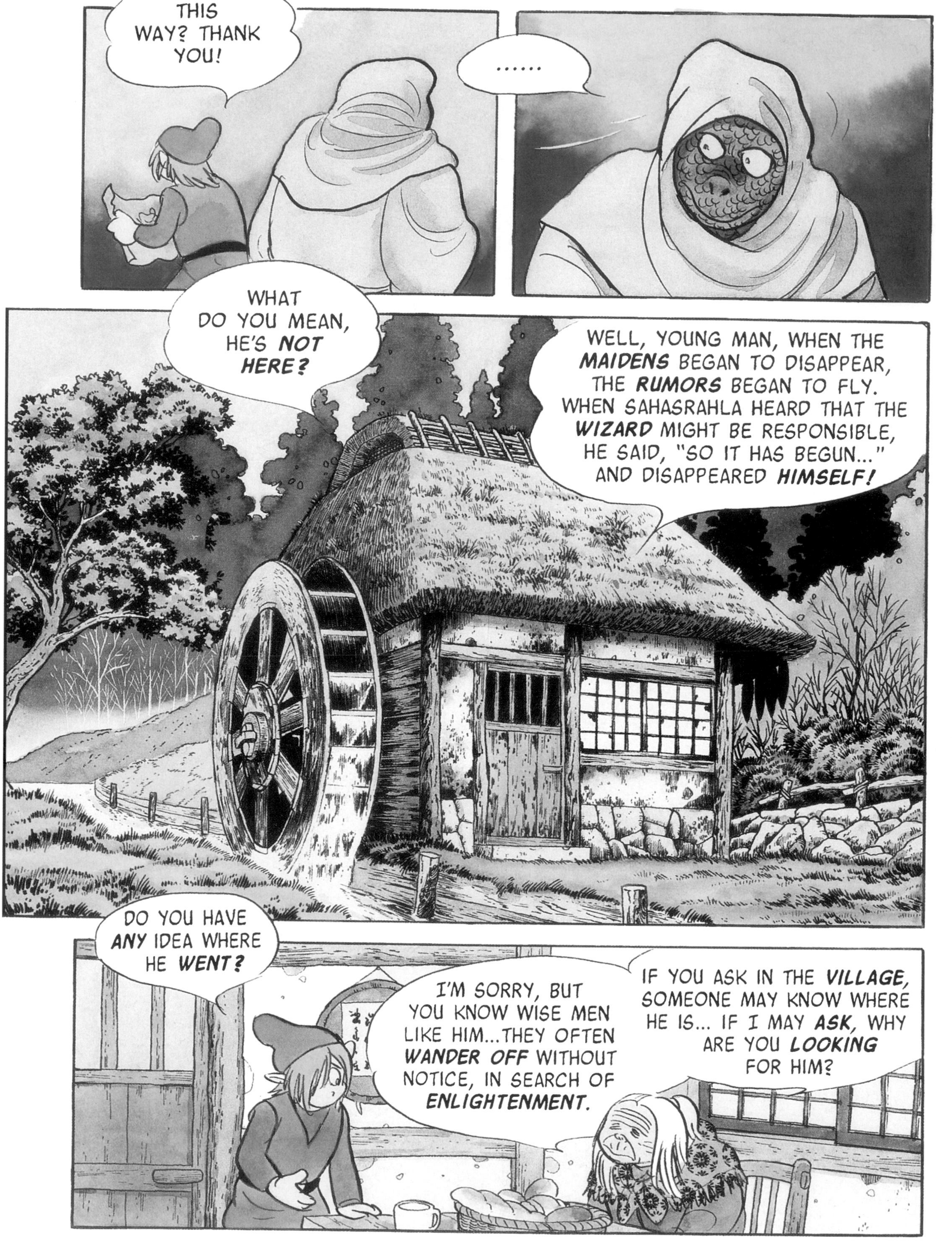
THIS WAY? THANK YOU!
......
WHAT DO YOU MEAN, HE'S **NOT HERE?**
WELL, YOUNG MAN, WHEN THE **MAIDENS** BEGAN TO DISAPPEAR, THE **RUMORS** BEGAN TO FLY. WHEN SAHASRAHLA HEARD THAT THE **WIZARD** MIGHT BE RESPONSIBLE, HE SAID, "SO IT HAS BEGUN..." AND DISAPPEARED **HIMSELF!**
DO YOU HAVE **ANY** IDEA WHERE HE **WENT?**
I'M SORRY, BUT YOU KNOW WISE MEN LIKE HIM...THEY OFTEN **WANDER OFF** WITHOUT NOTICE, IN SEARCH OF **ENLIGHTENMENT.**
IF YOU ASK IN THE **VILLAGE,** SOMEONE MAY KNOW WHERE HE IS... IF I MAY **ASK,** WHY ARE YOU **LOOKING** FOR HIM?

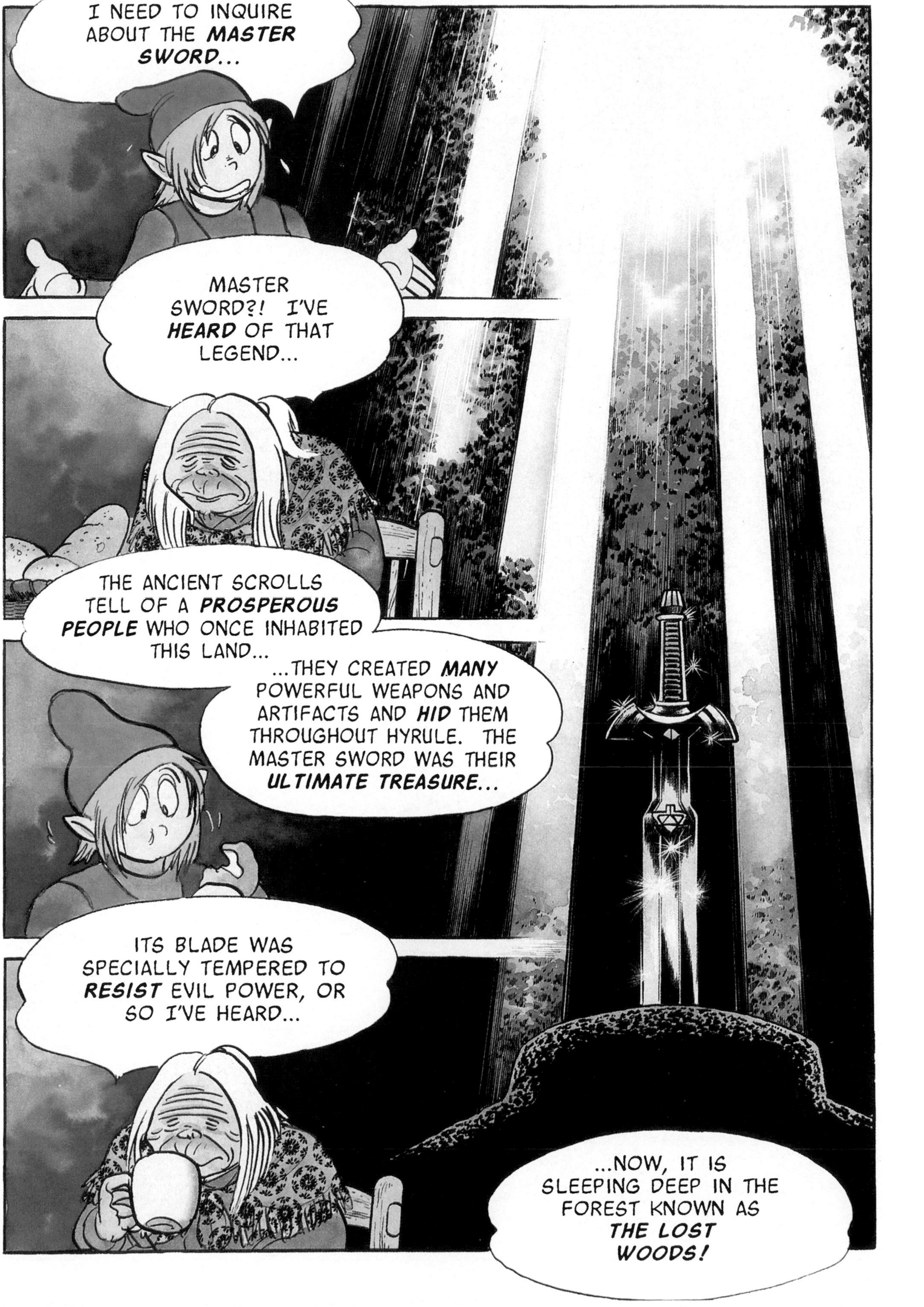
I NEED TO INQUIRE ABOUT THE ***MASTER SWORD...***
MASTER SWORD?! I'VE ***HEARD*** OF THAT LEGEND...
THE ANCIENT SCROLLS TELL OF A ***PROSPEROUS PEOPLE*** WHO ONCE INHABITED THIS LAND...
...THEY CREATED ***MANY*** POWERFUL WEAPONS AND ARTIFACTS AND ***HID*** THEM THROUGHOUT HYRULE. THE MASTER SWORD WAS THEIR ***ULTIMATE TREASURE...***
ITS BLADE WAS SPECIALLY TEMPERED TO ***RESIST*** EVIL POWER, OR SO I'VE HEARD...
...NOW, IT IS SLEEPING DEEP IN THE FOREST KNOWN AS ***THE LOST WOODS!***

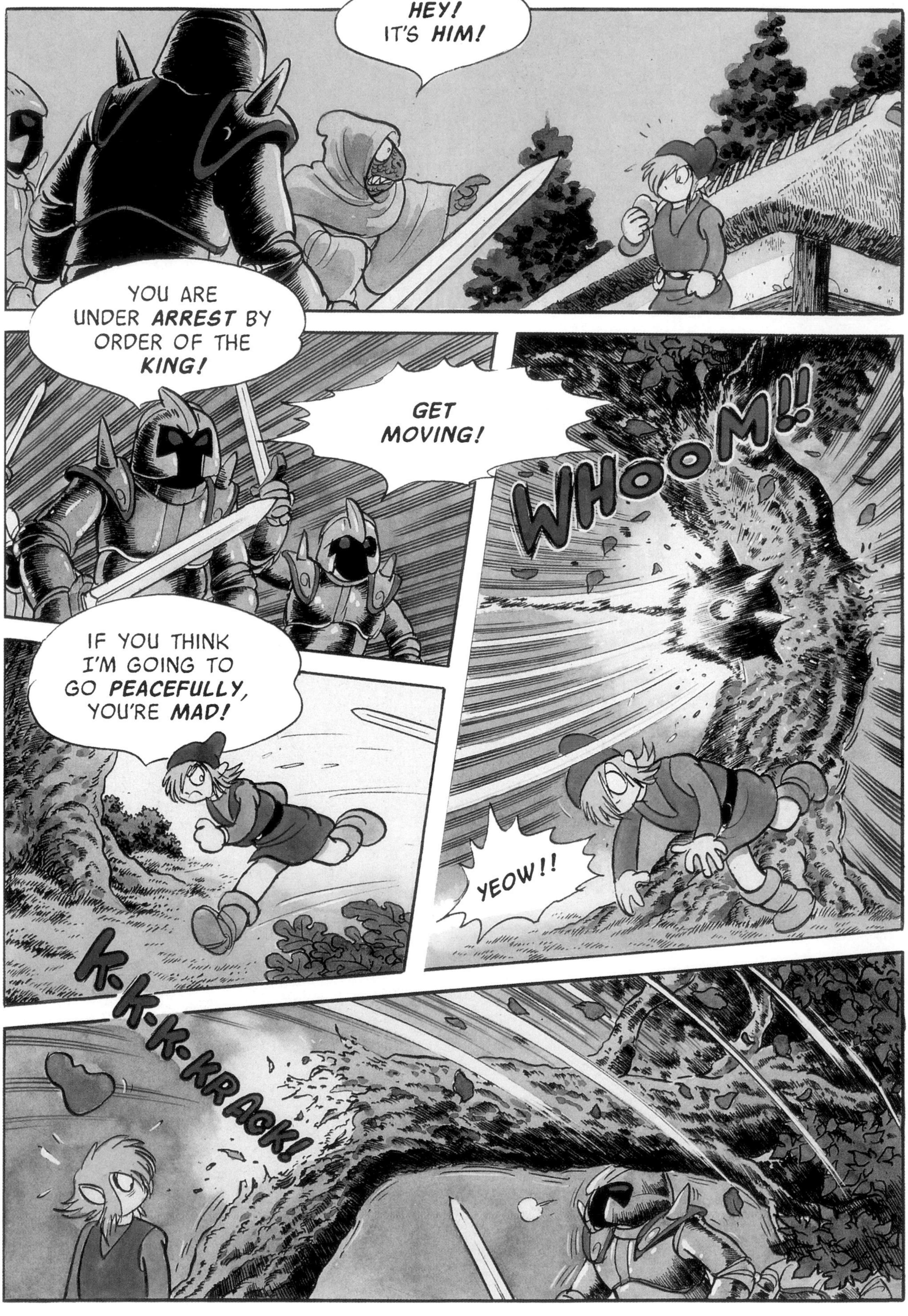
HEY! IT'S HIM!
YOU ARE UNDER ARREST BY ORDER OF THE KING!
GET MOVING!
WHOOOM!!
IF YOU THINK I'M GOING TO GO PEACEFULLY, YOU'RE MAD!
YEOW!!
K-K-K-KRACK!

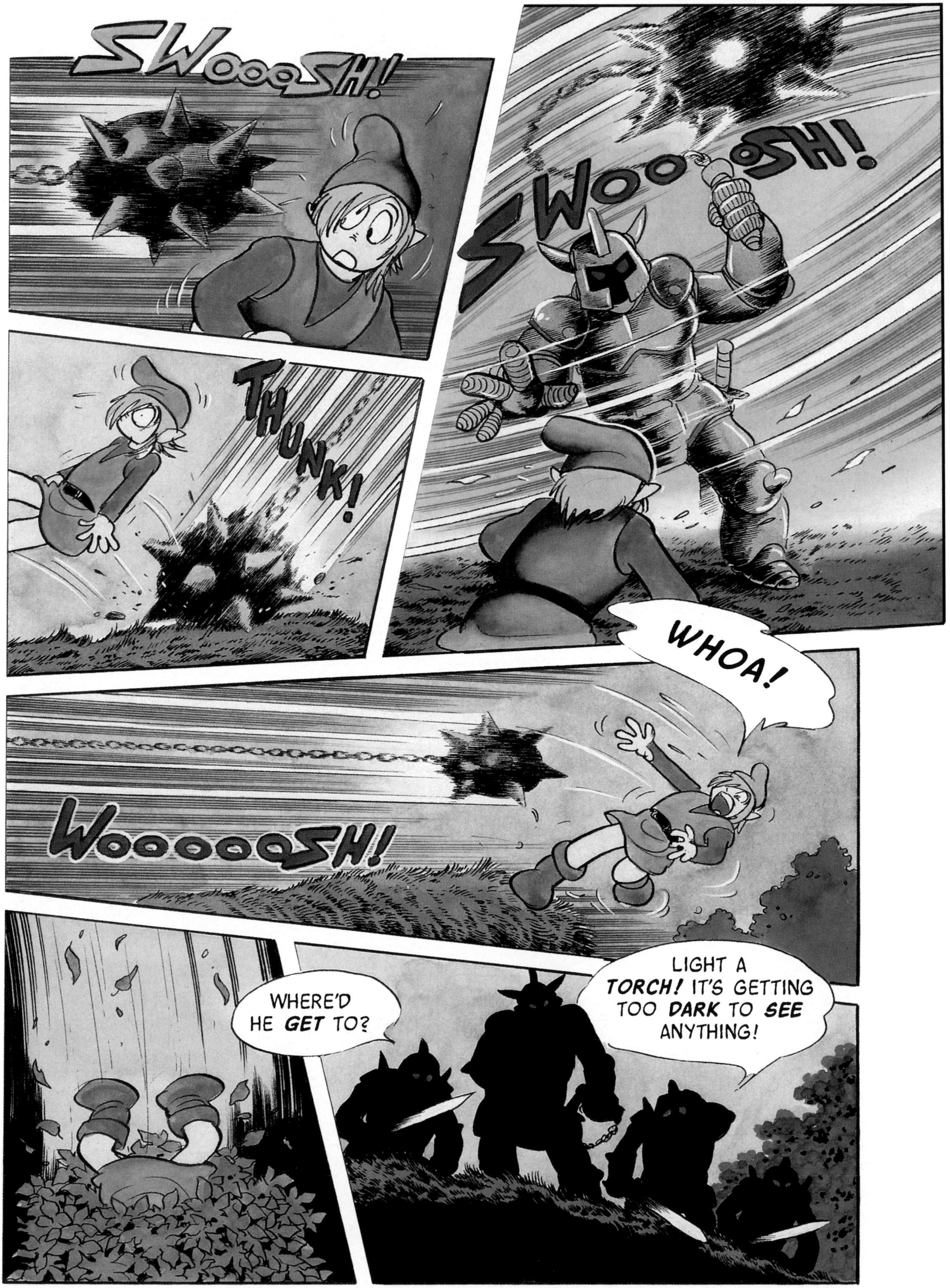
SWOOOSH!
THUNK!
SWOOOOSH!
WHOA!
WOOOOOOSH!
WHERE'D HE GET TO?
LIGHT A TORCH! IT'S GETTING TOO DARK TO SEE ANYTHING!

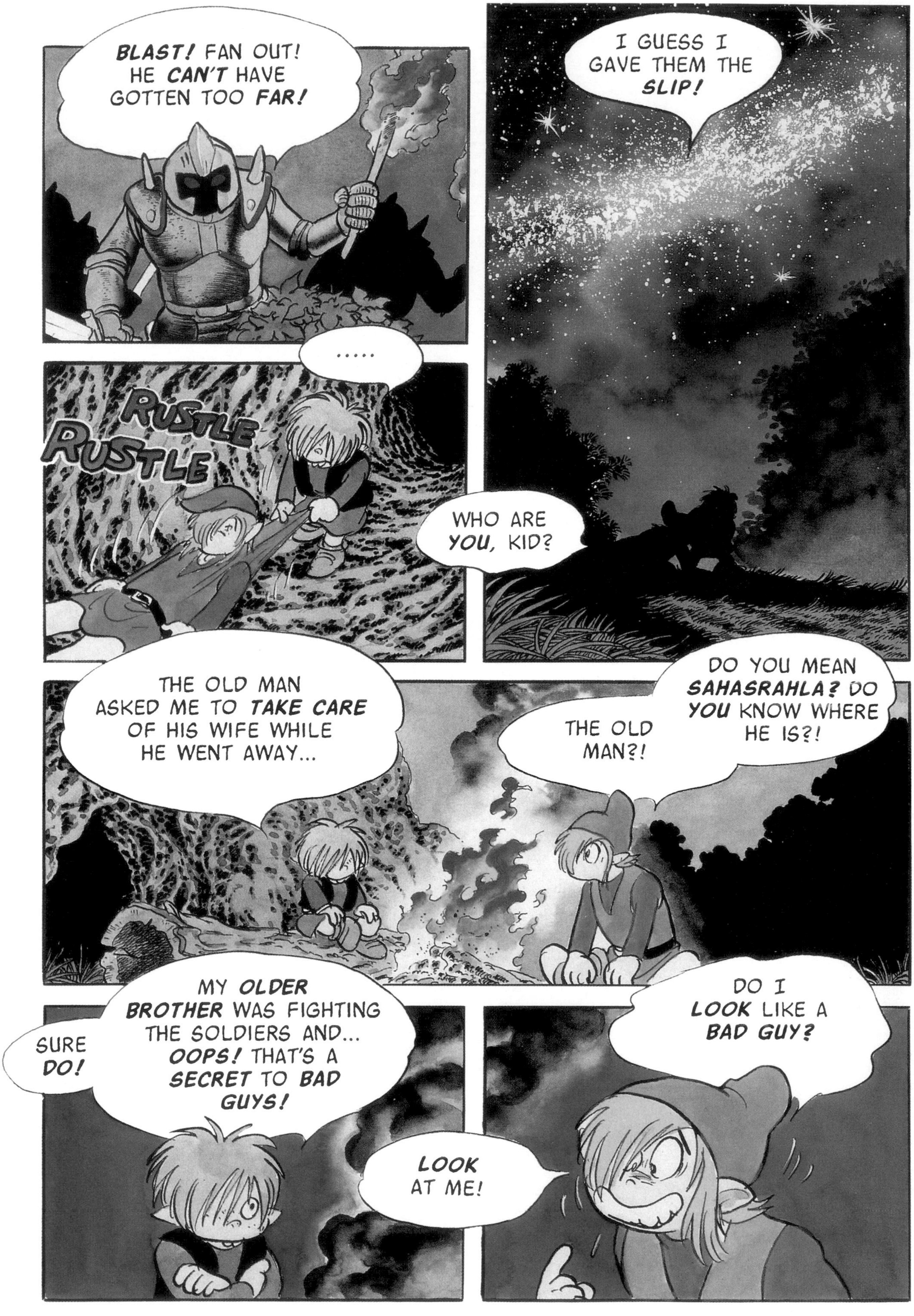
BLAST! FAN OUT! HE CAN'T HAVE GOTTEN TOO FAR!
.....
RUSTLE RUSTLE
I GUESS I GAVE THEM THE SLIP!
WHO ARE YOU, KID?
THE OLD MAN ASKED ME TO TAKE CARE OF HIS WIFE WHILE HE WENT AWAY...
THE OLD MAN?!
DO YOU MEAN SAHASRAHLA? DO YOU KNOW WHERE HE IS?!
MY OLDER BROTHER WAS FIGHTING THE SOLDIERS AND... OOPS! THAT'S A SECRET TO BAD GUYS!
SURE DO!
DO I LOOK LIKE A BAD GUY?
LOOK AT ME!

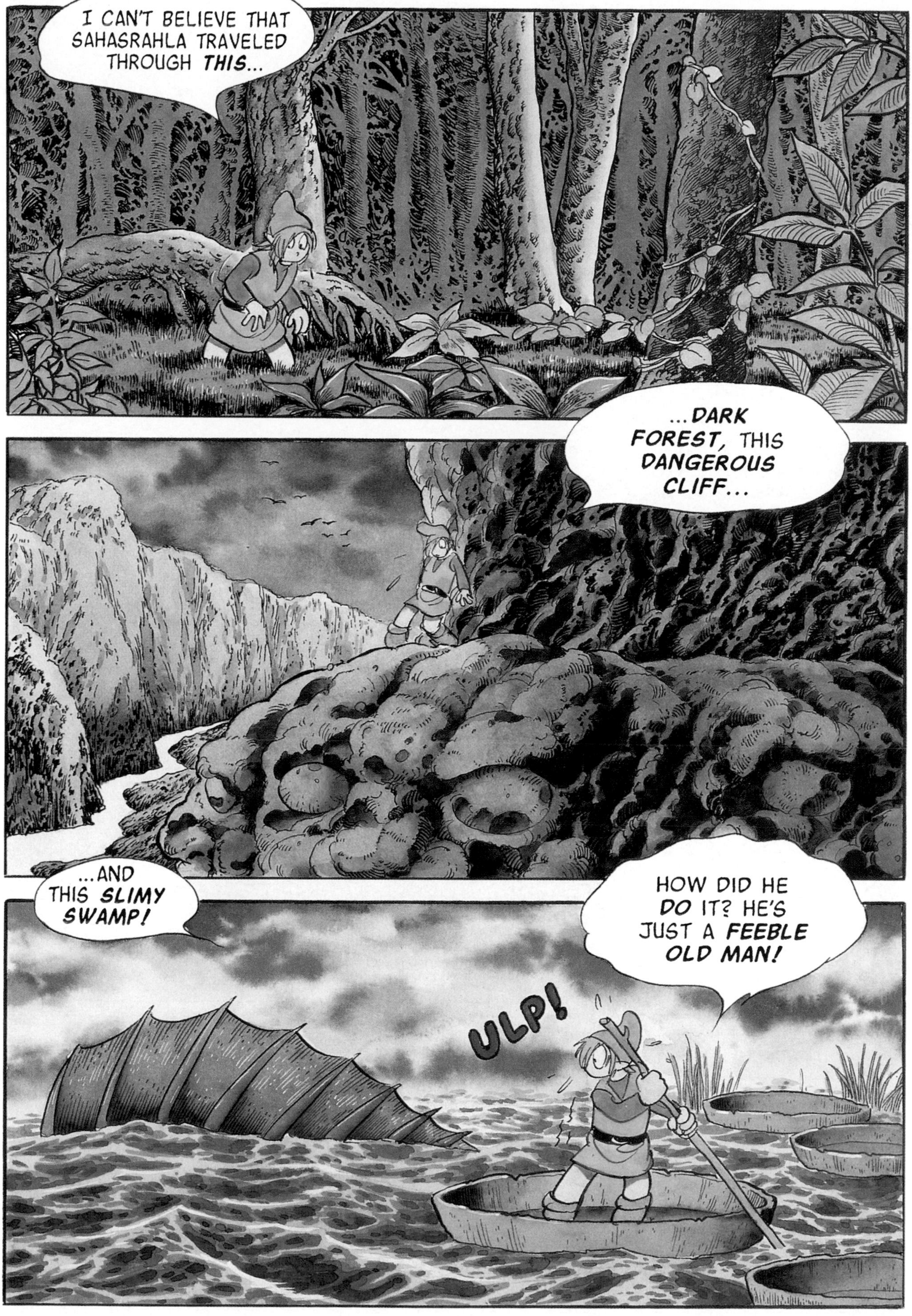
I CAN'T BELIEVE THAT SAHASRAHLA TRAVELED THROUGH **THIS**...
...**DARK FOREST,** THIS **DANGEROUS CLIFF**...
...AND THIS **SLIMY SWAMP!**
HOW DID HE **DO** IT? HE'S JUST A **FEEBLE OLD MAN!**
ULP!

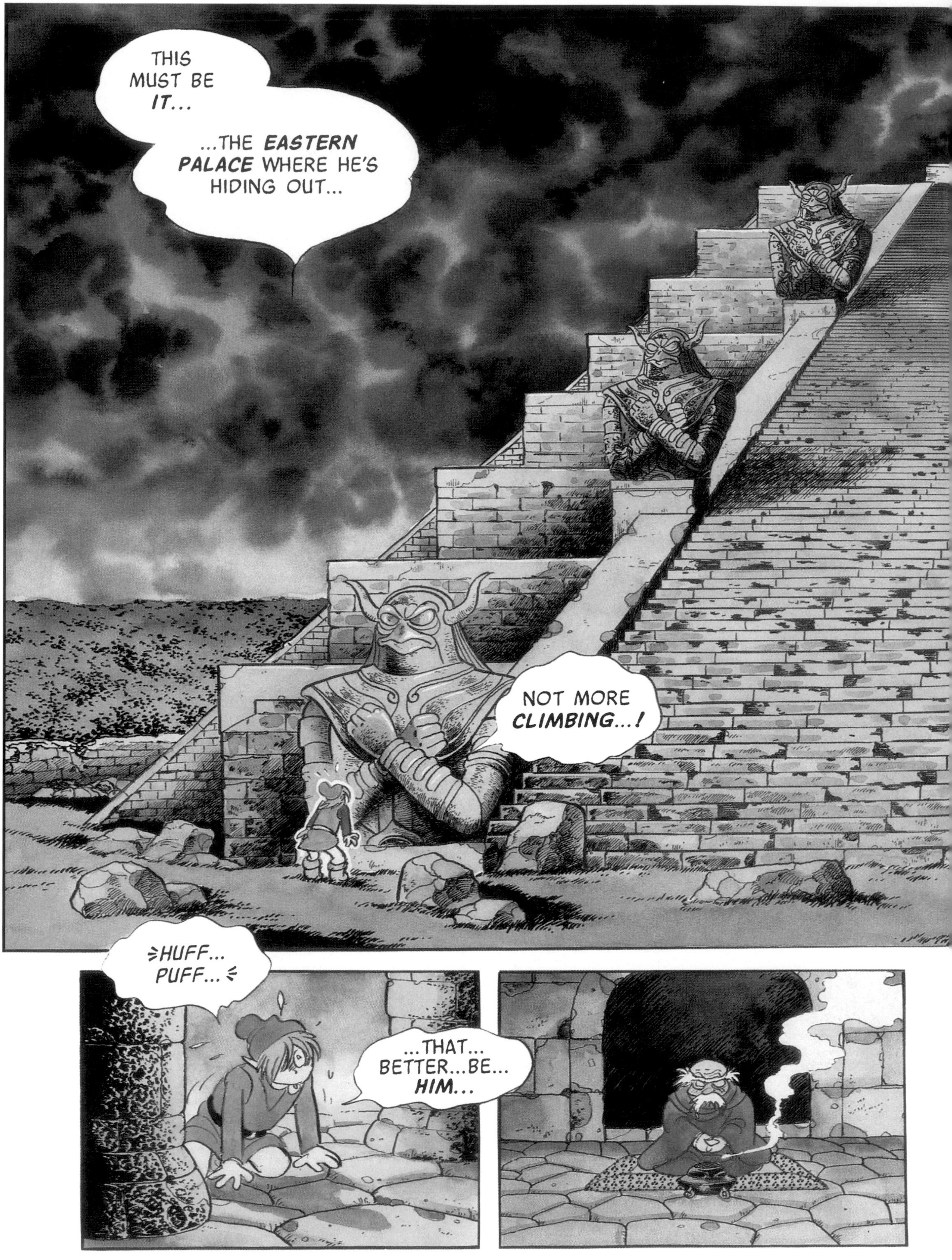
THIS MUST BE *IT*...
...THE ***EASTERN PALACE*** WHERE HE'S HIDING OUT...
NOT MORE ***CLIMBING***...!
HUFF... PUFF...
...THAT... BETTER...BE... ***HIM***...

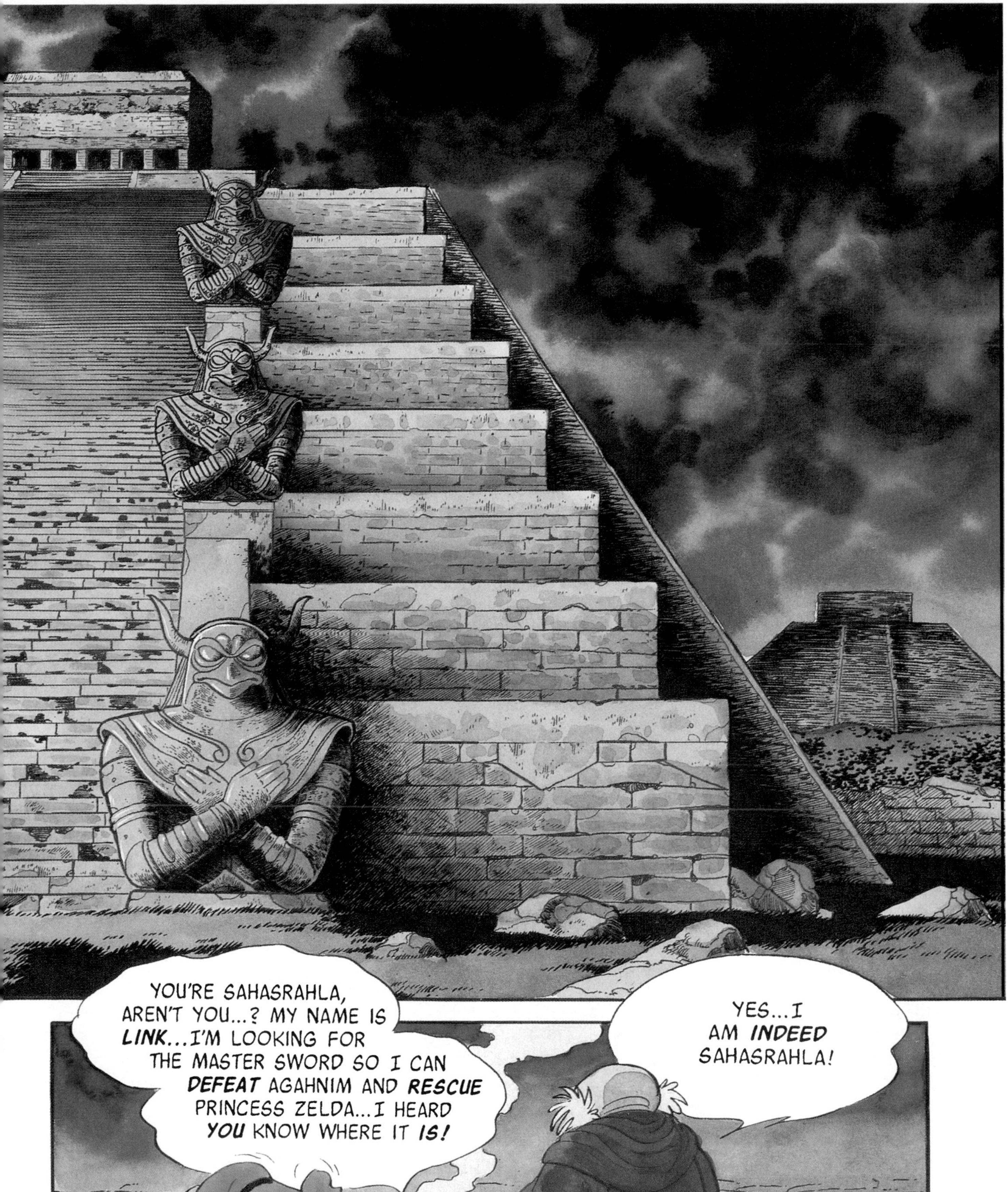

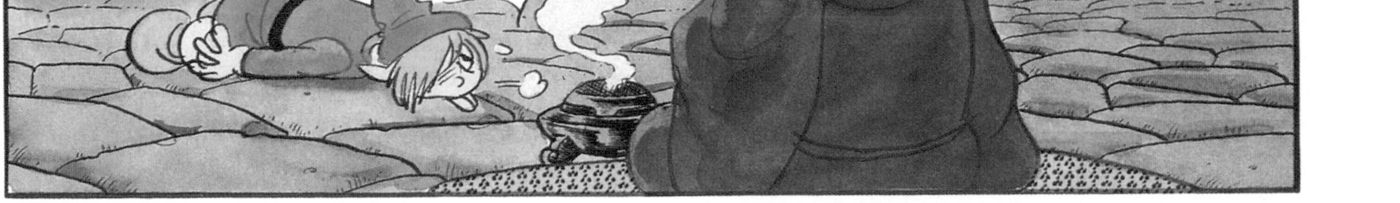

YOU'RE SAHASRAHLA, AREN'T YOU...? MY NAME IS **LINK**...I'M LOOKING FOR THE MASTER SWORD SO I CAN **DEFEAT** AGAHNIM AND **RESCUE** PRINCESS ZELDA...I HEARD **YOU** KNOW WHERE IT **IS!**
YES...I AM **INDEED** SAHASRAHLA!

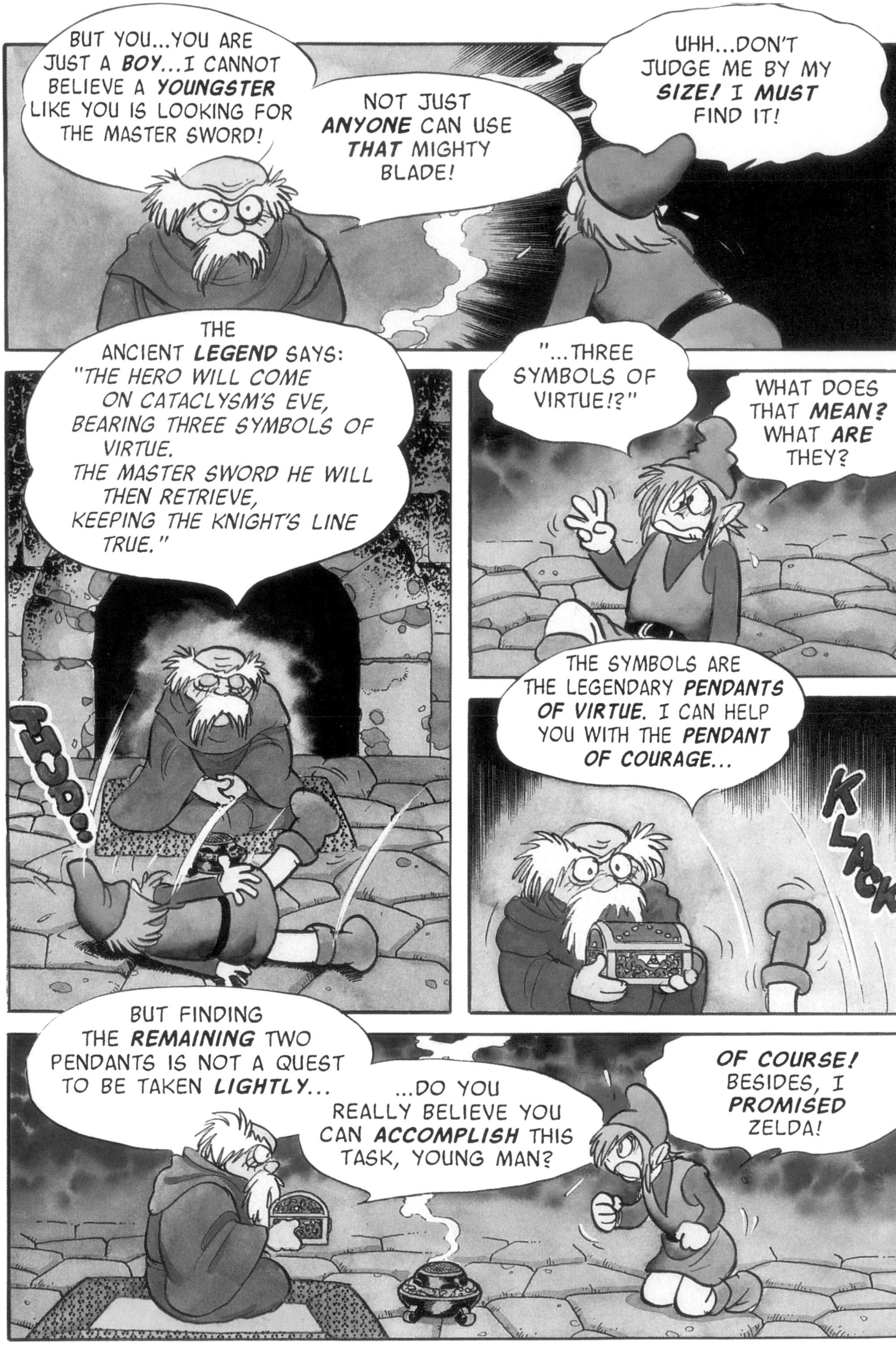
BUT YOU...YOU ARE JUST A BOY...I CANNOT BELIEVE A YOUNGSTER LIKE YOU IS LOOKING FOR THE MASTER SWORD!
NOT JUST ANYONE CAN USE THAT MIGHTY BLADE!
UHH...DON'T JUDGE ME BY MY SIZE! I MUST FIND IT!
THE ANCIENT LEGEND SAYS: "THE HERO WILL COME ON CATACLYSM'S EVE, BEARING THREE SYMBOLS OF VIRTUE. THE MASTER SWORD HE WILL THEN RETRIEVE, KEEPING THE KNIGHT'S LINE TRUE."
THUD!!
"...THREE SYMBOLS OF VIRTUE!?"
WHAT DOES THAT MEAN? WHAT ARE THEY?
THE SYMBOLS ARE THE LEGENDARY PENDANTS OF VIRTUE. I CAN HELP YOU WITH THE PENDANT OF COURAGE...
KLACK
BUT FINDING THE REMAINING TWO PENDANTS IS NOT A QUEST TO BE TAKEN LIGHTLY...
...DO YOU REALLY BELIEVE YOU CAN ACCOMPLISH THIS TASK, YOUNG MAN?
OF COURSE! BESIDES, I PROMISED ZELDA!

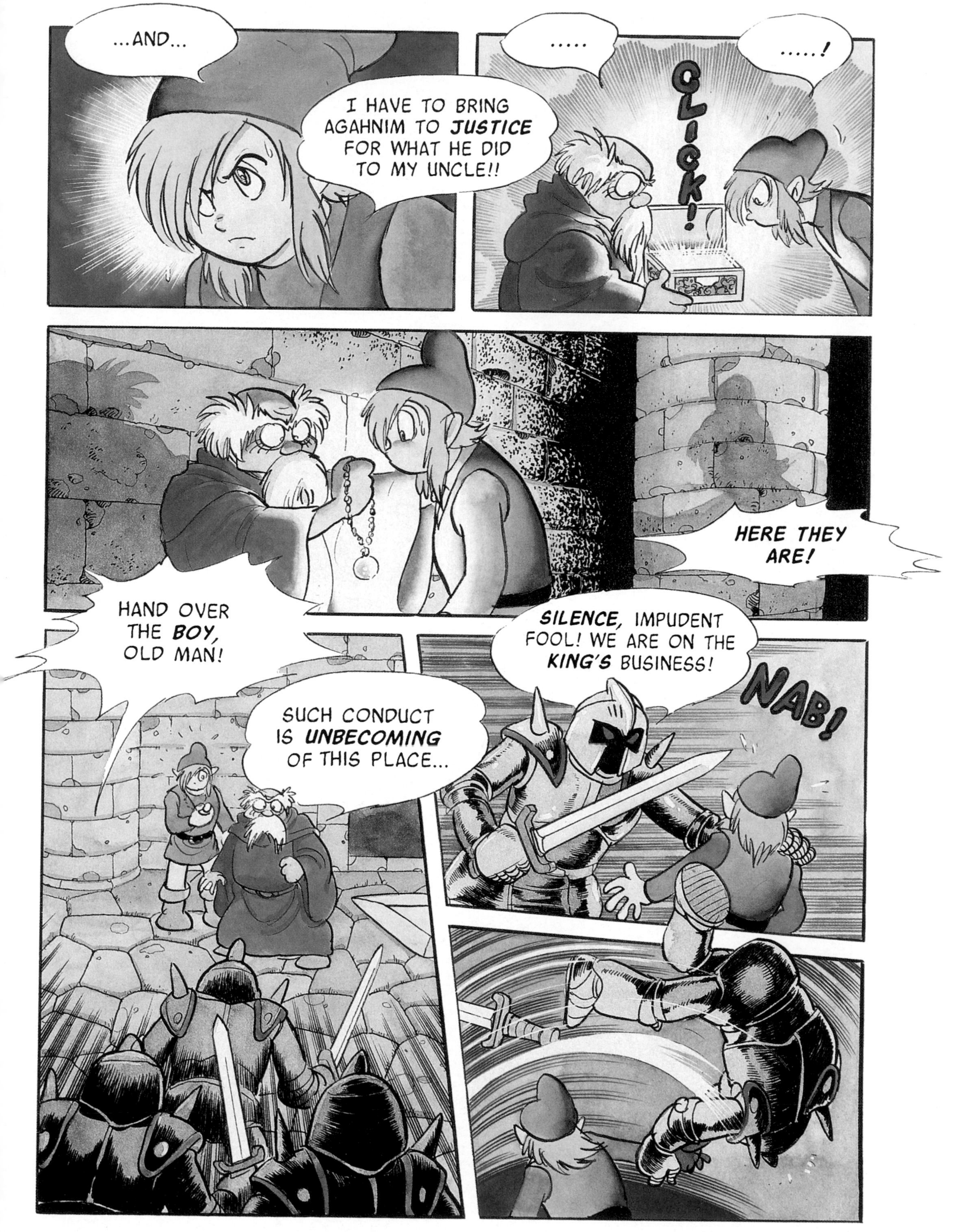
...AND...
I HAVE TO BRING AGAHNIM TO JUSTICE FOR WHAT HE DID TO MY UNCLE!!
.....
.....!
CLICK!
HERE THEY ARE!
HAND OVER THE BOY, OLD MAN!
SUCH CONDUCT IS UNBECOMING OF THIS PLACE...
SILENCE, IMPUDENT FOOL! WE ARE ON THE KING'S BUSINESS!
NAB!

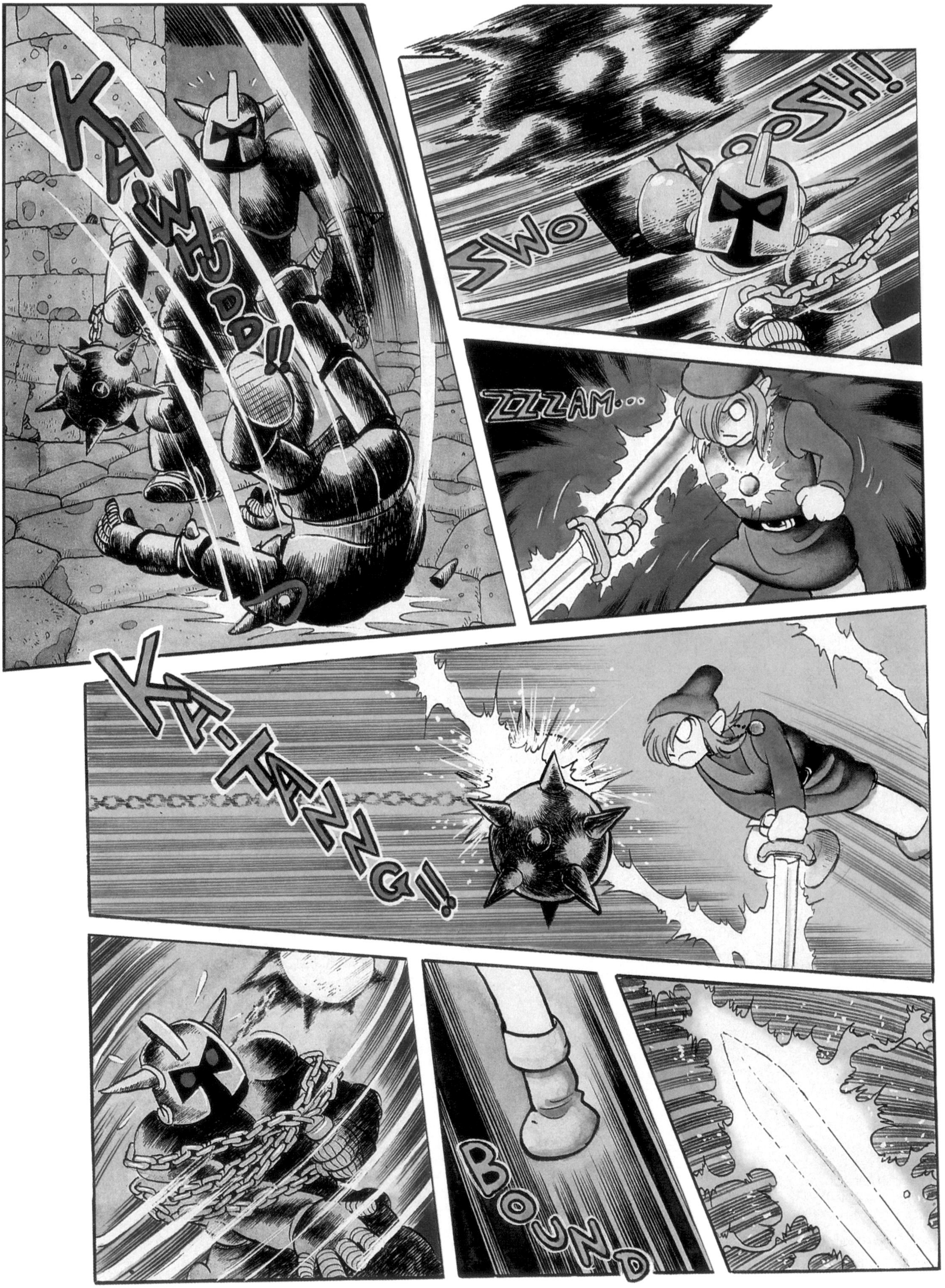
KA-WHUDD!!
SWOOOSH!
ZZZZAM...
KA-TANNG!!
BOUND

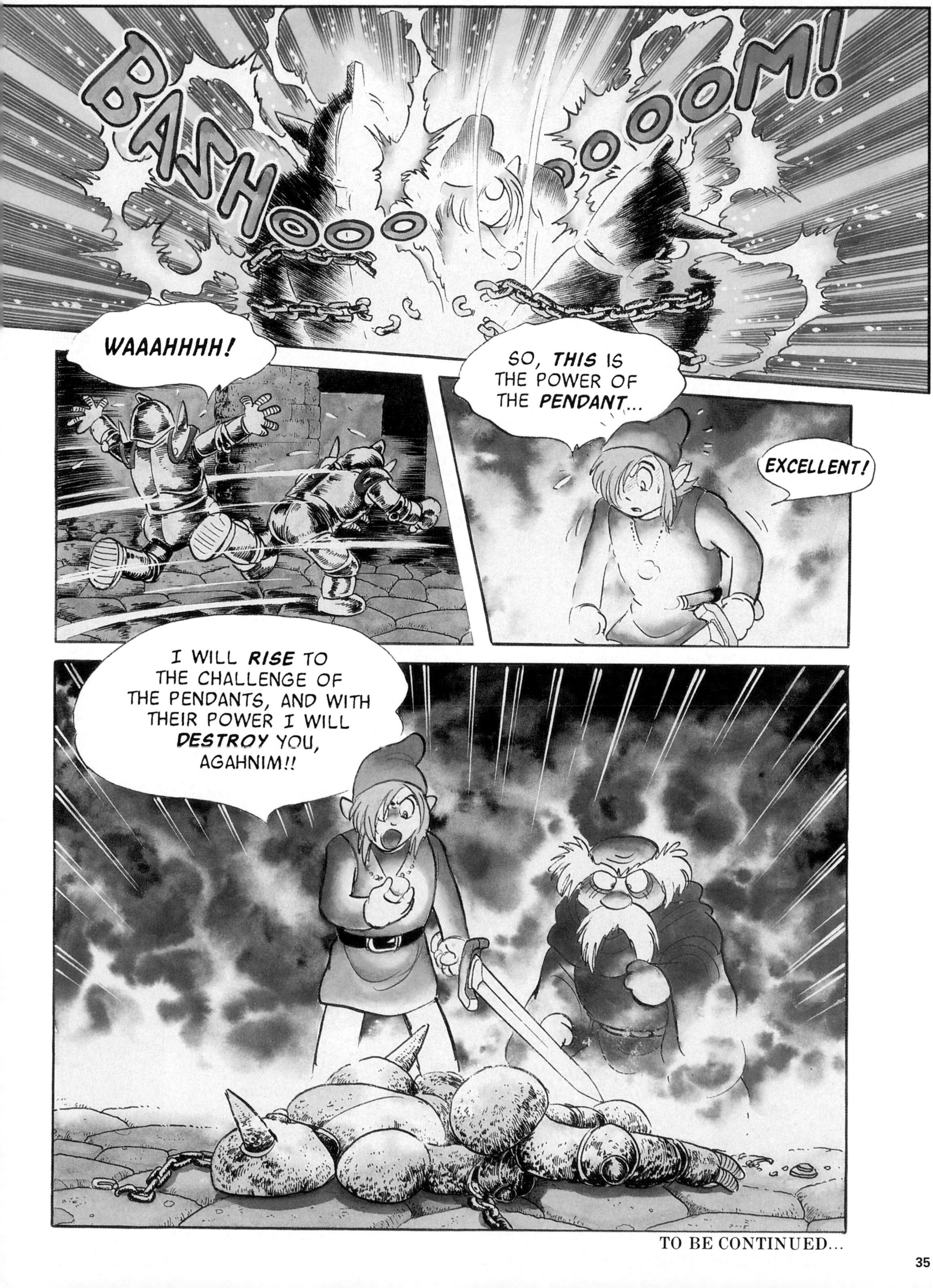
BASHOOOOOOOM!
WAAAHHHH!
SO, THIS IS THE POWER OF THE PENDANT...
EXCELLENT!
I WILL RISE TO THE CHALLENGE OF THE PENDANTS, AND WITH THEIR POWER I WILL DESTROY YOU, AGAHNIM!!

TO BE CONTINUED...

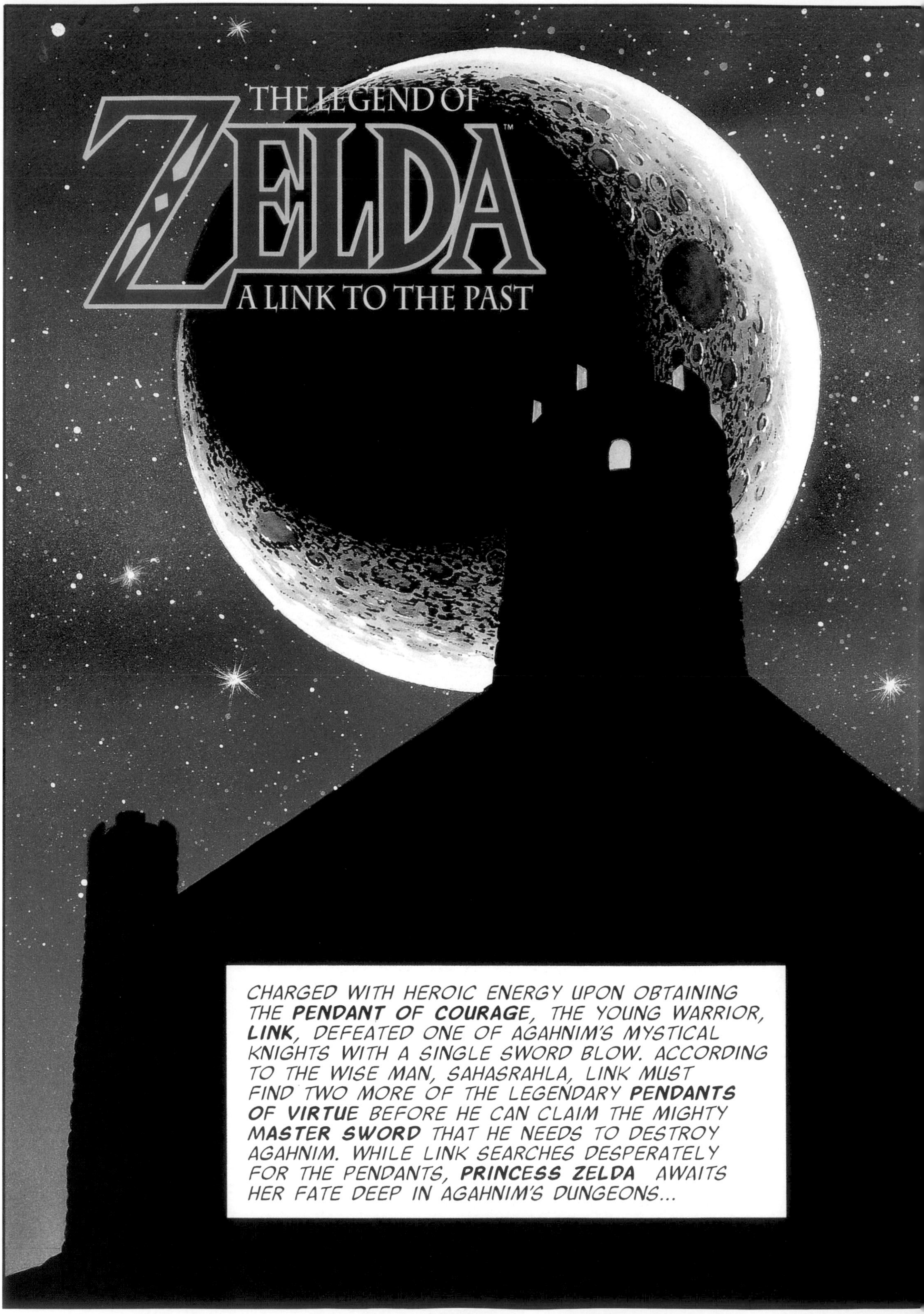
THE LEGEND OF
ZELDA™
A LINK TO THE PAST
CHARGED WITH HEROIC ENERGY UPON OBTAINING THE **PENDANT OF COURAGE**, THE YOUNG WARRIOR, **LINK**, DEFEATED ONE OF AGAHNIM'S MYSTICAL KNIGHTS WITH A SINGLE SWORD BLOW. ACCORDING TO THE WISE MAN, SAHASRAHLA, LINK MUST FIND TWO MORE OF THE LEGENDARY **PENDANTS OF VIRTUE** BEFORE HE CAN CLAIM THE MIGHTY **MASTER SWORD** THAT HE NEEDS TO DESTROY AGAHNIM. WHILE LINK SEARCHES DESPERATELY FOR THE PENDANTS, **PRINCESS ZELDA** AWAITS HER FATE DEEP IN AGAHNIM'S DUNGEONS...

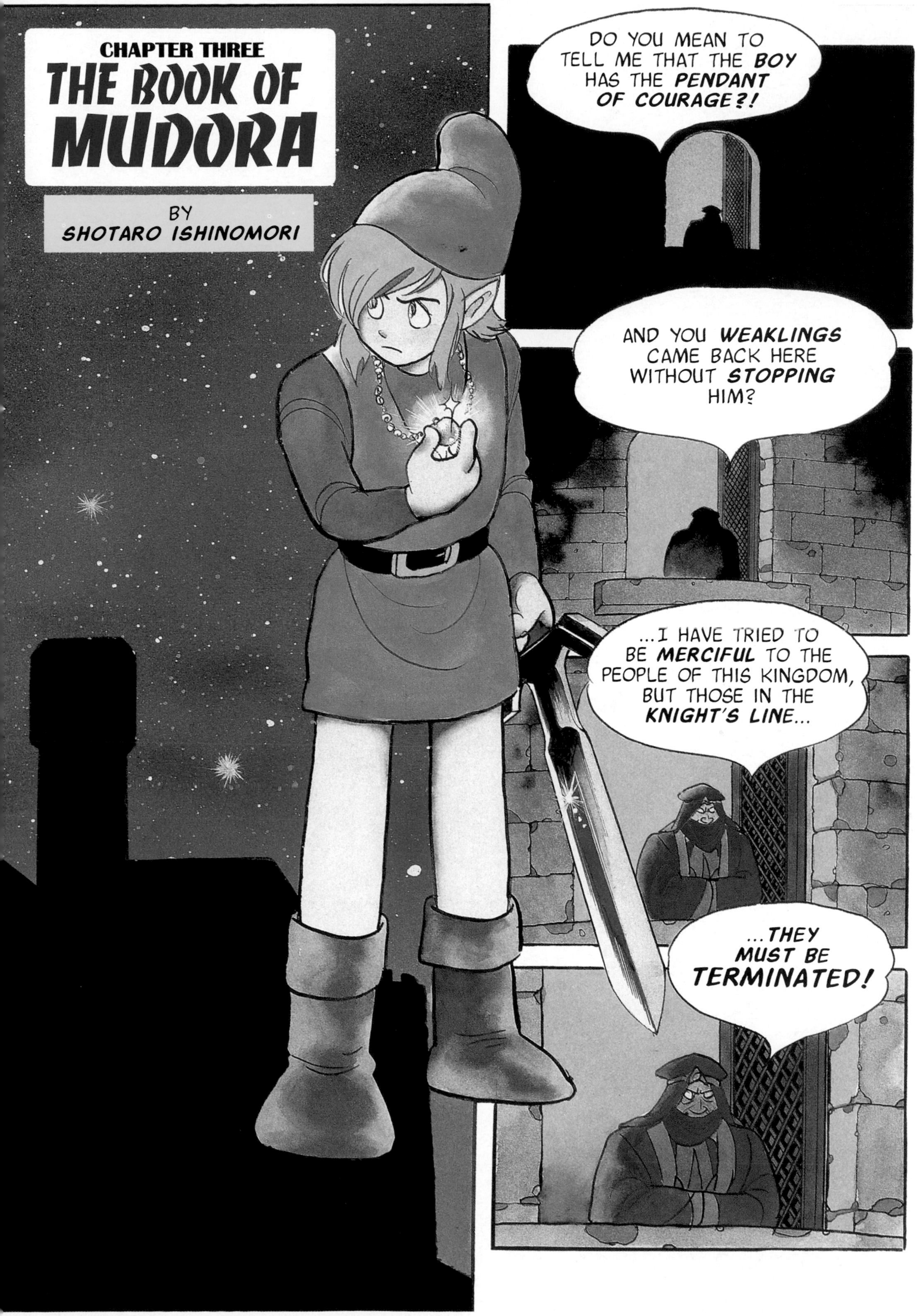
CHAPTER THREE
THE BOOK OF MUDORA
BY SHOTARO ISHINOMORI
DO YOU MEAN TO TELL ME THAT THE BOY HAS THE PENDANT OF COURAGE?!
AND YOU WEAKLINGS CAME BACK HERE WITHOUT STOPPING HIM?
...I HAVE TRIED TO BE MERCIFUL TO THE PEOPLE OF THIS KINGDOM, BUT THOSE IN THE KNIGHT'S LINE...
...THEY MUST BE TERMINATED!

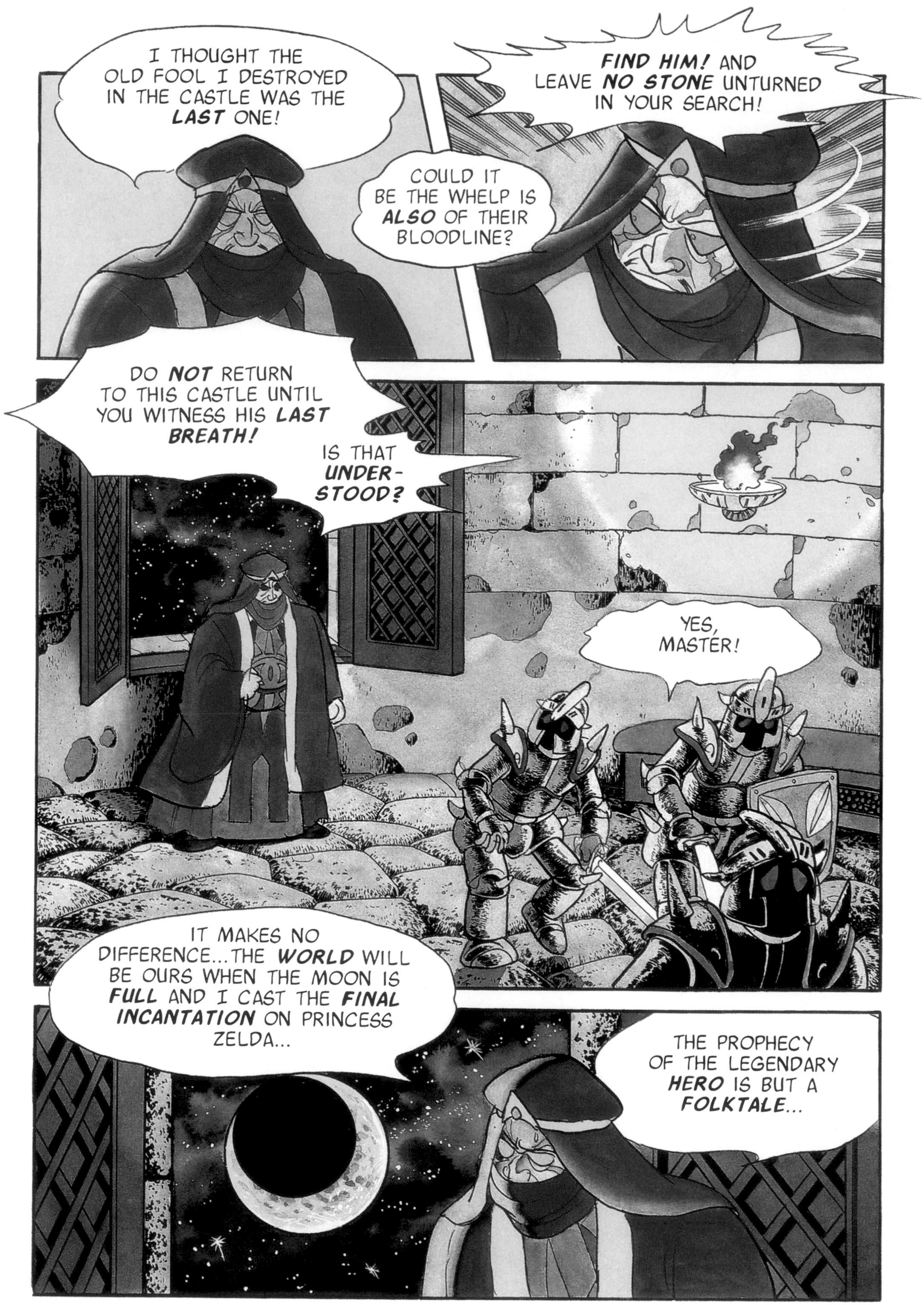
I THOUGHT THE OLD FOOL I DESTROYED IN THE CASTLE WAS THE LAST ONE!
FIND HIM! AND LEAVE NO STONE UNTURNED IN YOUR SEARCH!
COULD IT BE THE WHELP IS ALSO OF THEIR BLOODLINE?
DO NOT RETURN TO THIS CASTLE UNTIL YOU WITNESS HIS LAST BREATH!
IS THAT UNDER-STOOD?
YES, MASTER!
IT MAKES NO DIFFERENCE...THE WORLD WILL BE OURS WHEN THE MOON IS FULL AND I CAST THE FINAL INCANTATION ON PRINCESS ZELDA...
THE PROPHECY OF THE LEGENDARY HERO IS BUT A FOLKTALE...

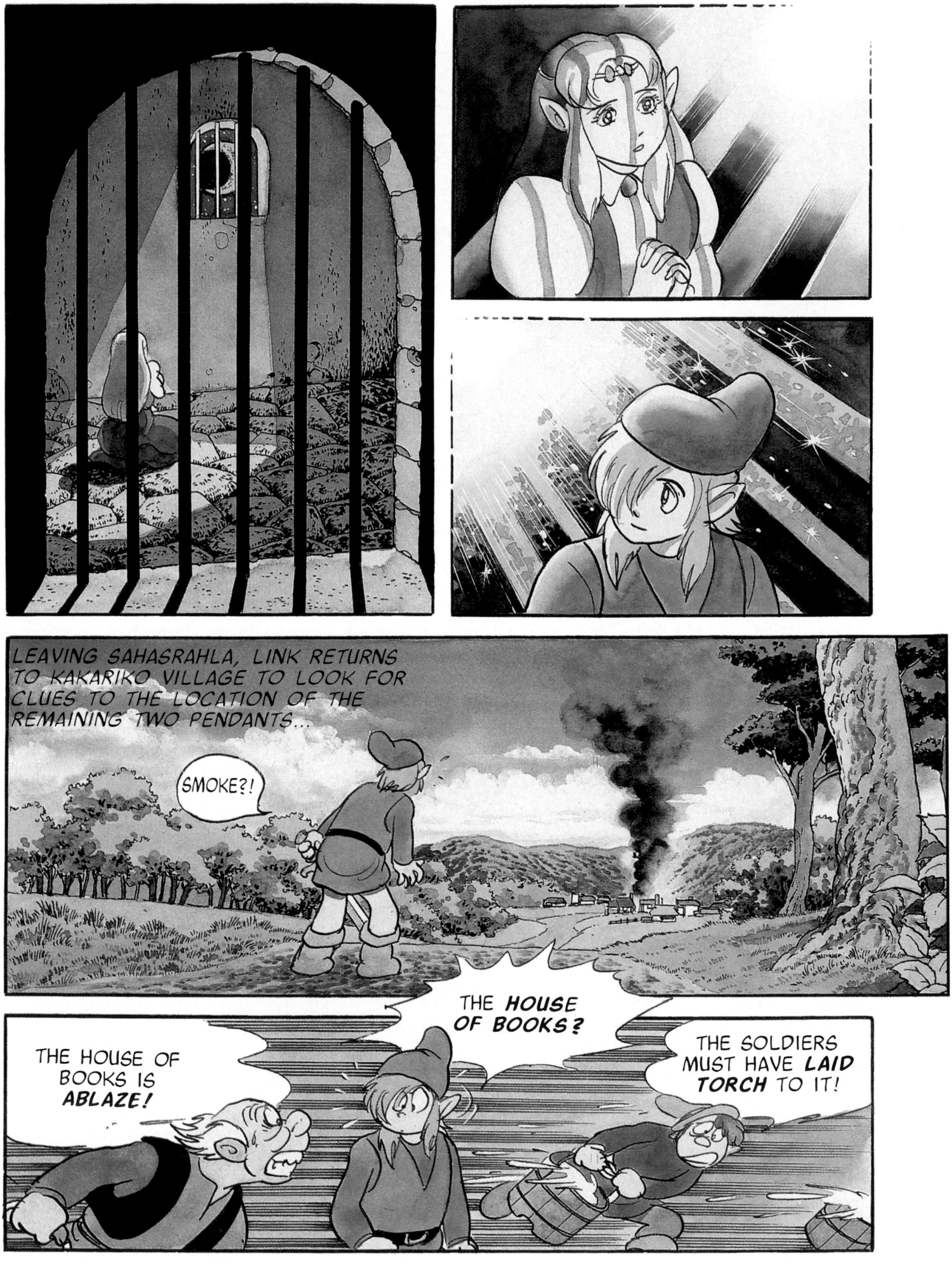
LEAVING SAHASRAHLA, LINK RETURNS TO KAKARIKO VILLAGE TO LOOK FOR CLUES TO THE LOCATION OF THE REMAINING TWO PENDANTS...
SMOKE?!
THE HOUSE OF BOOKS IS ABLAZE!
THE HOUSE OF BOOKS?
THE SOLDIERS MUST HAVE LAID TORCH TO IT!

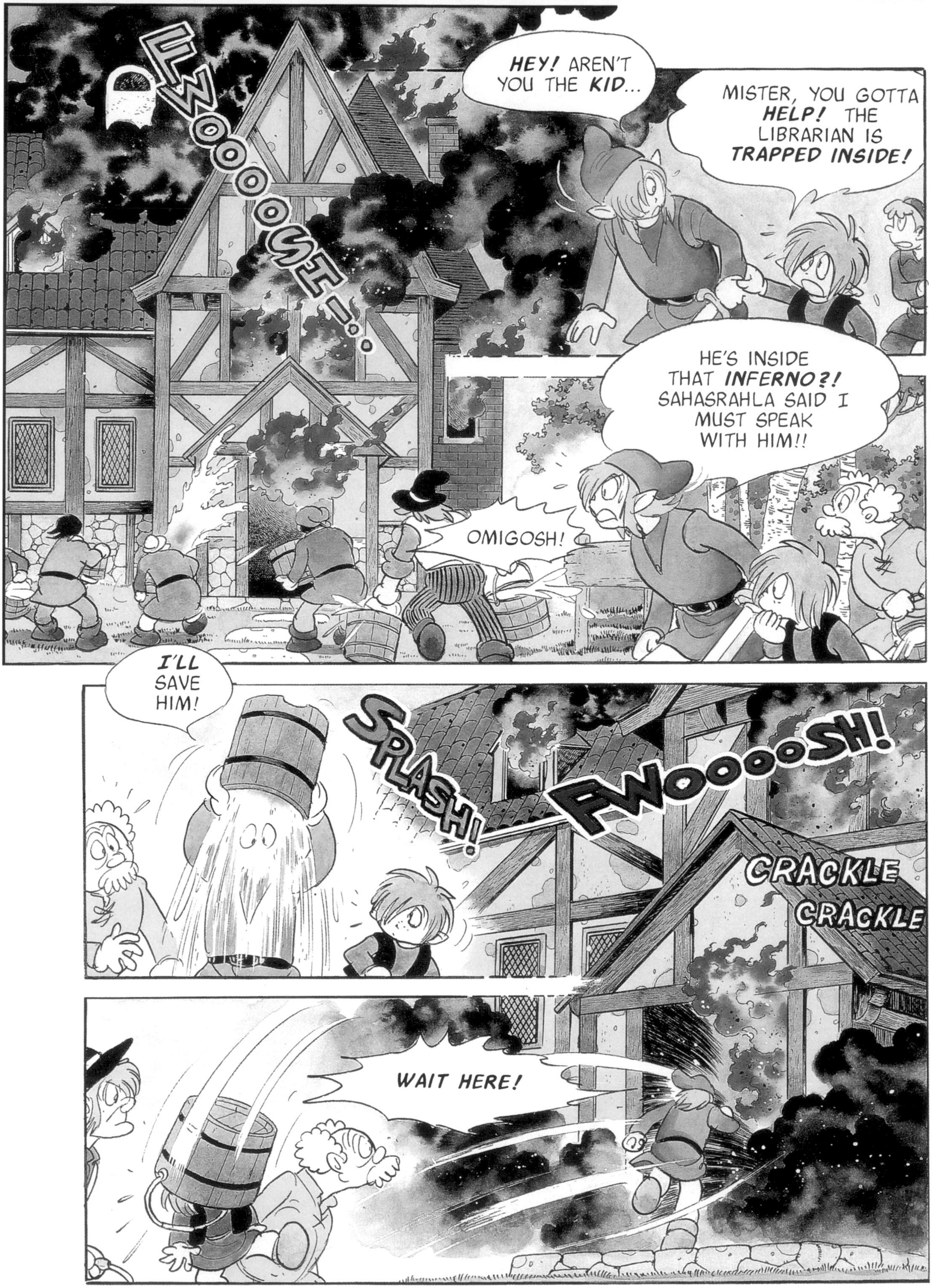
FWOOOOSH!..
HEY! AREN'T YOU THE KID...
MISTER, YOU GOTTA HELP! THE LIBRARIAN IS TRAPPED INSIDE!
HE'S INSIDE THAT INFERNO?! SAHASRAHLA SAID I MUST SPEAK WITH HIM!!
OMIGOSH!
I'LL SAVE HIM!
SPLASH!
FWOOOOSH!
CRACKLE
CRACKLE
WAIT HERE!

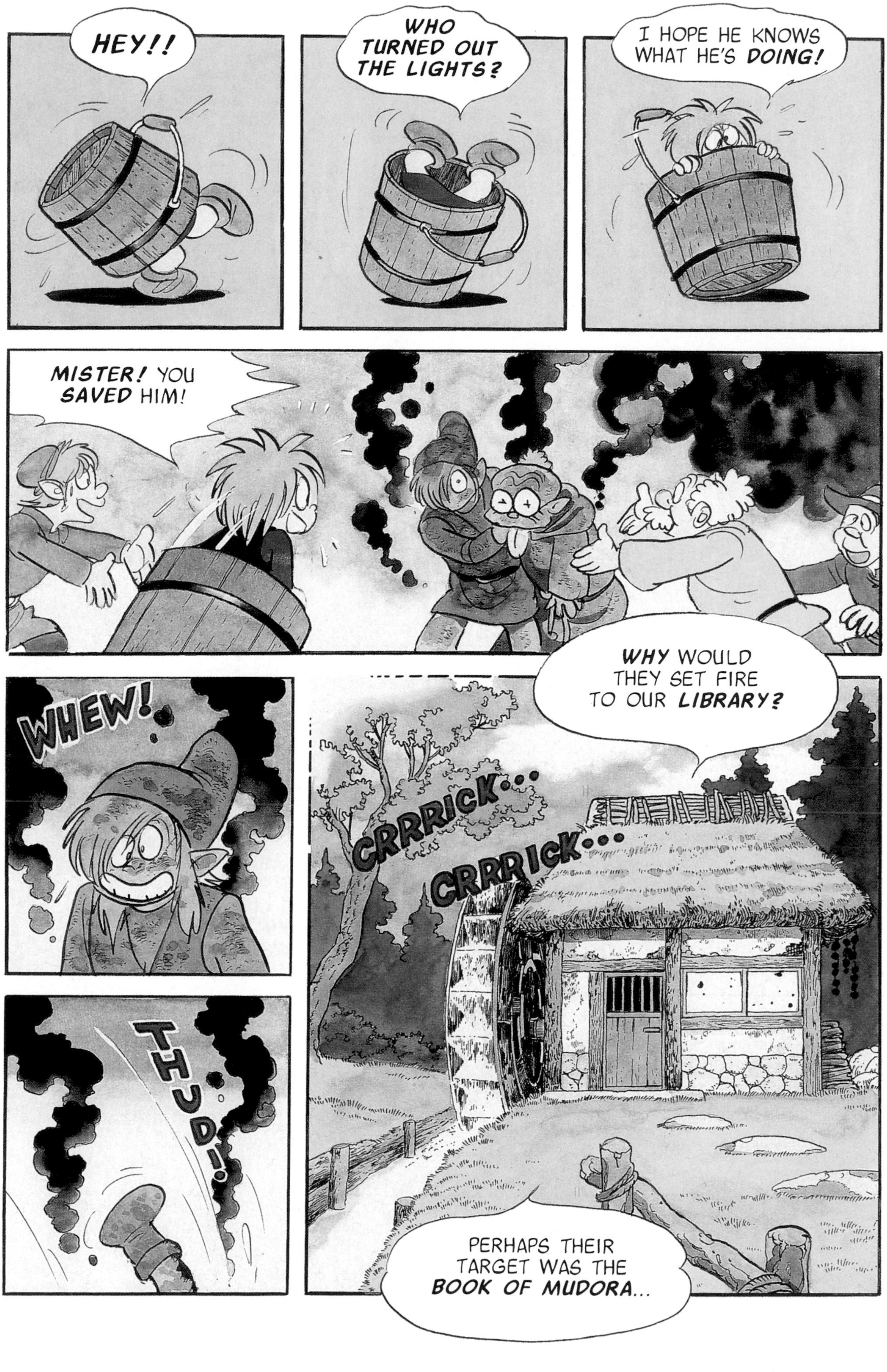
HEY!!
WHO TURNED OUT THE LIGHTS?
I HOPE HE KNOWS WHAT HE'S DOING!
MISTER! YOU SAVED HIM!
WHEW!
THUD!
WHY WOULD THEY SET FIRE TO OUR LIBRARY?
CRRRICK...
CRRRICK...
PERHAPS THEIR TARGET WAS THE BOOK OF MUDORA...

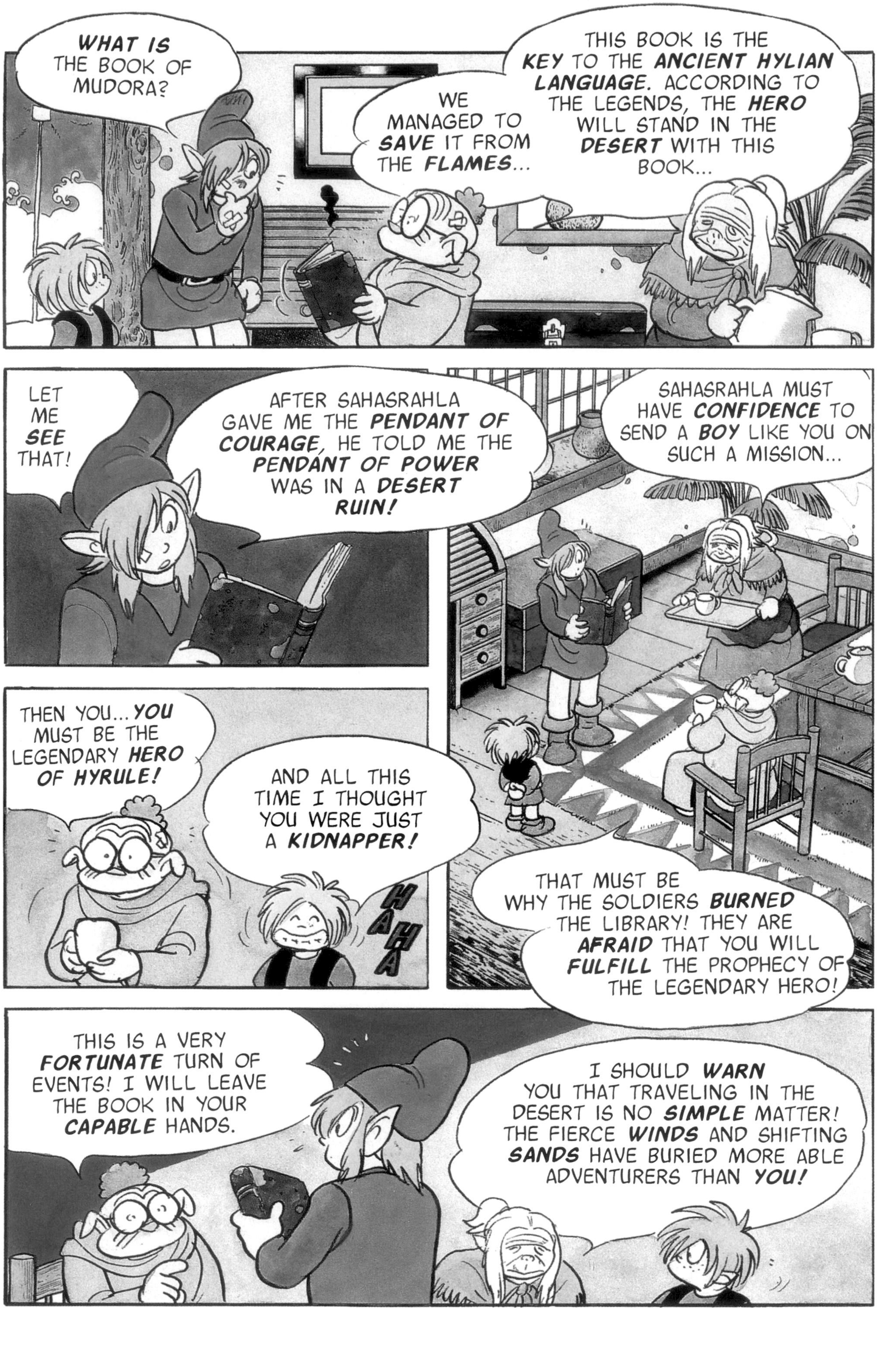
WHAT IS THE BOOK OF MUDORA?
WE MANAGED TO SAVE IT FROM THE FLAMES...
THIS BOOK IS THE KEY TO THE ANCIENT HYLIAN LANGUAGE. ACCORDING TO THE LEGENDS, THE HERO WILL STAND IN THE DESERT WITH THIS BOOK...
LET ME SEE THAT!
AFTER SAHASRAHLA GAVE ME THE PENDANT OF COURAGE, HE TOLD ME THE PENDANT OF POWER WAS IN A DESERT RUIN!
SAHASRAHLA MUST HAVE CONFIDENCE TO SEND A BOY LIKE YOU ON SUCH A MISSION...
THEN YOU...YOU MUST BE THE LEGENDARY HERO OF HYRULE!
AND ALL THIS TIME I THOUGHT YOU WERE JUST A KIDNAPPER!
HAHAHA
THAT MUST BE WHY THE SOLDIERS BURNED THE LIBRARY! THEY ARE AFRAID THAT YOU WILL FULFILL THE PROPHECY OF THE LEGENDARY HERO!
THIS IS A VERY FORTUNATE TURN OF EVENTS! I WILL LEAVE THE BOOK IN YOUR CAPABLE HANDS.
I SHOULD WARN YOU THAT TRAVELING IN THE DESERT IS NO SIMPLE MATTER! THE FIERCE WINDS AND SHIFTING SANDS HAVE BURIED MORE ABLE ADVENTURERS THAN YOU!

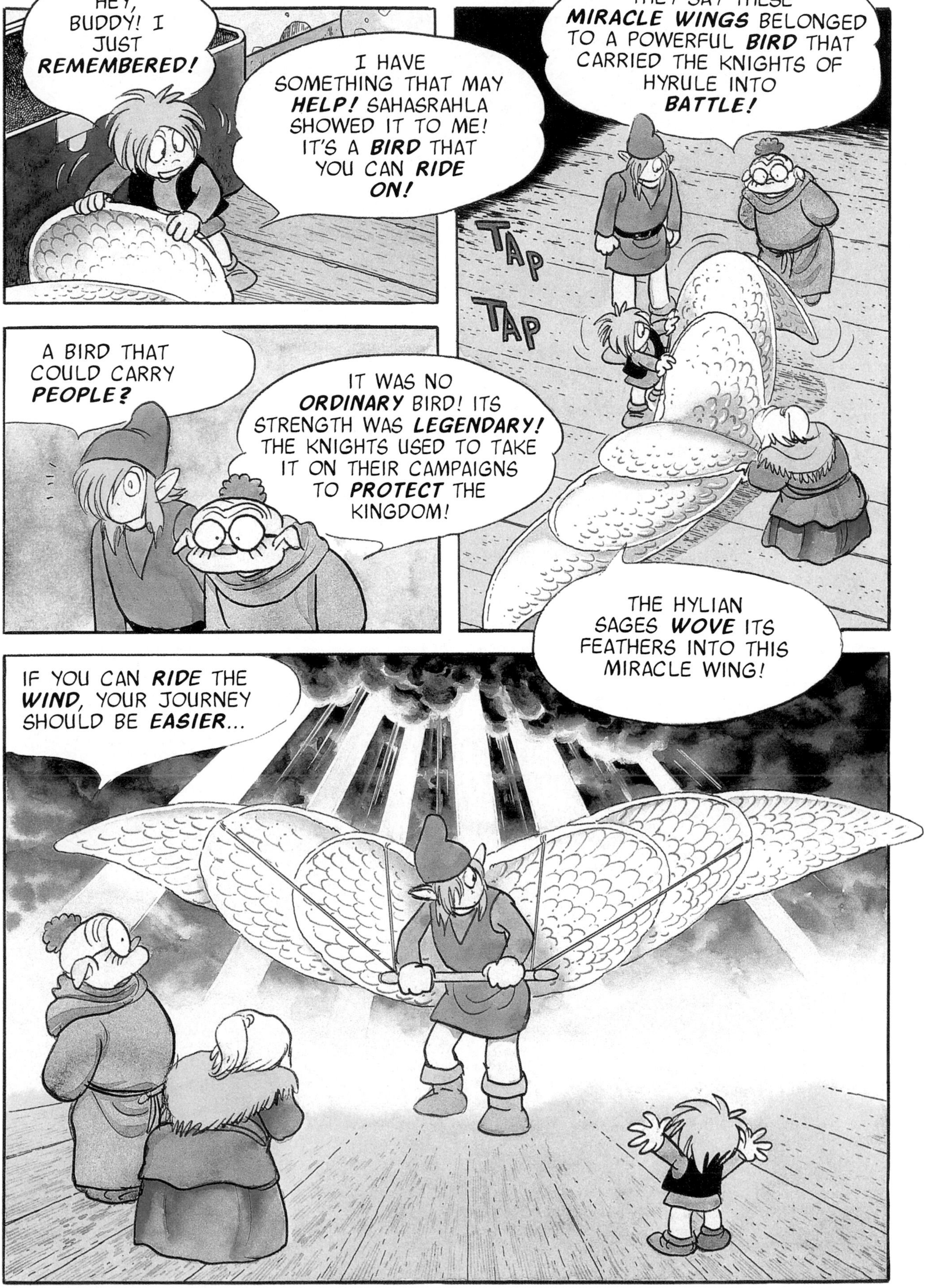
HEY, BUDDY! I JUST **REMEMBERED!**
I HAVE SOMETHING THAT MAY **HELP!** SAHASRAHLA SHOWED IT TO ME! IT'S A **BIRD** THAT YOU CAN **RIDE ON!**
THEY SAY THESE **MIRACLE WINGS** BELONGED TO A POWERFUL **BIRD** THAT CARRIED THE KNIGHTS OF HYRULE INTO **BATTLE!**
TAP
TAP
A BIRD THAT COULD CARRY **PEOPLE?**
IT WAS NO **ORDINARY** BIRD! ITS STRENGTH WAS **LEGENDARY!** THE KNIGHTS USED TO TAKE IT ON THEIR CAMPAIGNS TO **PROTECT** THE KINGDOM!
THE HYLIAN SAGES **WOVE** ITS FEATHERS INTO THIS MIRACLE WING!
IF YOU CAN **RIDE** THE **WIND**, YOUR JOURNEY SHOULD BE **EASIER**...

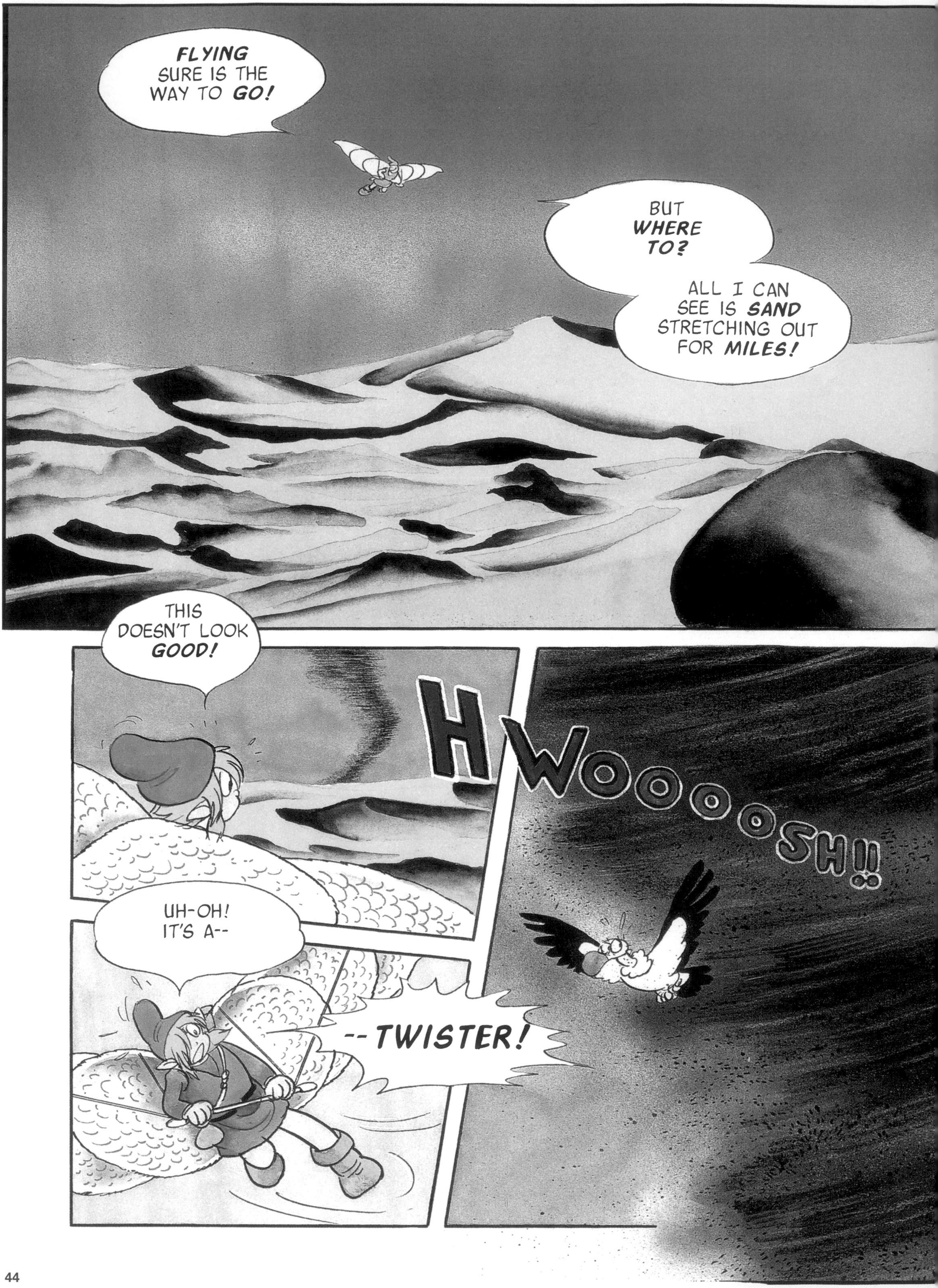
FLYING SURE IS THE WAY TO GO!
BUT WHERE TO?
ALL I CAN SEE IS SAND STRETCHING OUT FOR MILES!
THIS DOESN'T LOOK GOOD!
HWOOOOOSH!!
UH-OH! IT'S A--
--TWISTER!

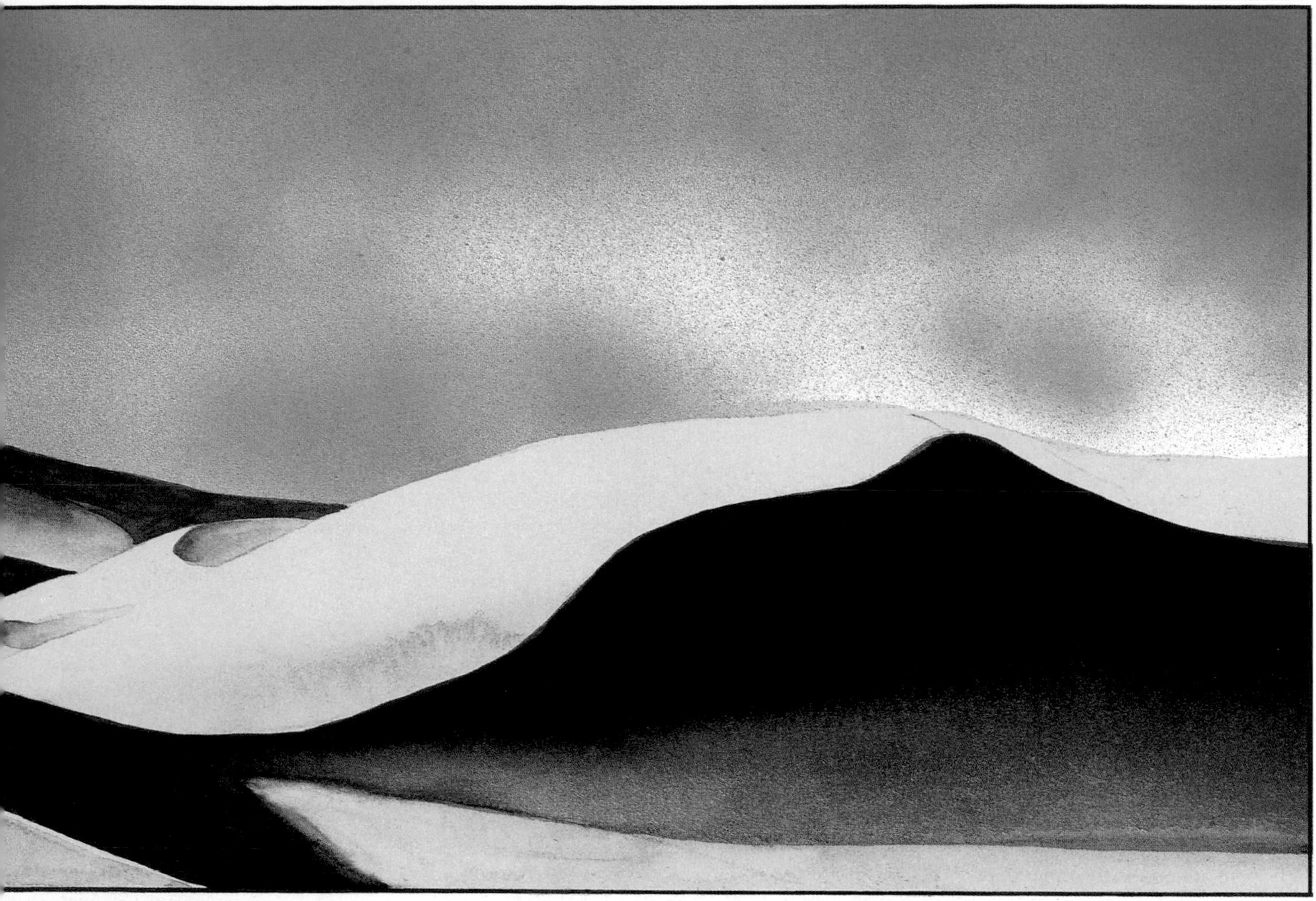

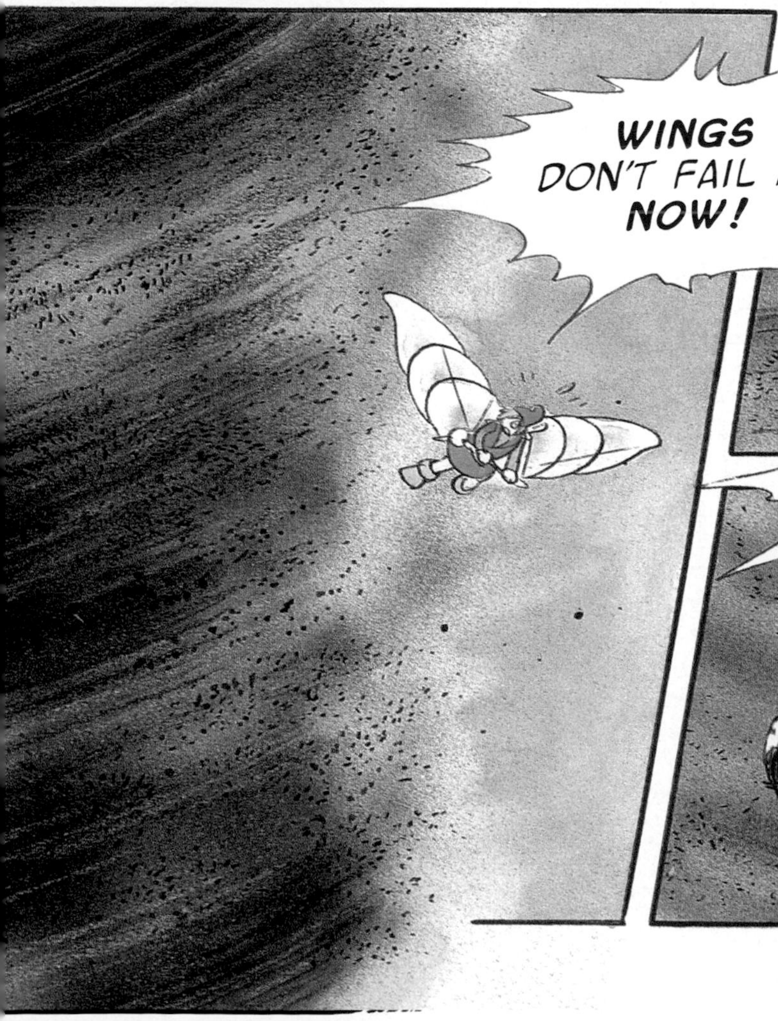
WINGS DON'T FAIL ME NOW!

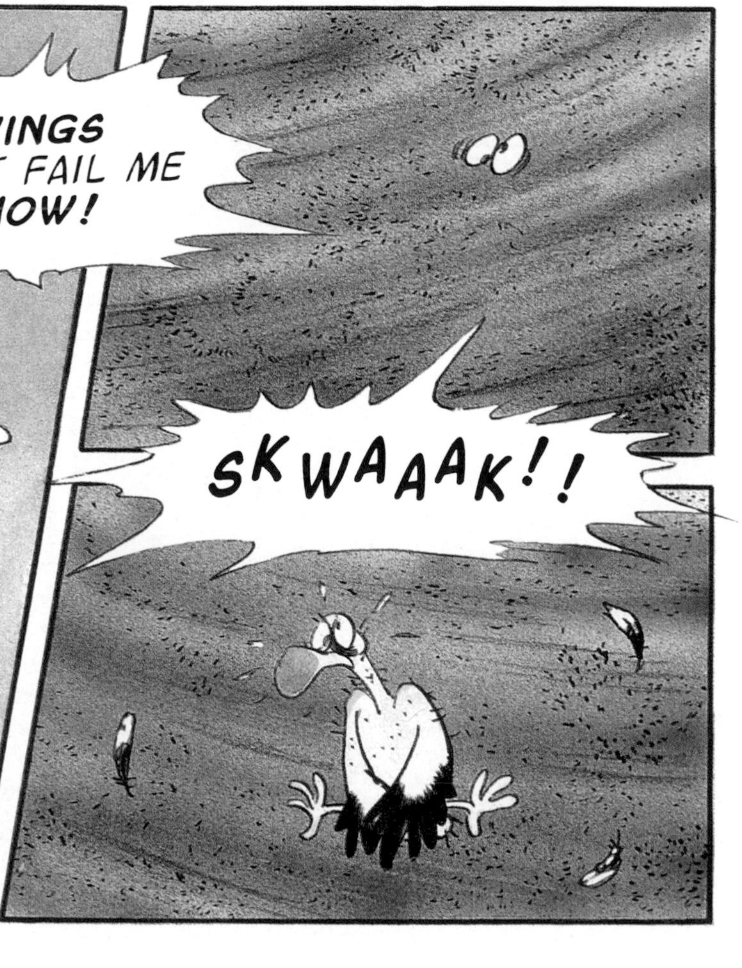
SKWAAAK!!

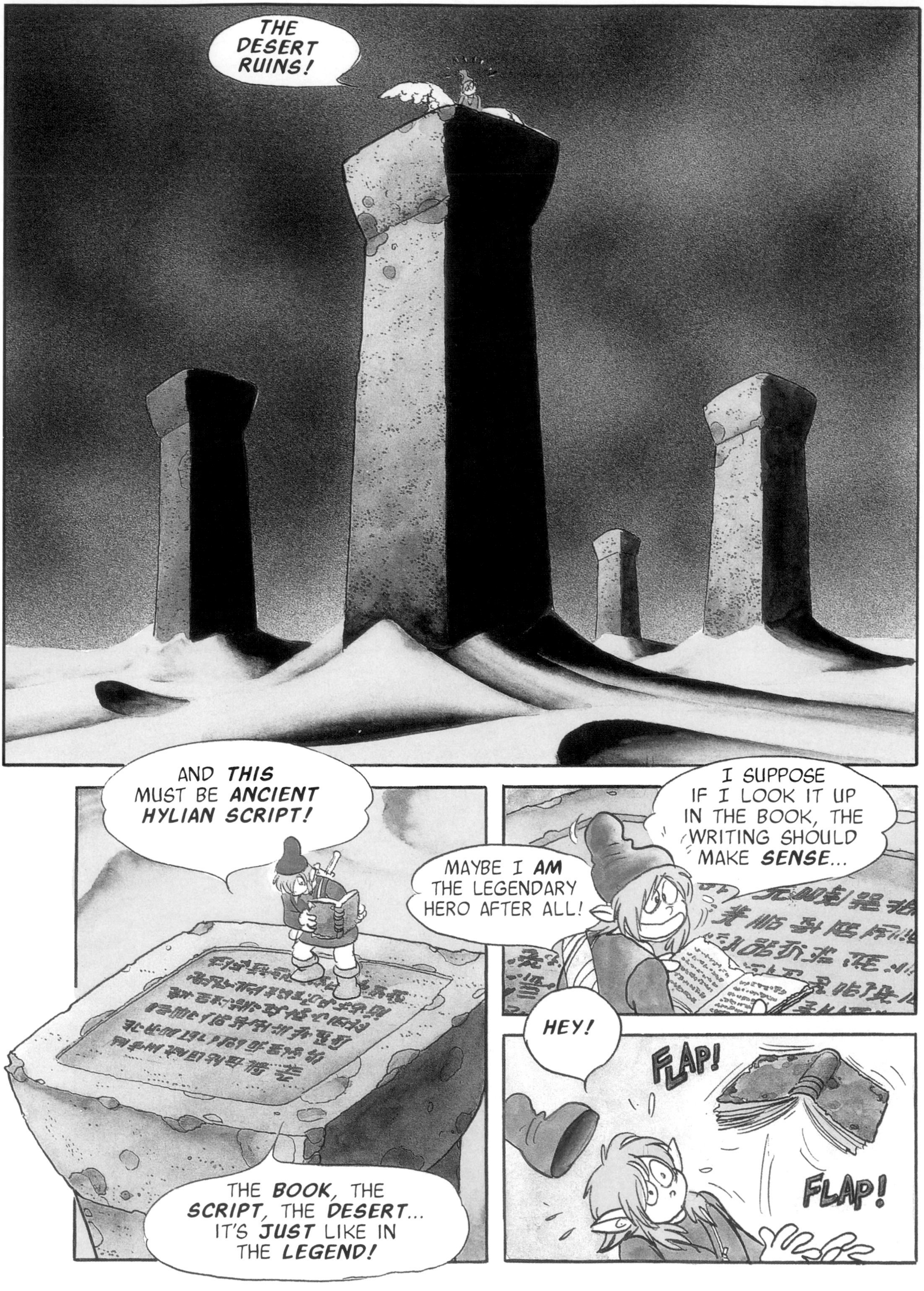
THE DESERT RUINS!
AND THIS MUST BE ANCIENT HYLIAN SCRIPT!
THE BOOK, THE SCRIPT, THE DESERT... IT'S JUST LIKE IN THE LEGEND!
I SUPPOSE IF I LOOK IT UP IN THE BOOK, THE WRITING SHOULD MAKE SENSE...
MAYBE I AM THE LEGENDARY HERO AFTER ALL!
HEY!
FLAP!
FLAP!

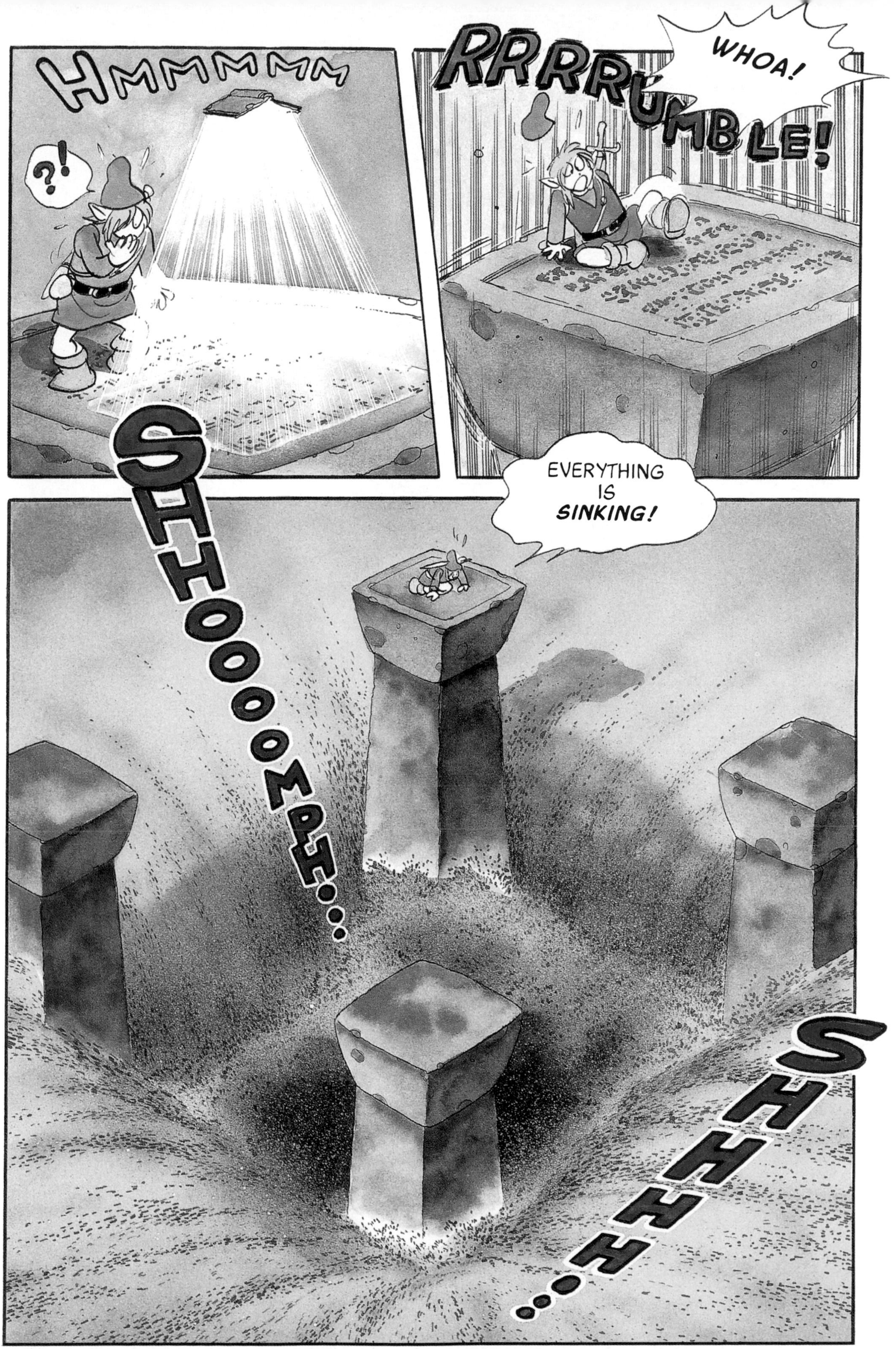
HMMMMM
?!
RRRRRUMBLE!
WHOA!
SHHOOOOOMPH...
EVERYTHING IS SINKING!
SHHHHH...

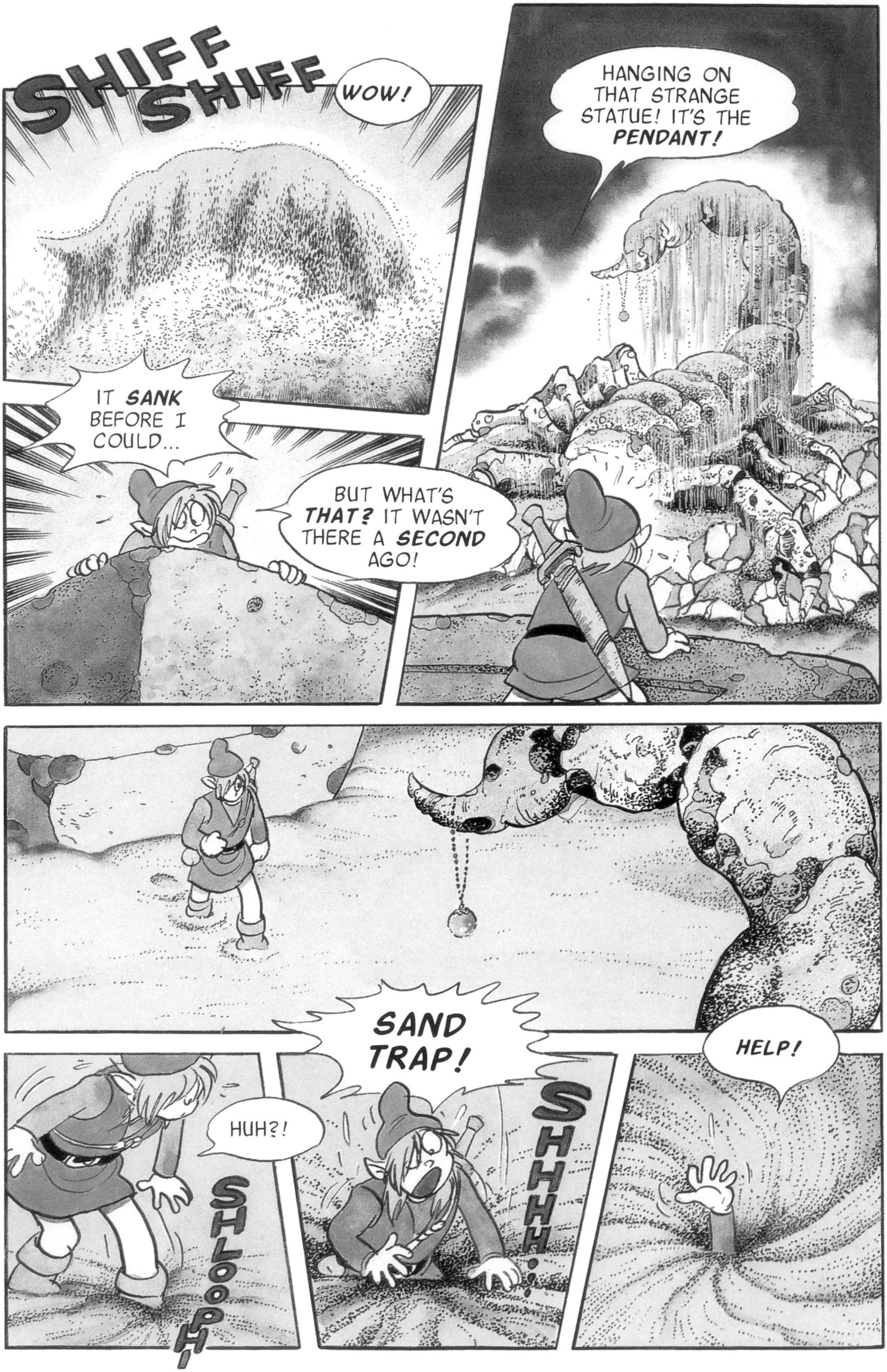

SHIFF SHIFF
WOW!
IT SANK BEFORE I COULD...
BUT WHAT'S THAT? IT WASN'T THERE A SECOND AGO!
HANGING ON THAT STRANGE STATUE! IT'S THE PENDANT!
HUH?!
SHLOOOPH!
SAND TRAP!
SHHHH...
HELP!

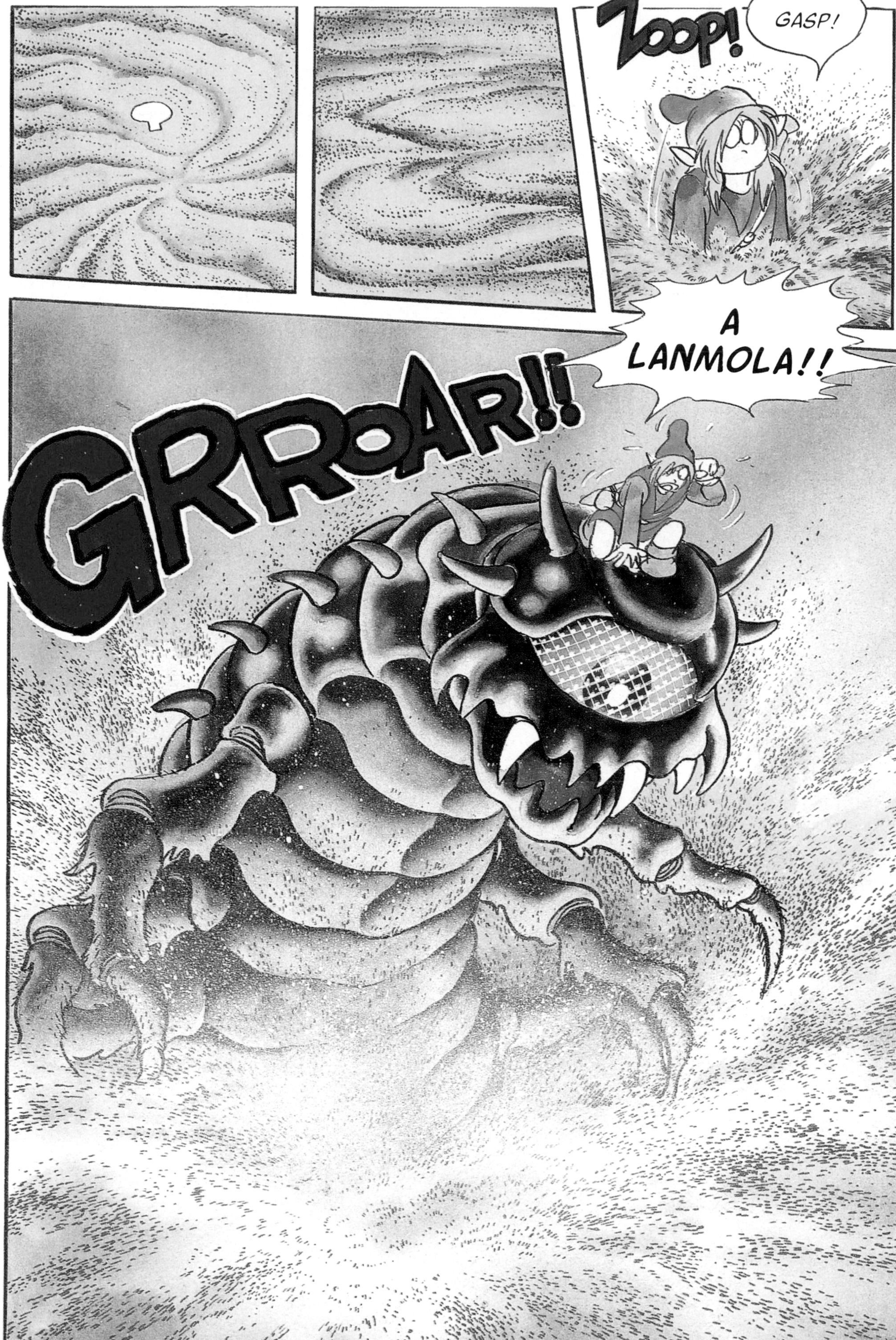
ZOOP!
GASP!
A LANMOLA!!
GRROAR!!

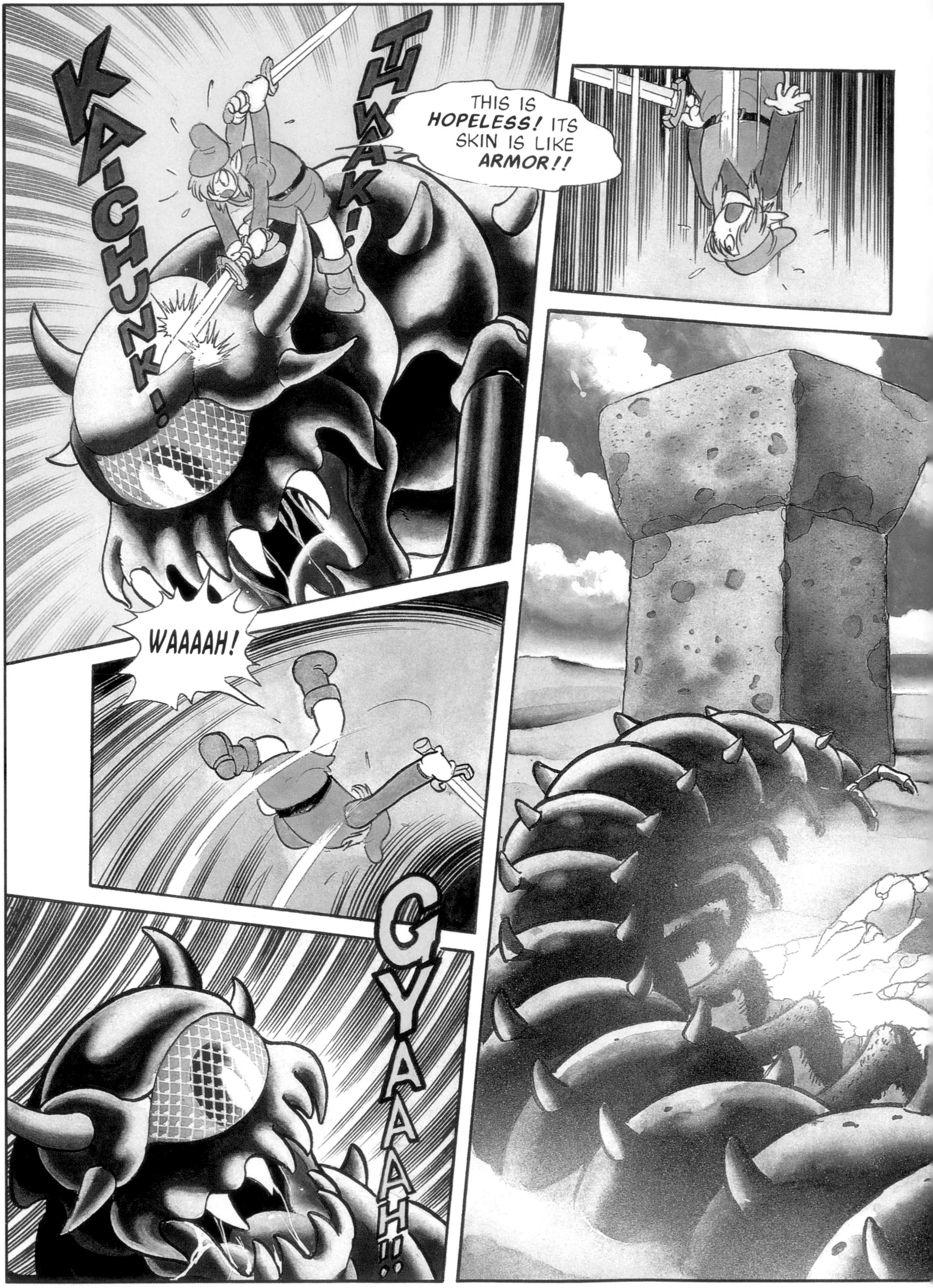
KA-CHUNK!!
THWAAK!!
THIS IS HOPELESS! ITS SKIN IS LIKE ARMOR!!
WAAAAH!
GYAAAH!!

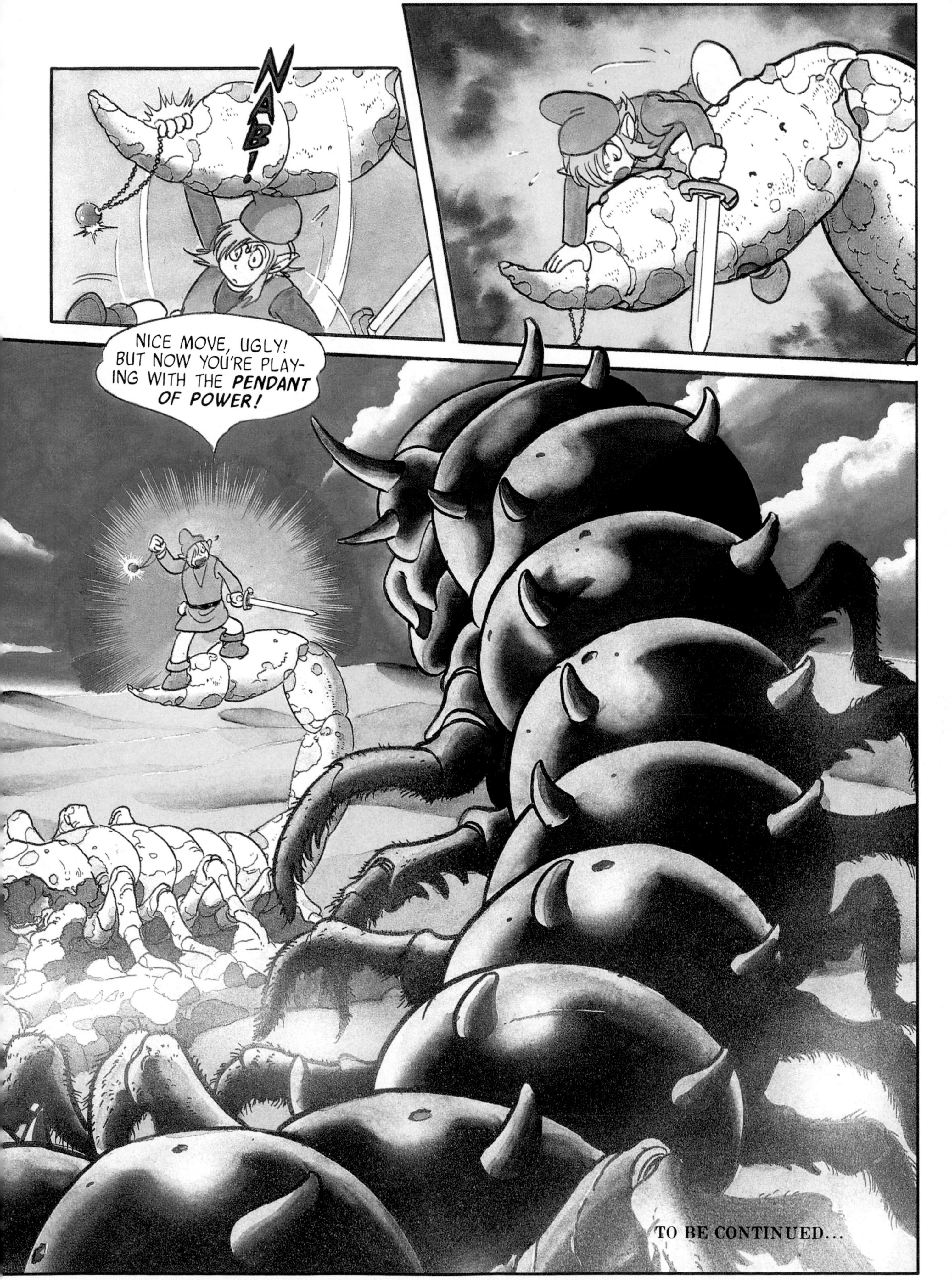
NAB!
NICE MOVE, UGLY! BUT NOW YOU'RE PLAYING WITH THE ***PENDANT OF POWER!***
TO BE CONTINUED...

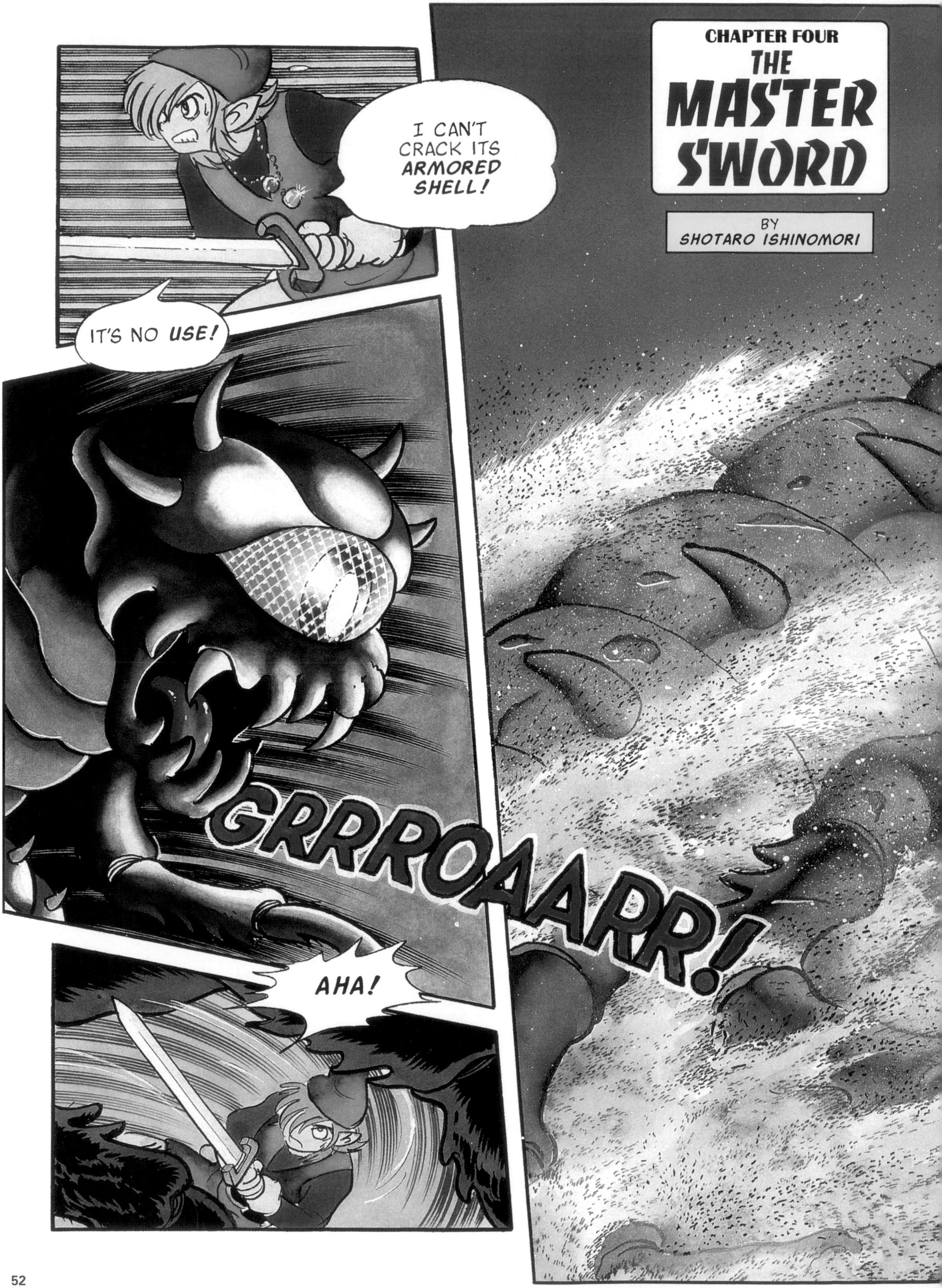
I CAN'T CRACK ITS ARMORED SHELL!
IT'S NO USE!
GRRROAARR!
AHA!
CHAPTER FOUR
THE MASTER SWORD
BY SHOTARO ISHINOMORI

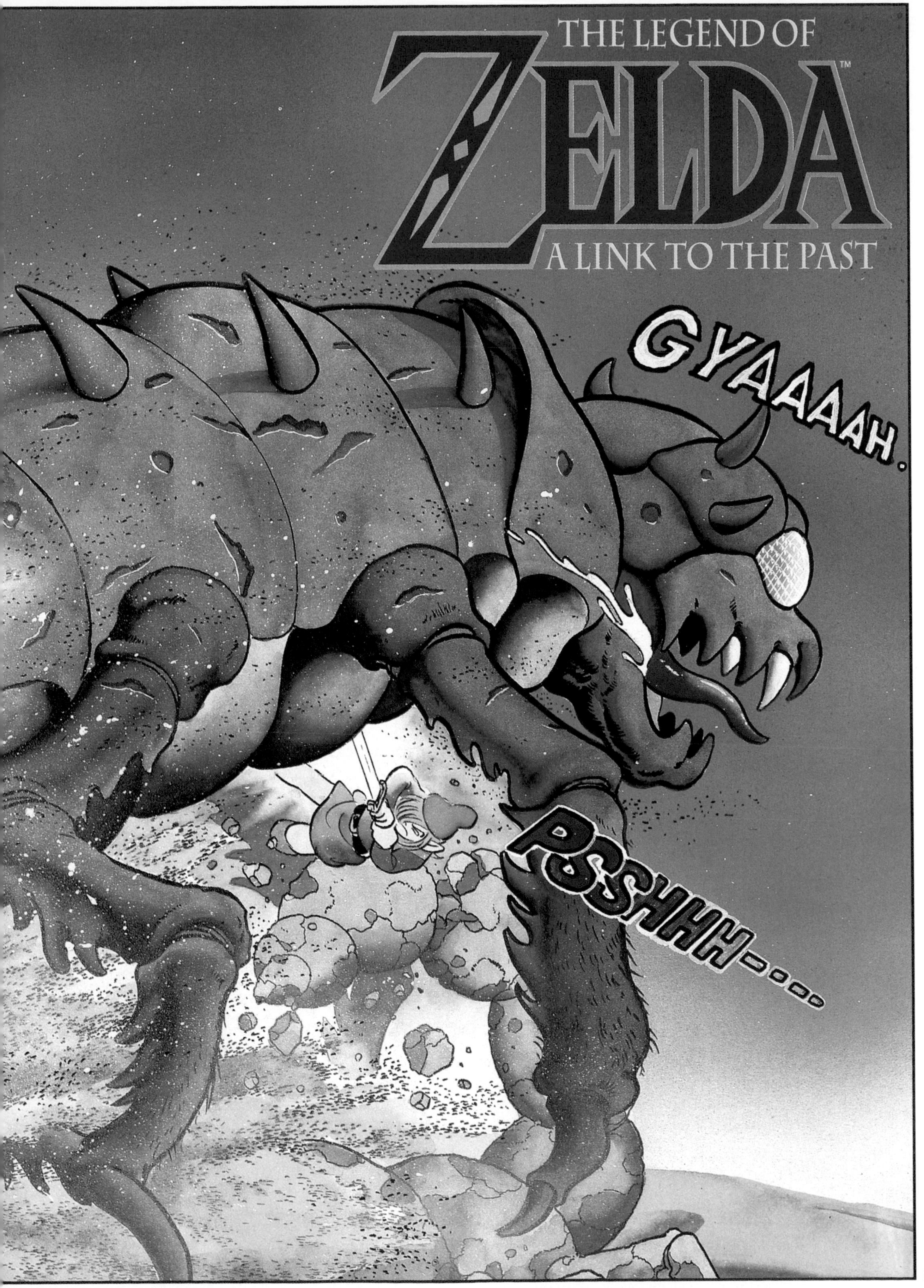
THE LEGEND OF
ZELDA™
A LINK TO THE PAST
GYAAAAH.
PSSHHH...

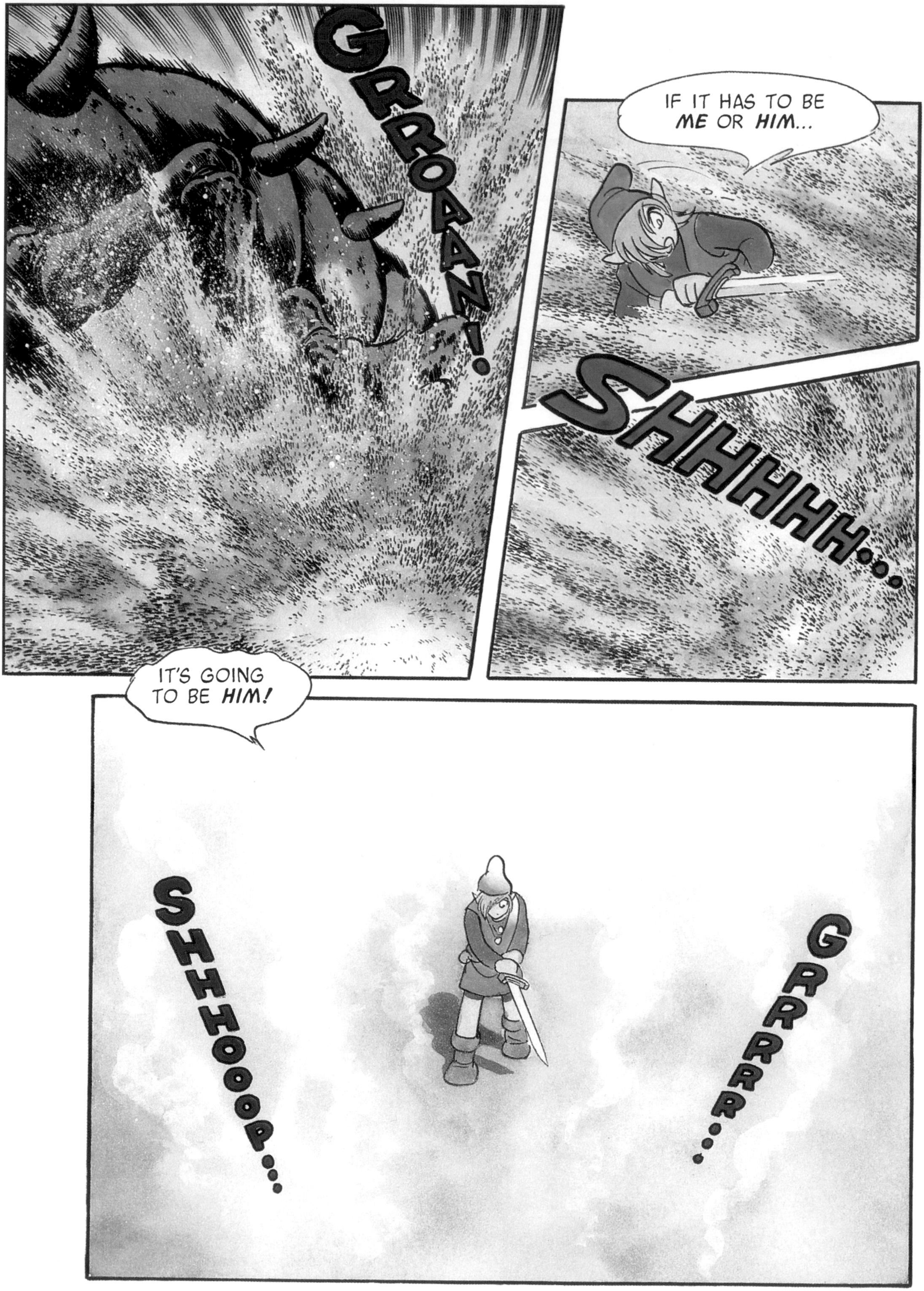
GRROAAN!
IF IT HAS TO BE *ME* OR *HIM*...
SHHHHHH...
IT'S GOING TO BE *HIM!*
SHHOOOP...
GRRRRR...

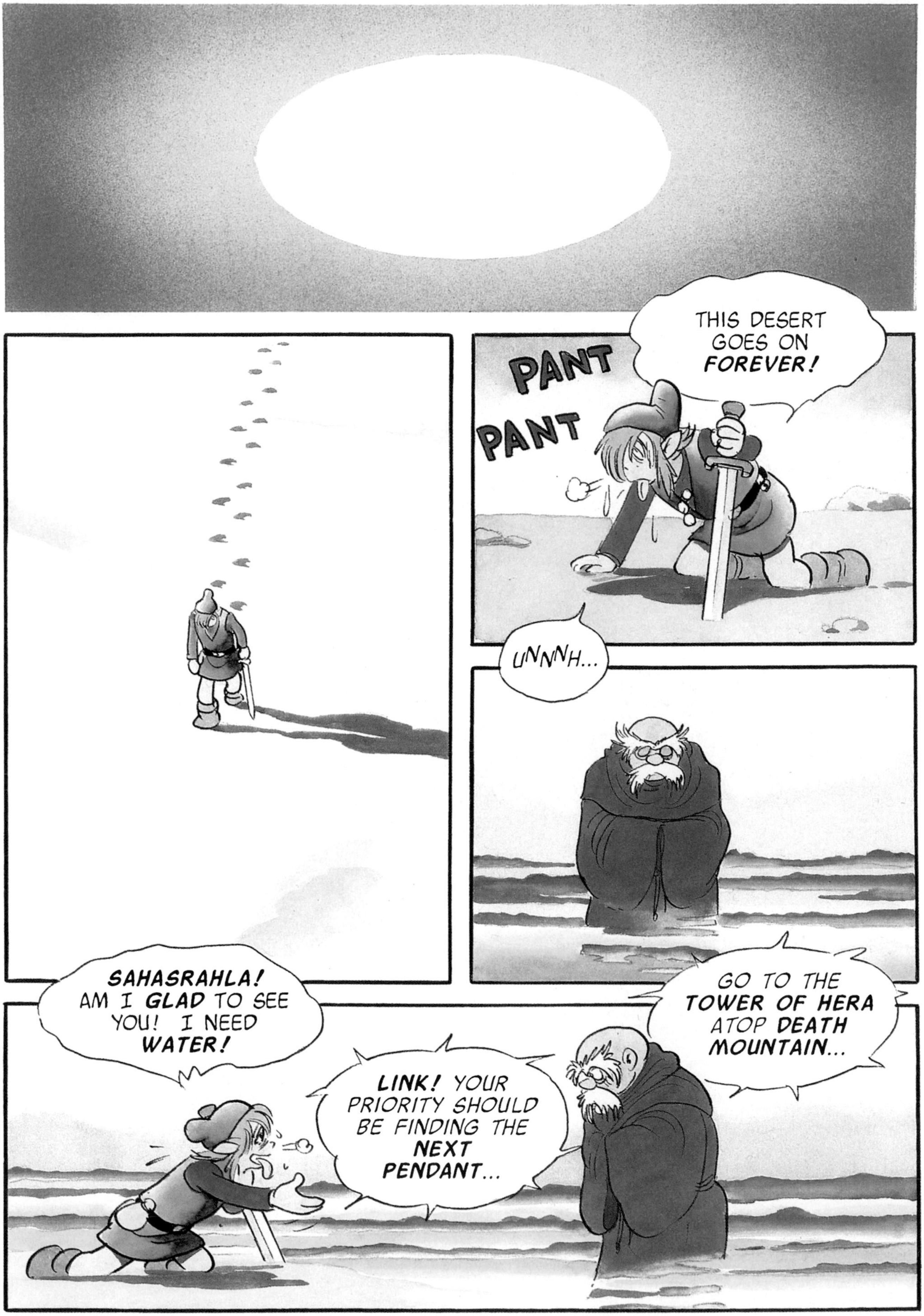

PANT
PANT
THIS DESERT GOES ON FOREVER!
UNNNH...
SAHASRAHLA! AM I GLAD TO SEE YOU! I NEED WATER!
LINK! YOUR PRIORITY SHOULD BE FINDING THE NEXT PENDANT...
GO TO THE TOWER OF HERA ATOP DEATH MOUNTAIN...

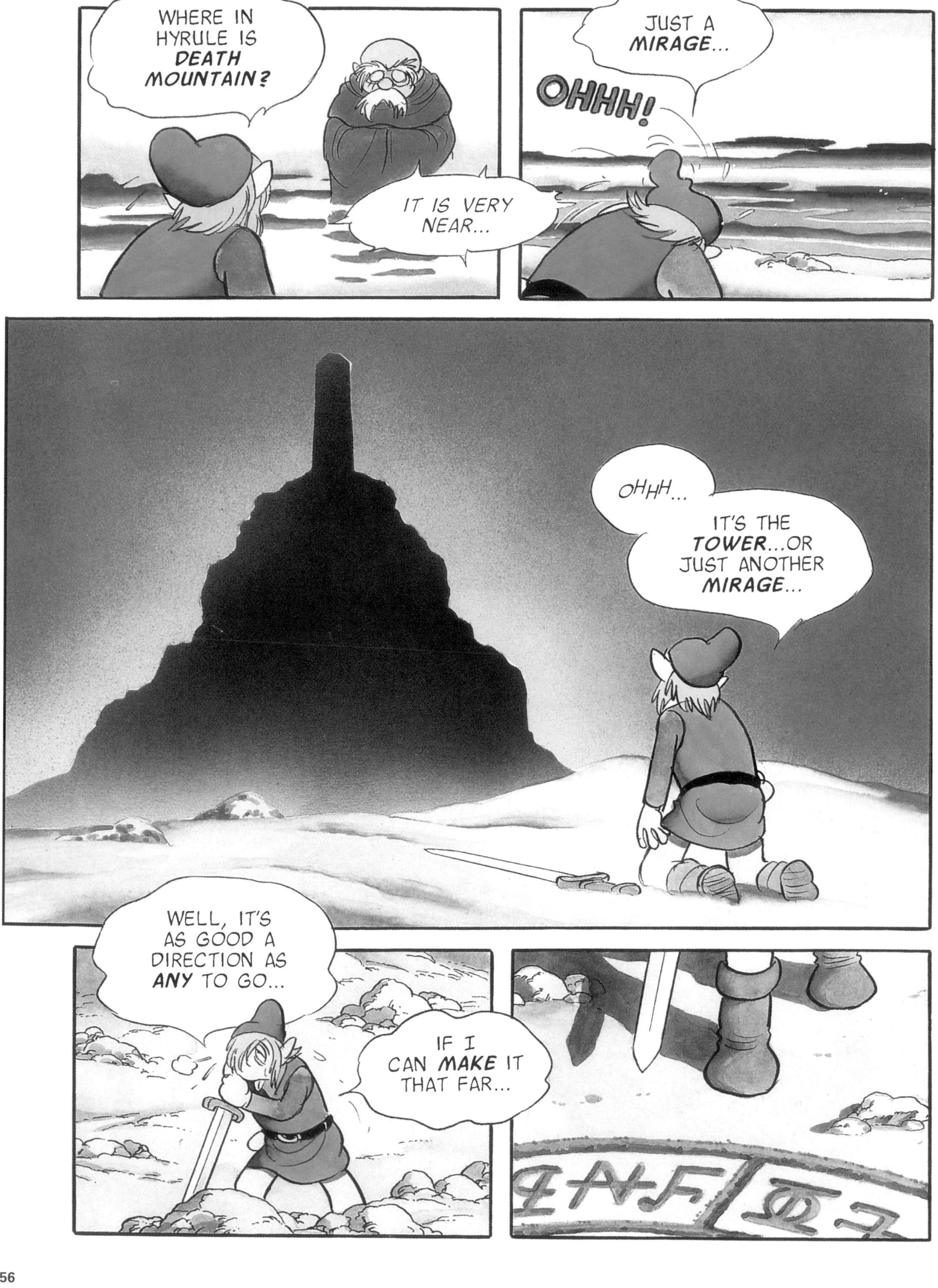
WHERE IN HYRULE IS **DEATH MOUNTAIN?**
IT IS VERY NEAR...
JUST A **MIRAGE**...
OHHH!
OHHH...
IT'S THE **TOWER**...OR JUST ANOTHER **MIRAGE**...
WELL, IT'S AS GOOD A DIRECTION AS **ANY** TO GO...
IF I CAN **MAKE** IT THAT FAR...

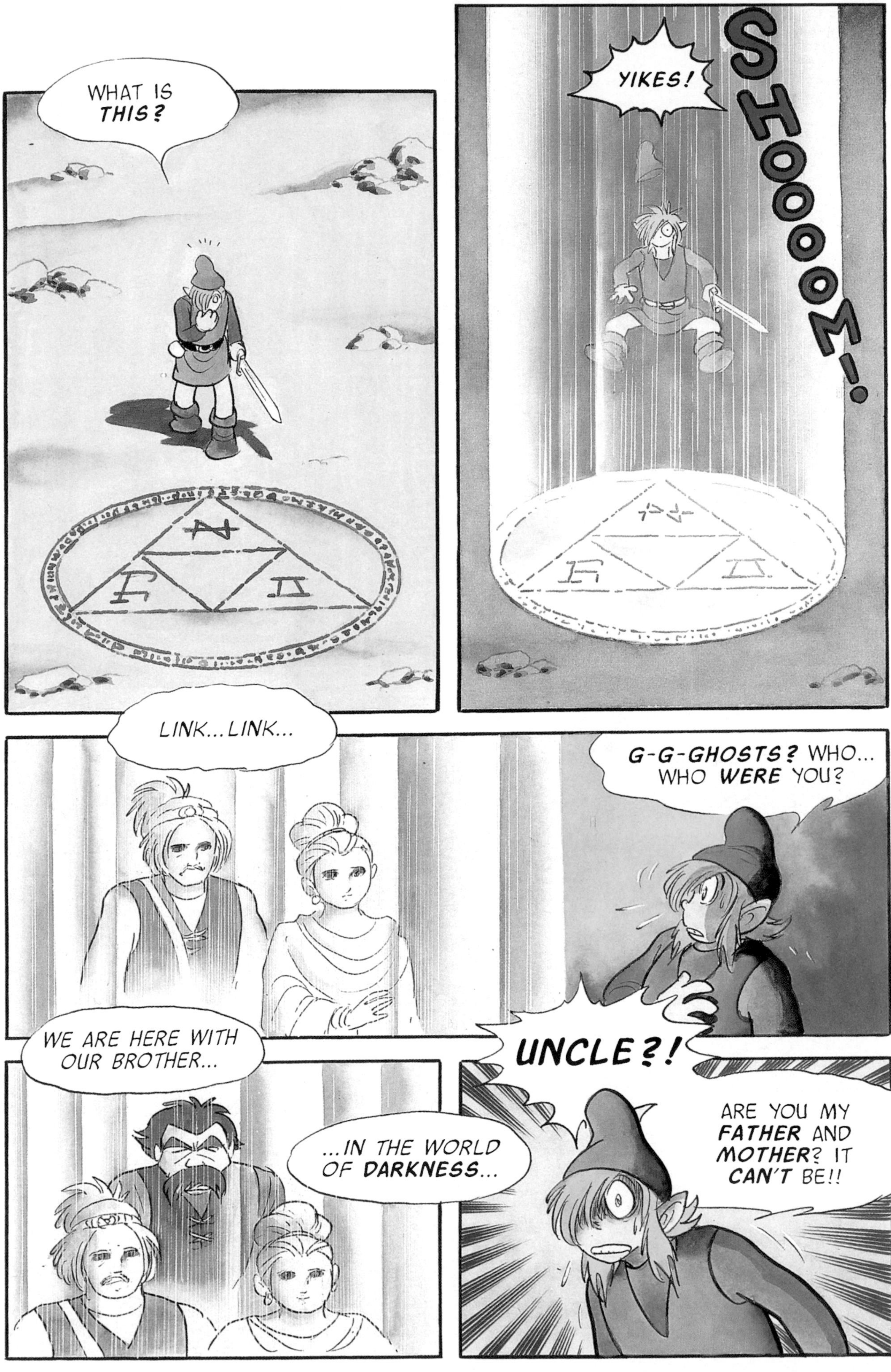
WHAT IS *THIS?*
YIKES!
SHOOOOOM!
LINK...LINK...
G-G-GHOSTS? WHO... WHO *WERE* YOU?
WE ARE HERE WITH OUR BROTHER...
...IN THE WORLD OF **DARKNESS**...
UNCLE?!
ARE YOU MY **FATHER** AND **MOTHER**? IT *CAN'T* BE!!

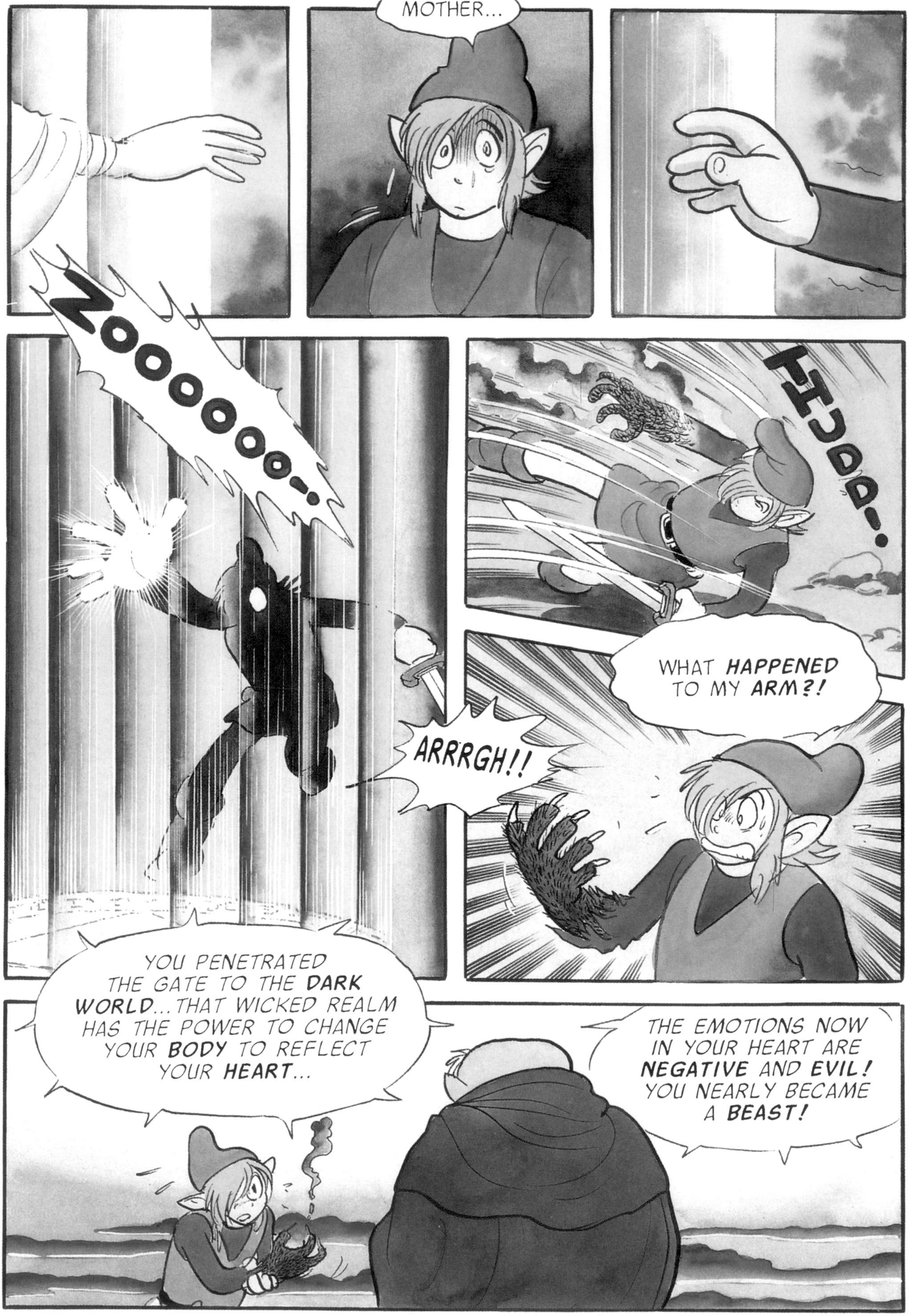
MOTHER...
ZOOOOOOO-!!
THUDD!
WHAT HAPPENED TO MY ARM?!
ARRRGH!!
YOU PENETRATED THE GATE TO THE DARK WORLD...THAT WICKED REALM HAS THE POWER TO CHANGE YOUR BODY TO REFLECT YOUR HEART...
THE EMOTIONS NOW IN YOUR HEART ARE NEGATIVE AND EVIL! YOU NEARLY BECAME A BEAST!

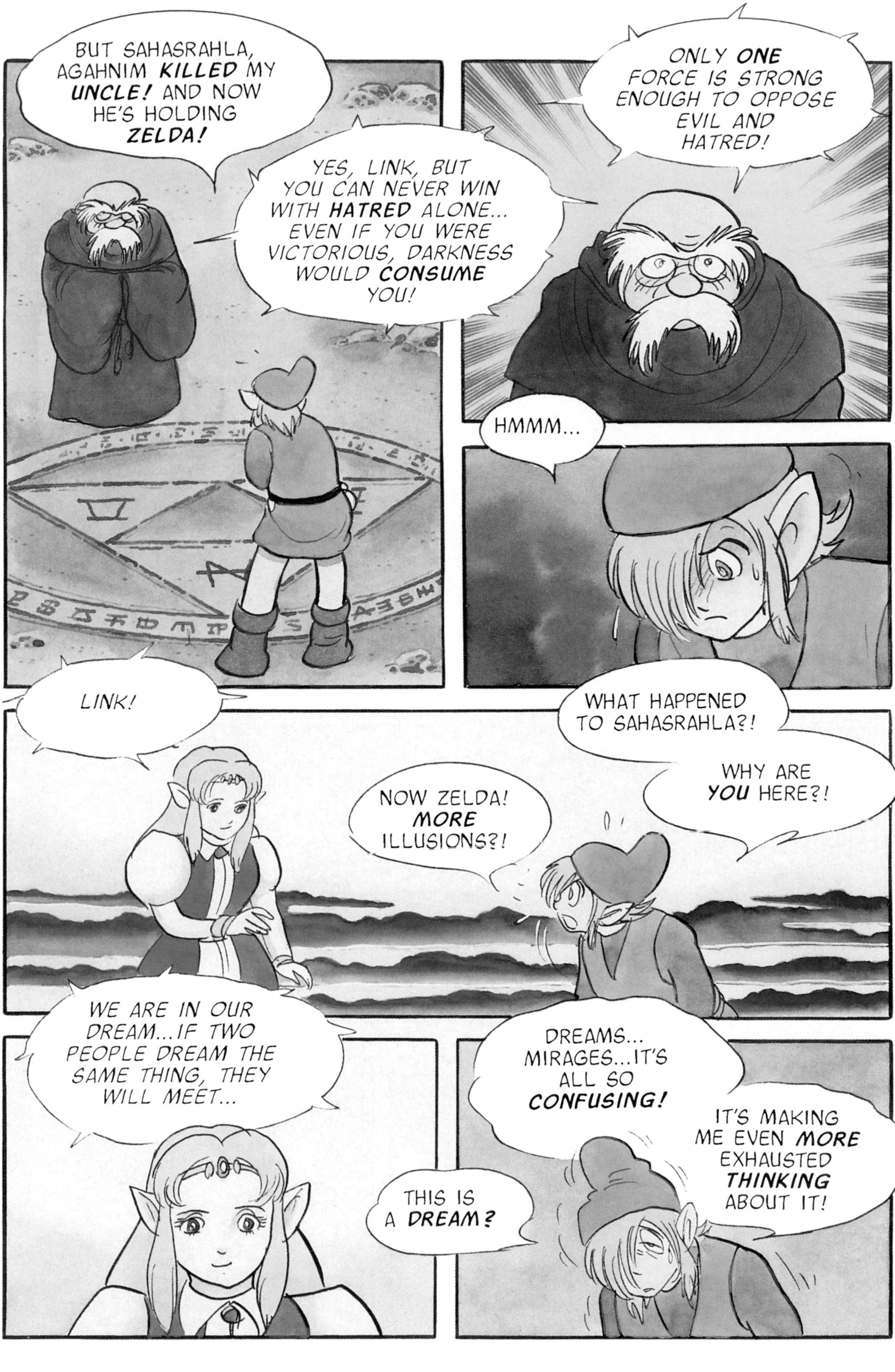
BUT SAHASRAHLA, AGAHNIM KILLED MY UNCLE! AND NOW HE'S HOLDING ZELDA!
YES, LINK, BUT YOU CAN NEVER WIN WITH HATRED ALONE... EVEN IF YOU WERE VICTORIOUS, DARKNESS WOULD CONSUME YOU!
ONLY ONE FORCE IS STRONG ENOUGH TO OPPOSE EVIL AND HATRED!
HMMM...
LINK!
WHAT HAPPENED TO SAHASRAHLA?!
WHY ARE YOU HERE?!
NOW ZELDA! MORE ILLUSIONS?!
WE ARE IN OUR DREAM...IF TWO PEOPLE DREAM THE SAME THING, THEY WILL MEET...
THIS IS A DREAM?
DREAMS... MIRAGES...IT'S ALL SO CONFUSING!
IT'S MAKING ME EVEN MORE EXHAUSTED THINKING ABOUT IT!

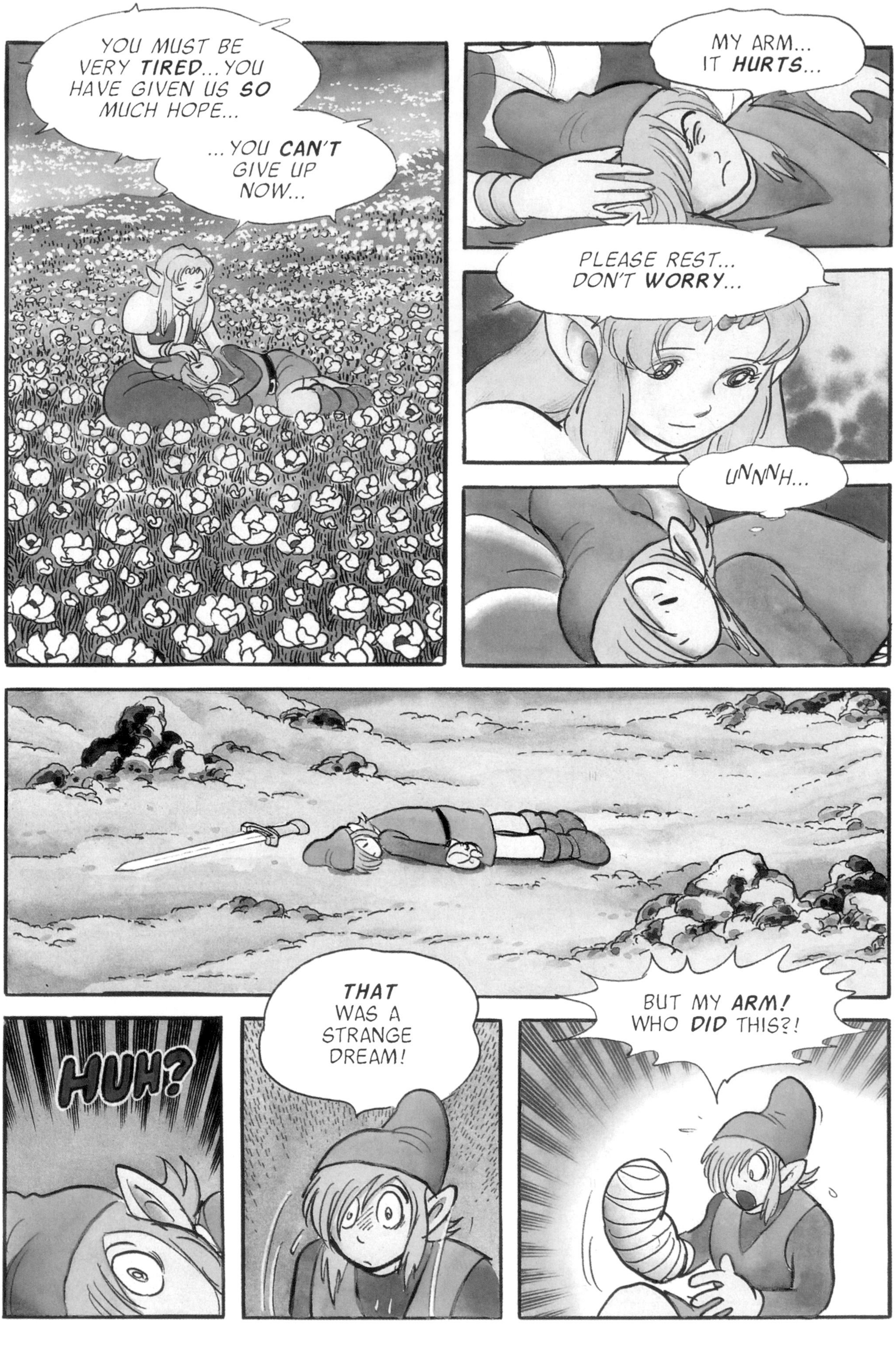
YOU MUST BE VERY TIRED... YOU HAVE GIVEN US SO MUCH HOPE...
...YOU CAN'T GIVE UP NOW...
MY ARM... IT HURTS...
PLEASE REST... DON'T WORRY...
UNNNH...
HUH?
THAT WAS A STRANGE DREAM!
BUT MY ARM! WHO DID THIS?!

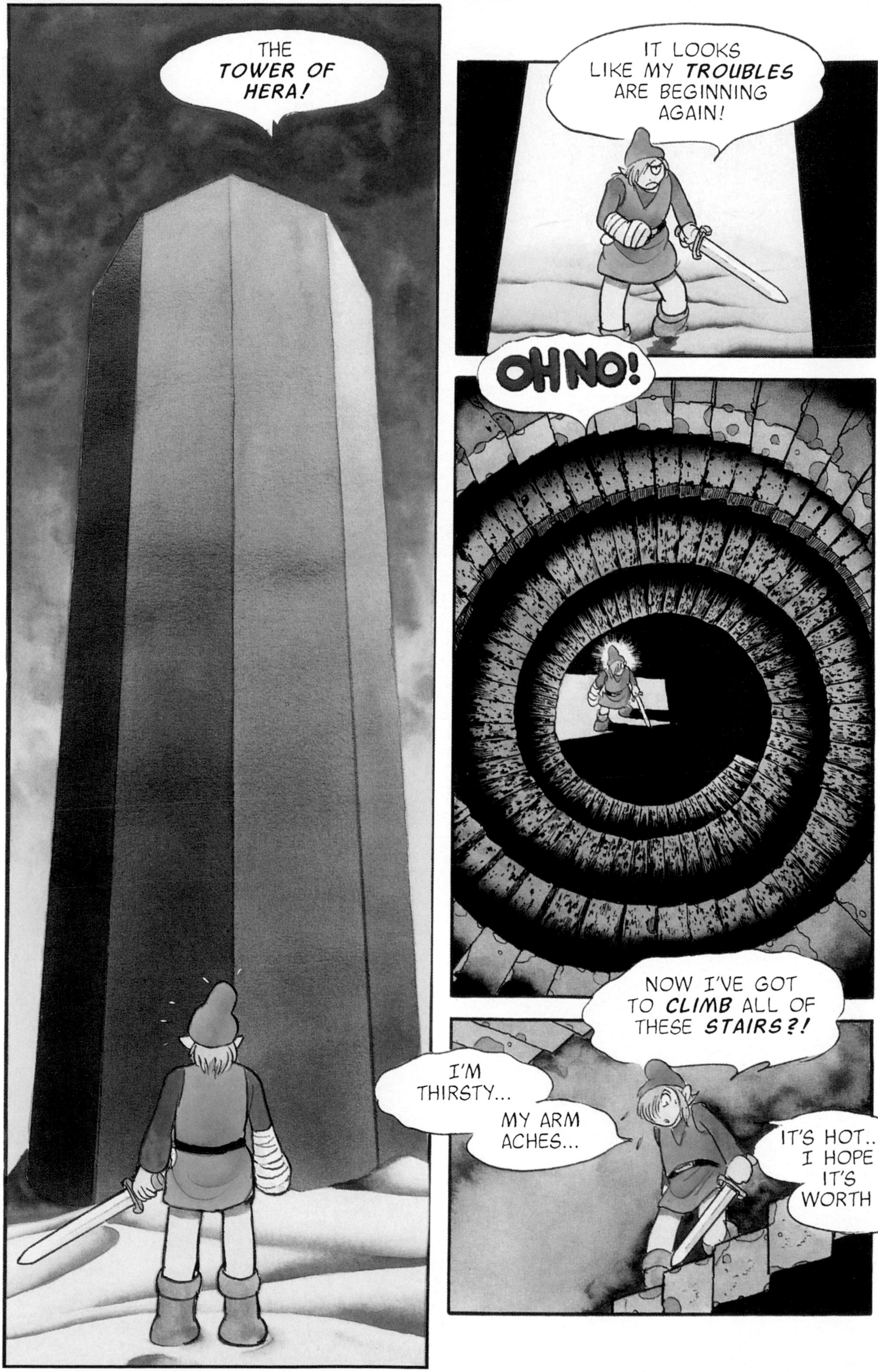
THE TOWER OF HERA!
IT LOOKS LIKE MY TROUBLES ARE BEGINNING AGAIN!
OH NO!
NOW I'VE GOT TO CLIMB ALL OF THESE STAIRS?!
I'M THIRSTY...
MY ARM ACHES...
IT'S HOT... I HOPE IT'S WORTH IT!

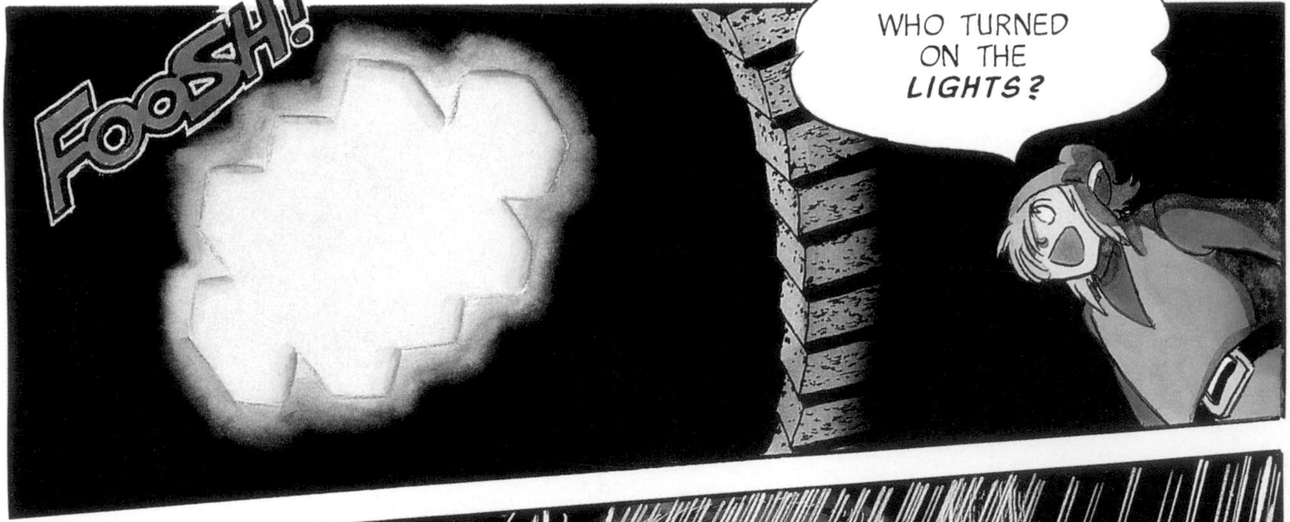
FOOSH!
WHO TURNED ON THE LIGHTS?
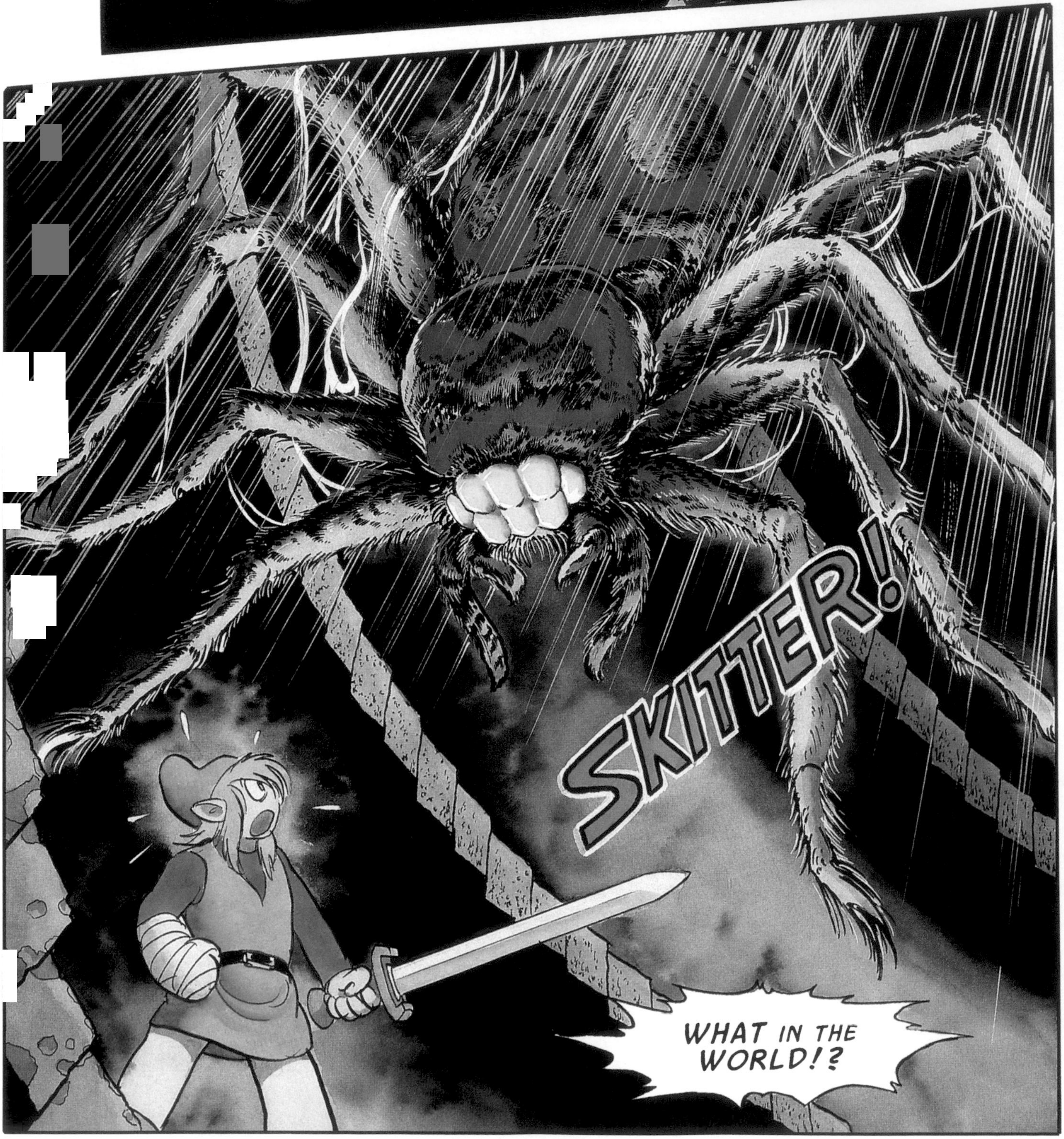
SKITTER!
WHAT IN THE WORLD!?

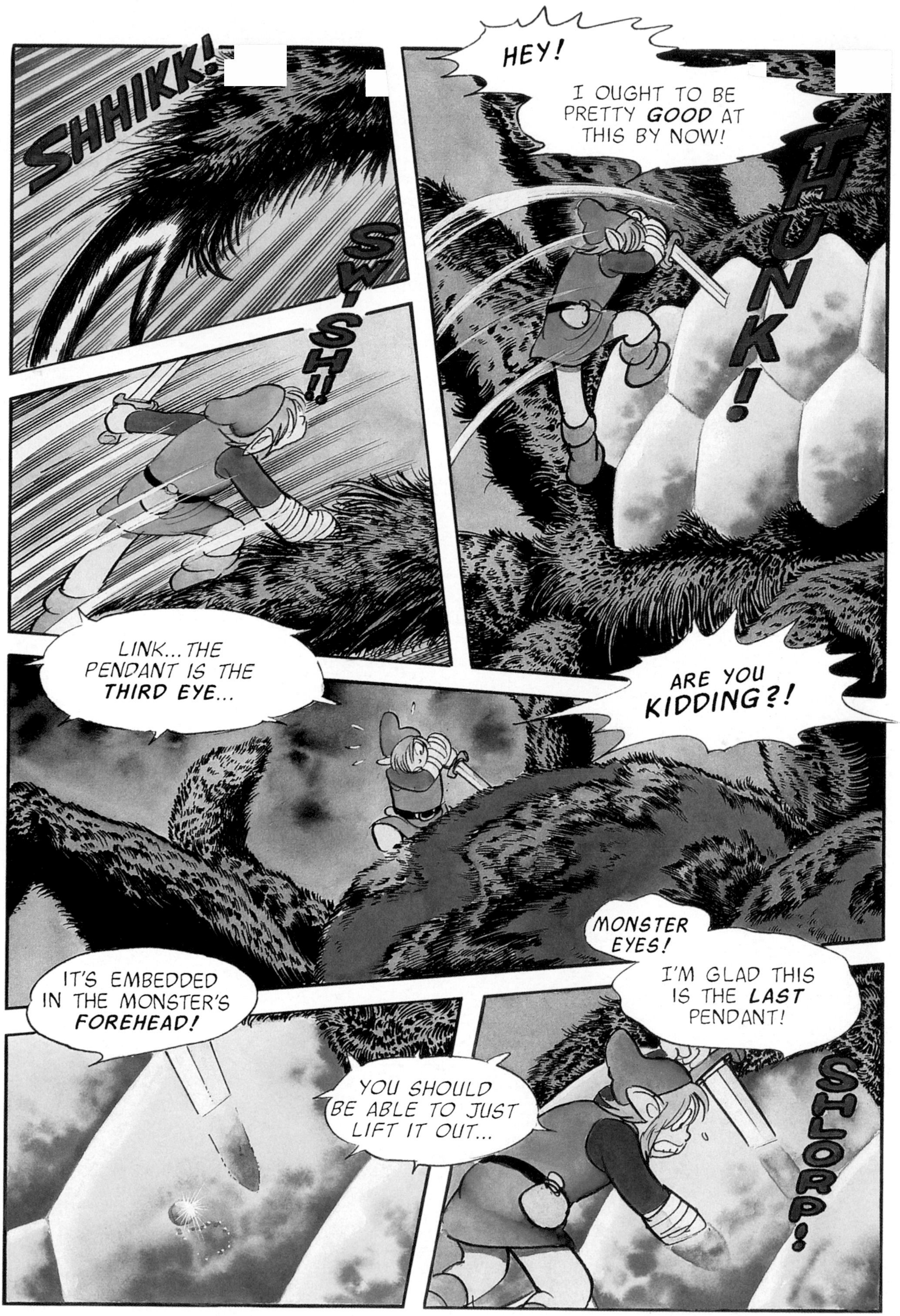
SHHIKK!
SWISH!!
HEY!
I OUGHT TO BE PRETTY GOOD AT THIS BY NOW!
THUNK!
LINK... THE PENDANT IS THE THIRD EYE...
ARE YOU KIDDING?!
MONSTER EYES!
IT'S EMBEDDED IN THE MONSTER'S FOREHEAD!
YOU SHOULD BE ABLE TO JUST LIFT IT OUT...
I'M GLAD THIS IS THE LAST PENDANT!
SHLORP!

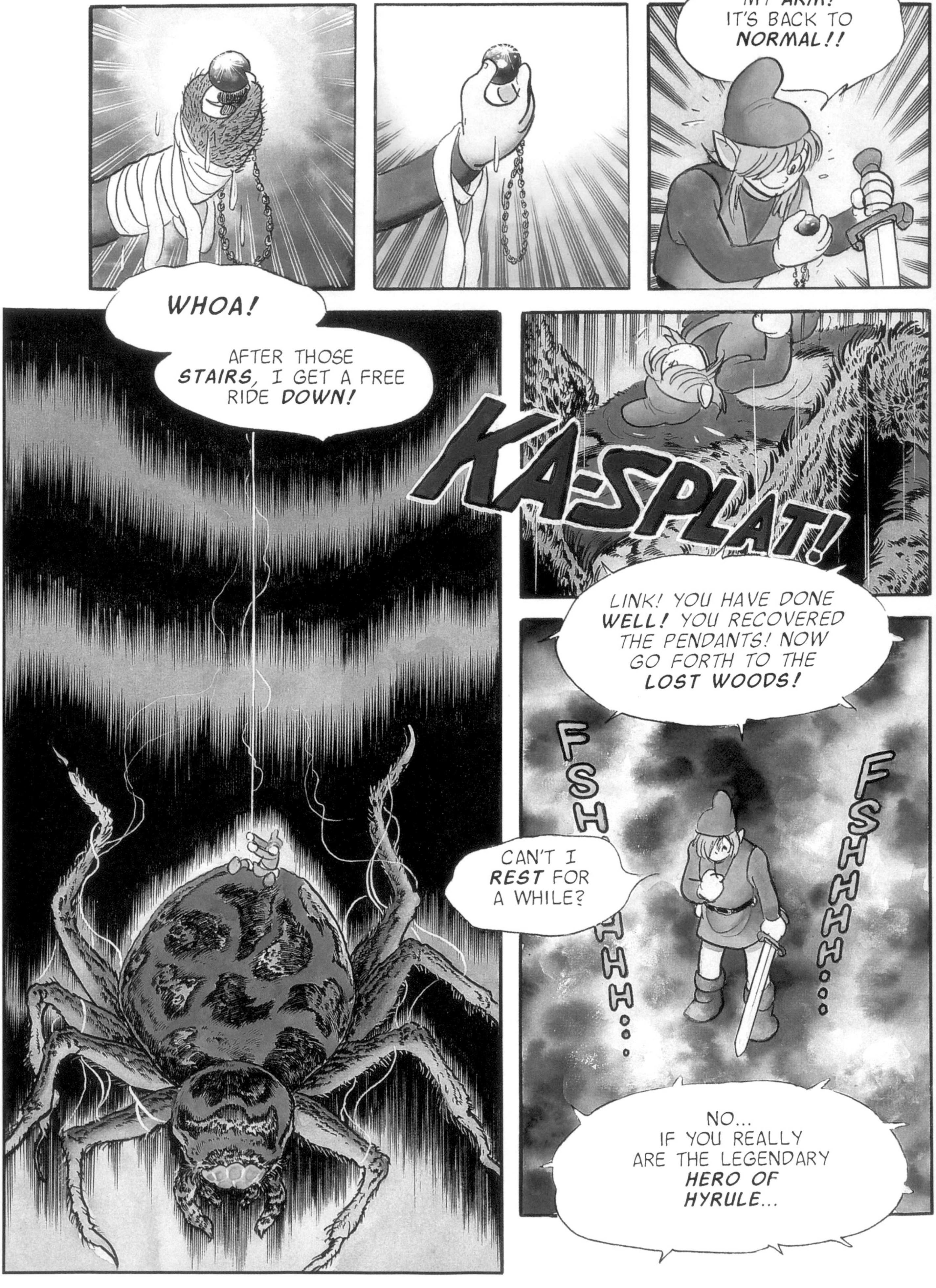

MY ARM! IT'S BACK TO NORMAL!!
WHOA!
AFTER THOSE STAIRS, I GET A FREE RIDE DOWN!
KA-SPLAT!
LINK! YOU HAVE DONE WELL! YOU RECOVERED THE PENDANTS! NOW GO FORTH TO THE LOST WOODS!
CAN'T I REST FOR A WHILE?
FSHHHHH...
FSHHHHH...
NO... IF YOU REALLY ARE THE LEGENDARY HERO OF HYRULE...

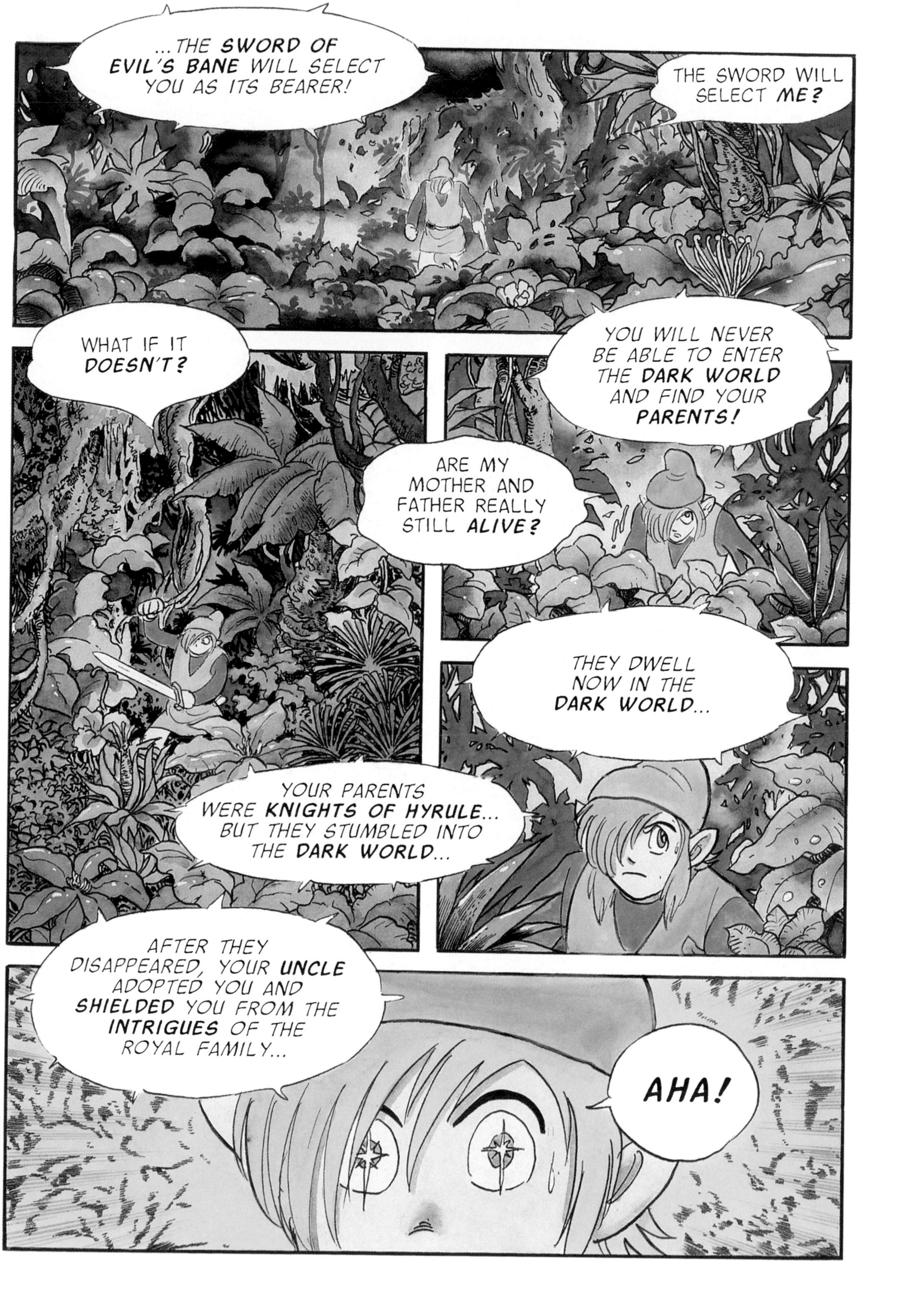
...THE SWORD OF EVIL'S BANE WILL SELECT YOU AS ITS BEARER!
THE SWORD WILL SELECT ME?
WHAT IF IT DOESN'T?
YOU WILL NEVER BE ABLE TO ENTER THE DARK WORLD AND FIND YOUR PARENTS!
ARE MY MOTHER AND FATHER REALLY STILL ALIVE?
THEY DWELL NOW IN THE DARK WORLD...
YOUR PARENTS WERE KNIGHTS OF HYRULE... BUT THEY STUMBLED INTO THE DARK WORLD...
AFTER THEY DISAPPEARED, YOUR UNCLE ADOPTED YOU AND SHIELDED YOU FROM THE INTRIGUES OF THE ROYAL FAMILY...
AHA!

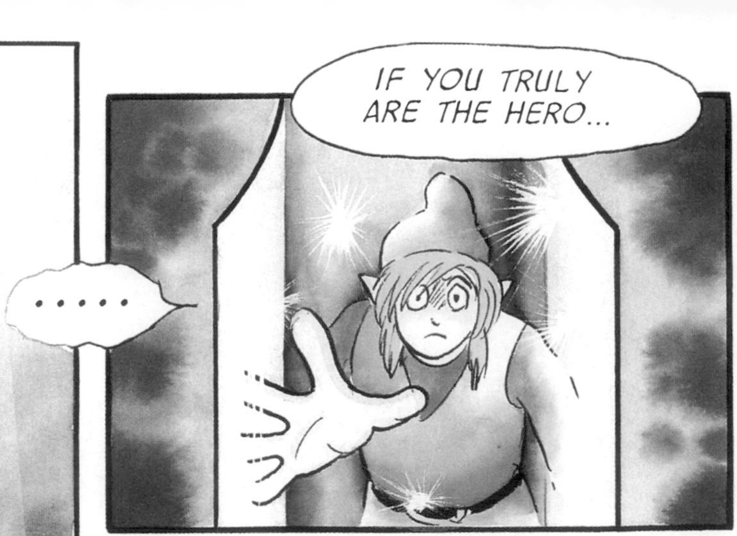
IF YOU TRULY ARE THE HERO...
.....

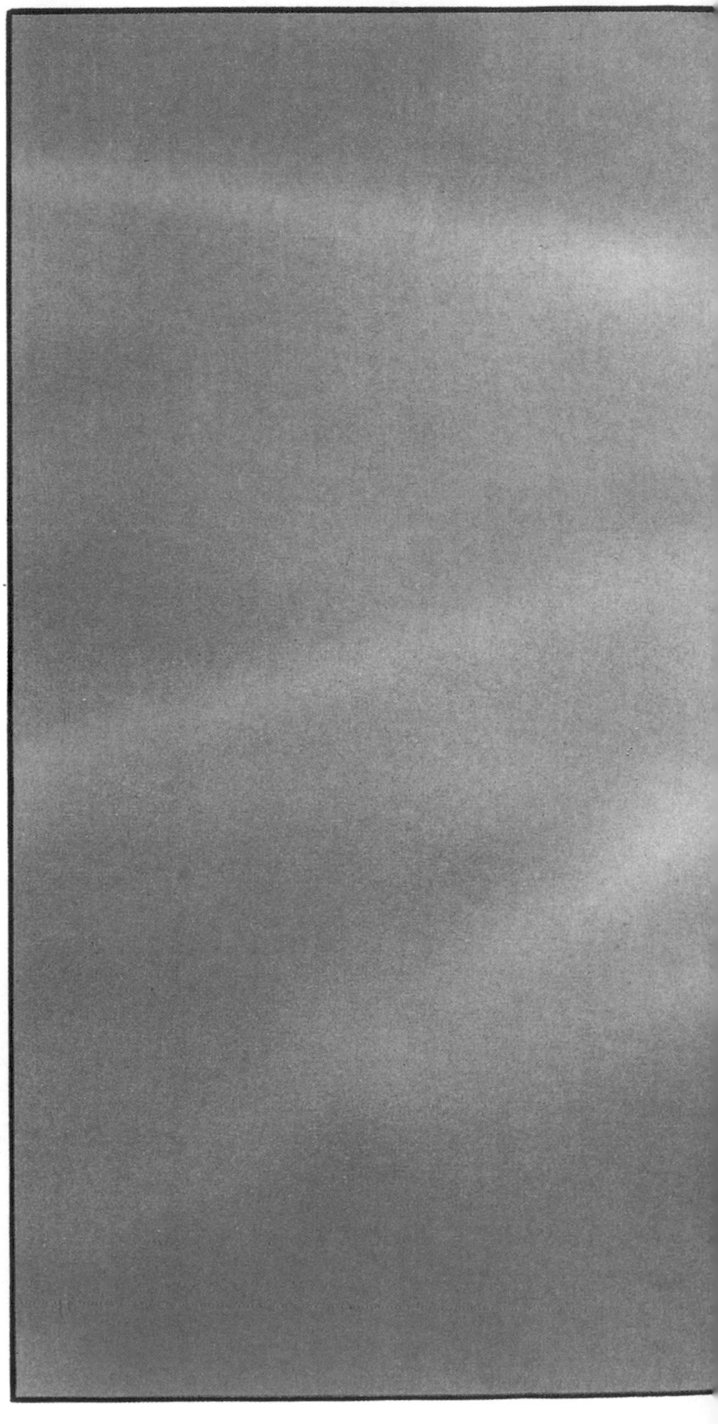

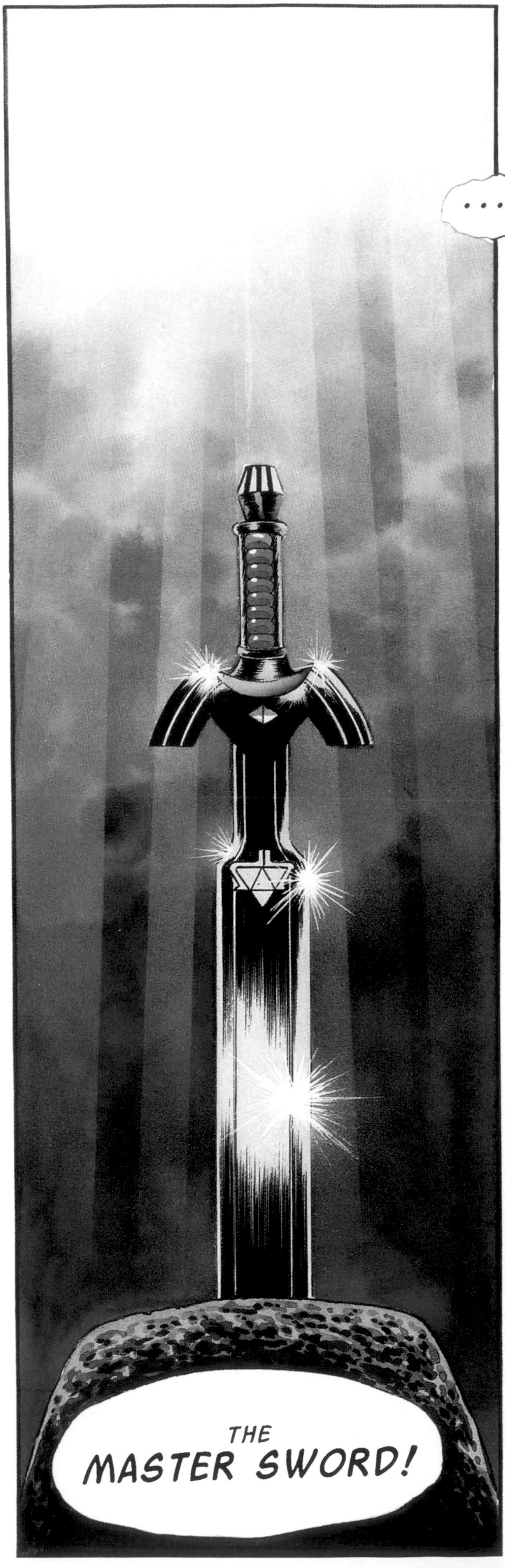
THE MASTER SWORD!

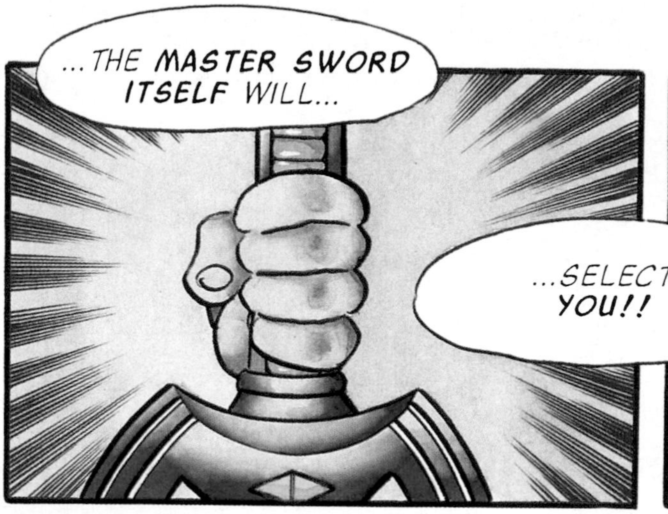
...THE MASTER SWORD ITSELF WILL...
...SELECT YOU!!
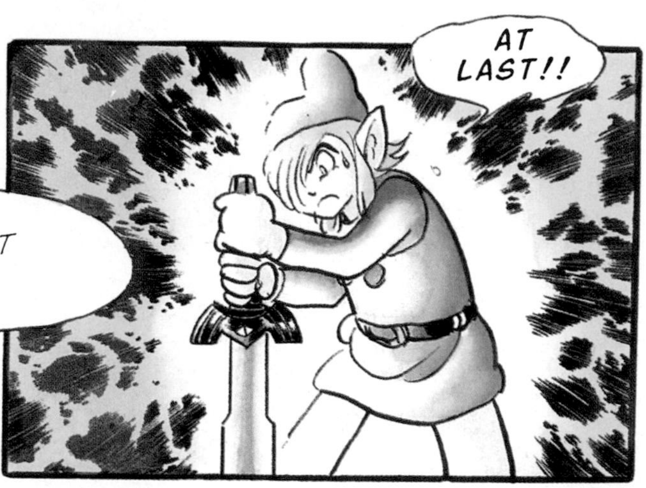
AT LAST!!
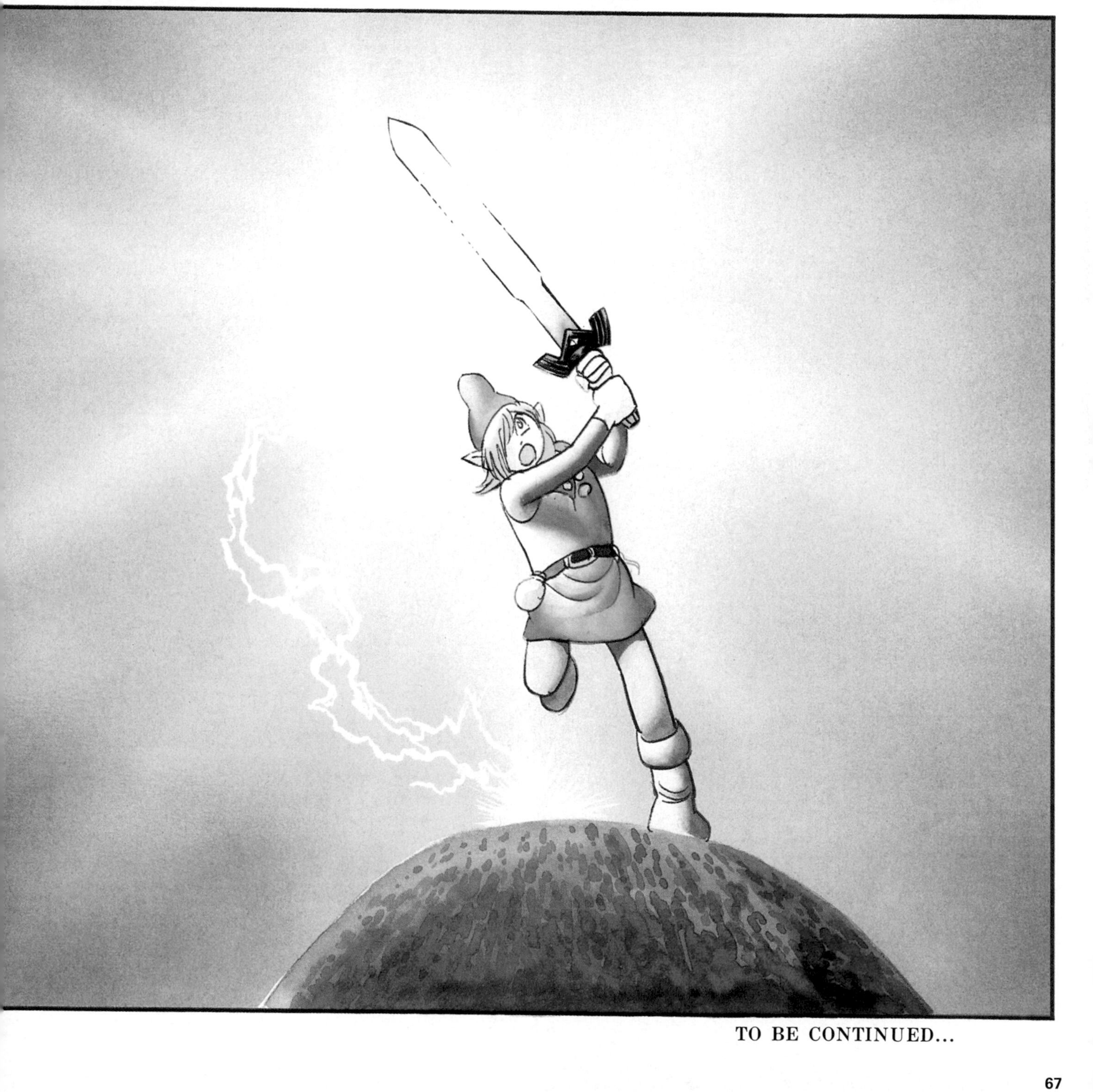

TO BE CONTINUED...

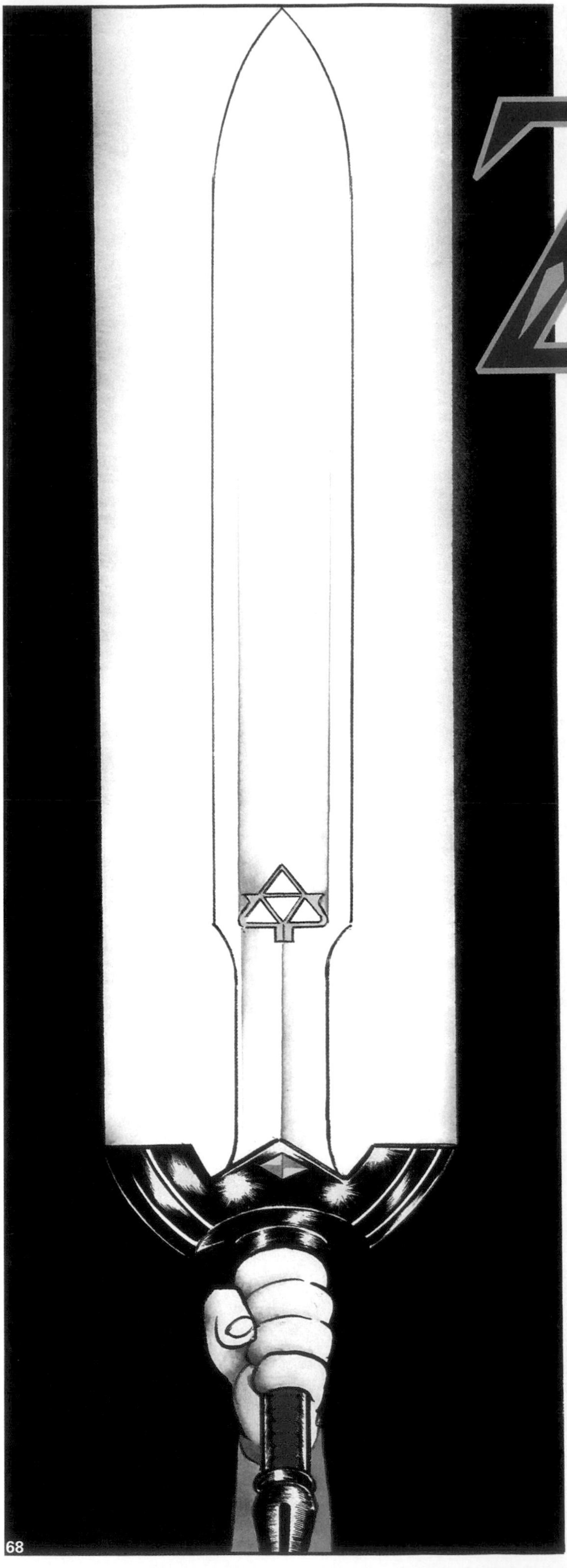
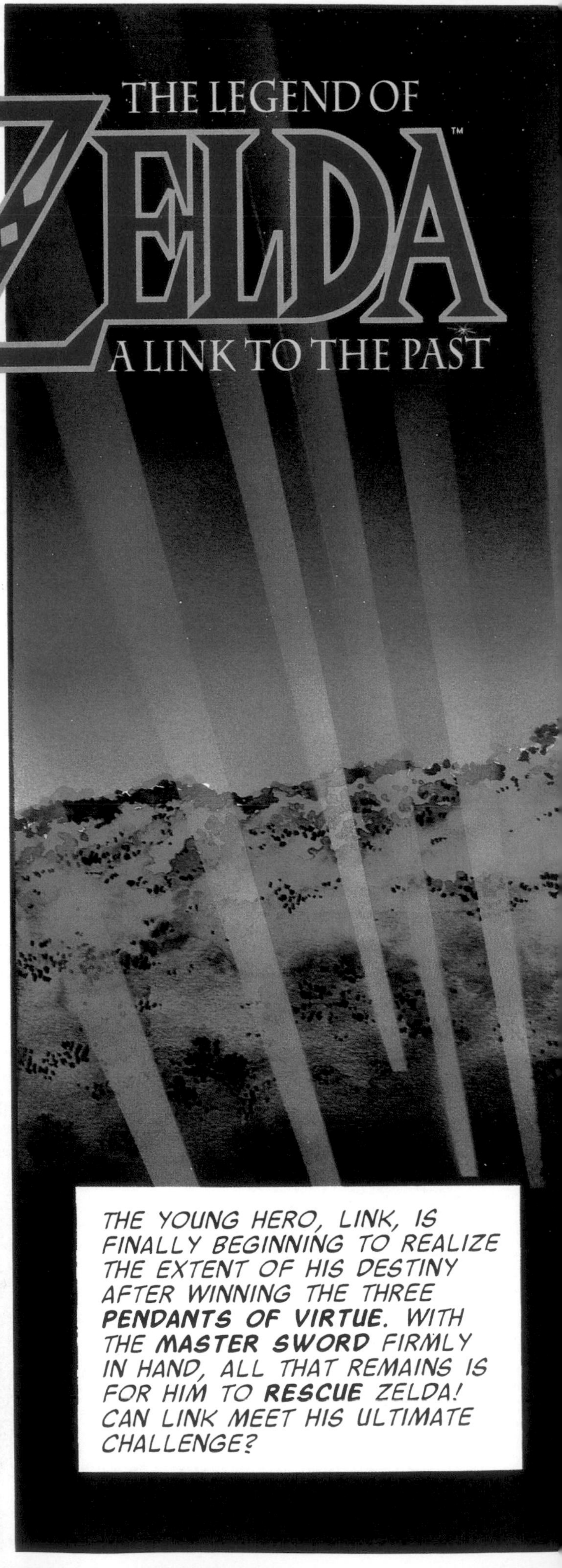
THE LEGEND OF
ZELDA™
A LINK TO THE PAST
THE YOUNG HERO, LINK, IS FINALLY BEGINNING TO REALIZE THE EXTENT OF HIS DESTINY AFTER WINNING THE THREE **PENDANTS OF VIRTUE.** WITH THE **MASTER SWORD** FIRMLY IN HAND, ALL THAT REMAINS IS FOR HIM TO **RESCUE** ZELDA! CAN LINK MEET HIS ULTIMATE CHALLENGE?

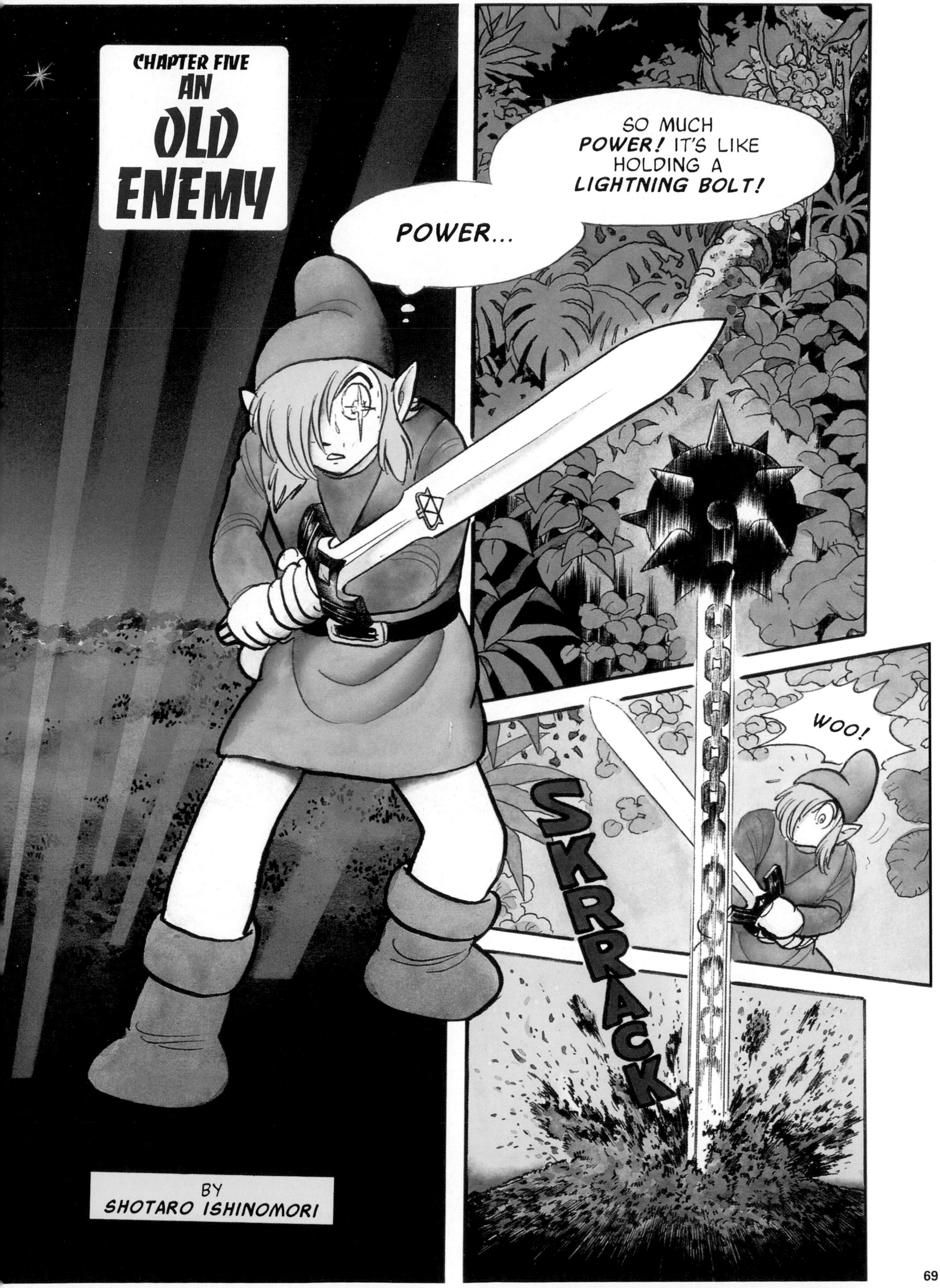
CHAPTER FIVE
AN OLD ENEMY
BY
SHOTARO ISHINOMORI
POWER...
SO MUCH POWER! IT'S LIKE HOLDING A LIGHTNING BOLT!
WOO!
SKRRACK

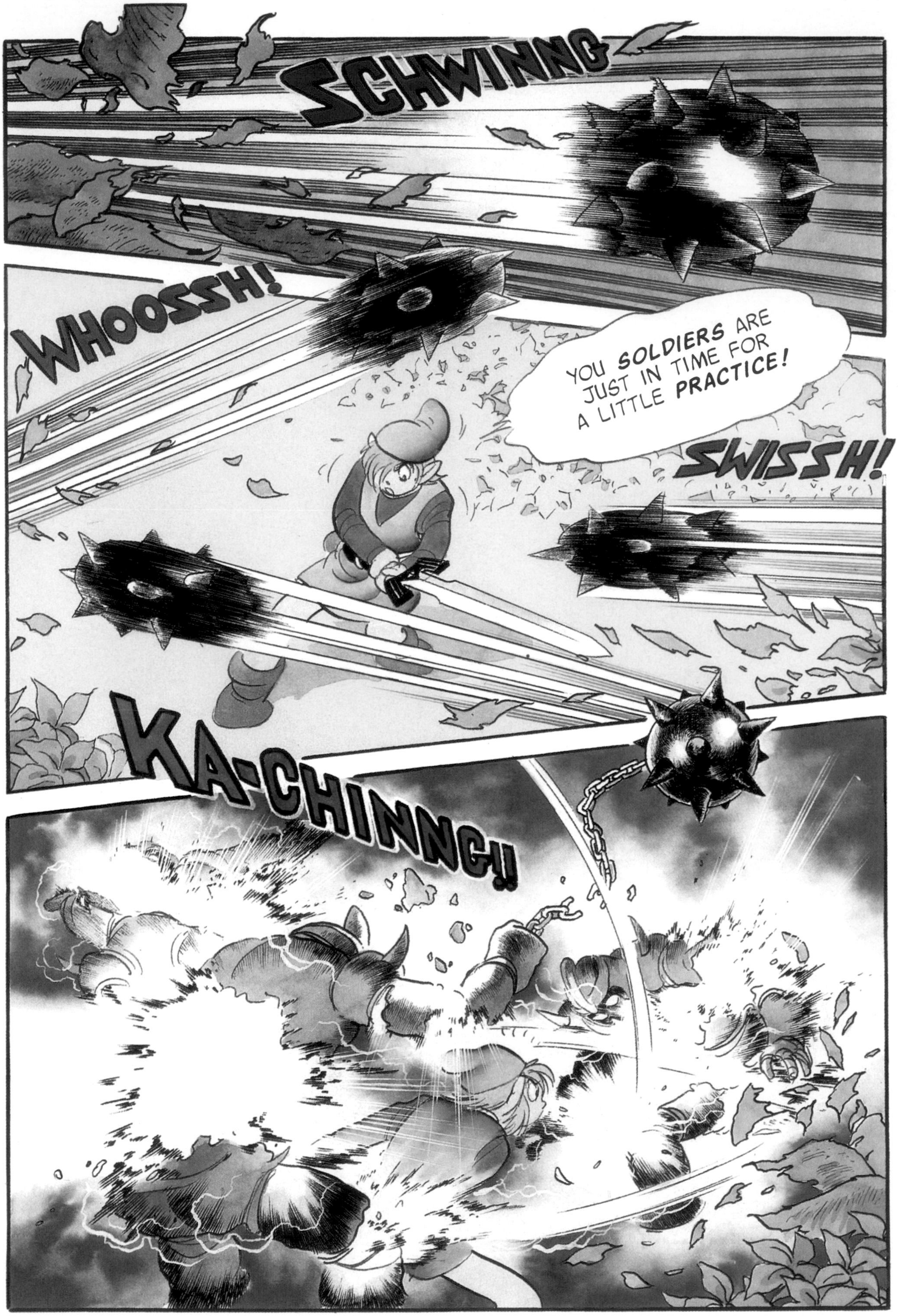
SCHWINNG
WHOOSSH!
YOU SOLDIERS ARE JUST IN TIME FOR A LITTLE PRACTICE!
SWISSH!
KA-CHINNG!!

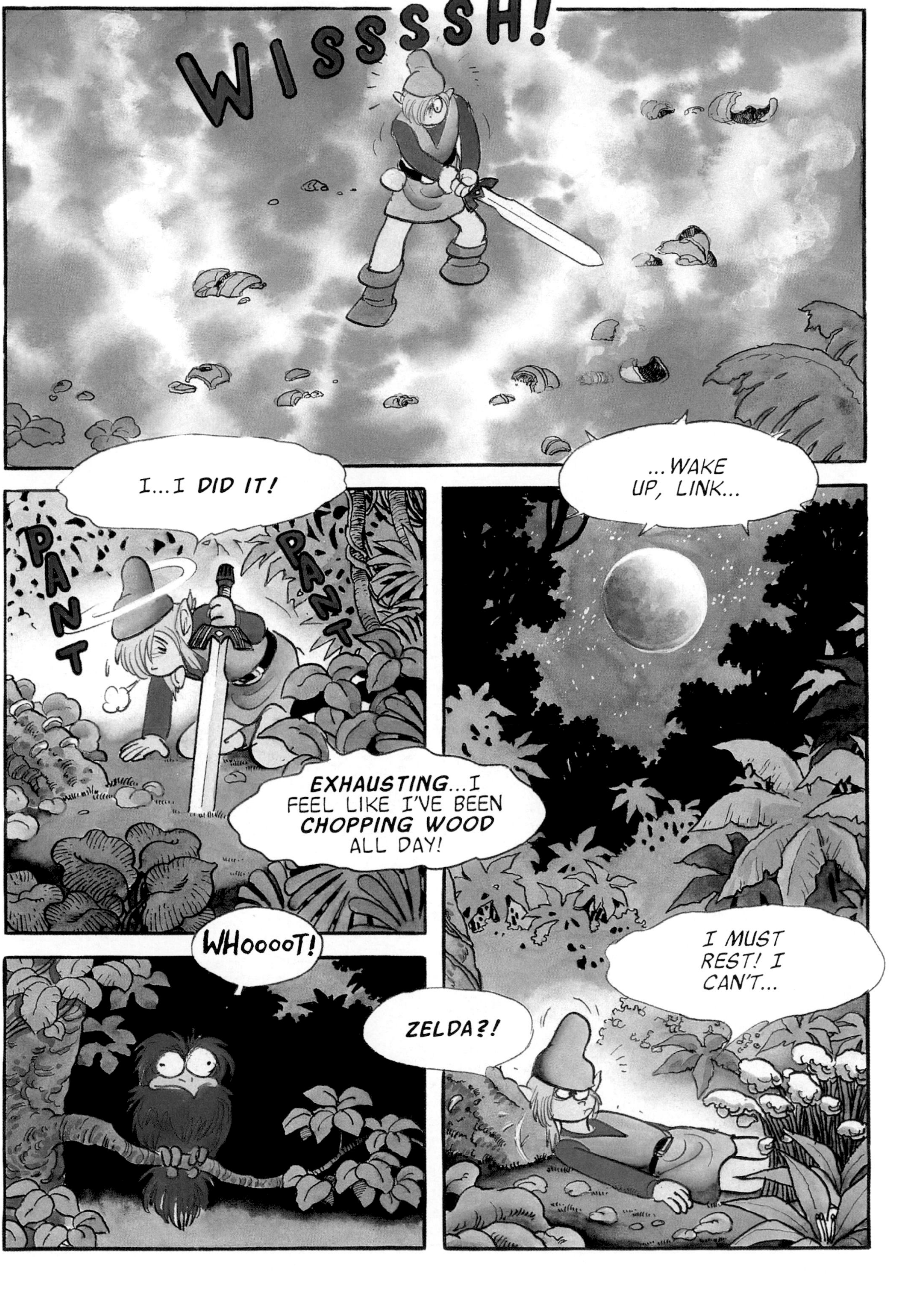
WISSSSH!
I...I DID IT!
PANT
PANT
EXHAUSTING...I FEEL LIKE I'VE BEEN CHOPPING WOOD ALL DAY!
...WAKE UP, LINK...
WHOOOOT!
I MUST REST! I CAN'T...
ZELDA?!

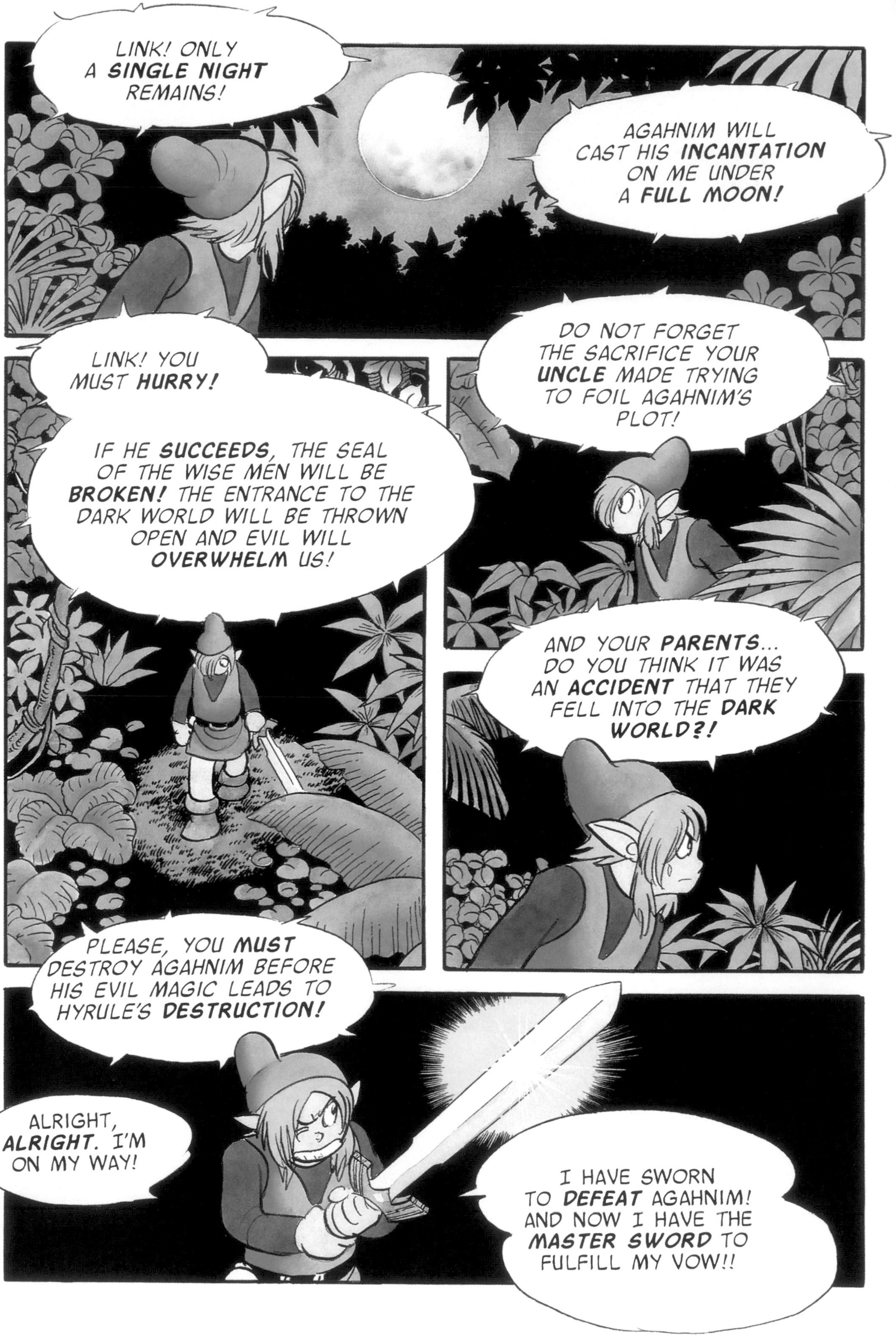
LINK! ONLY A SINGLE NIGHT REMAINS!
AGAHNIM WILL CAST HIS INCANTATION ON ME UNDER A FULL MOON!
LINK! YOU MUST HURRY!
IF HE SUCCEEDS, THE SEAL OF THE WISE MEN WILL BE BROKEN! THE ENTRANCE TO THE DARK WORLD WILL BE THROWN OPEN AND EVIL WILL OVERWHELM US!
DO NOT FORGET THE SACRIFICE YOUR UNCLE MADE TRYING TO FOIL AGAHNIM'S PLOT!
AND YOUR PARENTS... DO YOU THINK IT WAS AN ACCIDENT THAT THEY FELL INTO THE DARK WORLD?!
PLEASE, YOU MUST DESTROY AGAHNIM BEFORE HIS EVIL MAGIC LEADS TO HYRULE'S DESTRUCTION!
ALRIGHT, ALRIGHT. I'M ON MY WAY!
I HAVE SWORN TO DEFEAT AGAHNIM! AND NOW I HAVE THE MASTER SWORD TO FULFILL MY VOW!!

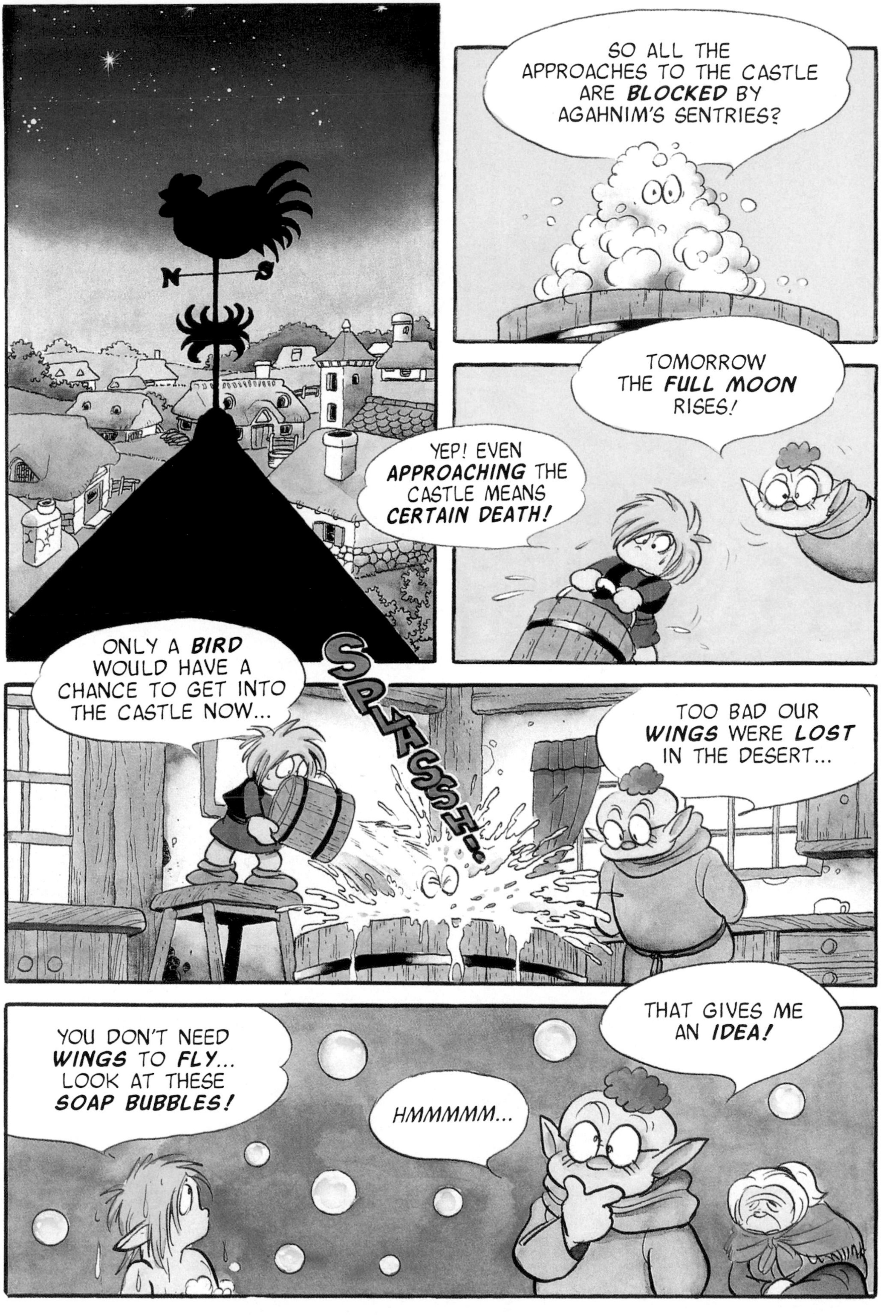
SO ALL THE APPROACHES TO THE CASTLE ARE **BLOCKED** BY AGAHNIM'S SENTRIES?
YEP! EVEN **APPROACHING** THE CASTLE MEANS **CERTAIN DEATH!**
TOMORROW THE **FULL MOON** RISES!
ONLY A **BIRD** WOULD HAVE A CHANCE TO GET INTO THE CASTLE NOW...
SPLASSSH!!
TOO BAD OUR **WINGS** WERE **LOST** IN THE DESERT...
YOU DON'T NEED **WINGS** TO **FLY**... LOOK AT THESE **SOAP BUBBLES!**
HMMMMM...
THAT GIVES ME AN **IDEA!**

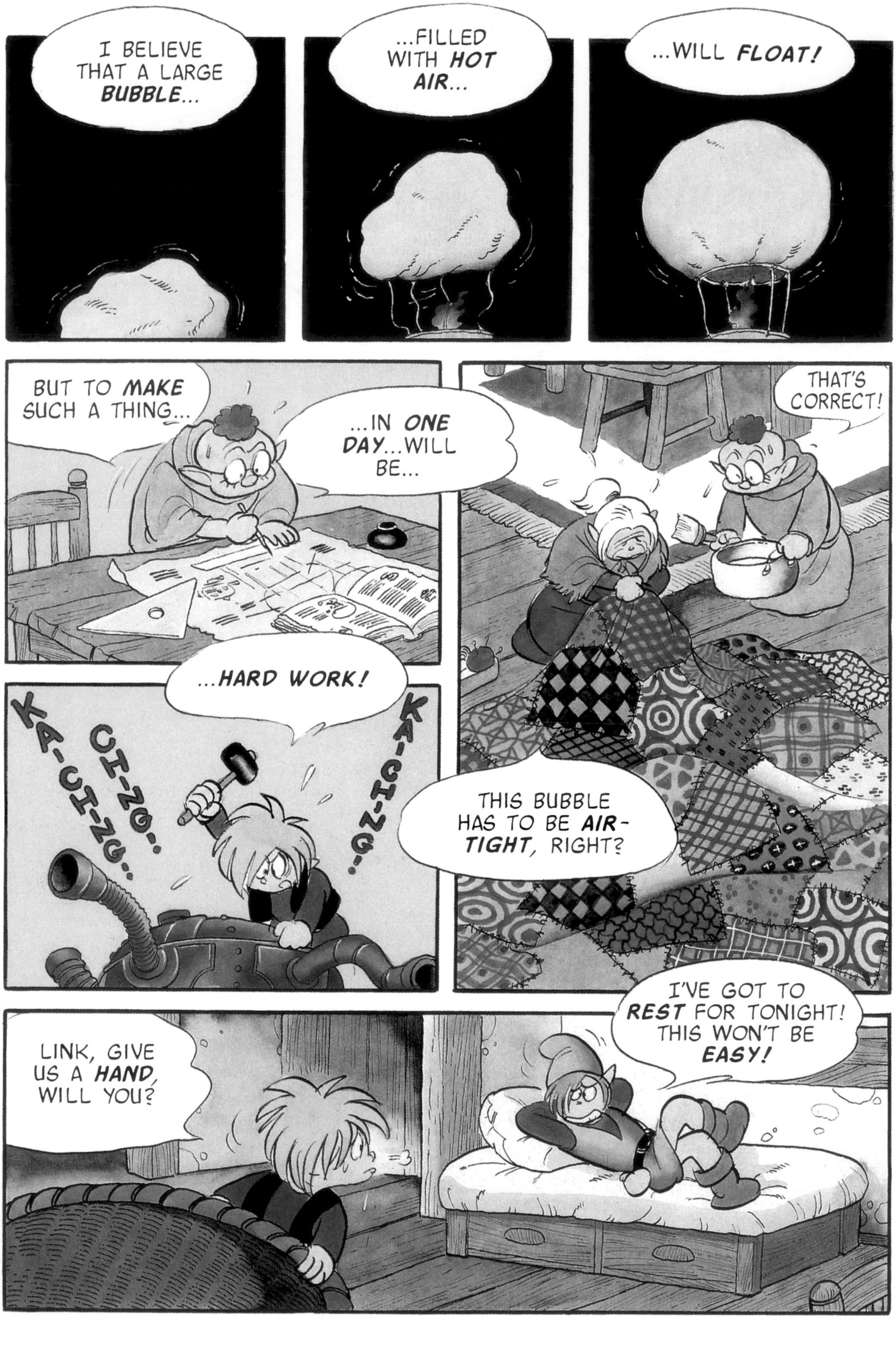
I BELIEVE THAT A LARGE BUBBLE...
...FILLED WITH HOT AIR...
...WILL FLOAT!
BUT TO MAKE SUCH A THING...
...IN ONE DAY...WILL BE...
...HARD WORK!
KA-CHING...
CHING...
KA-CHING!
THAT'S CORRECT!
THIS BUBBLE HAS TO BE AIR-TIGHT, RIGHT?
LINK, GIVE US A HAND, WILL YOU?
I'VE GOT TO REST FOR TONIGHT! THIS WON'T BE EASY!

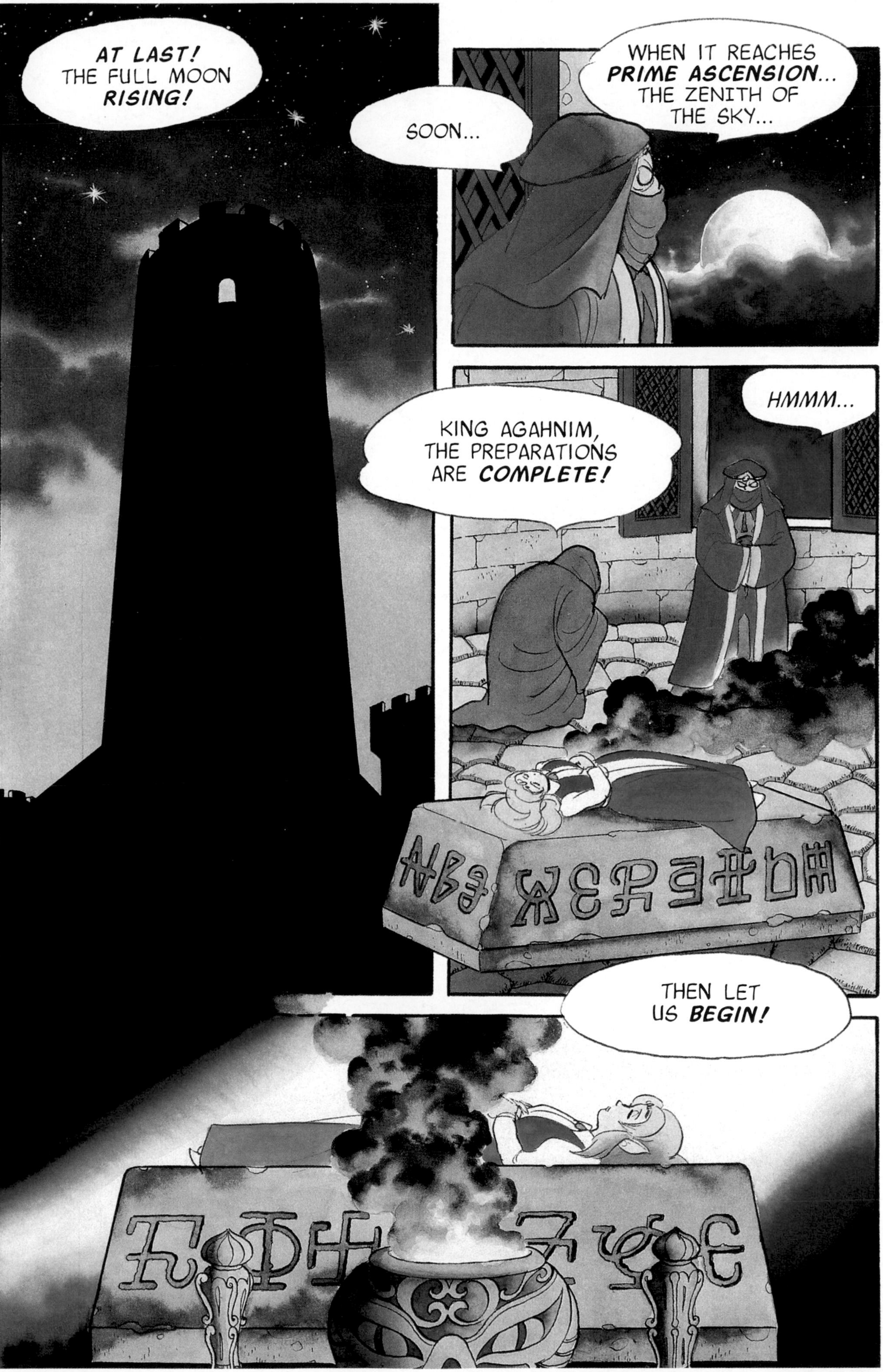

AT LAST! THE FULL MOON ***RISING!***
SOON...
WHEN IT REACHES ***PRIME ASCENSION***... THE ZENITH OF THE SKY...
KING AGAHNIM, THE PREPARATIONS ARE ***COMPLETE!***
HMMM...
THEN LET US ***BEGIN!***

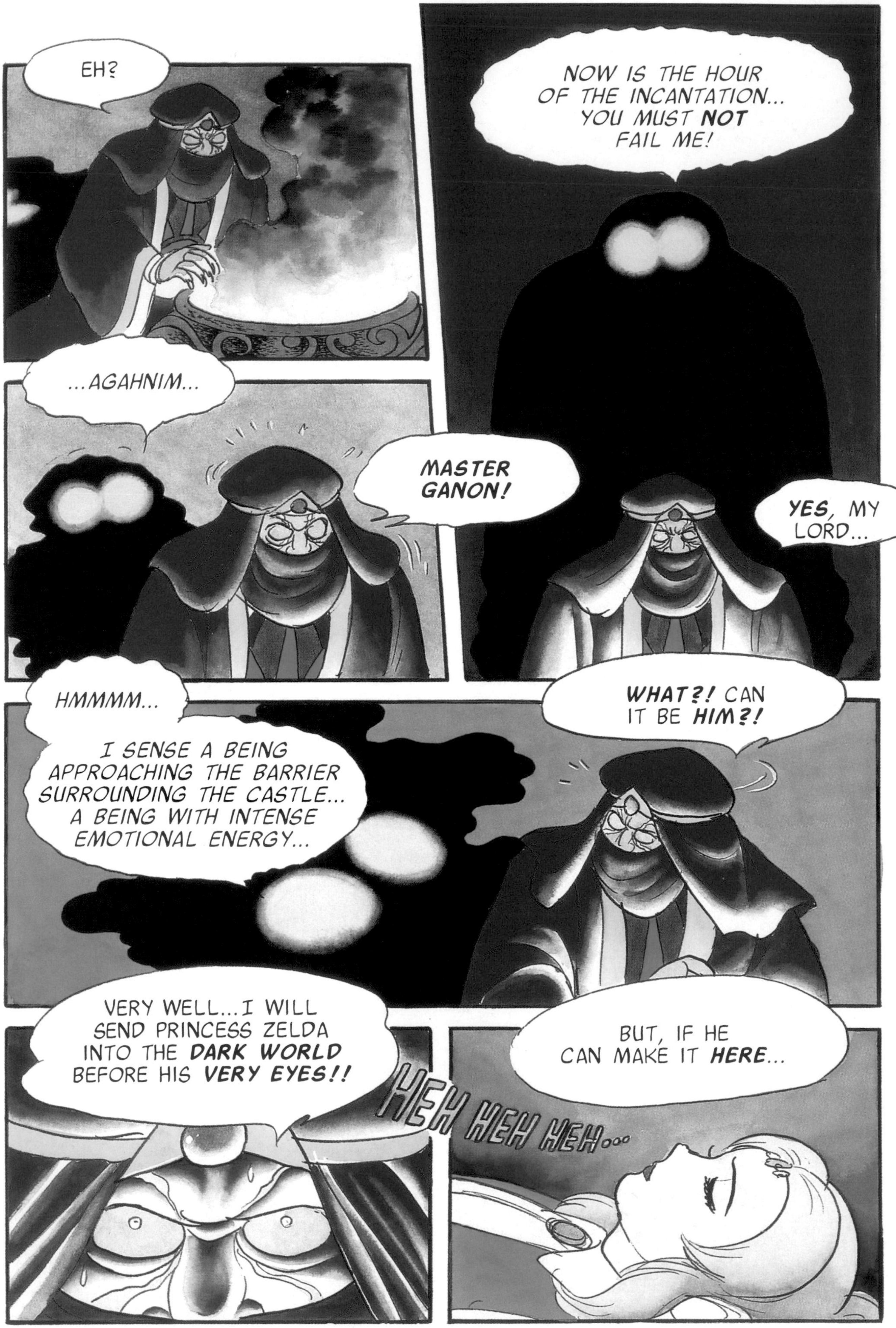
EH?
...AGAHNIM...
MASTER GANON!
NOW IS THE HOUR OF THE INCANTATION... YOU MUST NOT FAIL ME!
YES, MY LORD...
HMMMM...
I SENSE A BEING APPROACHING THE BARRIER SURROUNDING THE CASTLE... A BEING WITH INTENSE EMOTIONAL ENERGY...
WHAT?! CAN IT BE HIM?!
VERY WELL...I WILL SEND PRINCESS ZELDA INTO THE DARK WORLD BEFORE HIS VERY EYES!!
BUT, IF HE CAN MAKE IT HERE...
HEH HEH HEH...

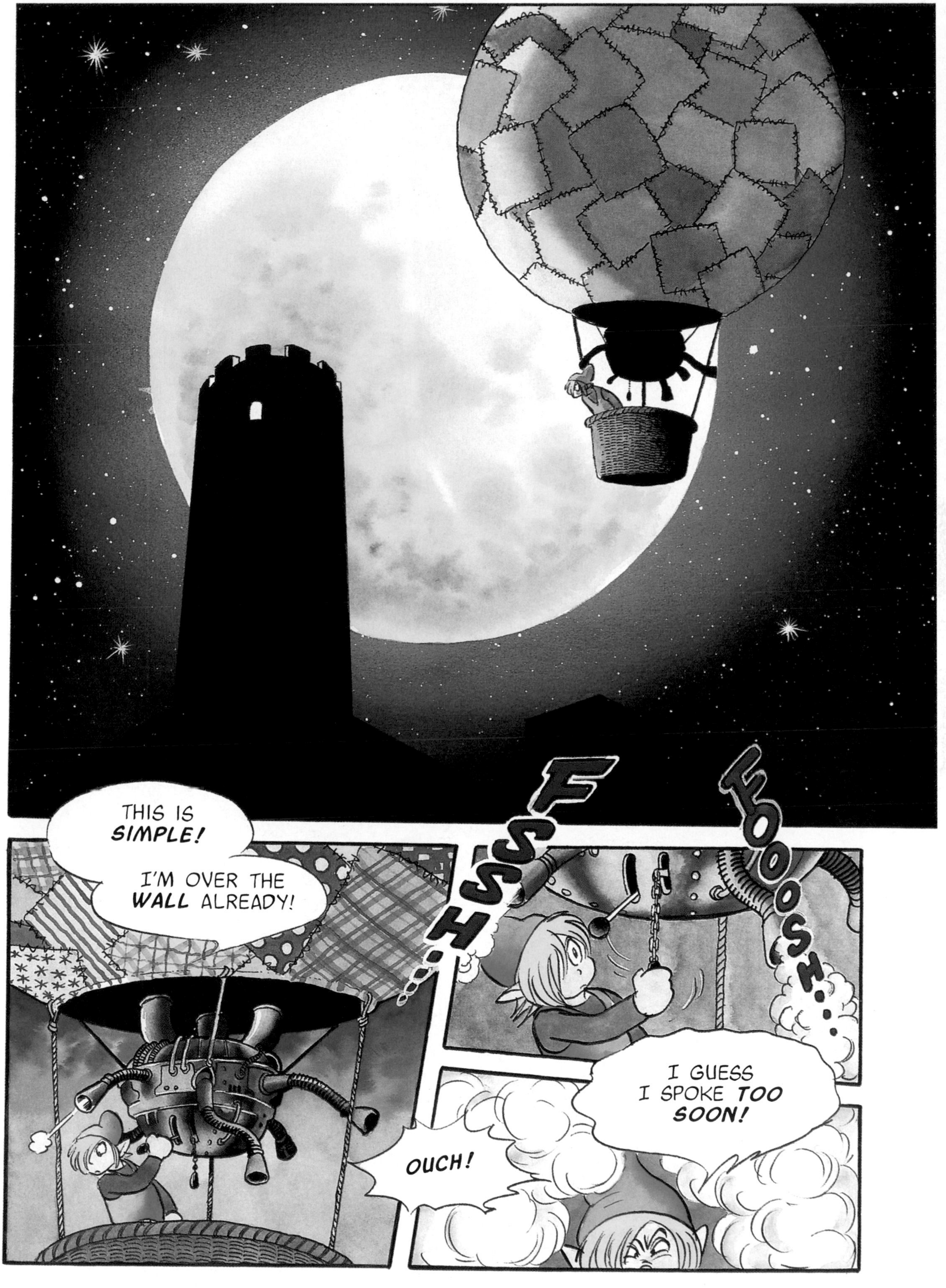
THIS IS SIMPLE!
I'M OVER THE WALL ALREADY!
FSSH...
FOOOSH...
OUCH!
I GUESS I SPOKE TOO SOON!

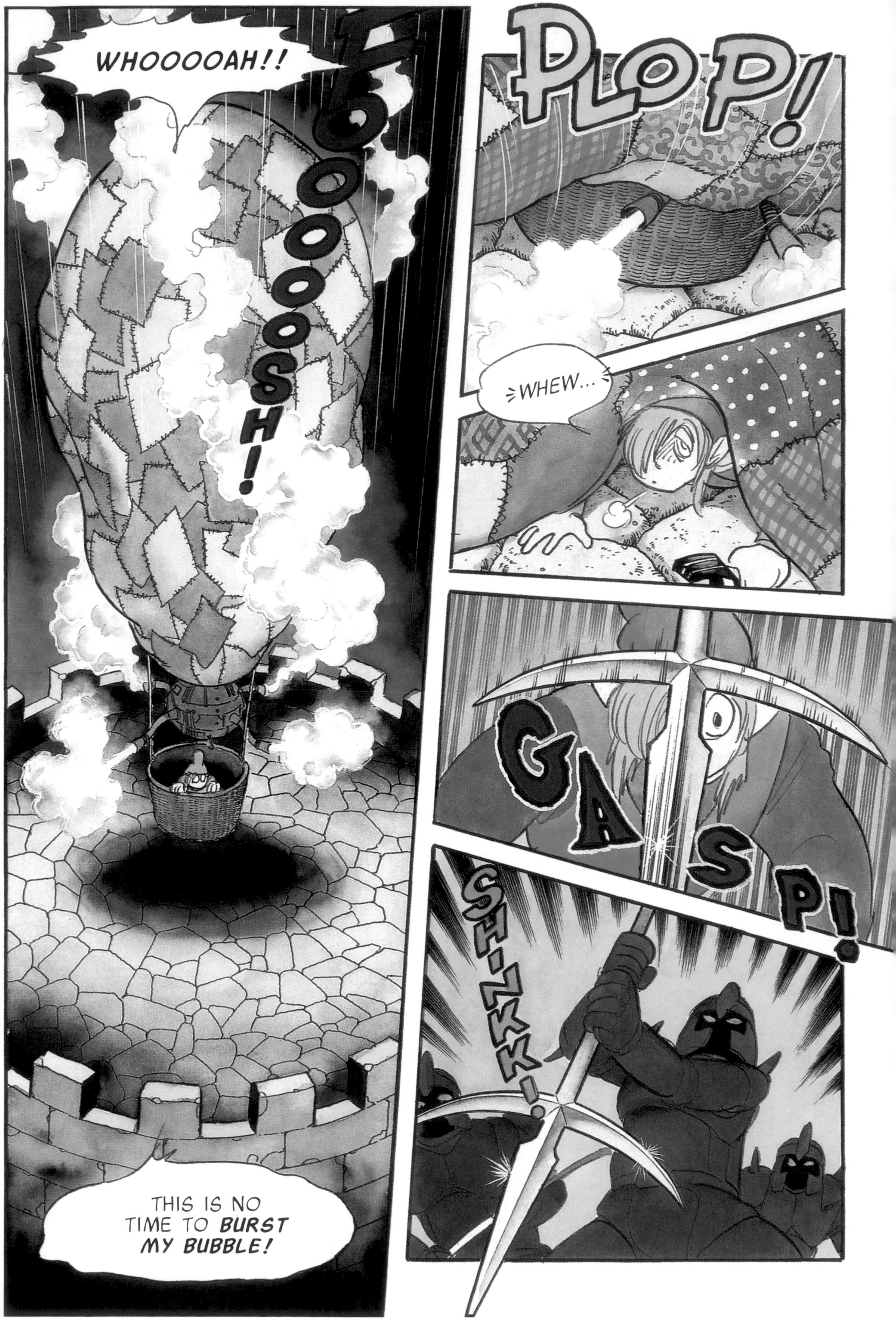
WHOOOOAH!!
FOOOOOSH!
THIS IS NO TIME TO BURST MY BUBBLE!
PLOP!
WHEW...
GASP!
SHIZKK!

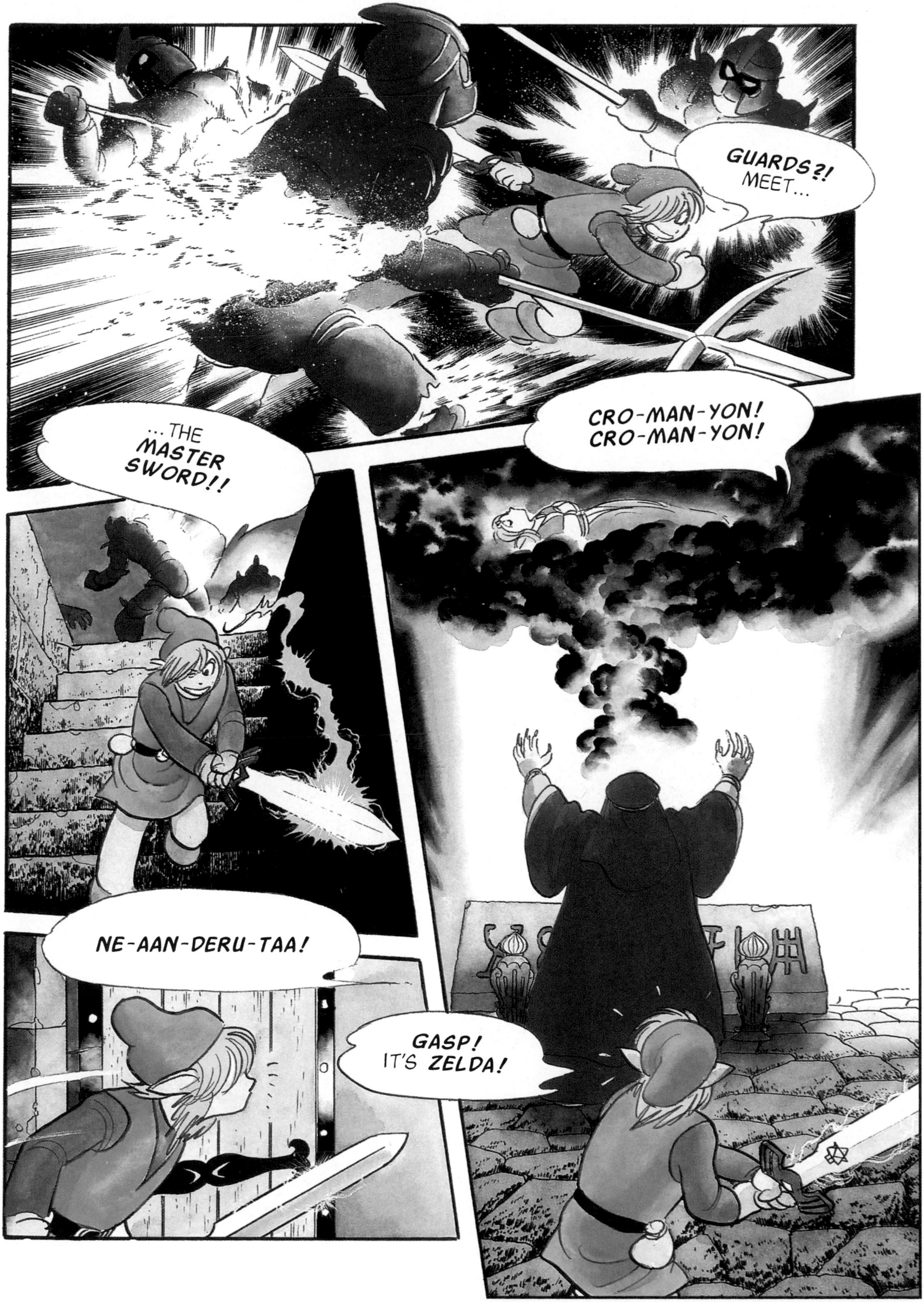
GUARDS?! MEET...
...THE MASTER SWORD!!
CRO-MAN-YON! CRO-MAN-YON!
NE-AAN-DERU-TAA!
GASP! IT'S ZELDA!

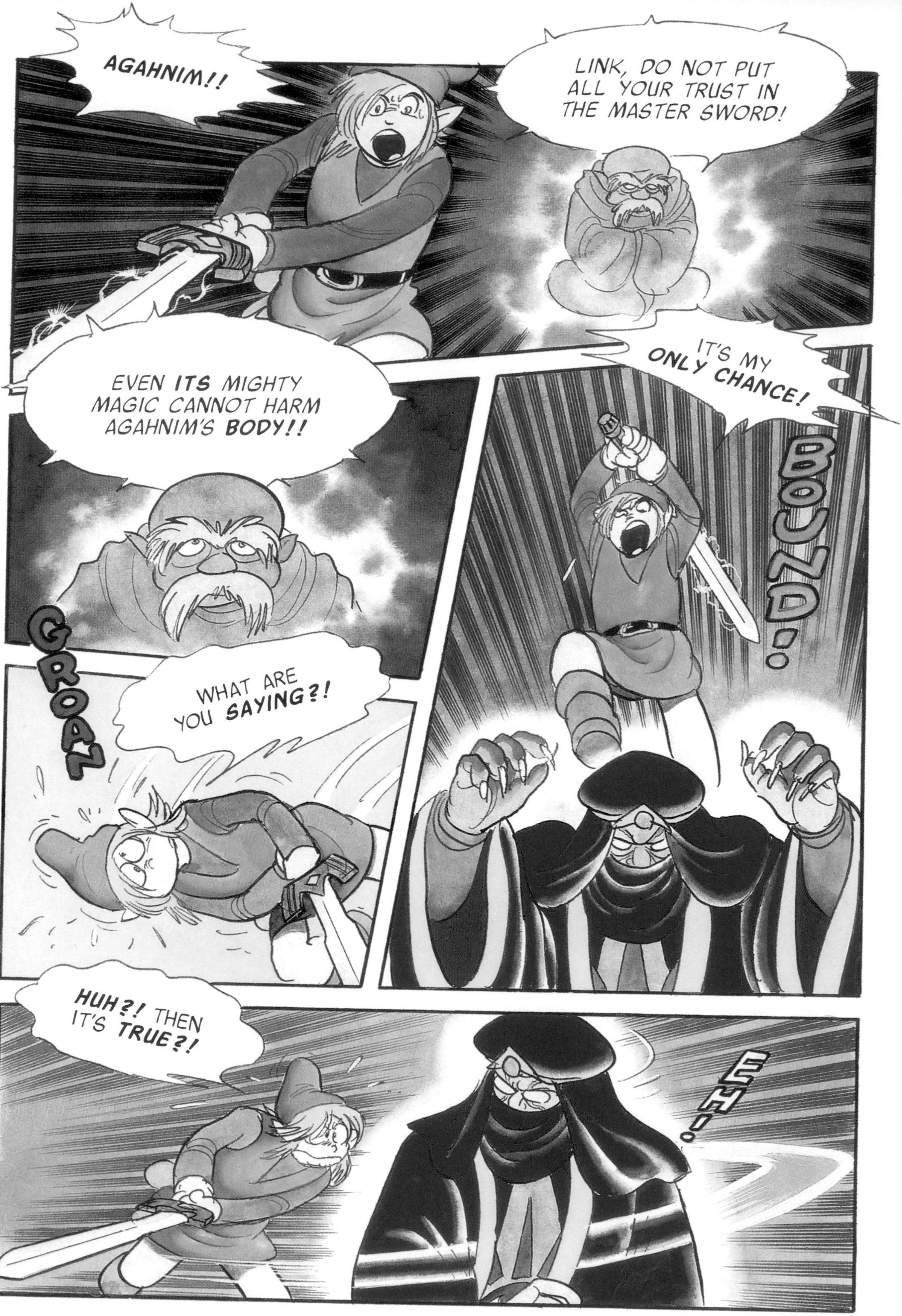
AGAHNIM!!
LINK, DO NOT PUT ALL YOUR TRUST IN THE MASTER SWORD!
EVEN ITS MIGHTY MAGIC CANNOT HARM AGAHNIM'S BODY!!
GROAZ
WHAT ARE YOU SAYING?!
IT'S MY ONLY CHANCE!
BOUND!
HUH?! THEN IT'S TRUE?!
EH!

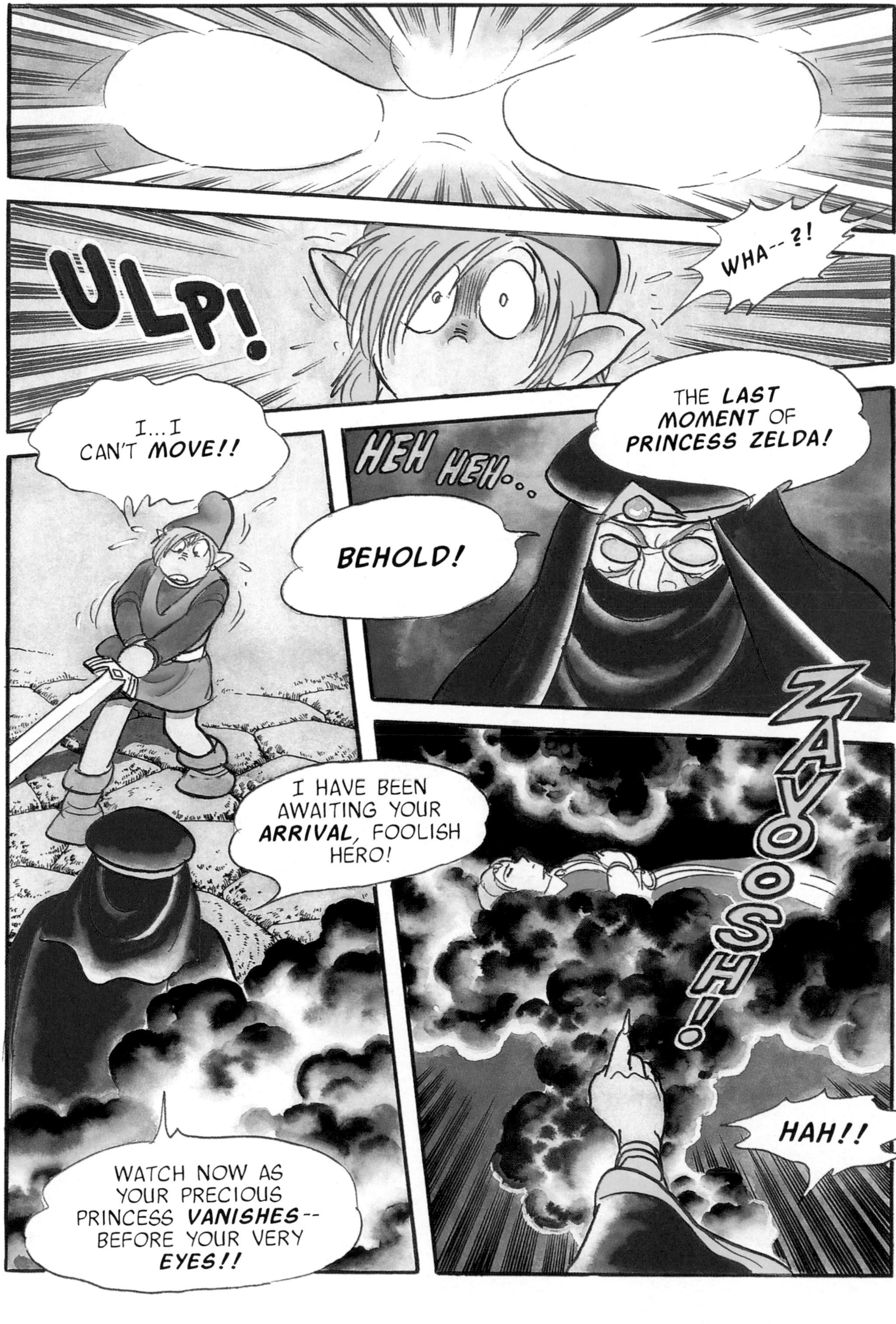
ULP!
WHA--?!
I...I CAN'T MOVE!!
HEH HEH...
THE LAST MOMENT OF PRINCESS ZELDA!
BEHOLD!
I HAVE BEEN AWAITING YOUR ARRIVAL, FOOLISH HERO!
WATCH NOW AS YOUR PRECIOUS PRINCESS VANISHES--BEFORE YOUR VERY EYES!!
ZAVOOSH!
HAH!!

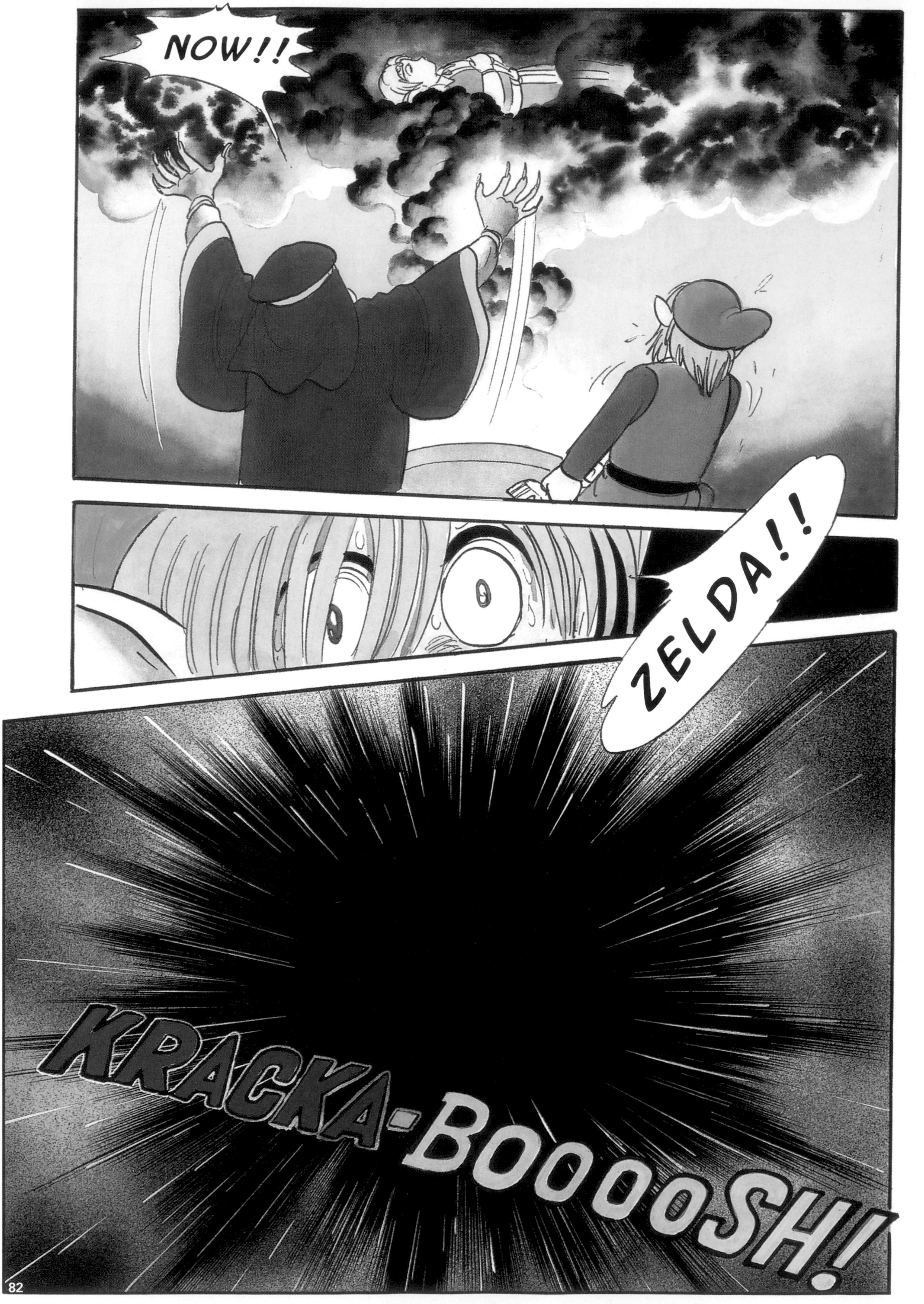
NOW!!
ZELDA!!
KRACKA-BOOOOOSH!

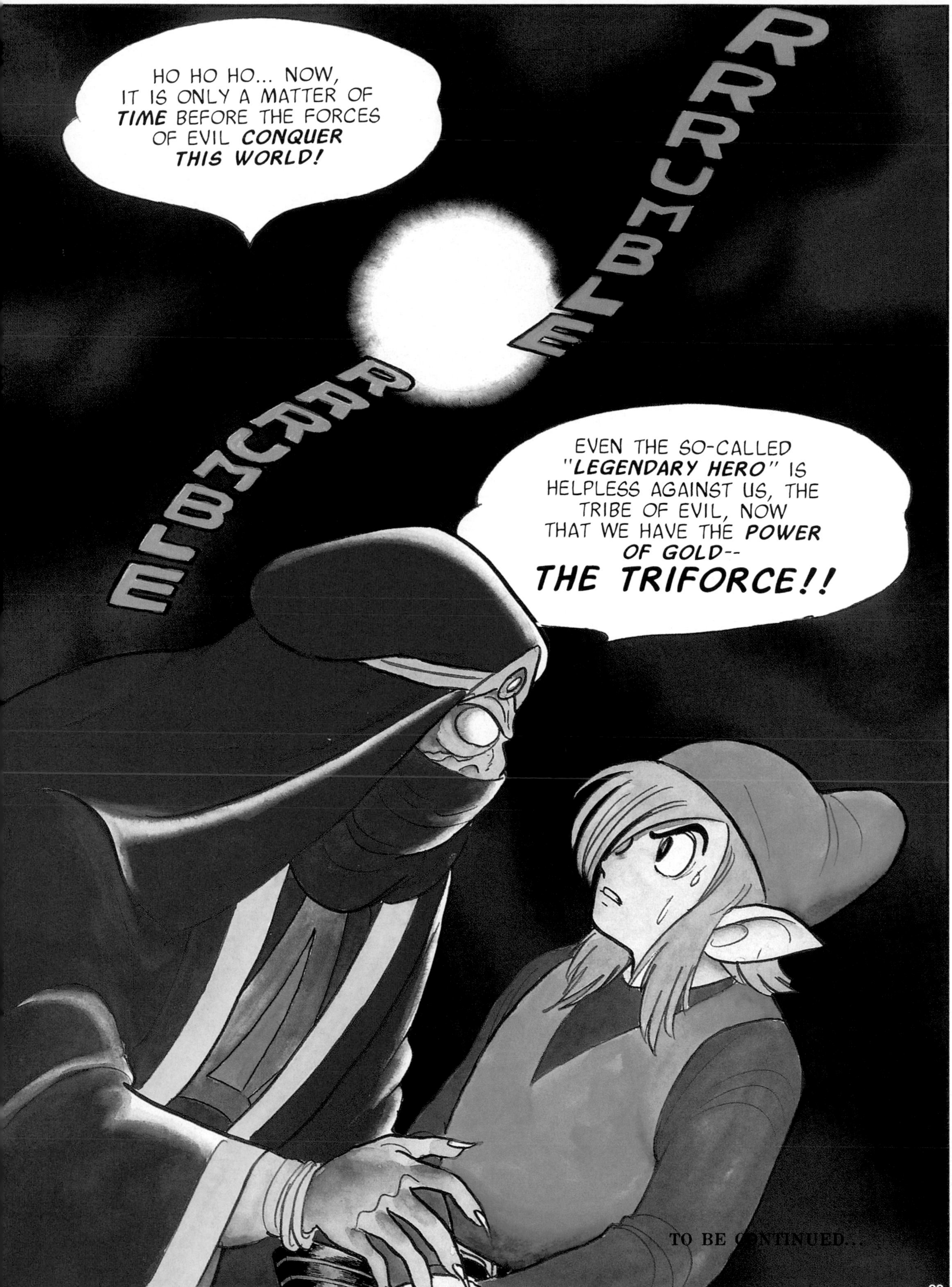
HO HO HO... NOW, IT IS ONLY A MATTER OF TIME BEFORE THE FORCES OF EVIL CONQUER THIS WORLD!
RRRUMBLE
RRRUMBLE
EVEN THE SO-CALLED "LEGENDARY HERO" IS HELPLESS AGAINST US, THE TRIBE OF EVIL, NOW THAT WE HAVE THE POWER OF GOLD-- THE TRIFORCE!!
TO BE CONTINUED...

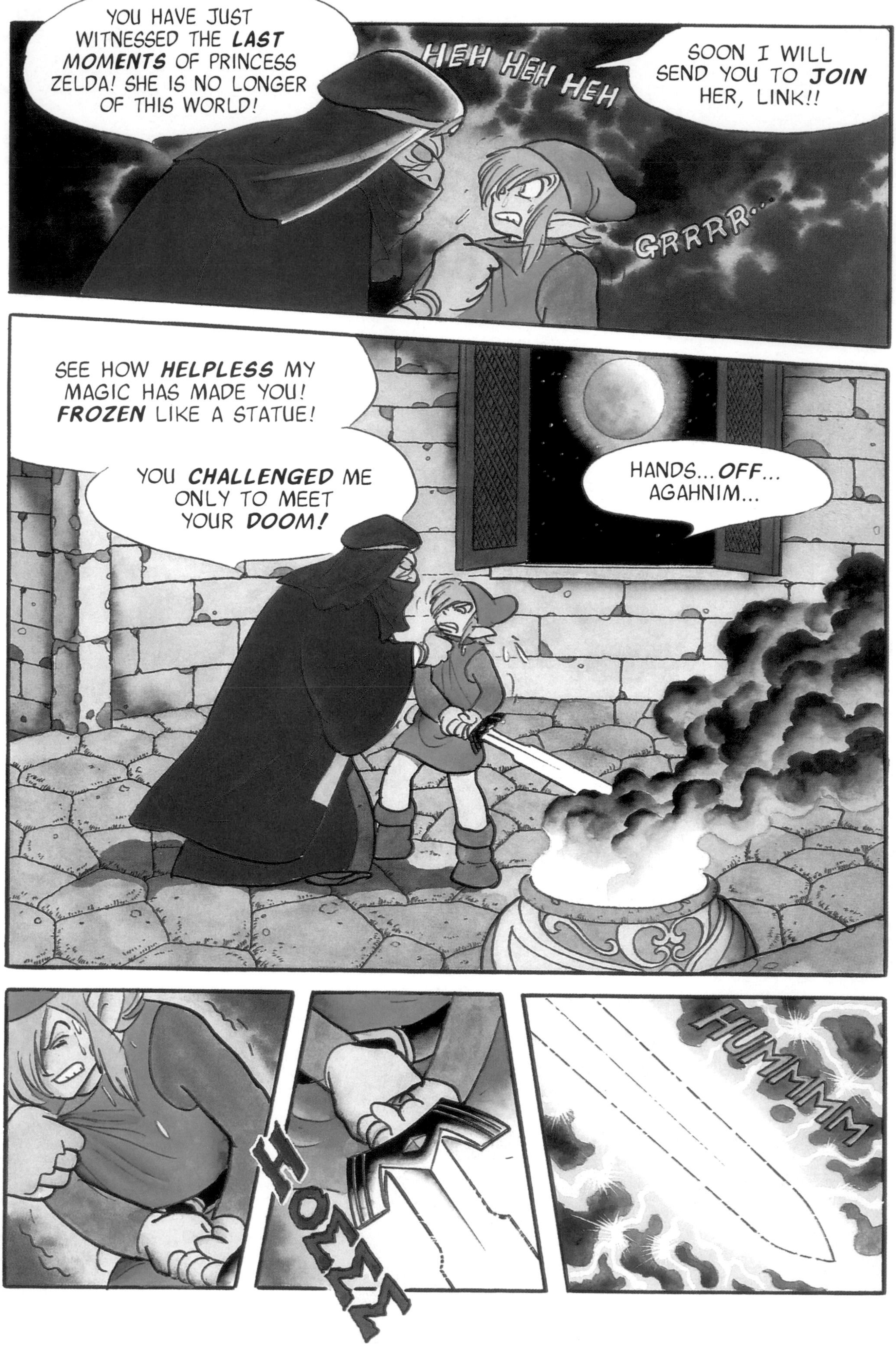
YOU HAVE JUST WITNESSED THE **LAST MOMENTS** OF PRINCESS ZELDA! SHE IS NO LONGER OF THIS WORLD!
HEH HEH HEH
SOON I WILL SEND YOU TO **JOIN** HER, LINK!!
GRRRR...
SEE HOW **HELPLESS** MY MAGIC HAS MADE YOU! **FROZEN** LIKE A STATUE!
YOU **CHALLENGED** ME ONLY TO MEET YOUR **DOOM!**
HANDS... **OFF**... AGAHNIM...
HOMMM
HUMMMM

THE LEGEND OF ZELDA

A LINK TO THE PAST

Illustrated adventures based on the legendary game series

WHAT IS THIS?!!

BY
SHOTARO ISHINOMORI

CHAPTER SIX
A
FOOL
IN THE
SHAPE
OF A
TREE

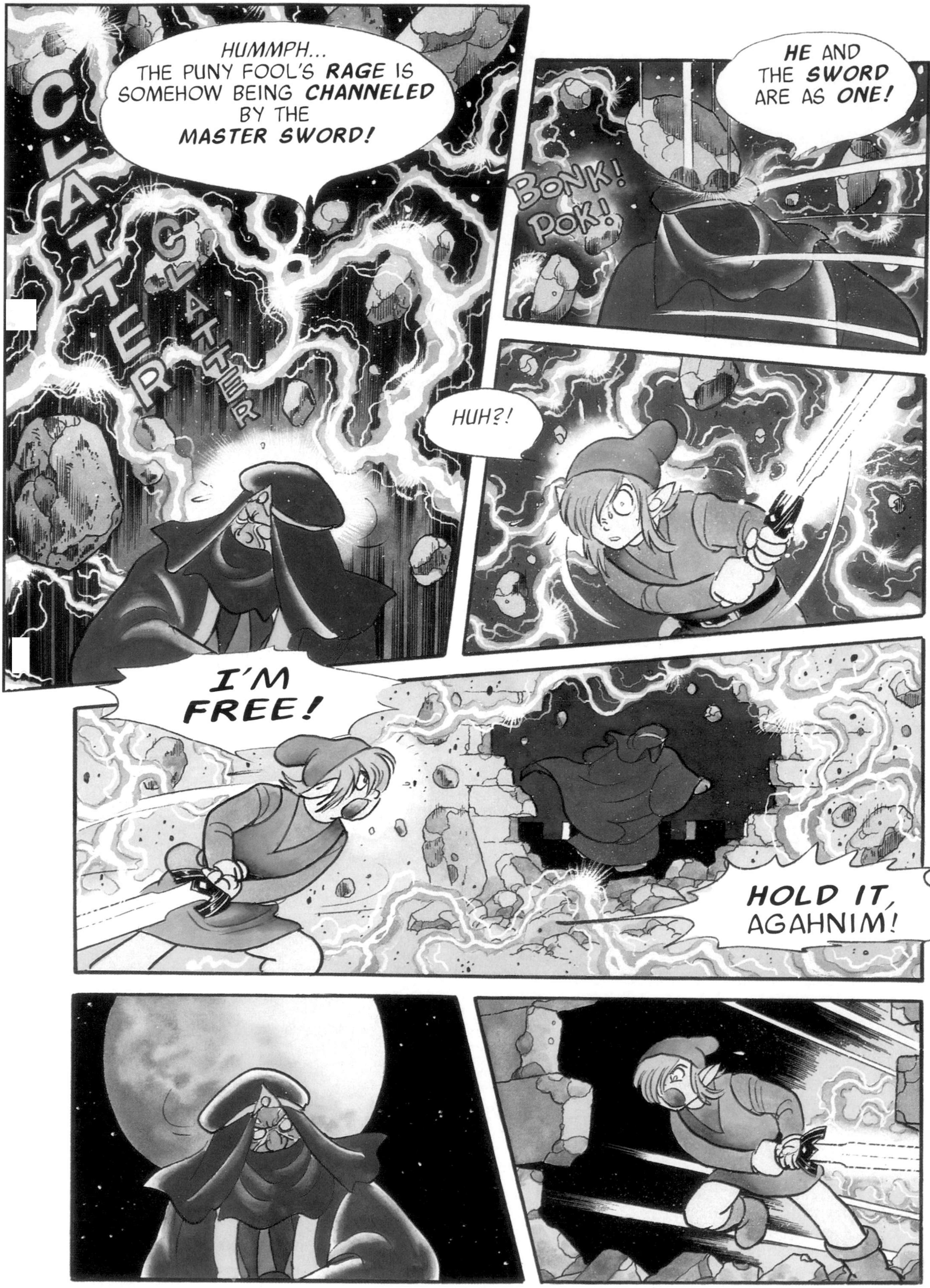
HUMMPH... THE PUNY FOOL'S **RAGE** IS SOMEHOW BEING **CHANNELED** BY THE **MASTER SWORD!**
CLATTER
CLATTER
HE AND THE **SWORD** ARE AS **ONE!**
BONK! POK!
HUH?!
I'M FREE!
HOLD IT, AGAHNIM!

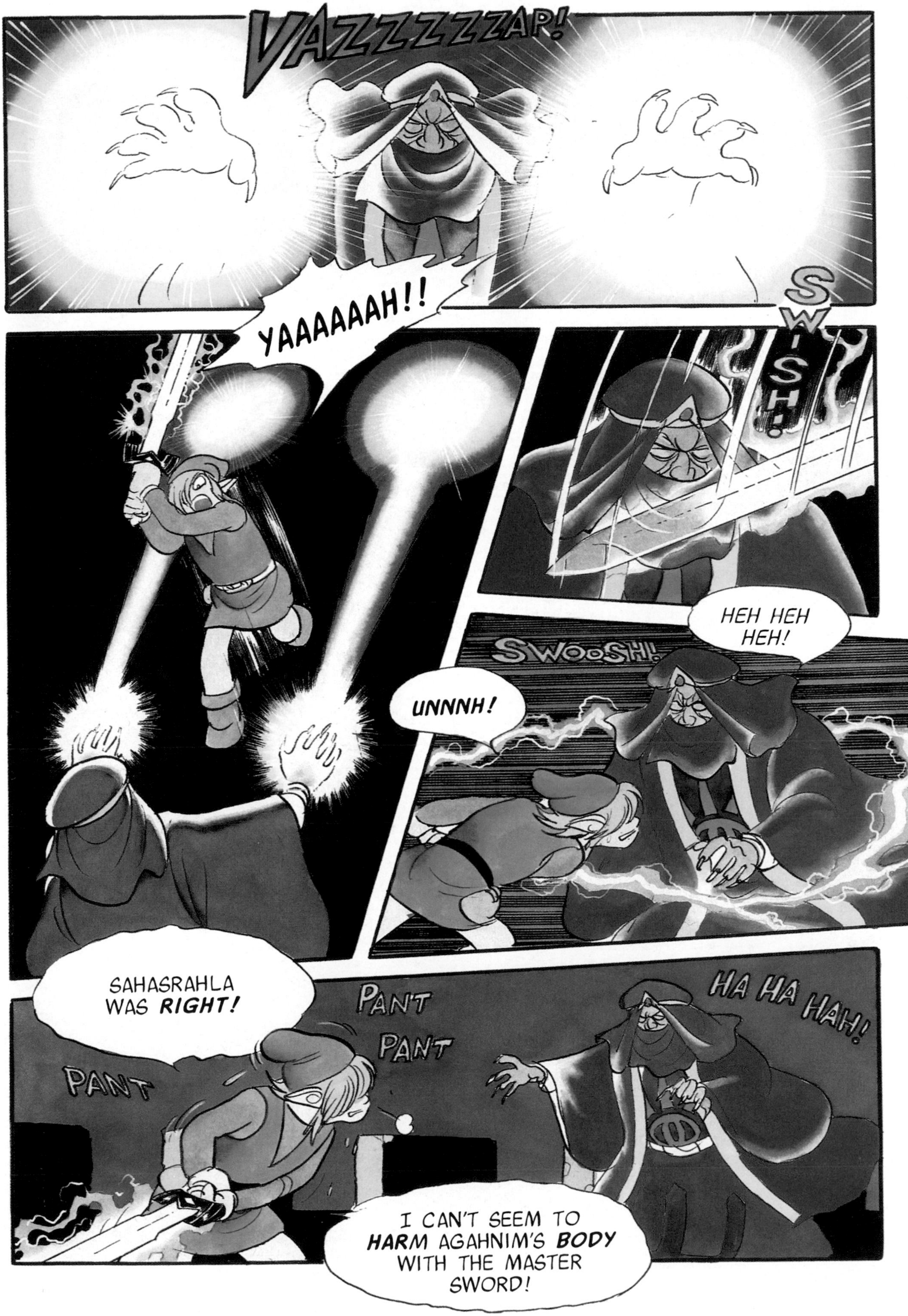
VAZZZZZZAP!
YAAAAAAH!!
SWISH!
SWOOSH!
HEH HEH HEH!
UNNNH!
SAHASRAHLA WAS **RIGHT!**
PANT
PANT
PANT
HA HA HAH!
I CAN'T SEEM TO **HARM** AGAHNIM'S **BODY** WITH THE MASTER SWORD!

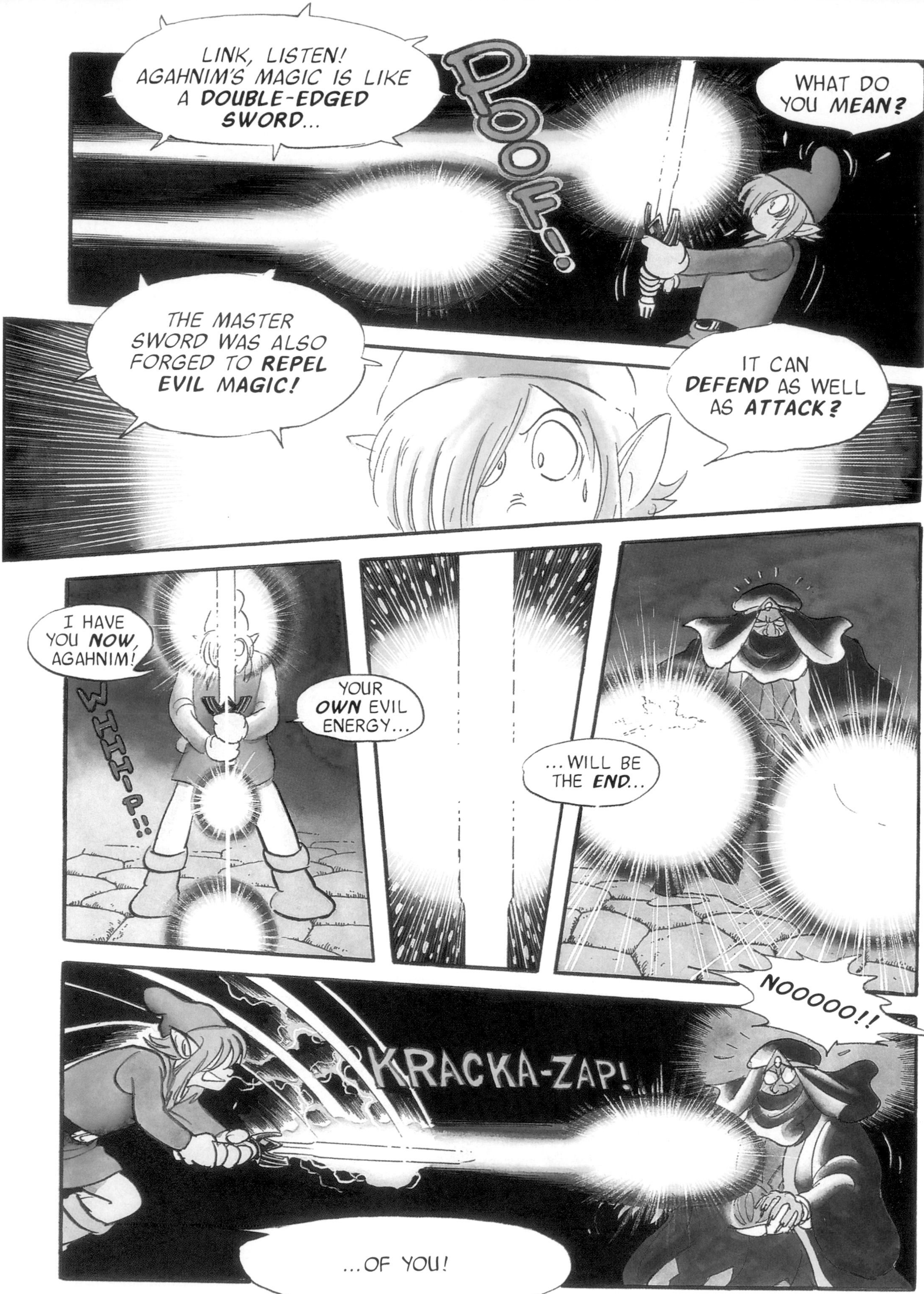
LINK, LISTEN! AGAHNIM'S MAGIC IS LIKE A DOUBLE-EDGED SWORD...
POOF!
WHAT DO YOU MEAN?
THE MASTER SWORD WAS ALSO FORGED TO REPEL EVIL MAGIC!
IT CAN DEFEND AS WELL AS ATTACK?
I HAVE YOU NOW, AGAHNIM!
WHHHIP!!
YOUR OWN EVIL ENERGY...
...WILL BE THE END...
NOOOOO!!
KRACKA-ZAP!
...OF YOU!

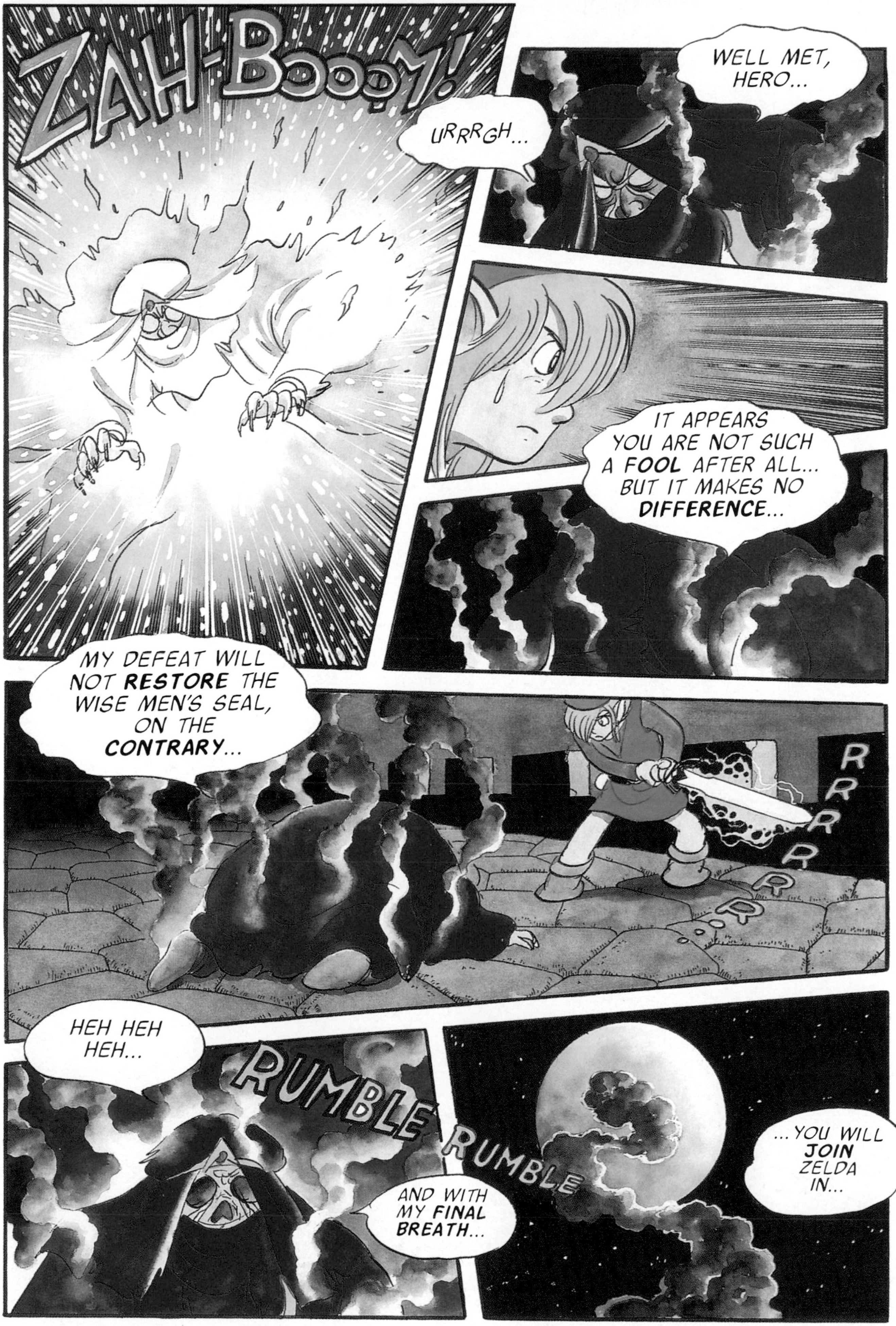
ZAH-BOOOOM!
URRRGH...
WELL MET, HERO...
IT APPEARS YOU ARE NOT SUCH A **FOOL** AFTER ALL... BUT IT MAKES NO **DIFFERENCE**...
MY DEFEAT WILL NOT **RESTORE** THE WISE MEN'S SEAL, ON THE **CONTRARY**...
RRRRRR...
HEH HEH HEH...
RUMBLE
RUMBLE
AND WITH MY **FINAL BREATH**...
...YOU WILL **JOIN** ZELDA IN...

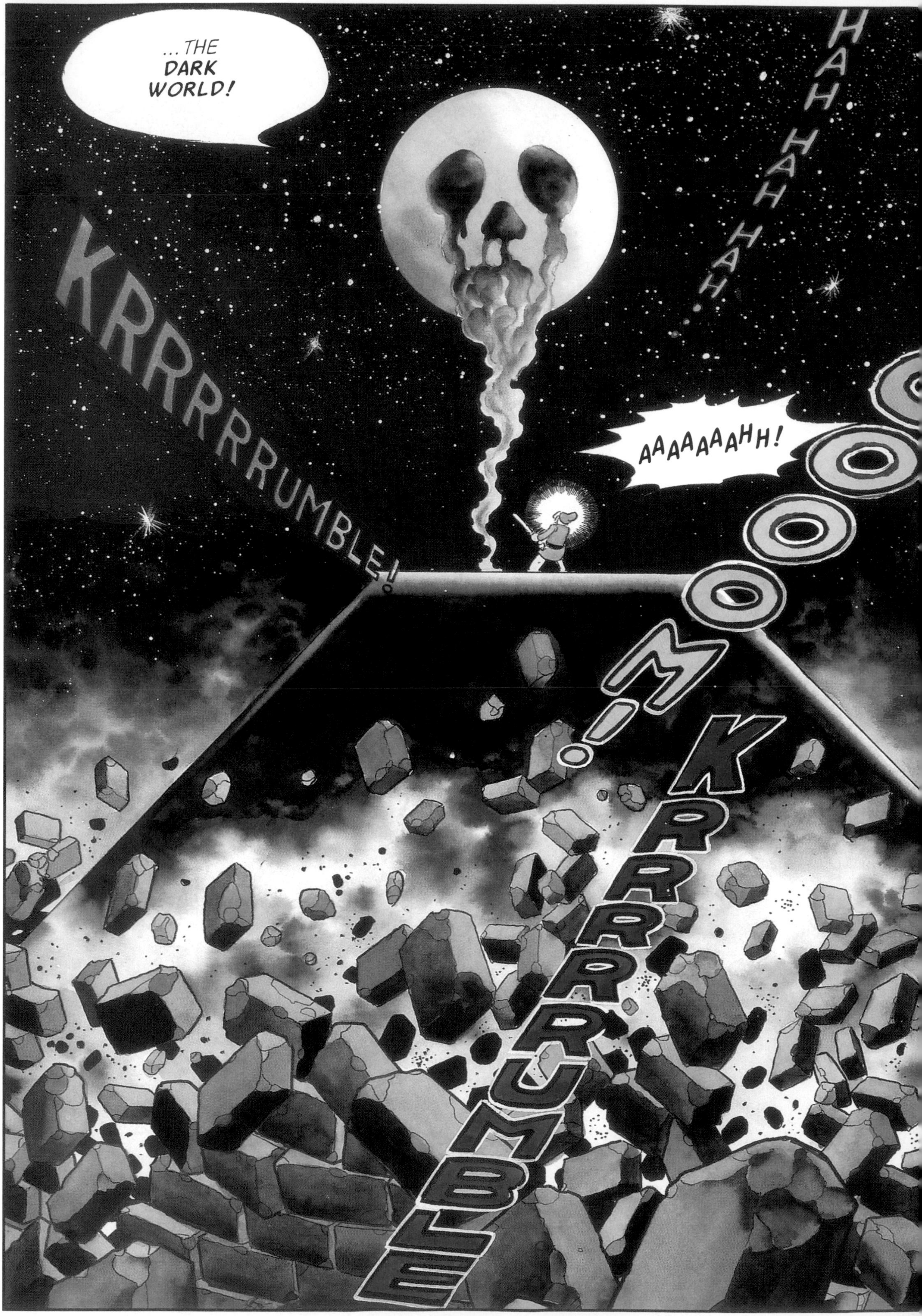
...THE DARK WORLD!
KRRRRRRUMBLE!
HAH HAH HAH HAH!
AAAAAAAHH!
OOOOOM!
KRRRRRRUMBLE

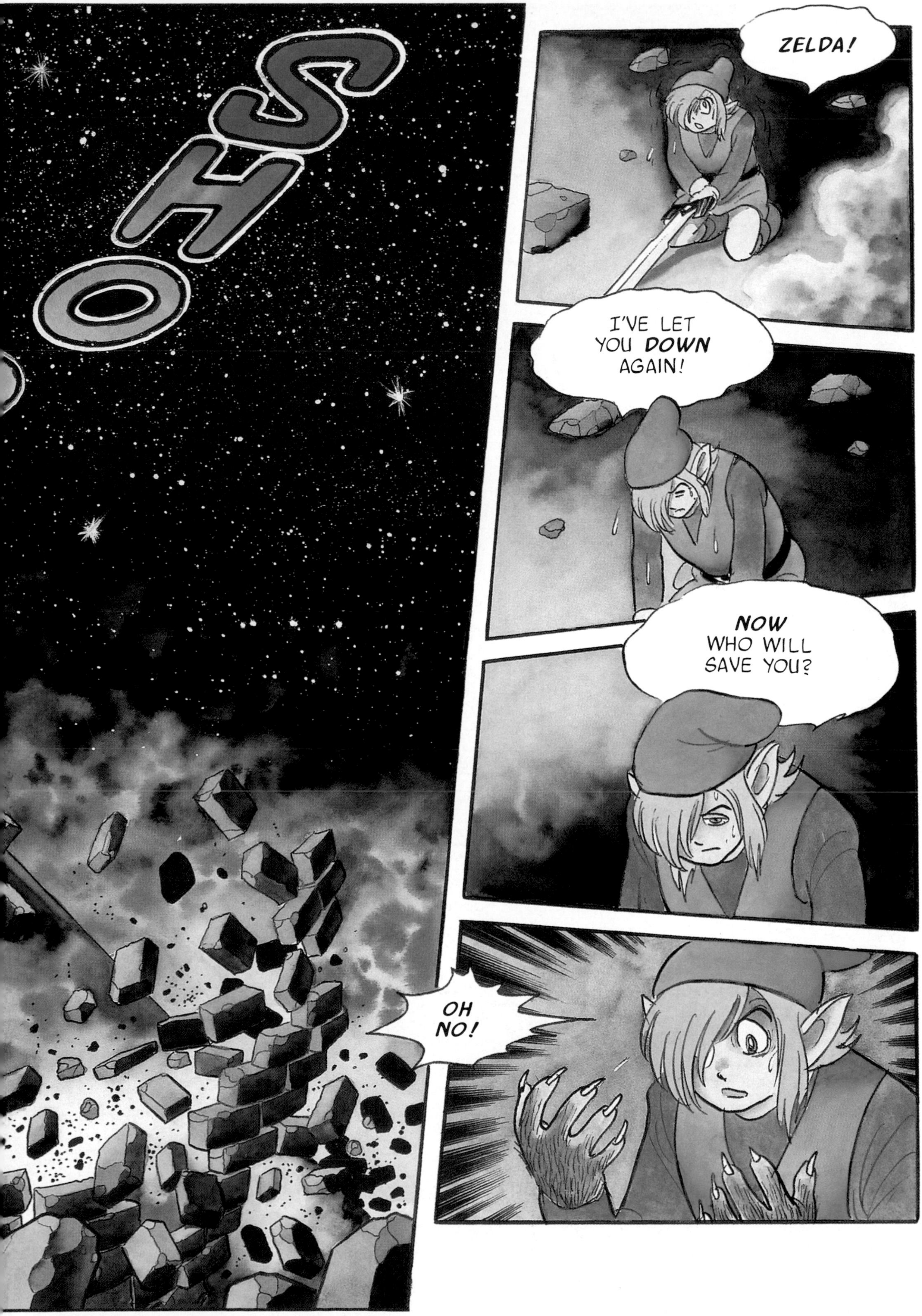
ZELDA!
I'VE LET YOU DOWN AGAIN!
NOW WHO WILL SAVE YOU?
OH NO!

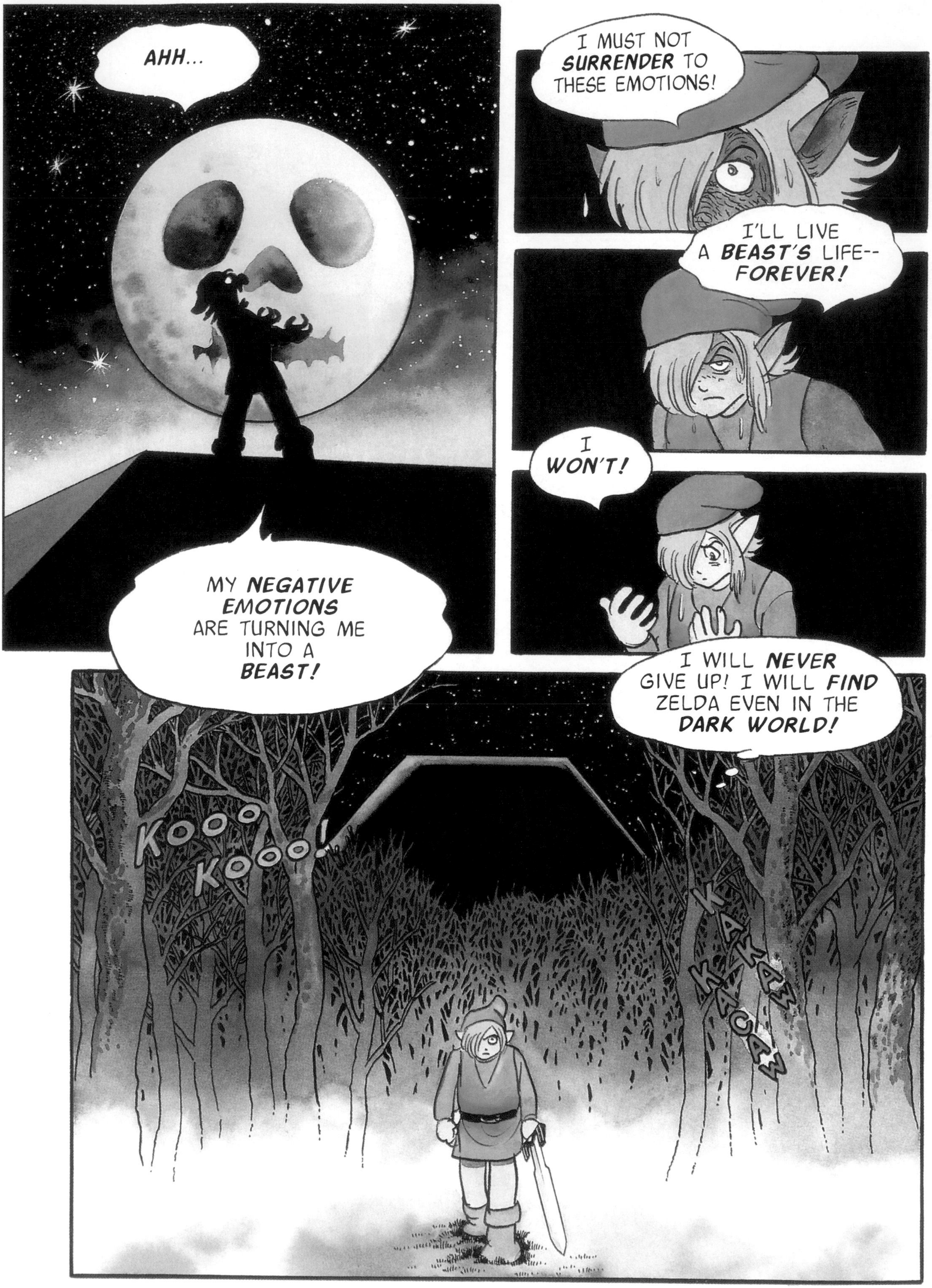

AHH...
MY **NEGATIVE EMOTIONS** ARE TURNING ME INTO A **BEAST!**
I MUST NOT **SURRENDER** TO THESE EMOTIONS!
I'LL LIVE A **BEAST'S** LIFE-- **FOREVER!**
I **WON'T!**
KOOO KOOO!
I WILL **NEVER** GIVE UP! I WILL **FIND** ZELDA EVEN IN THE **DARK WORLD!**
KAKAW KACAW

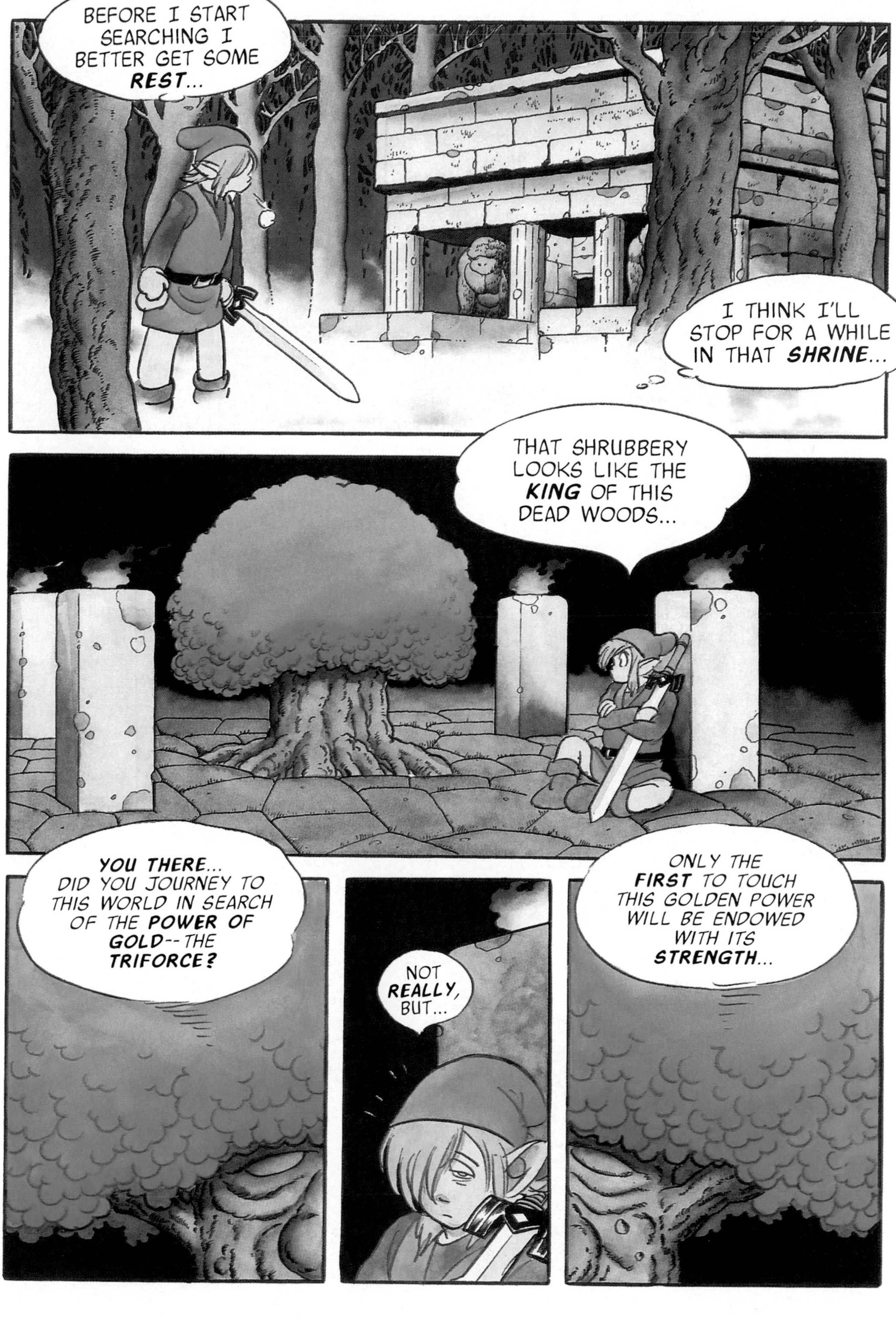
BEFORE I START SEARCHING I BETTER GET SOME **REST**...
I THINK I'LL STOP FOR A WHILE IN THAT **SHRINE**...
THAT SHRUBBERY LOOKS LIKE THE **KING** OF THIS DEAD WOODS...
YOU THERE... DID YOU JOURNEY TO THIS WORLD IN SEARCH OF THE **POWER OF GOLD**--THE **TRIFORCE?**
NOT **REALLY**, BUT...
ONLY THE **FIRST** TO TOUCH THIS GOLDEN POWER WILL BE ENDOWED WITH ITS **STRENGTH**...

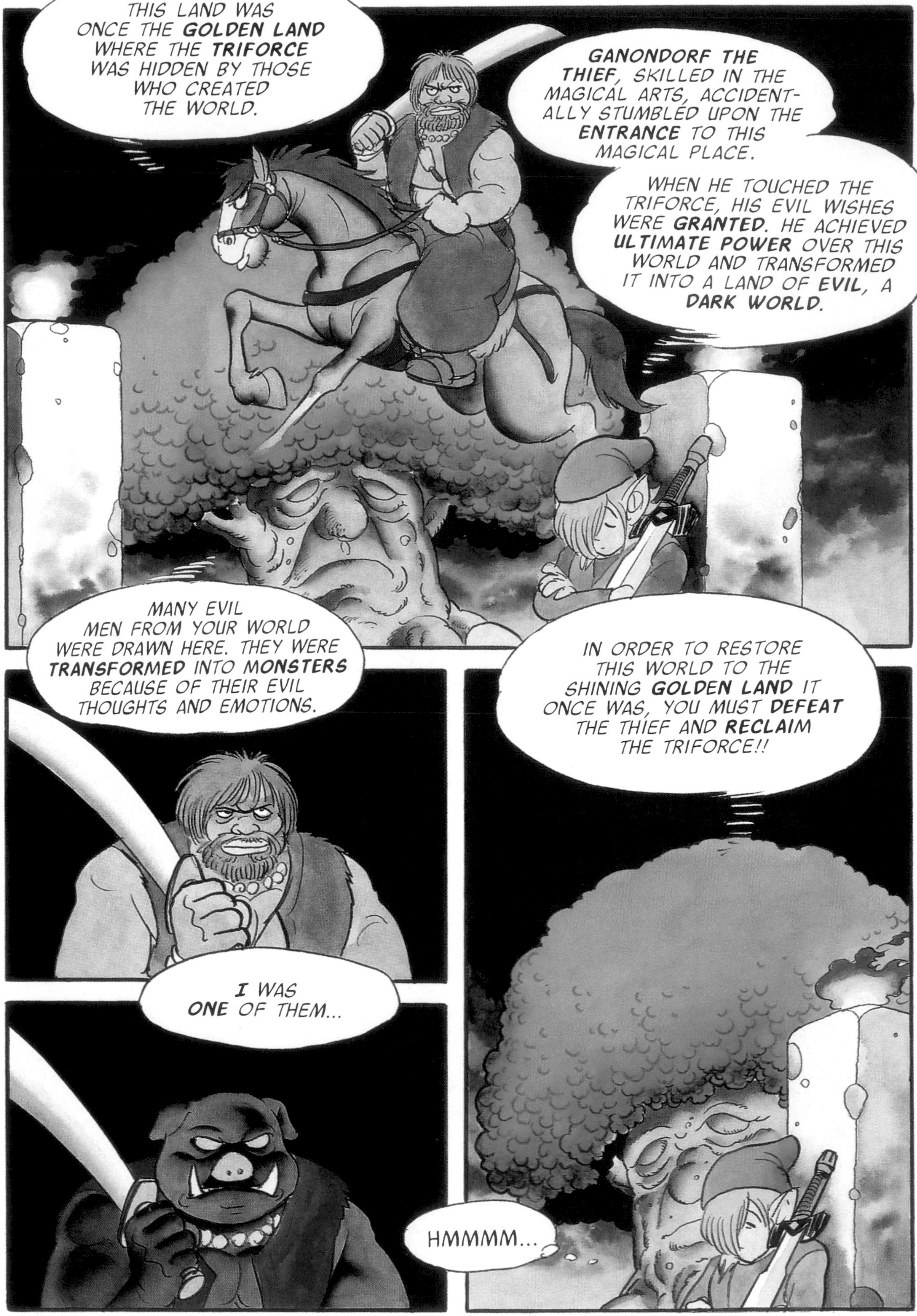
THIS LAND WAS ONCE THE **GOLDEN LAND** WHERE THE **TRIFORCE** WAS HIDDEN BY THOSE WHO CREATED THE WORLD.
GANONDORF THE THIEF, SKILLED IN THE MAGICAL ARTS, ACCIDENTALLY STUMBLED UPON THE **ENTRANCE** TO THIS MAGICAL PLACE.
WHEN HE TOUCHED THE TRIFORCE, HIS EVIL WISHES WERE **GRANTED**. HE ACHIEVED **ULTIMATE POWER** OVER THIS WORLD AND TRANSFORMED IT INTO A LAND OF **EVIL**, A **DARK WORLD**.
MANY EVIL MEN FROM YOUR WORLD WERE DRAWN HERE. THEY WERE **TRANSFORMED** INTO **MONSTERS** BECAUSE OF THEIR EVIL THOUGHTS AND EMOTIONS.
I WAS **ONE** OF THEM...
IN ORDER TO RESTORE THIS WORLD TO THE SHINING **GOLDEN LAND** IT ONCE WAS, YOU MUST **DEFEAT** THE THIEF AND **RECLAIM** THE TRIFORCE!!
HMMMM...

UNTIL THEN...
I REMAIN A FOOL IN THE SHAPE OF A TREE...
DOOMED NEVER TO LEAVE THE DARK WORLD...
A TALKING TREE? GANONDORF?
WAS IT A DREAM?
BLIP!
WHOA!

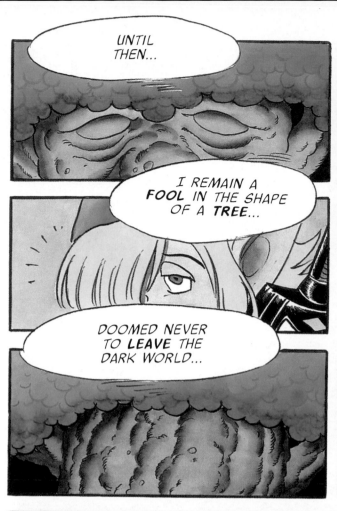

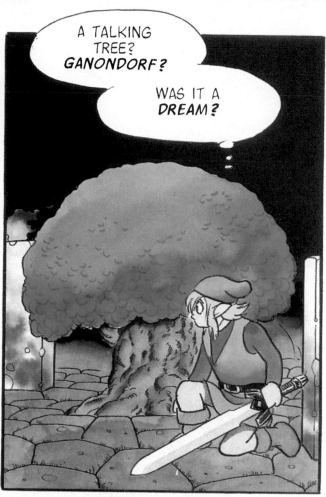

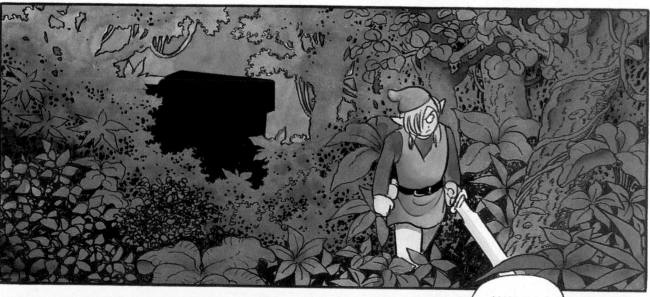

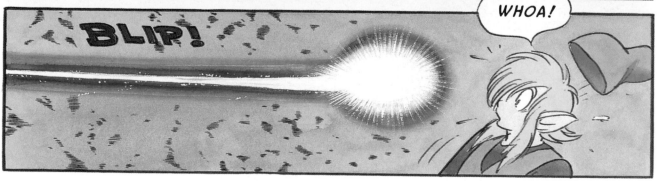

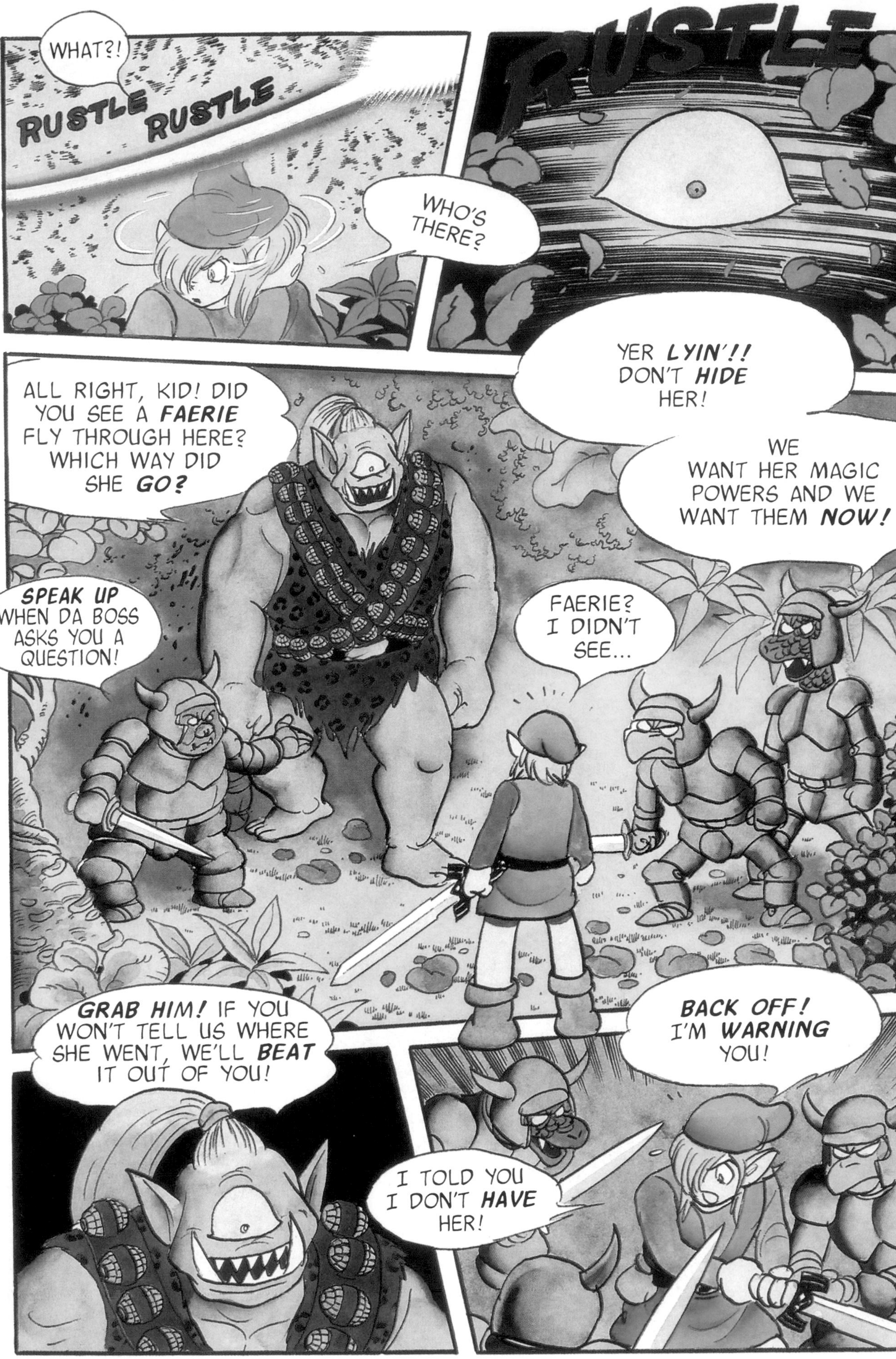
WHAT?!
RUSTLE RUSTLE
WHO'S THERE?
RUSTLE
ALL RIGHT, KID! DID YOU SEE A **FAERIE** FLY THROUGH HERE? WHICH WAY DID SHE **GO?**
YER **LYIN'!!** DON'T **HIDE** HER!
WE WANT HER MAGIC POWERS AND WE WANT THEM **NOW!**
SPEAK UP WHEN DA BOSS ASKS YOU A QUESTION!
FAERIE? I DIDN'T SEE...
GRAB HIM! IF YOU WON'T TELL US WHERE SHE WENT, WE'LL **BEAT** IT OUT OF YOU!
BACK OFF! I'M **WARNING** YOU!
I TOLD YOU I DON'T **HAVE** HER!

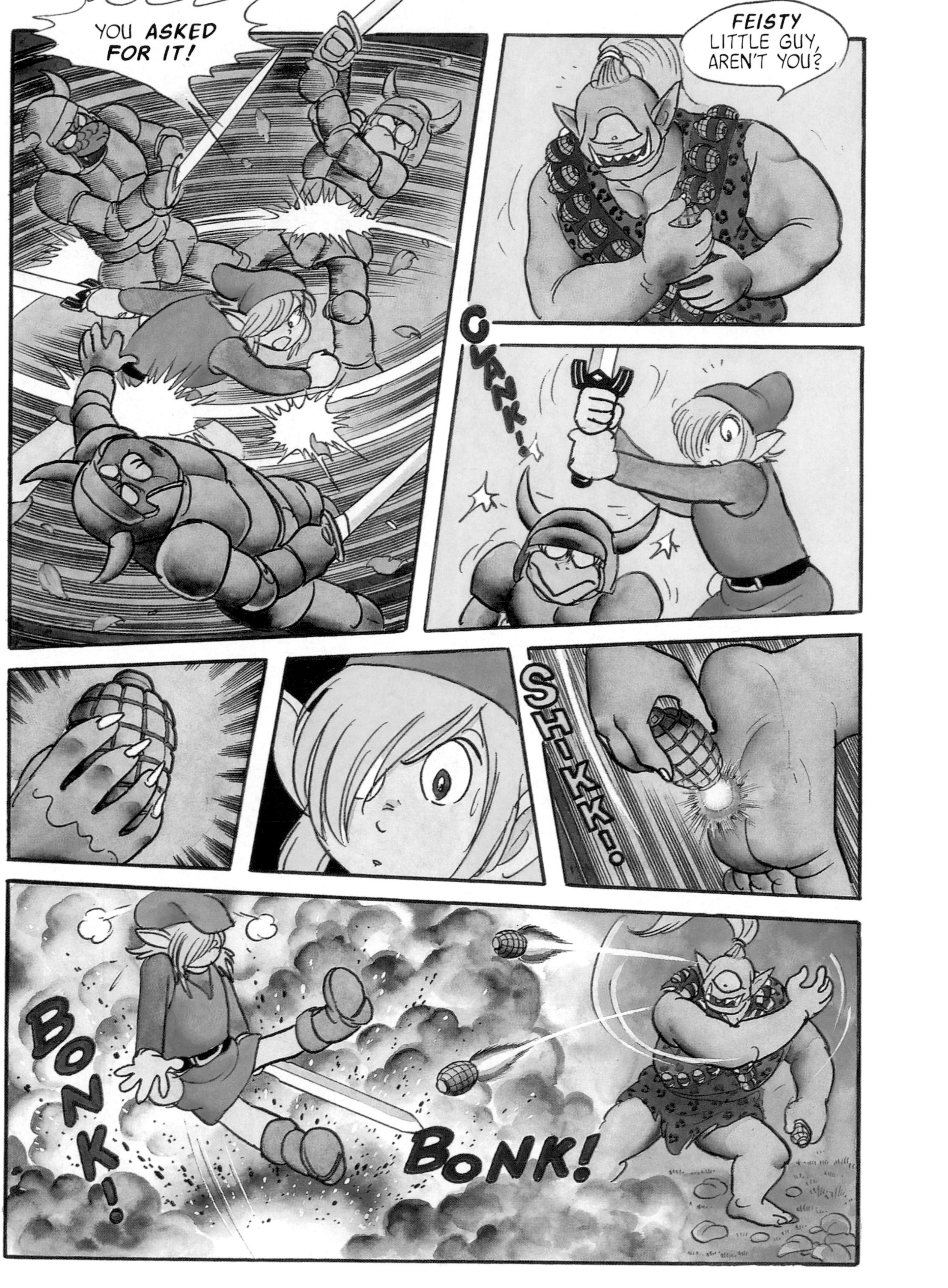
YOU ASKED FOR IT!
FEISTY LITTLE GUY, AREN'T YOU?
GVANK!
SHI-KKK!
BONK!
BONK!

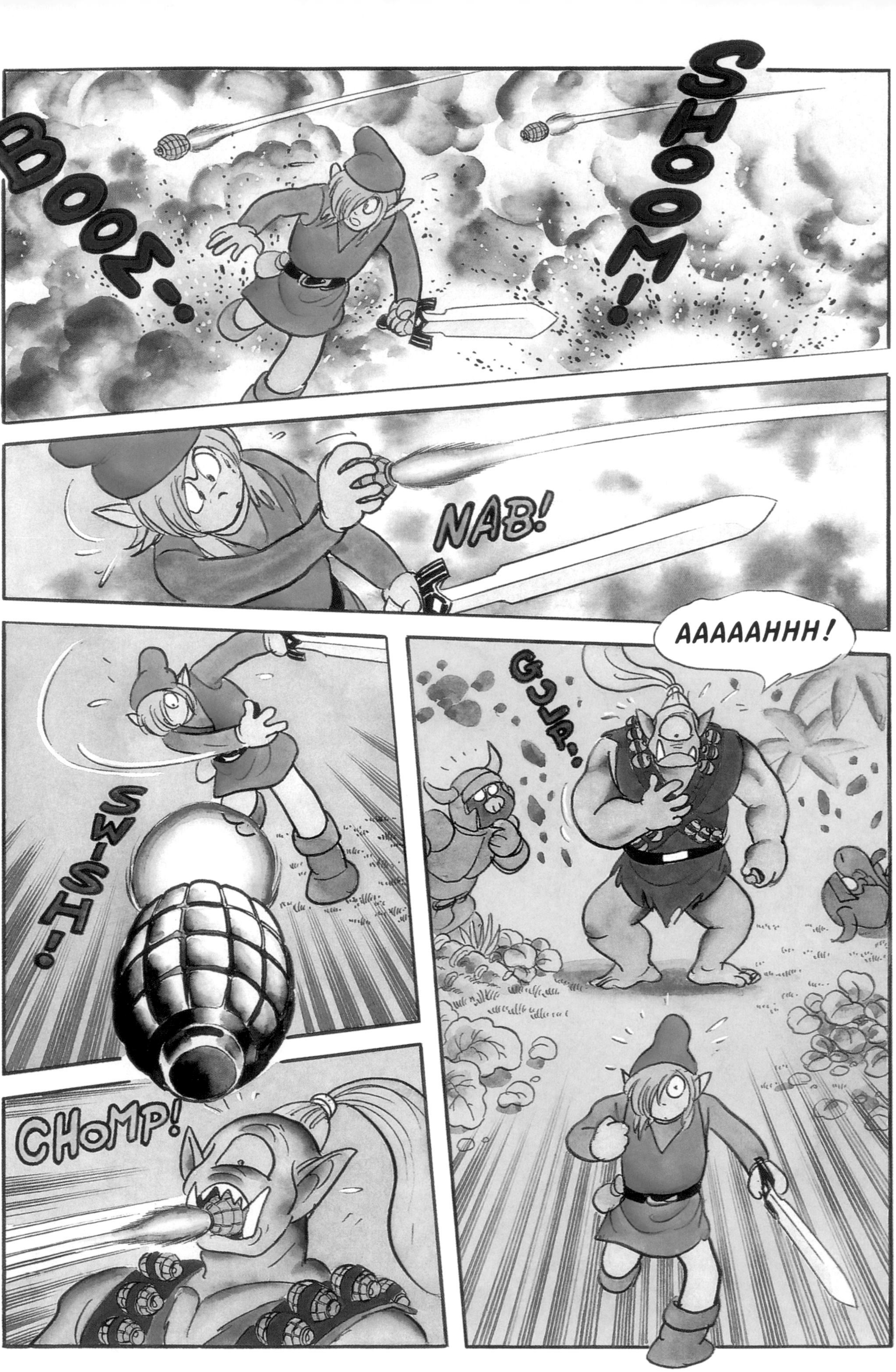
BOOOM!!
SHOOOM!
NAB!
SWISH!
AAAAAHHH!
GULP..
CHOMP!

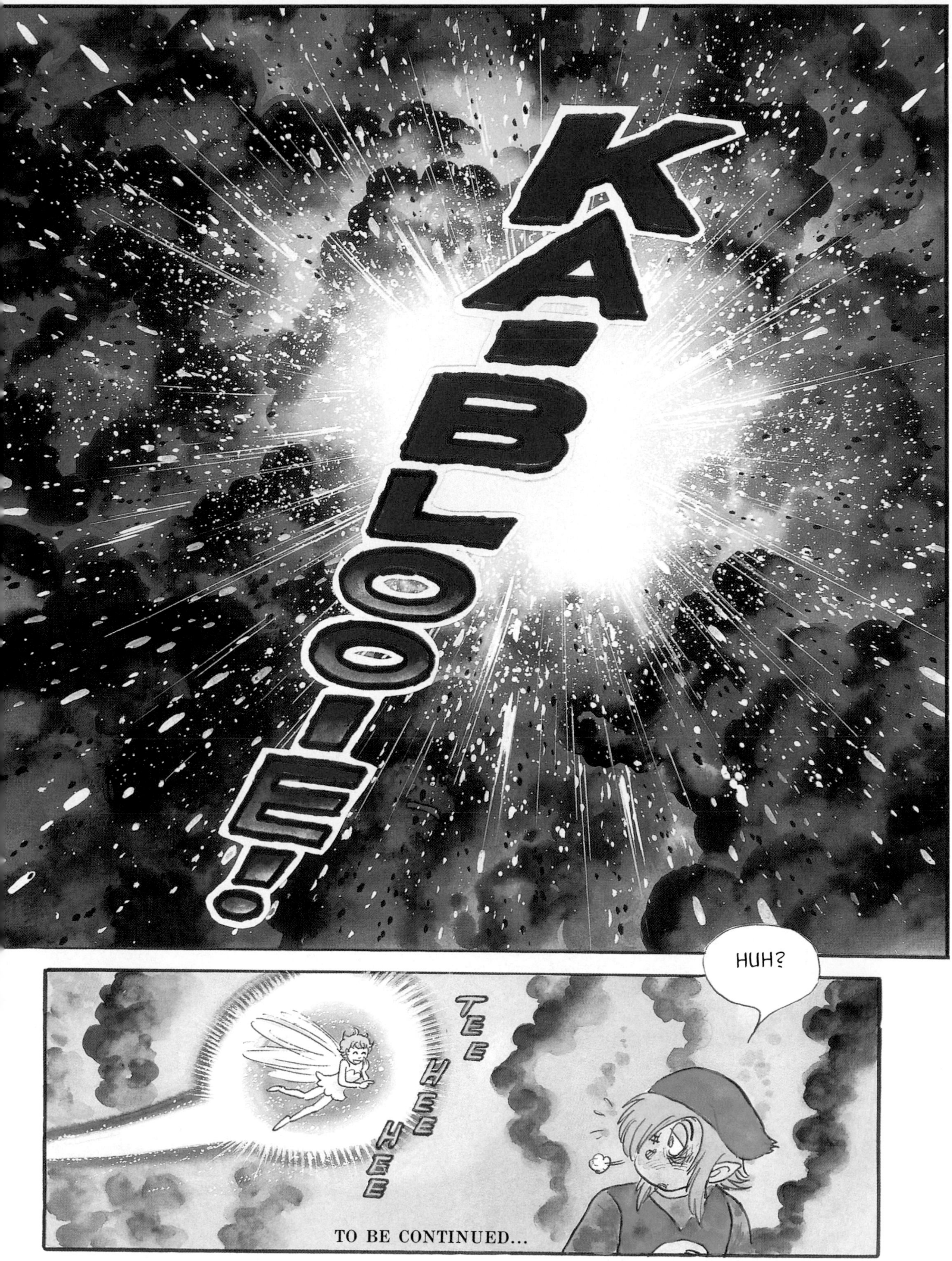
KA-BLOOOIE!!
TEE HEE HEE HEE
HUH?
TO BE CONTINUED...

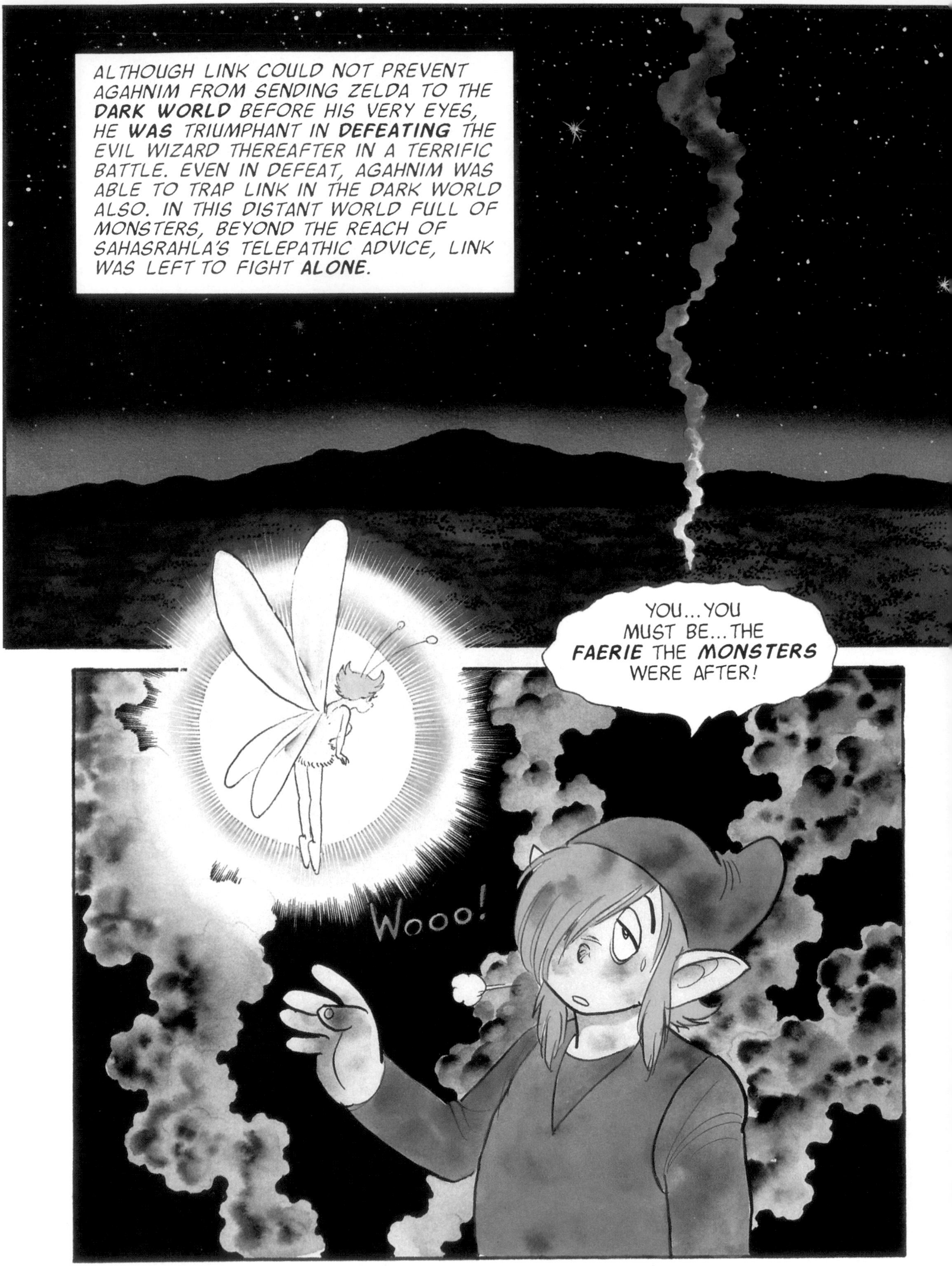
ALTHOUGH LINK COULD NOT PREVENT AGAHNIM FROM SENDING ZELDA TO THE DARK WORLD BEFORE HIS VERY EYES, HE WAS TRIUMPHANT IN DEFEATING THE EVIL WIZARD THEREAFTER IN A TERRIFIC BATTLE. EVEN IN DEFEAT, AGAHNIM WAS ABLE TO TRAP LINK IN THE DARK WORLD ALSO. IN THIS DISTANT WORLD FULL OF MONSTERS, BEYOND THE REACH OF SAHASRAHLA'S TELEPATHIC ADVICE, LINK WAS LEFT TO FIGHT ALONE.
YOU... YOU MUST BE... THE FAERIE THE MONSTERS WERE AFTER!
Wooo!

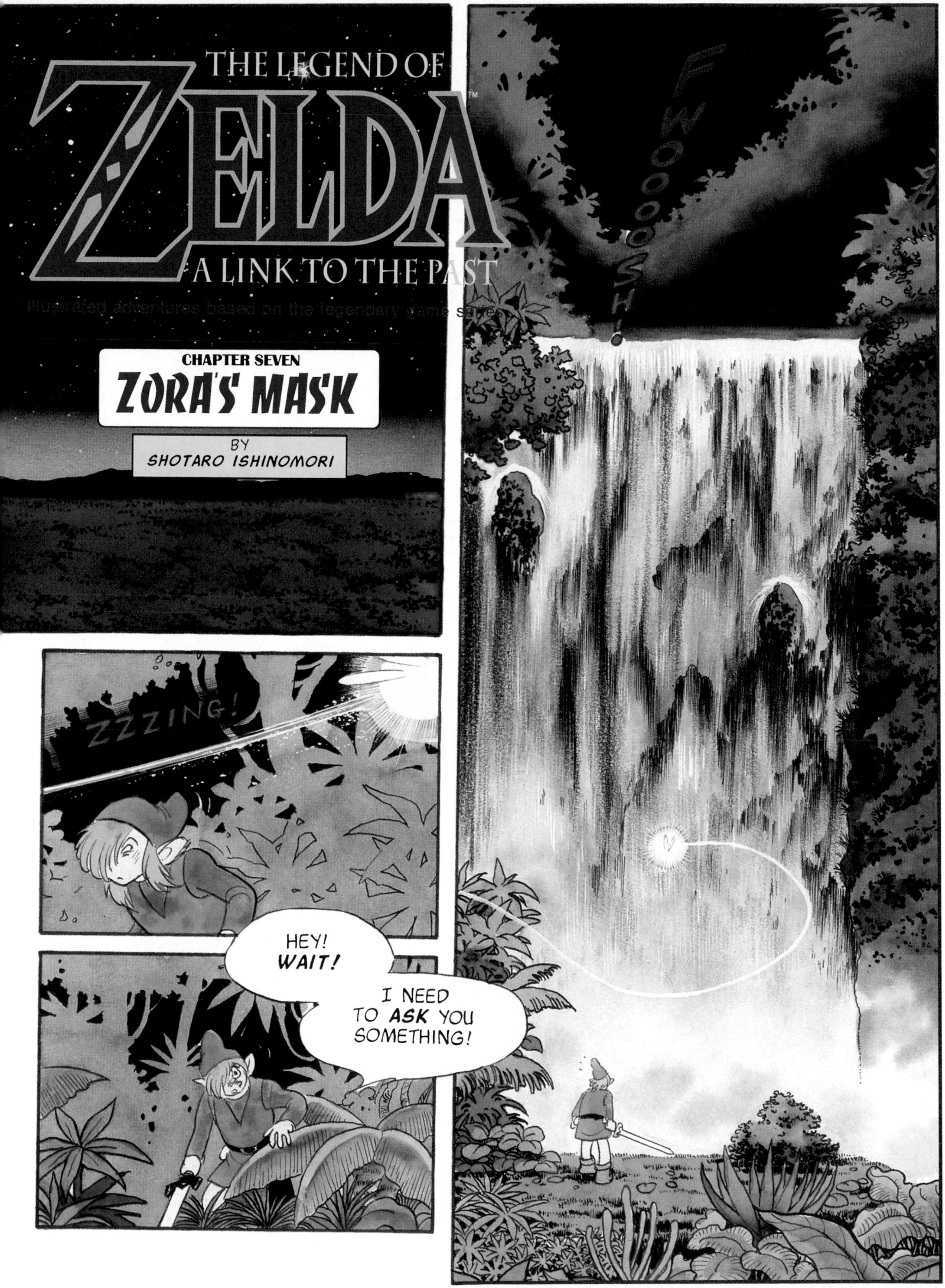
THE LEGEND OF
ZELDA™
A LINK TO THE PAST
Illustrated adventures based on the legendary game series
CHAPTER SEVEN
ZORA'S MASK
BY
SHOTARO ISHINOMORI
ZZZING!
HEY! WAIT!
I NEED TO ASK YOU SOMETHING!
FWOOOOOSH!

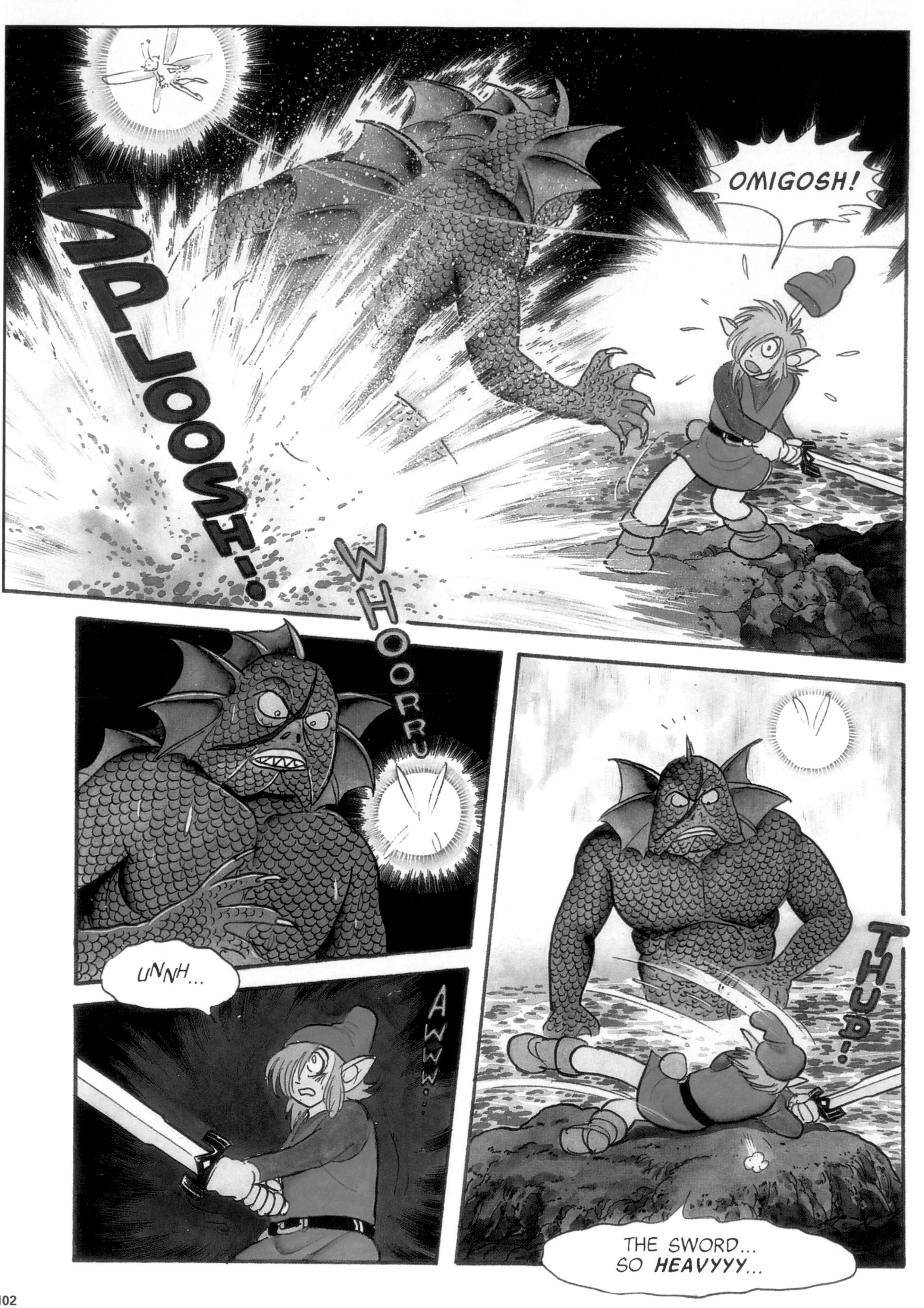
SPLOOSH!!
OMIGOSH!
WHOORRU
UNNH...
AWWW...
THUD!!
THE SWORD...
SO HEAVYYY...

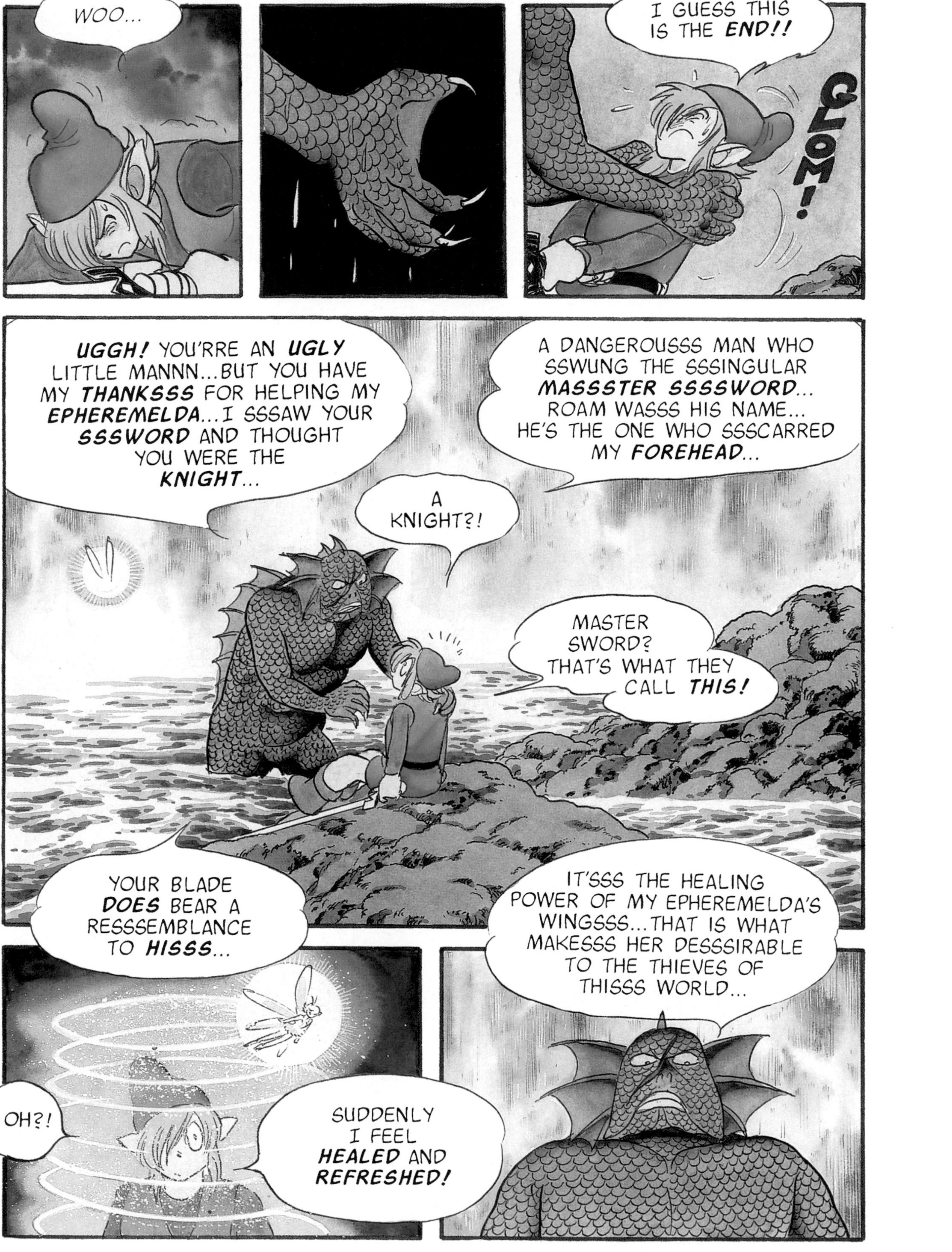
WOO...
I GUESS THIS IS THE END!!
GLOM!
UGGH! YOU'RRE AN UGLY LITTLE MANNN...BUT YOU HAVE MY THANKSSS FOR HELPING MY EPHEREMELDA...I SSSAW YOUR SSSWORD AND THOUGHT YOU WERE THE KNIGHT...
A DANGEROUSSS MAN WHO SSWUNG THE SSSINGULAR MASSSTER SSSSWORD... ROAM WASSS HIS NAME... HE'S THE ONE WHO SSSCARRED MY FOREHEAD...
A KNIGHT?!
MASTER SWORD? THAT'S WHAT THEY CALL THIS!
YOUR BLADE DOES BEAR A RESSSEMBLANCE TO HISSS...
OH?!
SUDDENLY I FEEL HEALED AND REFRESHED!
IT'SSS THE HEALING POWER OF MY EPHEREMELDA'S WINGSSS...THAT IS WHAT MAKESSS HER DESSSIRABLE TO THE THIEVES OF THISSS WORLD...

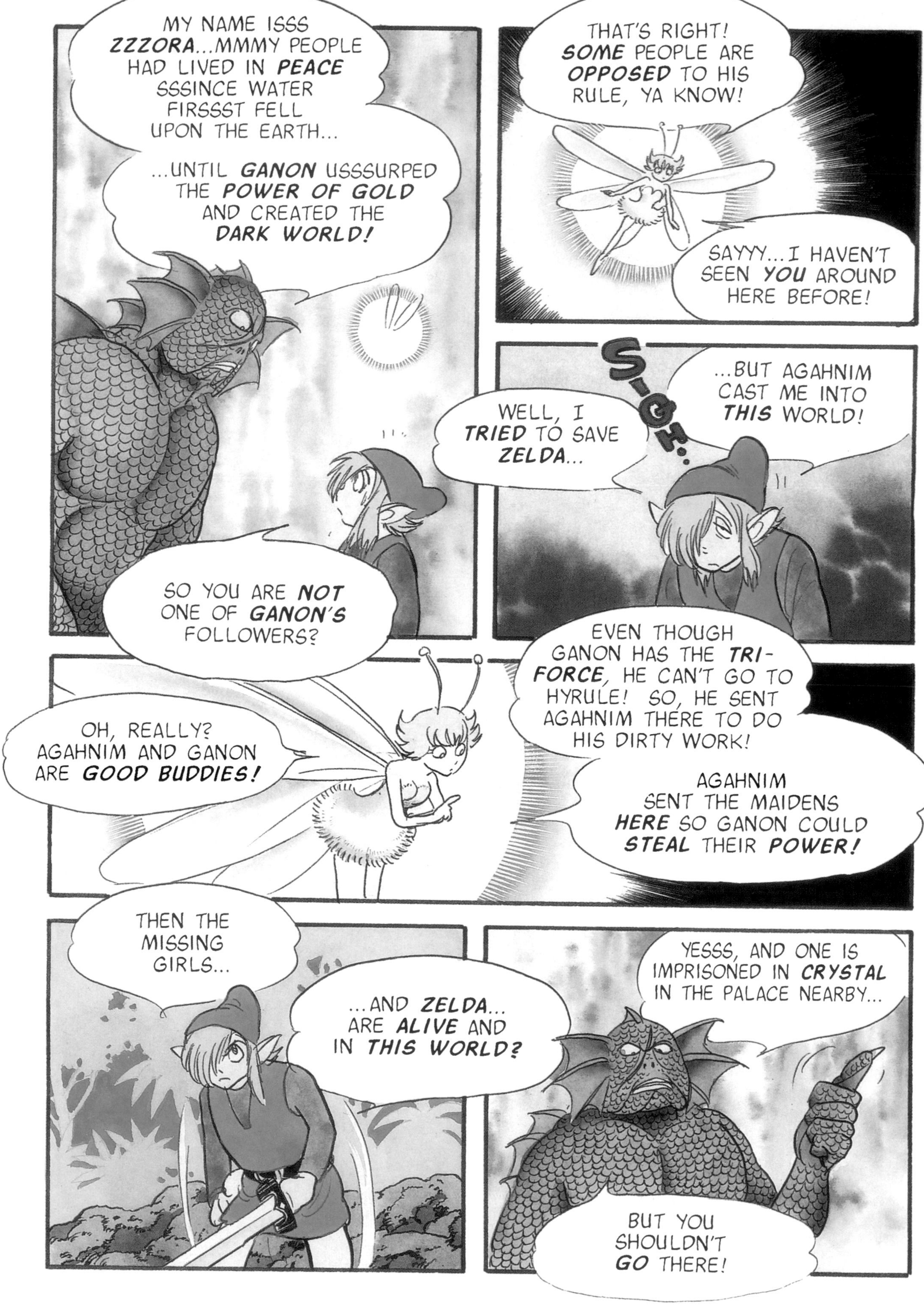

MY NAME ISSS ZZZORA...MMMY PEOPLE HAD LIVED IN PEACE SSSINCE WATER FIRSSST FELL UPON THE EARTH...
...UNTIL GANON USSSURPED THE POWER OF GOLD AND CREATED THE DARK WORLD!
THAT'S RIGHT! SOME PEOPLE ARE OPPOSED TO HIS RULE, YA KNOW!
SAYYY...I HAVEN'T SEEN YOU AROUND HERE BEFORE!
SIGH..
WELL, I TRIED TO SAVE ZELDA...
...BUT AGAHNIM CAST ME INTO THIS WORLD!
SO YOU ARE NOT ONE OF GANON'S FOLLOWERS?
OH, REALLY? AGAHNIM AND GANON ARE GOOD BUDDIES!
EVEN THOUGH GANON HAS THE TRI-FORCE, HE CAN'T GO TO HYRULE! SO, HE SENT AGAHNIM THERE TO DO HIS DIRTY WORK!
AGAHNIM SENT THE MAIDENS HERE SO GANON COULD STEAL THEIR POWER!
THEN THE MISSING GIRLS...
...AND ZELDA... ARE ALIVE AND IN THIS WORLD?
YESSS, AND ONE IS IMPRISONED IN CRYSTAL IN THE PALACE NEARBY...
BUT YOU SHOULDN'T GO THERE!

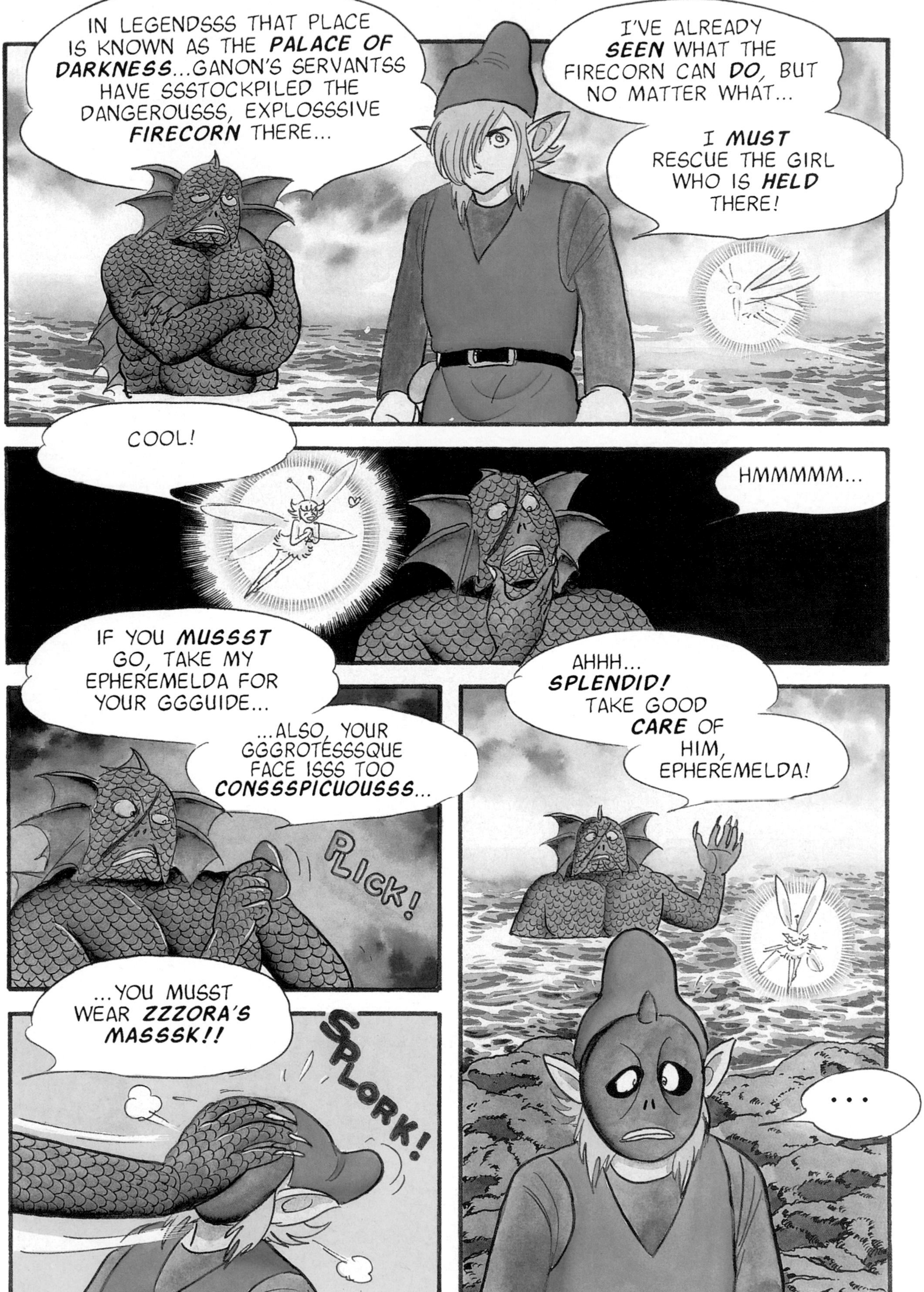
IN LEGENDSSS THAT PLACE IS KNOWN AS THE **PALACE OF DARKNESS**...GANON'S SERVANTSS HAVE SSSTOCKPILED THE DANGEROUSSS, EXPLOSSSIVE **FIRECORN** THERE...
I'VE ALREADY **SEEN** WHAT THE FIRECORN CAN **DO**, BUT NO MATTER WHAT...
I **MUST** RESCUE THE GIRL WHO IS **HELD** THERE!
COOL!
HMMMMM...
IF YOU **MUSSST** GO, TAKE MY EPHEREMELDA FOR YOUR GGGUIDE...
...ALSO, YOUR GGGROTESSSQUE FACE ISSS TOO **CONSSSPICUOUSSS**...
PLICK!
...YOU MUSST WEAR **ZZZORA'S MASSSK!!**
SPLORK!
AHHH... **SPLENDID!** TAKE GOOD **CARE** OF HIM, EPHEREMELDA!
...

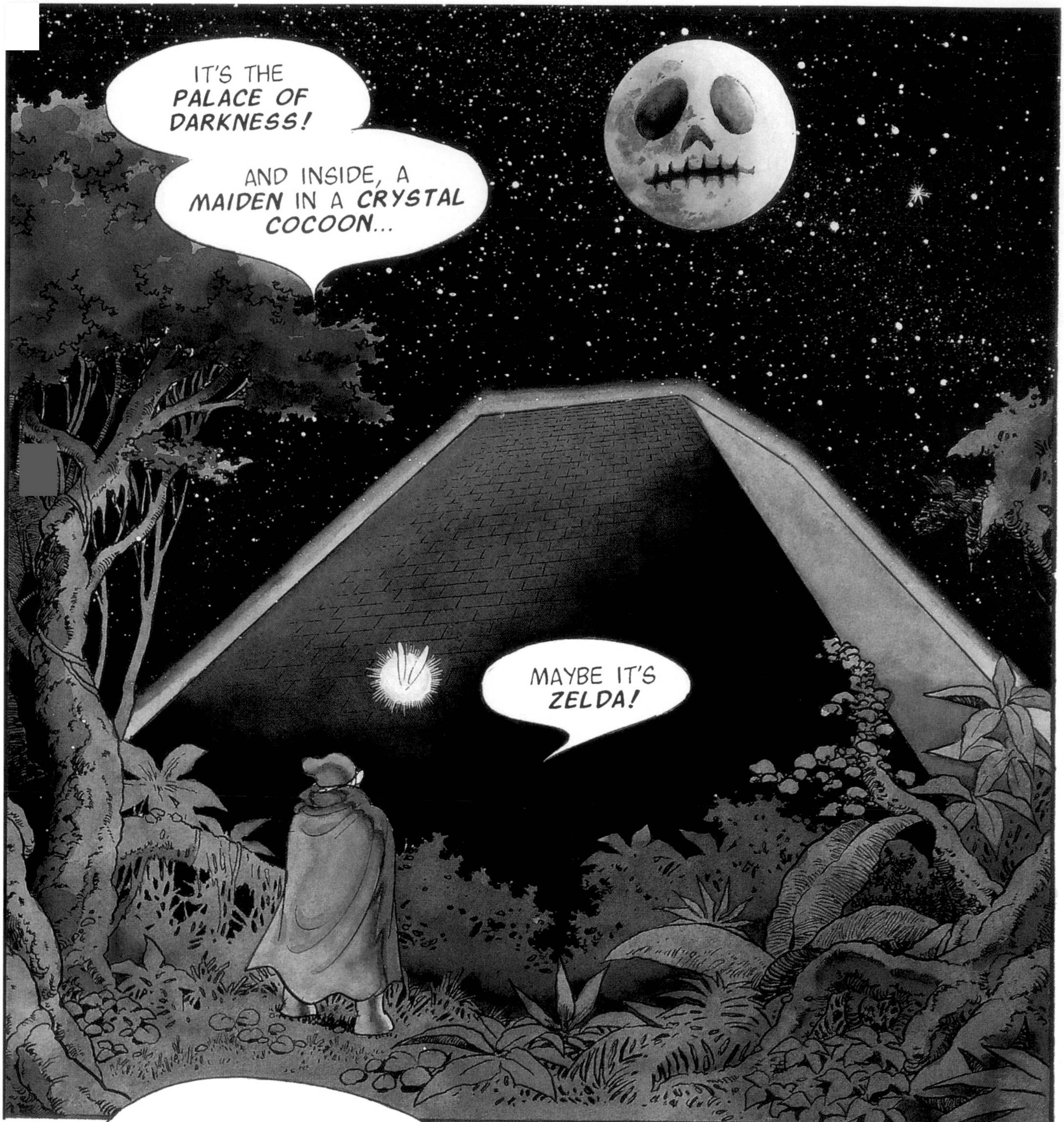
IT'S THE PALACE OF DARKNESS!
AND INSIDE, A MAIDEN IN A CRYSTAL COCOON...
MAYBE IT'S ZELDA!
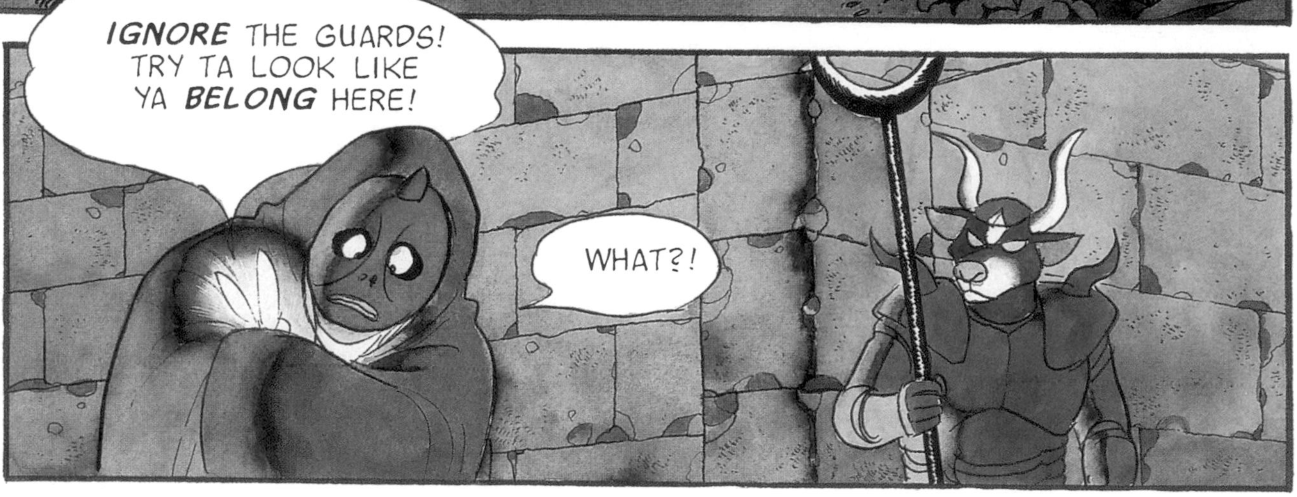
IGNORE THE GUARDS! TRY TA LOOK LIKE YA BELONG HERE!
WHAT?!

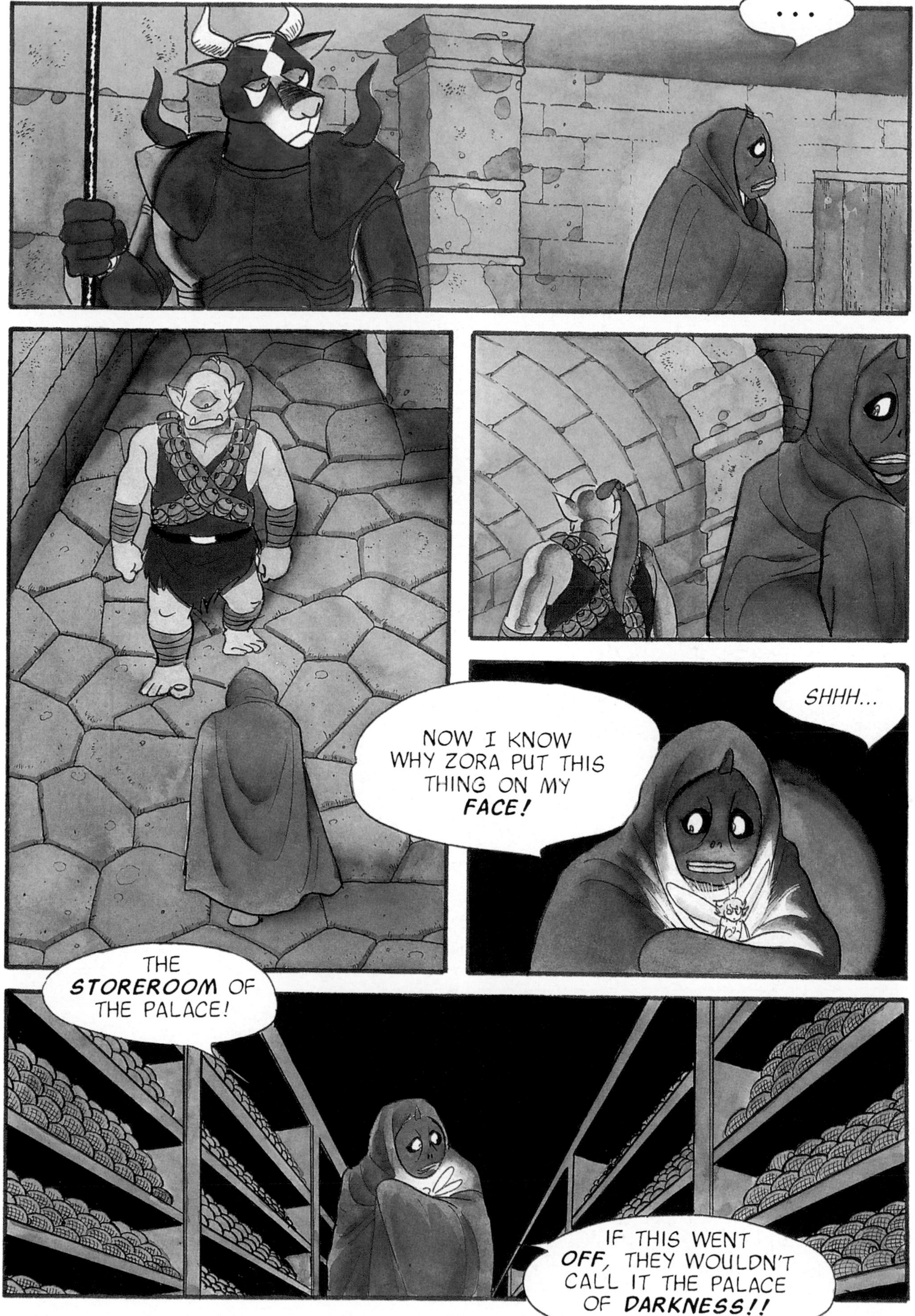
...
NOW I KNOW WHY ZORA PUT THIS THING ON MY **FACE!**
SHHH...
THE **STOREROOM** OF THE PALACE!
IF THIS WENT **OFF**, THEY WOULDN'T CALL IT THE PALACE OF **DARKNESS!!**

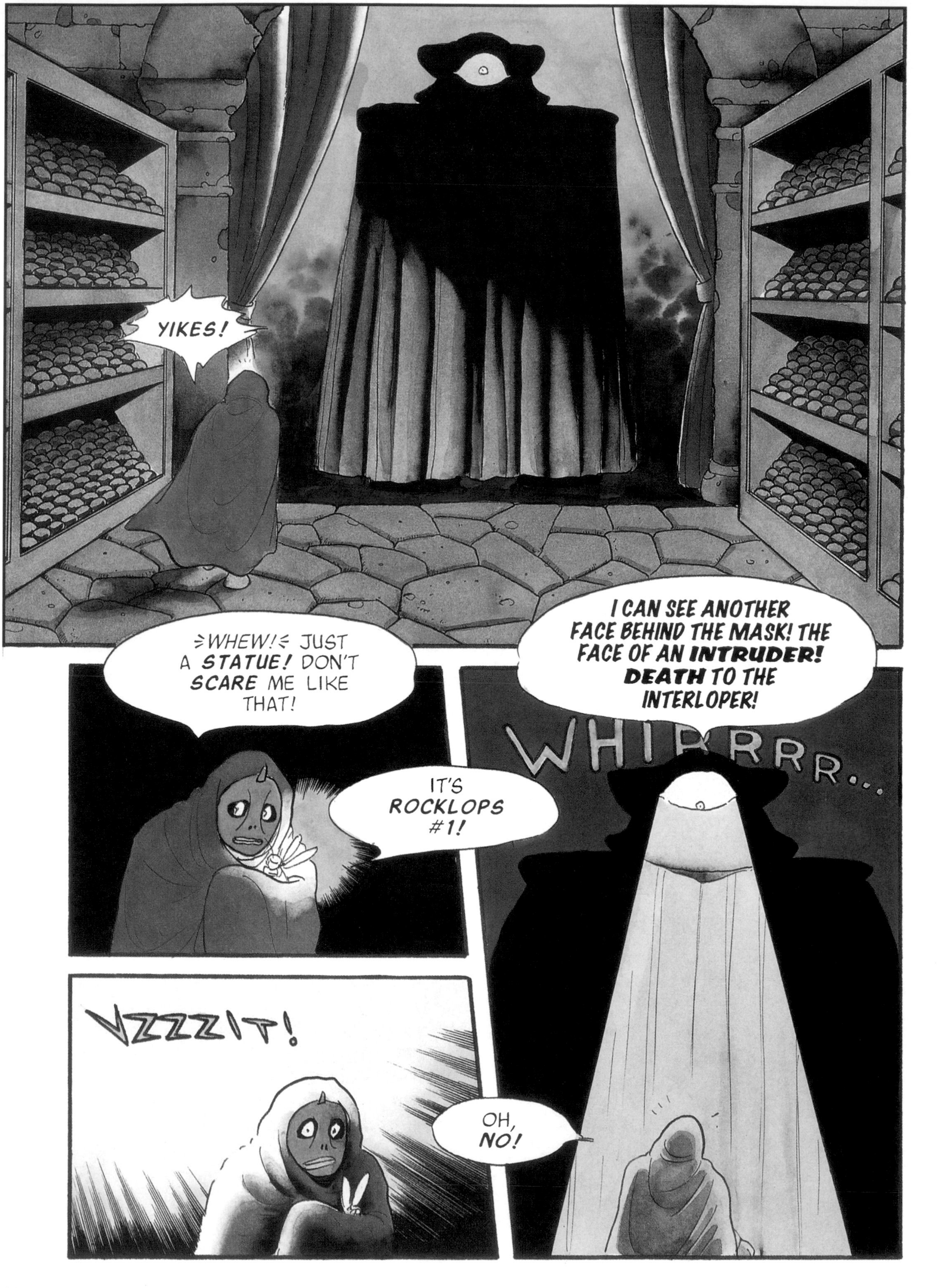
YIKES!
≠WHEW!≠ JUST A STATUE! DON'T SCARE ME LIKE THAT!
IT'S ROCKLOPS #1!
VZZZIT!
OH, NO!
I CAN SEE ANOTHER FACE BEHIND THE MASK! THE FACE OF AN INTRUDER! DEATH TO THE INTERLOPER!
WHIRRRR...

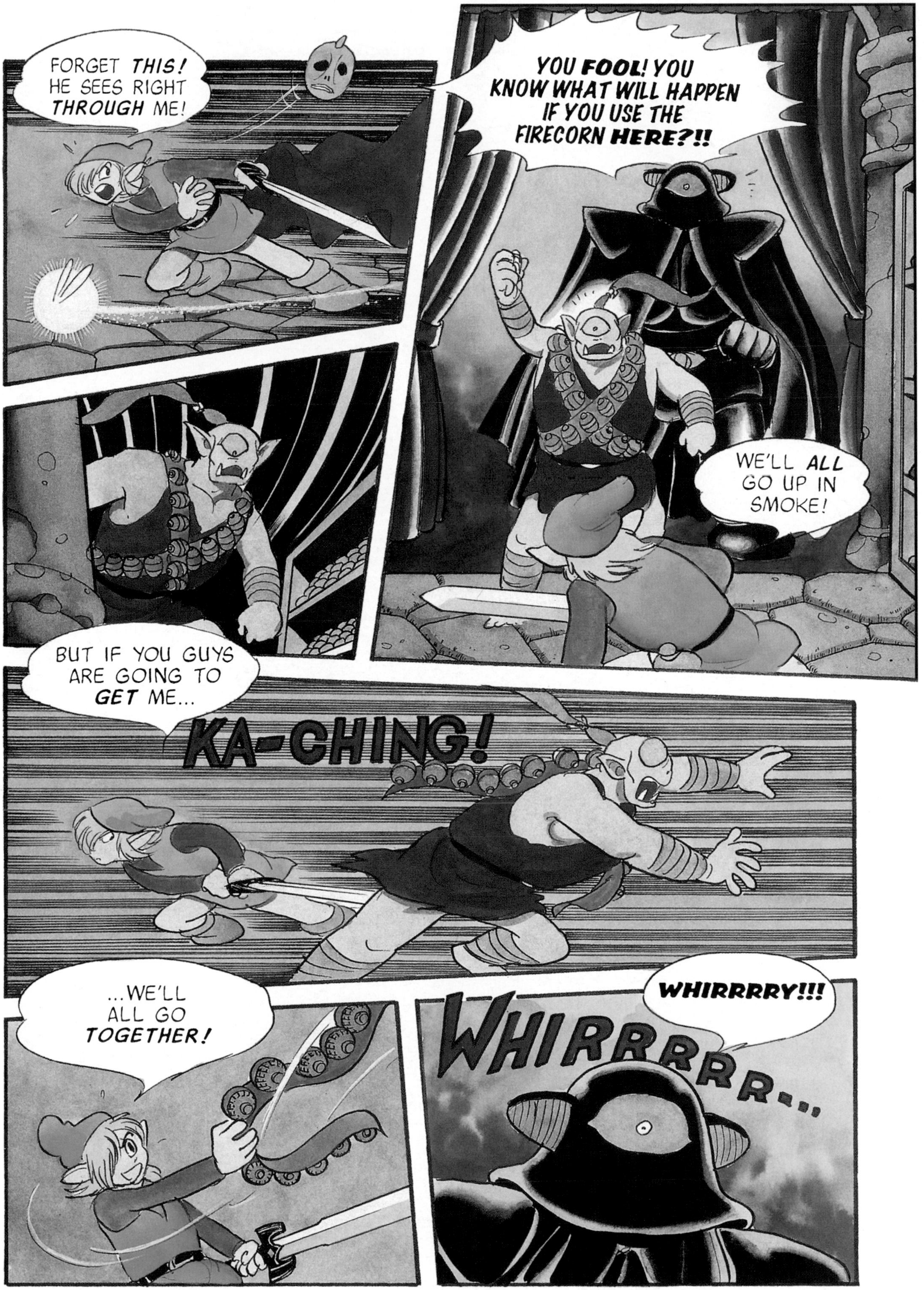
FORGET THIS! HE SEES RIGHT THROUGH ME!
YOU FOOL! YOU KNOW WHAT WILL HAPPEN IF YOU USE THE FIRECORN HERE?!!
WE'LL ALL GO UP IN SMOKE!
BUT IF YOU GUYS ARE GOING TO GET ME...
KA-CHING!
...WE'LL ALL GO TOGETHER!
WHIRRRRY!!!
WHIRRRRRR...

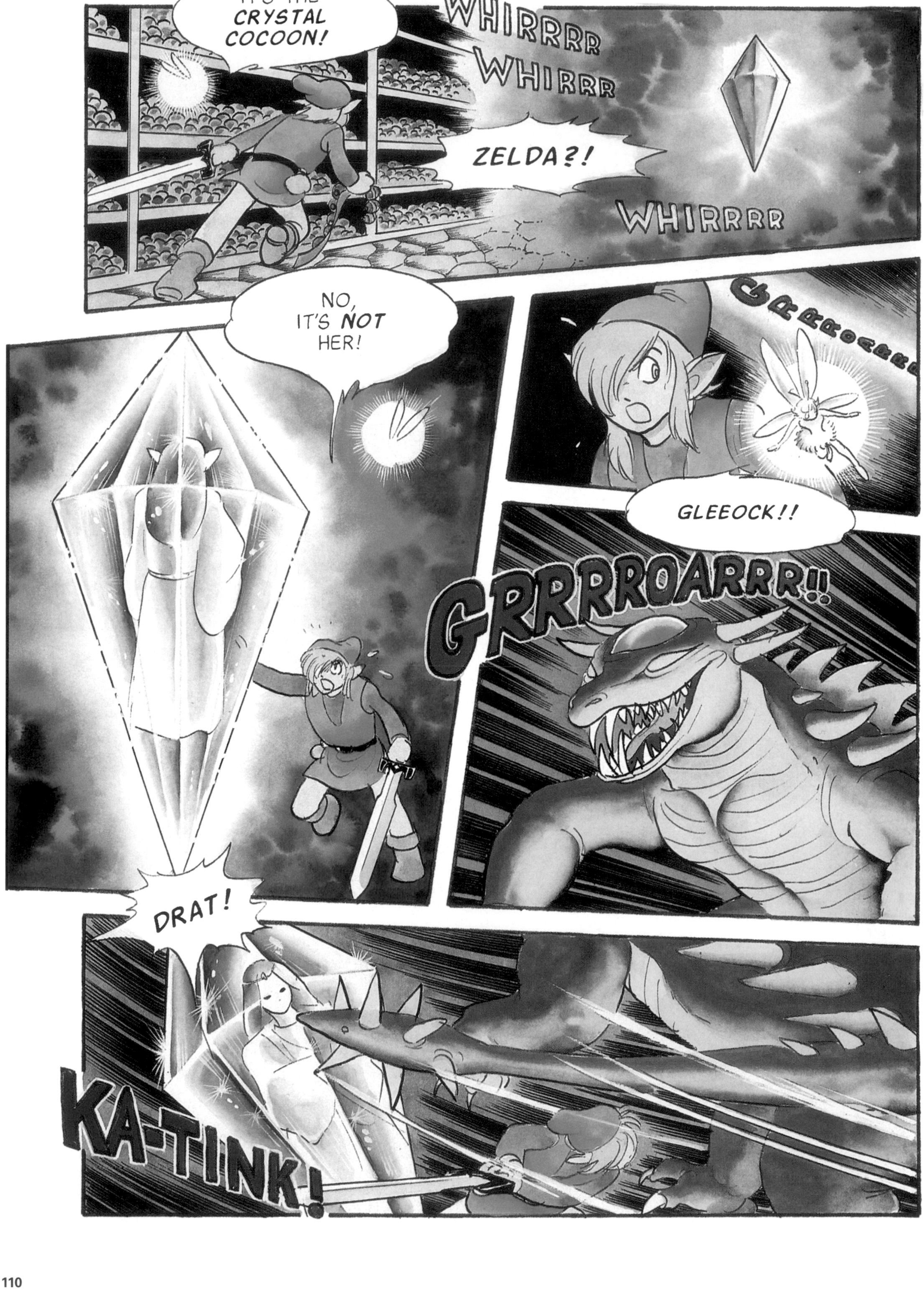
IT'S THE **CRYSTAL COCOON!**
WHIRRRRR
WHIRRRR
ZELDA?!
WHIRRRRR
NO, IT'S **NOT** HER!
GLEEOCK!!
GRRRROARRR!!
DRAT!
KA-TINK!

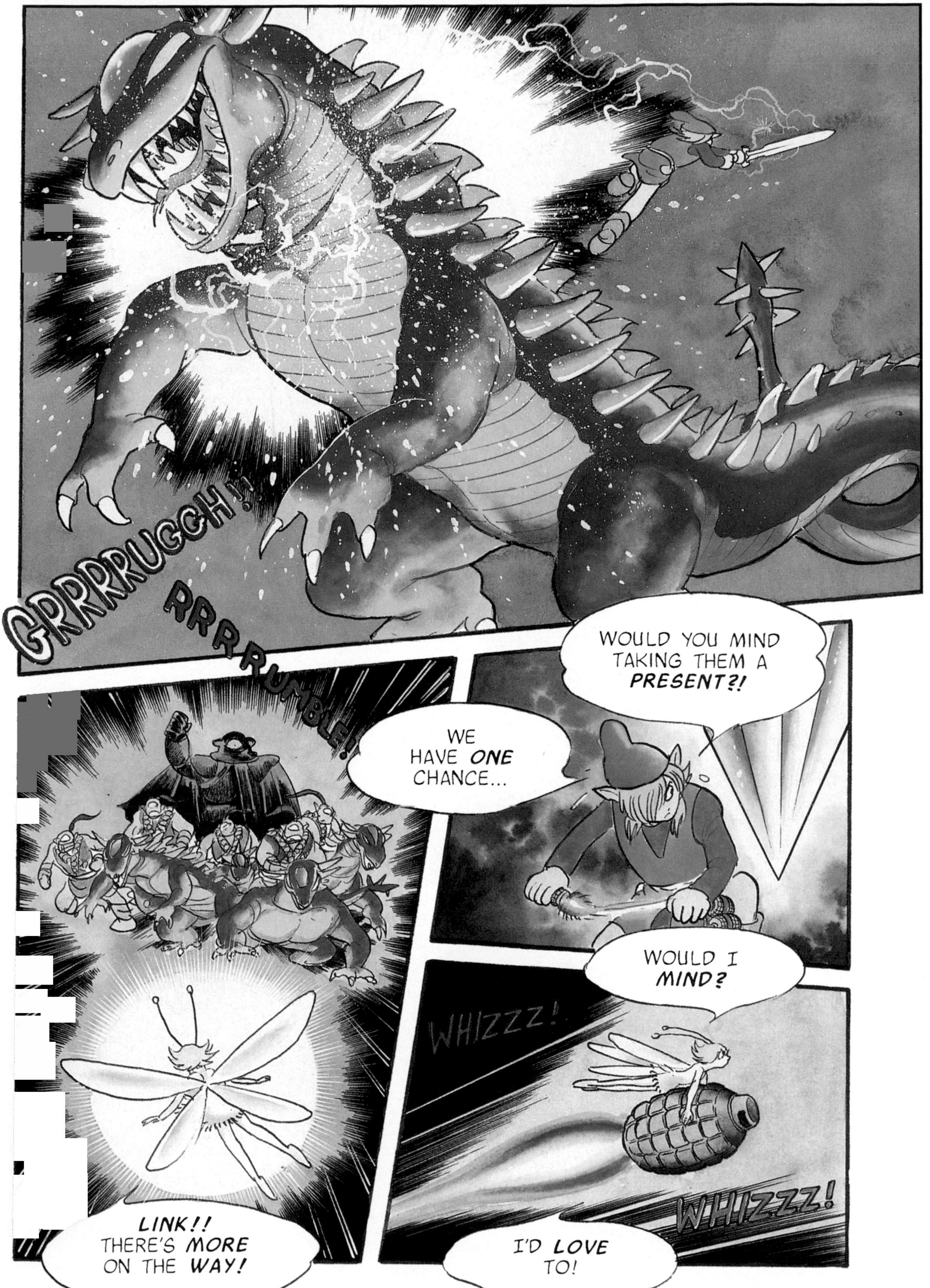
GRRRRUGCH!!
RRRRRUMBLE!
LINK!! THERE'S MORE ON THE WAY!
WE HAVE ONE CHANCE...
WOULD YOU MIND TAKING THEM A PRESENT?!
WOULD I MIND?
WHIZZZ!
WHIZZZ!
I'D LOVE TO!

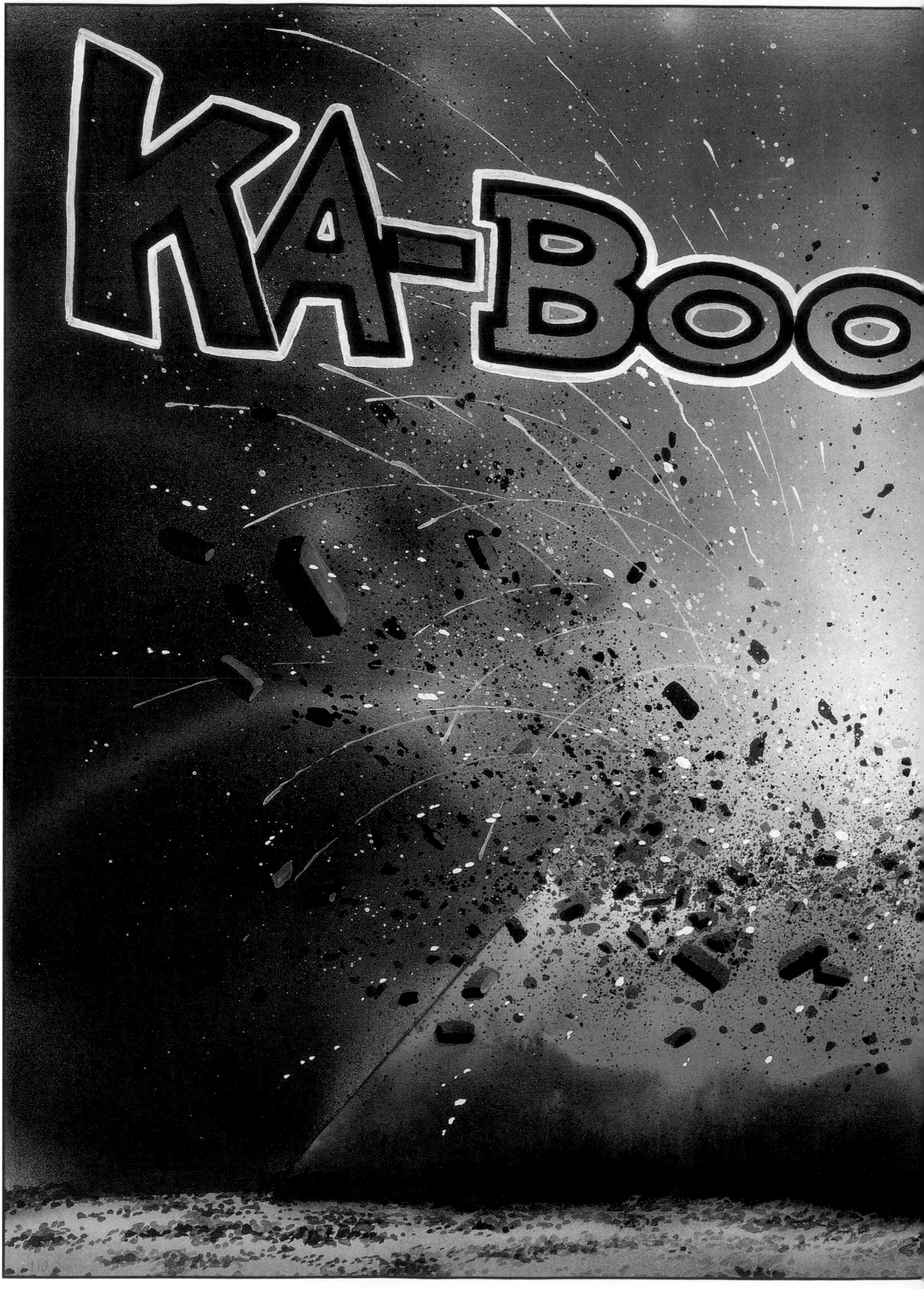
KA-BOO

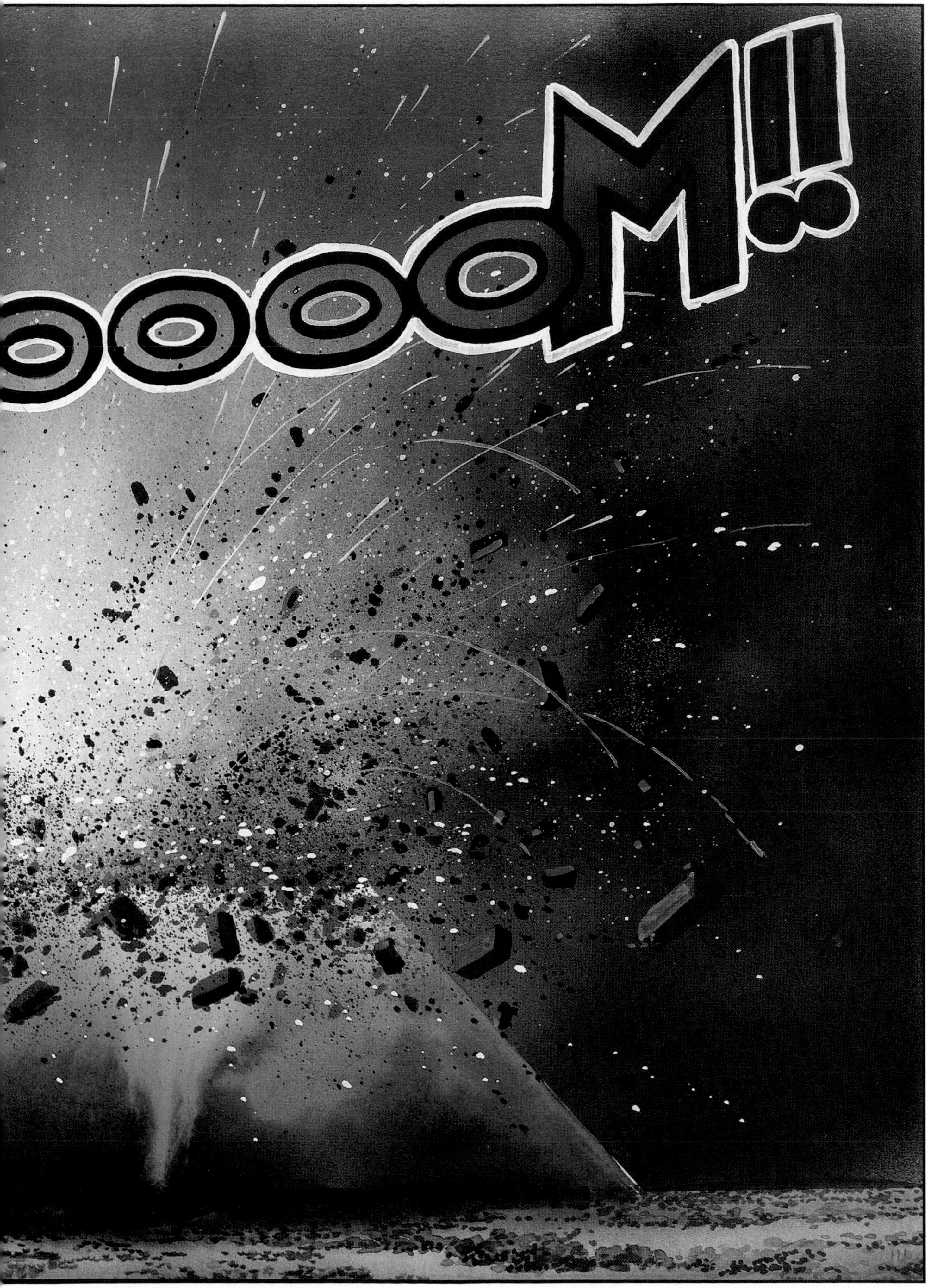
OOOOM!!

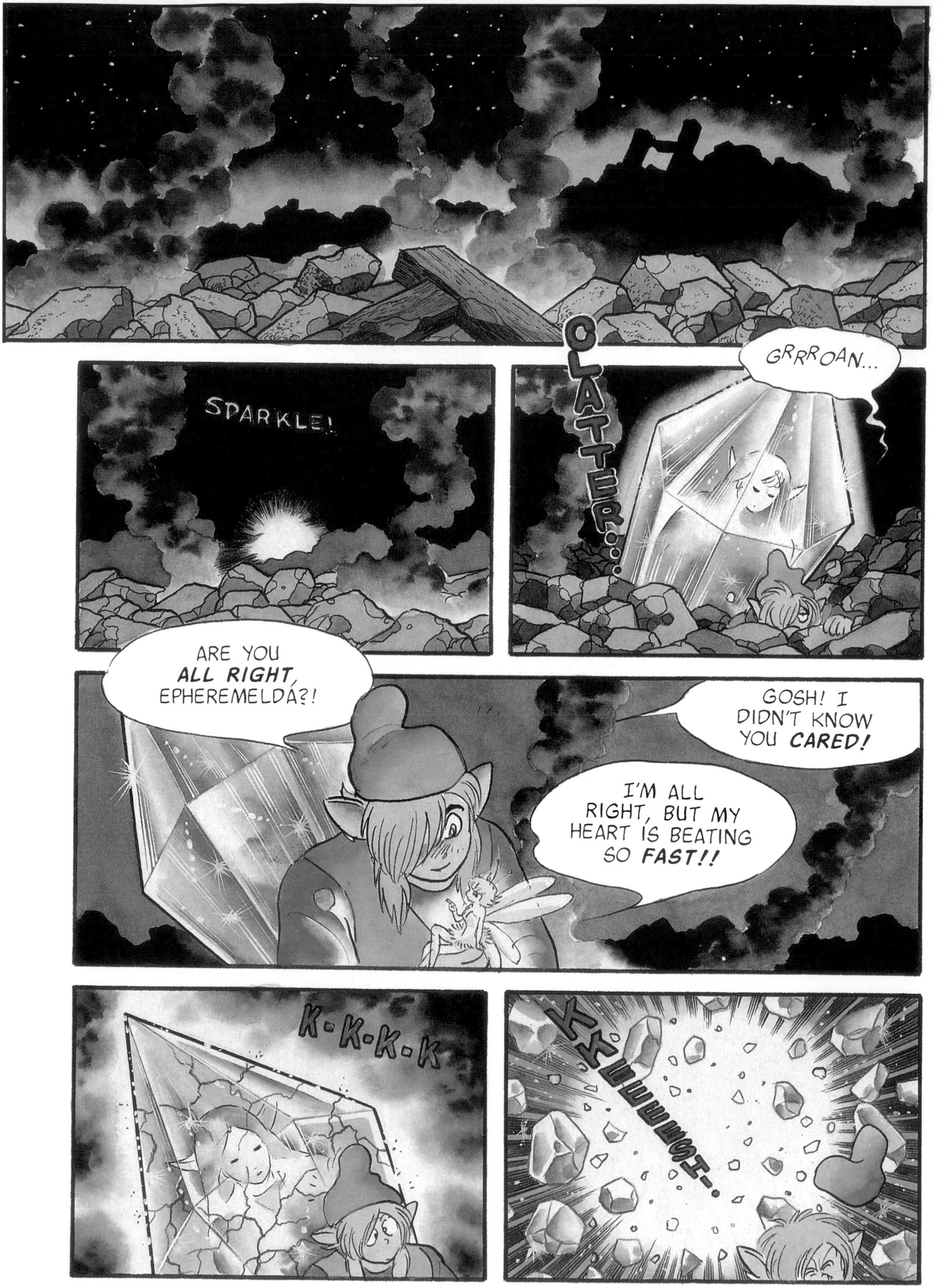
SPARKLE!
CLATTER...
GRRROAN...
ARE YOU ALL RIGHT, EPHEREMELDA?!
GOSH! I DIDN'T KNOW YOU CARED!
I'M ALL RIGHT, BUT MY HEART IS BEATING SO FAST!!
K-K-K-K
KKEEEESH!!

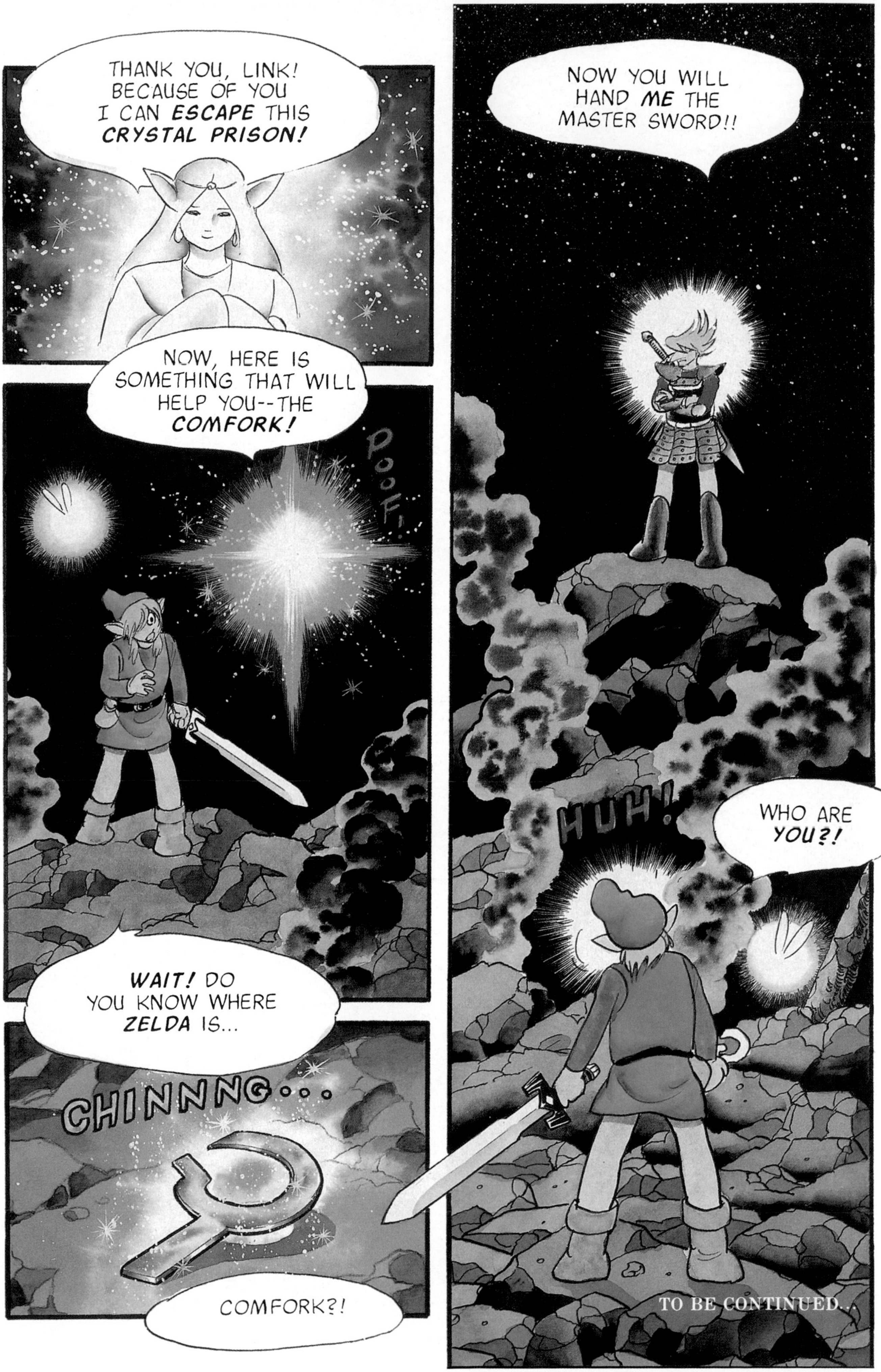
THANK YOU, LINK! BECAUSE OF YOU I CAN ESCAPE THIS CRYSTAL PRISON!
NOW, HERE IS SOMETHING THAT WILL HELP YOU--THE COMFORK!
POOF!
WAIT! DO YOU KNOW WHERE ZELDA IS...
CHINNNG...
COMFORK?!
NOW YOU WILL HAND ME THE MASTER SWORD!!
HUH!
WHO ARE YOU?!
TO BE CONTINUED...

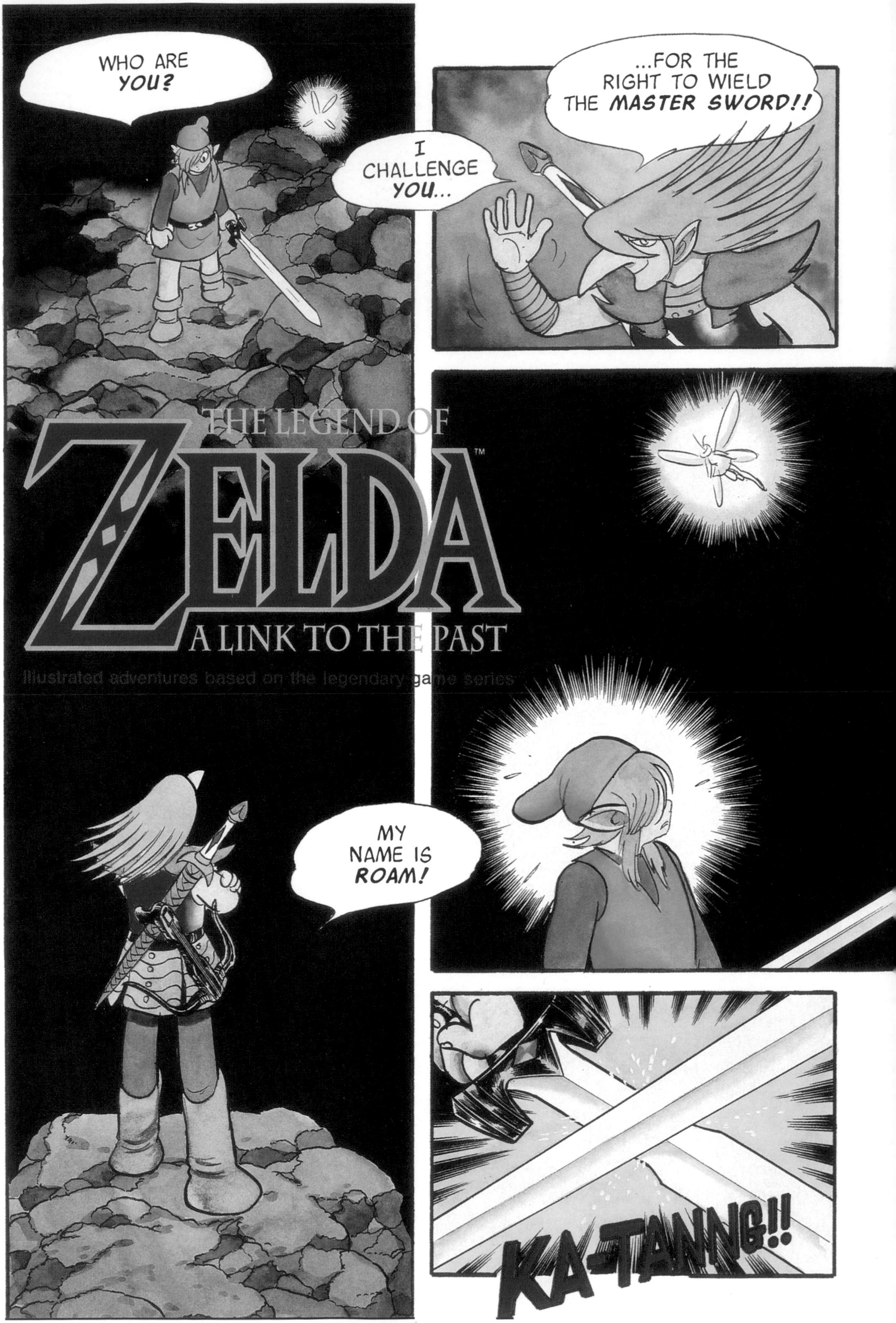
WHO ARE YOU?
I CHALLENGE YOU...
...FOR THE RIGHT TO WIELD THE MASTER SWORD!!
THE LEGEND OF ZELDA™ A LINK TO THE PAST
Illustrated adventures based on the legendary game series
MY NAME IS ROAM!
KA-TANNG!!

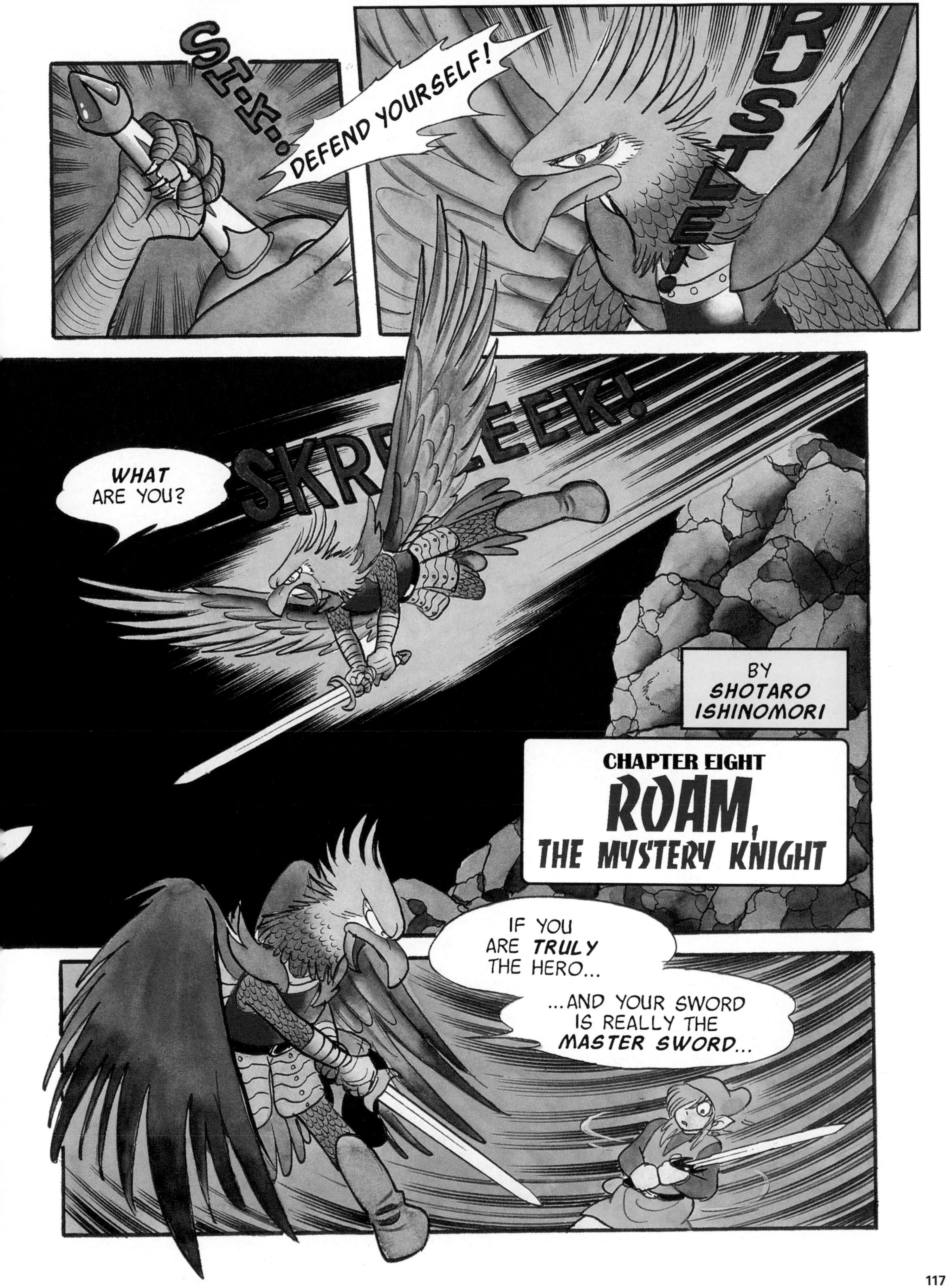
SHK..
DEFEND YOURSELF!
RUSTLE!
WHAT ARE YOU?
SKRREEEK!
BY SHOTARO ISHINOMORI
CHAPTER EIGHT
ROAM, THE MYSTERY KNIGHT
IF YOU ARE TRULY THE HERO...
...AND YOUR SWORD IS REALLY THE MASTER SWORD...

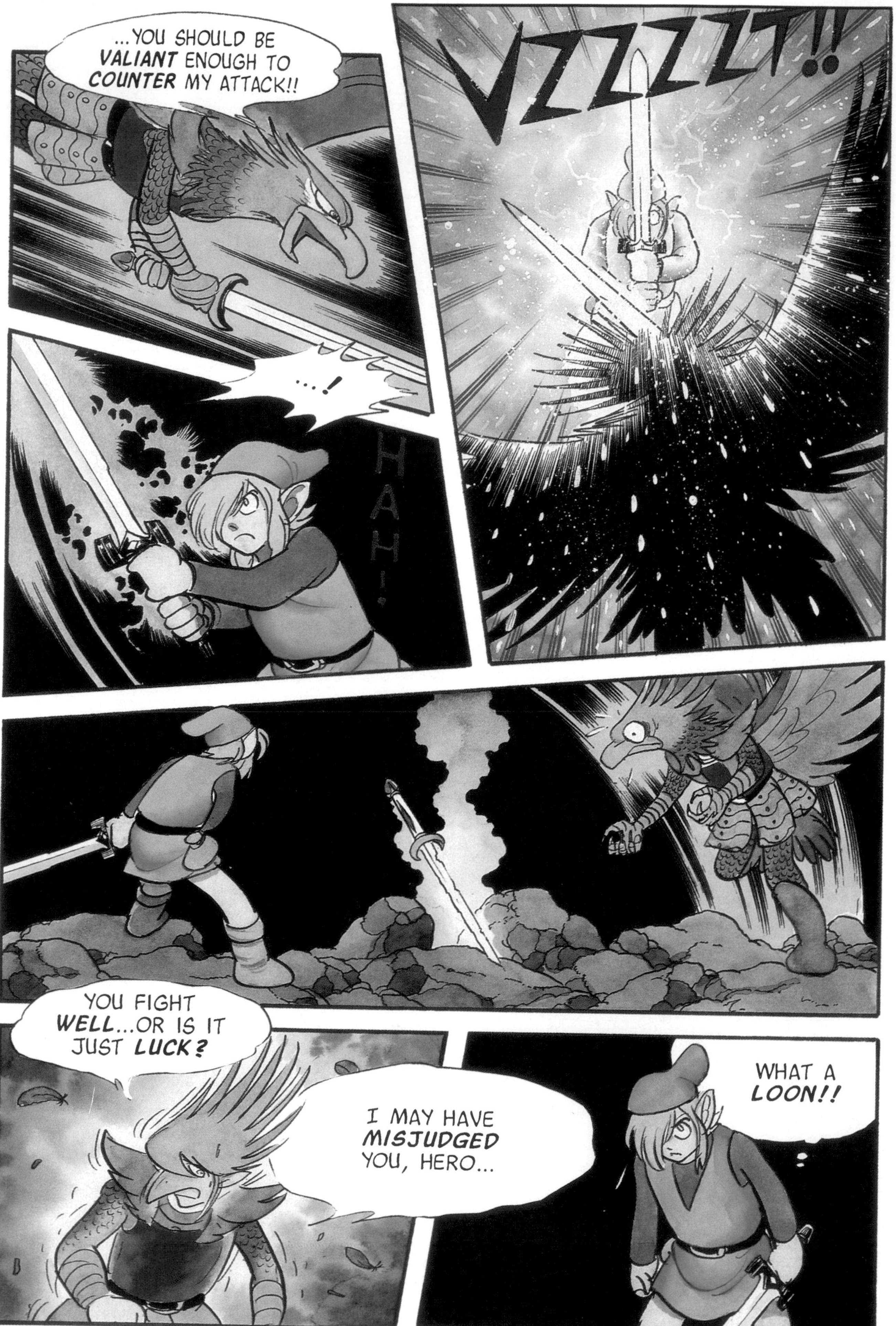
...YOU SHOULD BE VALIANT ENOUGH TO COUNTER MY ATTACK!!
VZZZZZT!!
...!
HAH!
YOU FIGHT WELL...OR IS IT JUST LUCK?
I MAY HAVE MISJUDGED YOU, HERO...
WHAT A LOON!!

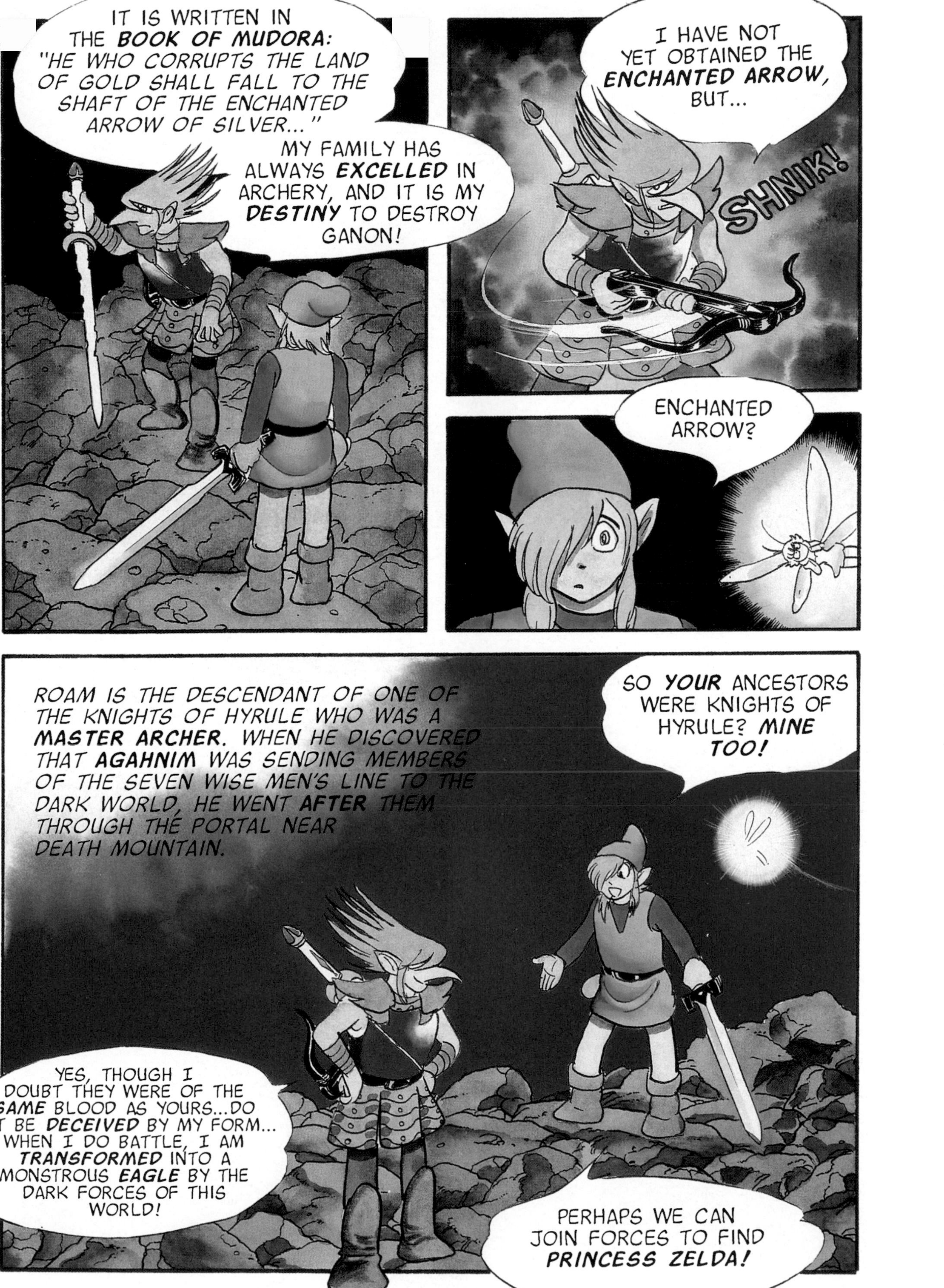
IT IS WRITTEN IN THE BOOK OF MUDORA: "HE WHO CORRUPTS THE LAND OF GOLD SHALL FALL TO THE SHAFT OF THE ENCHANTED ARROW OF SILVER..."
MY FAMILY HAS ALWAYS EXCELLED IN ARCHERY, AND IT IS MY DESTINY TO DESTROY GANON!
I HAVE NOT YET OBTAINED THE ENCHANTED ARROW, BUT...
SHNIK!
ENCHANTED ARROW?
ROAM IS THE DESCENDANT OF ONE OF THE KNIGHTS OF HYRULE WHO WAS A MASTER ARCHER. WHEN HE DISCOVERED THAT AGAHNIM WAS SENDING MEMBERS OF THE SEVEN WISE MEN'S LINE TO THE DARK WORLD, HE WENT AFTER THEM THROUGH THE PORTAL NEAR DEATH MOUNTAIN.
SO YOUR ANCESTORS WERE KNIGHTS OF HYRULE? MINE TOO!
YES, THOUGH I DOUBT THEY WERE OF THE SAME BLOOD AS YOURS...DO NOT BE DECEIVED BY MY FORM... WHEN I DO BATTLE, I AM TRANSFORMED INTO A MONSTROUS EAGLE BY THE DARK FORCES OF THIS WORLD!
PERHAPS WE CAN JOIN FORCES TO FIND PRINCESS ZELDA!

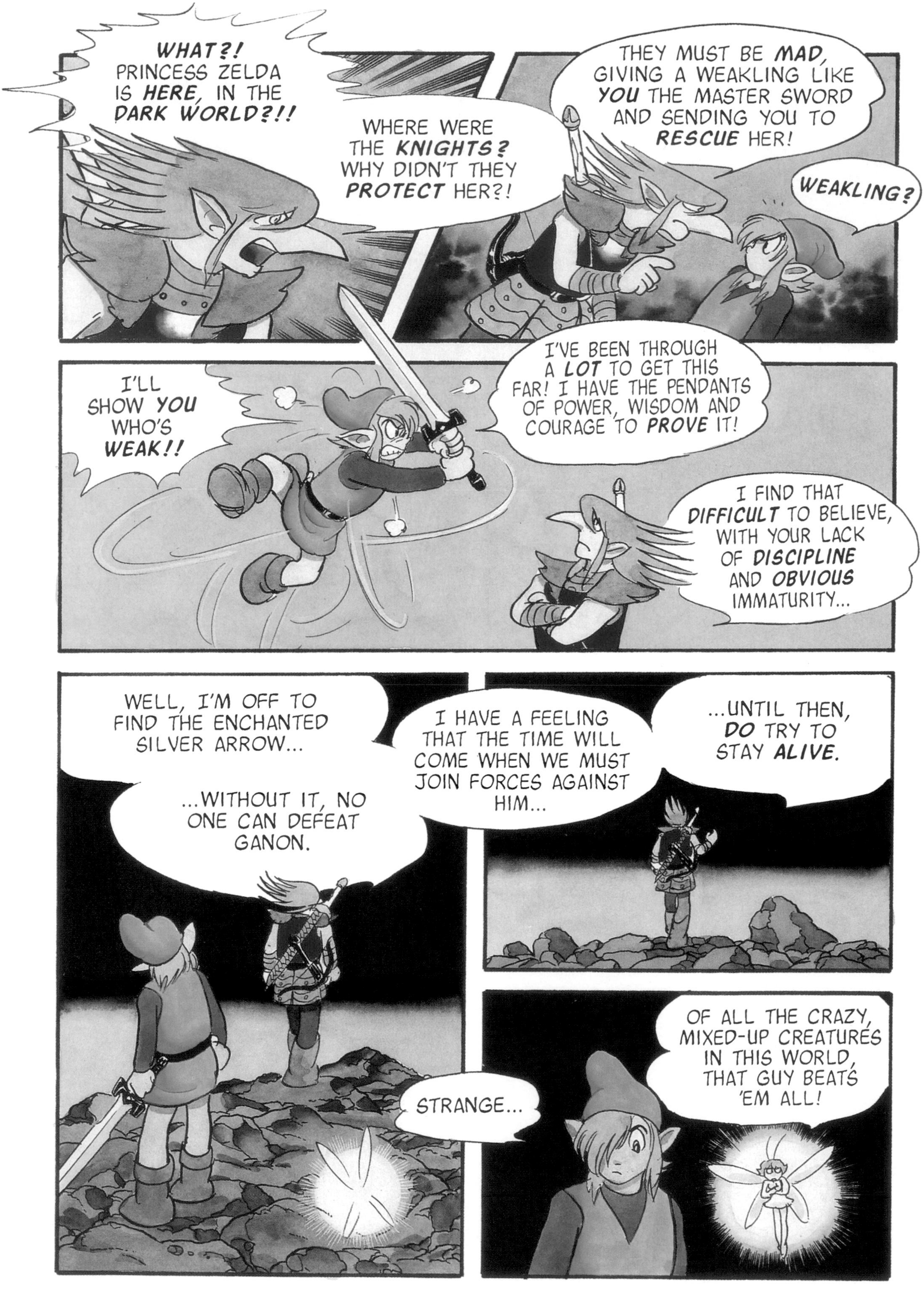
WHAT?! PRINCESS ZELDA IS HERE, IN THE DARK WORLD?!!
WHERE WERE THE KNIGHTS? WHY DIDN'T THEY PROTECT HER?!
THEY MUST BE MAD, GIVING A WEAKLING LIKE YOU THE MASTER SWORD AND SENDING YOU TO RESCUE HER!
WEAKLING?
I'LL SHOW YOU WHO'S WEAK!!
I'VE BEEN THROUGH A LOT TO GET THIS FAR! I HAVE THE PENDANTS OF POWER, WISDOM AND COURAGE TO PROVE IT!
I FIND THAT DIFFICULT TO BELIEVE, WITH YOUR LACK OF DISCIPLINE AND OBVIOUS IMMATURITY...
WELL, I'M OFF TO FIND THE ENCHANTED SILVER ARROW...
...WITHOUT IT, NO ONE CAN DEFEAT GANON.
I HAVE A FEELING THAT THE TIME WILL COME WHEN WE MUST JOIN FORCES AGAINST HIM...
...UNTIL THEN, DO TRY TO STAY ALIVE.
STRANGE...
OF ALL THE CRAZY, MIXED-UP CREATURES IN THIS WORLD, THAT GUY BEATS 'EM ALL!

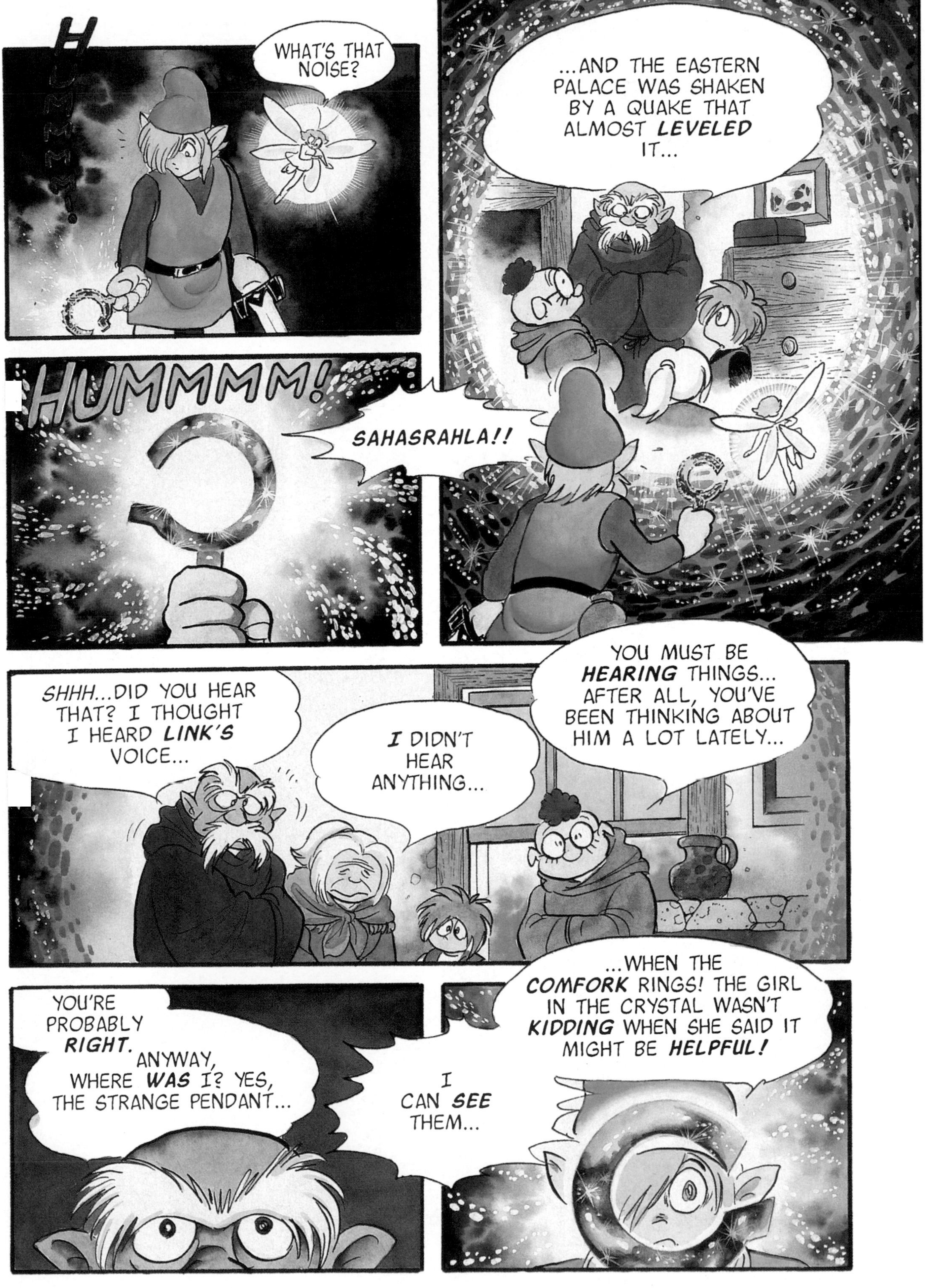
HUMMMM!
WHAT'S THAT NOISE?
...AND THE EASTERN PALACE WAS SHAKEN BY A QUAKE THAT ALMOST **LEVELED** IT...
HUMMMM!
SAHASRAHLA!!
SHHH...DID YOU HEAR THAT? I THOUGHT I HEARD **LINK'S** VOICE...
I DIDN'T HEAR ANYTHING...
YOU MUST BE **HEARING** THINGS... AFTER ALL, YOU'VE BEEN THINKING ABOUT HIM A LOT LATELY...
YOU'RE PROBABLY **RIGHT.** ANYWAY, WHERE **WAS** I? YES, THE STRANGE PENDANT...
...WHEN THE **COMFORK** RINGS! THE GIRL IN THE CRYSTAL WASN'T **KIDDING** WHEN SHE SAID IT MIGHT BE **HELPFUL!**
I CAN **SEE** THEM...

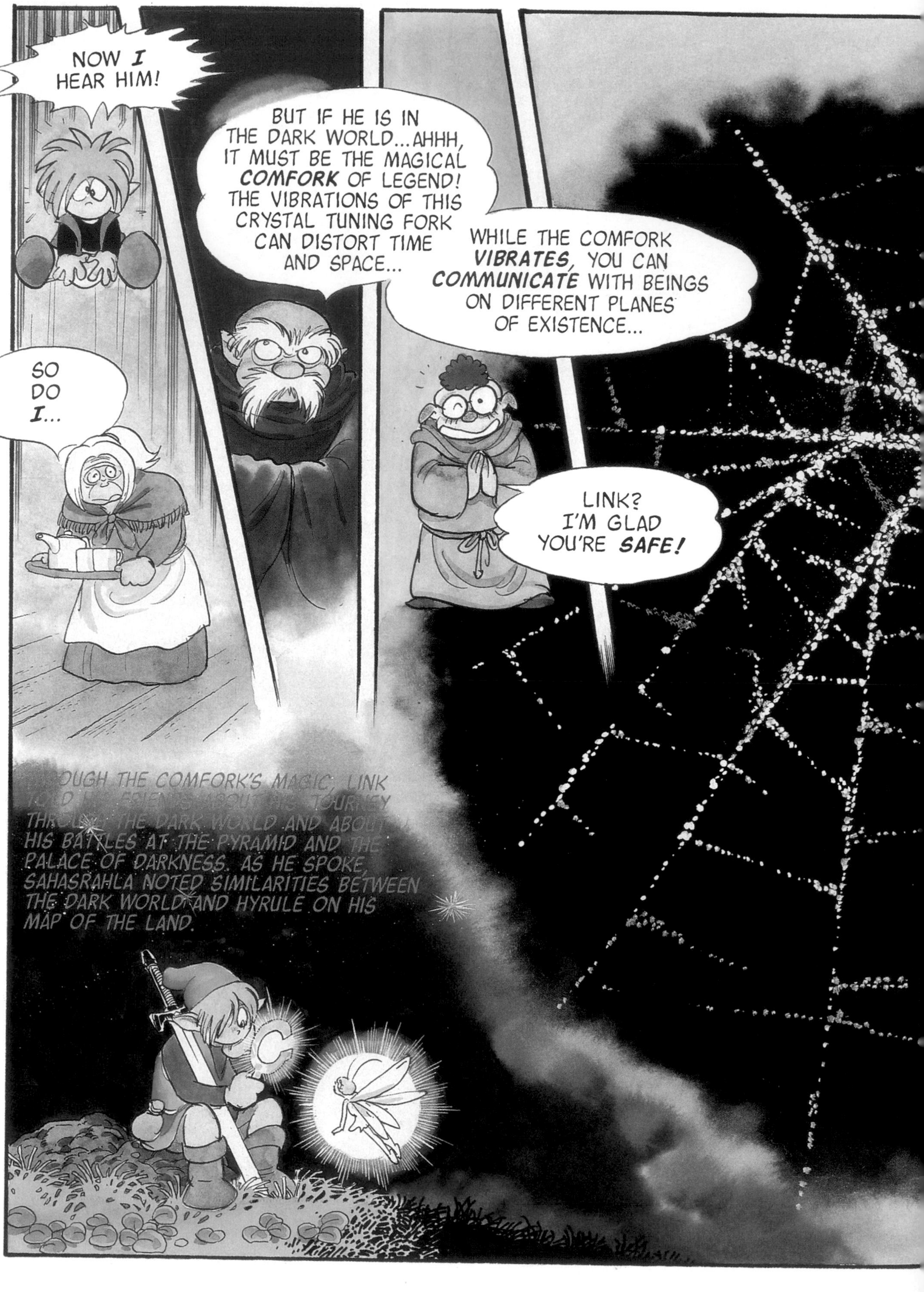
NOW *I* HEAR HIM!
SO DO *I*...
BUT IF HE IS IN THE DARK WORLD...AHHH, IT MUST BE THE MAGICAL **COMFORK** OF LEGEND! THE VIBRATIONS OF THIS CRYSTAL TUNING FORK CAN DISTORT TIME AND SPACE...
WHILE THE COMFORK **VIBRATES**, YOU CAN **COMMUNICATE** WITH BEINGS ON DIFFERENT PLANES OF EXISTENCE...
LINK? I'M GLAD YOU'RE **SAFE!**
THROUGH THE COMFORK'S MAGIC, LINK TOLD HIS FRIENDS ABOUT HIS JOURNEY THROUGH THE DARK WORLD AND ABOUT HIS BATTLES AT THE PYRAMID AND THE PALACE OF DARKNESS. AS HE SPOKE, SAHASRAHLA NOTED SIMILARITIES BETWEEN THE DARK WORLD AND HYRULE ON HIS MAP OF THE LAND.

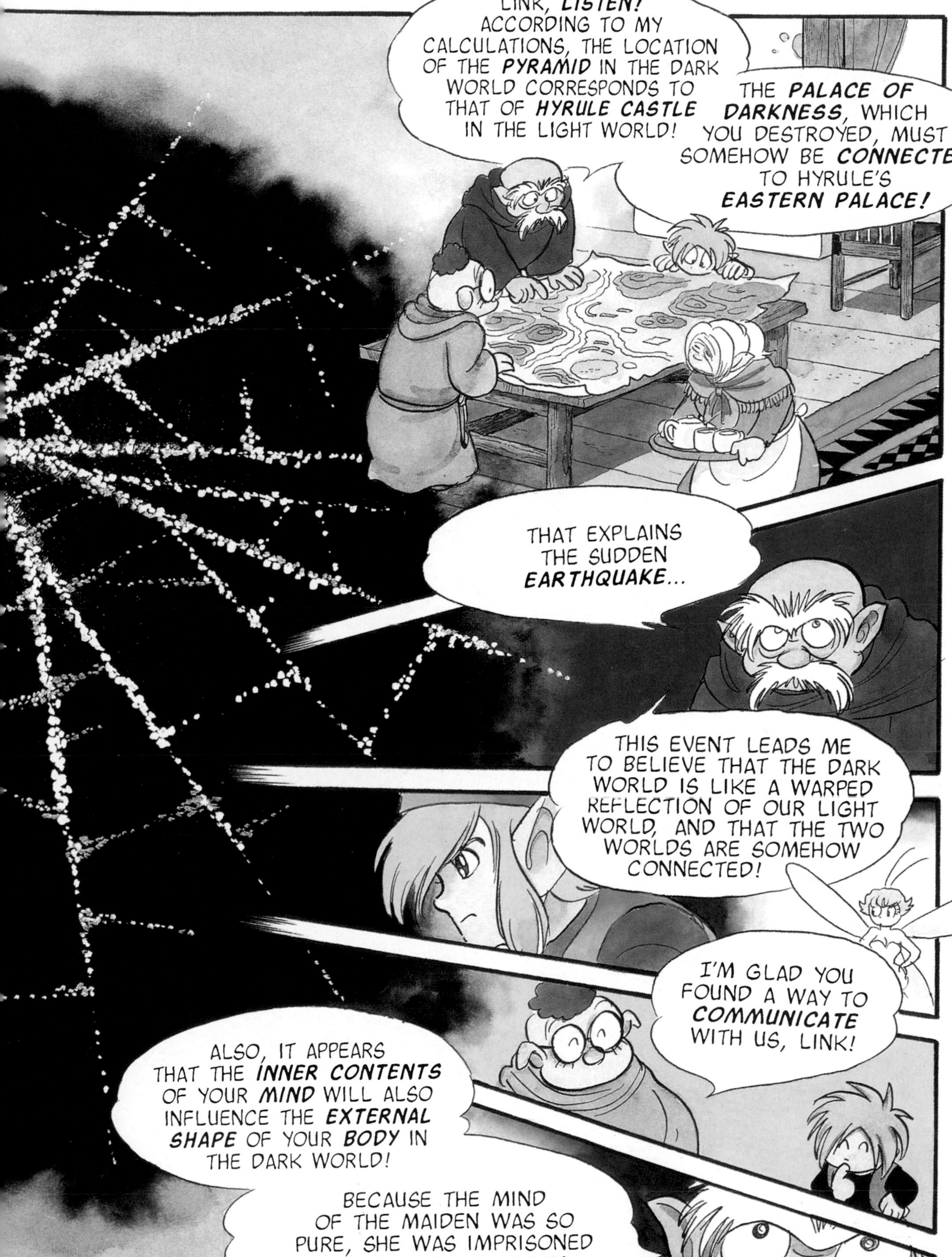
LINK, LISTEN! ACCORDING TO MY CALCULATIONS, THE LOCATION OF THE PYRAMID IN THE DARK WORLD CORRESPONDS TO THAT OF HYRULE CASTLE IN THE LIGHT WORLD!
THE PALACE OF DARKNESS, WHICH YOU DESTROYED, MUST SOMEHOW BE CONNECTED TO HYRULE'S EASTERN PALACE!
THAT EXPLAINS THE SUDDEN EARTHQUAKE...
THIS EVENT LEADS ME TO BELIEVE THAT THE DARK WORLD IS LIKE A WARPED REFLECTION OF OUR LIGHT WORLD, AND THAT THE TWO WORLDS ARE SOMEHOW CONNECTED!
I'M GLAD YOU FOUND A WAY TO COMMUNICATE WITH US, LINK!
ALSO, IT APPEARS THAT THE INNER CONTENTS OF YOUR MIND WILL ALSO INFLUENCE THE EXTERNAL SHAPE OF YOUR BODY IN THE DARK WORLD!
BECAUSE THE MIND OF THE MAIDEN WAS SO PURE, SHE WAS IMPRISONED IN THE CRYSTAL COCOON...

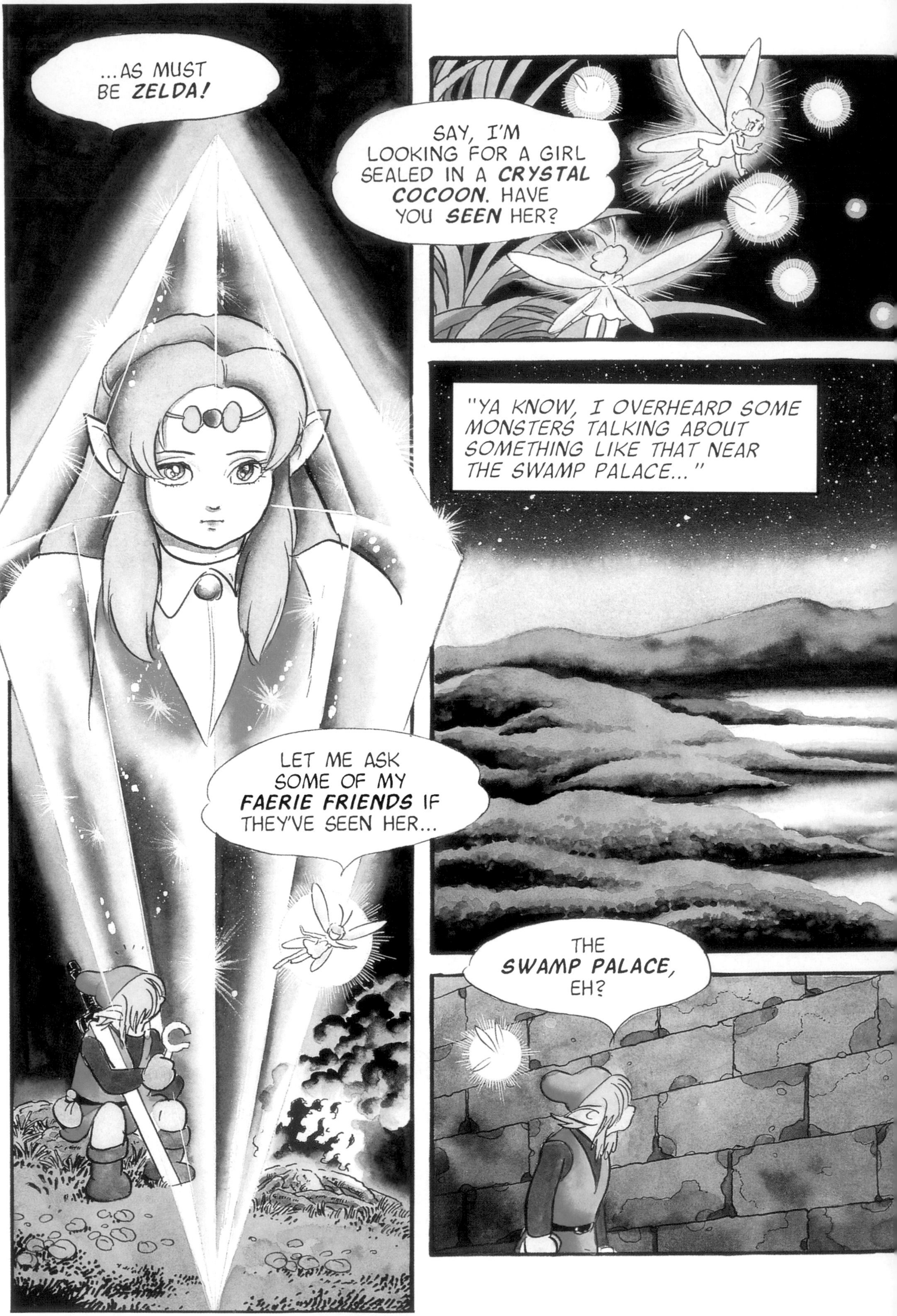
...AS MUST BE **ZELDA!**
LET ME ASK SOME OF MY **FAERIE FRIENDS** IF THEY'VE SEEN HER...
SAY, I'M LOOKING FOR A GIRL SEALED IN A **CRYSTAL COCOON**. HAVE YOU **SEEN** HER?
"YA KNOW, I OVERHEARD SOME MONSTERS TALKING ABOUT SOMETHING LIKE THAT NEAR THE SWAMP PALACE..."
THE **SWAMP PALACE,** EH?

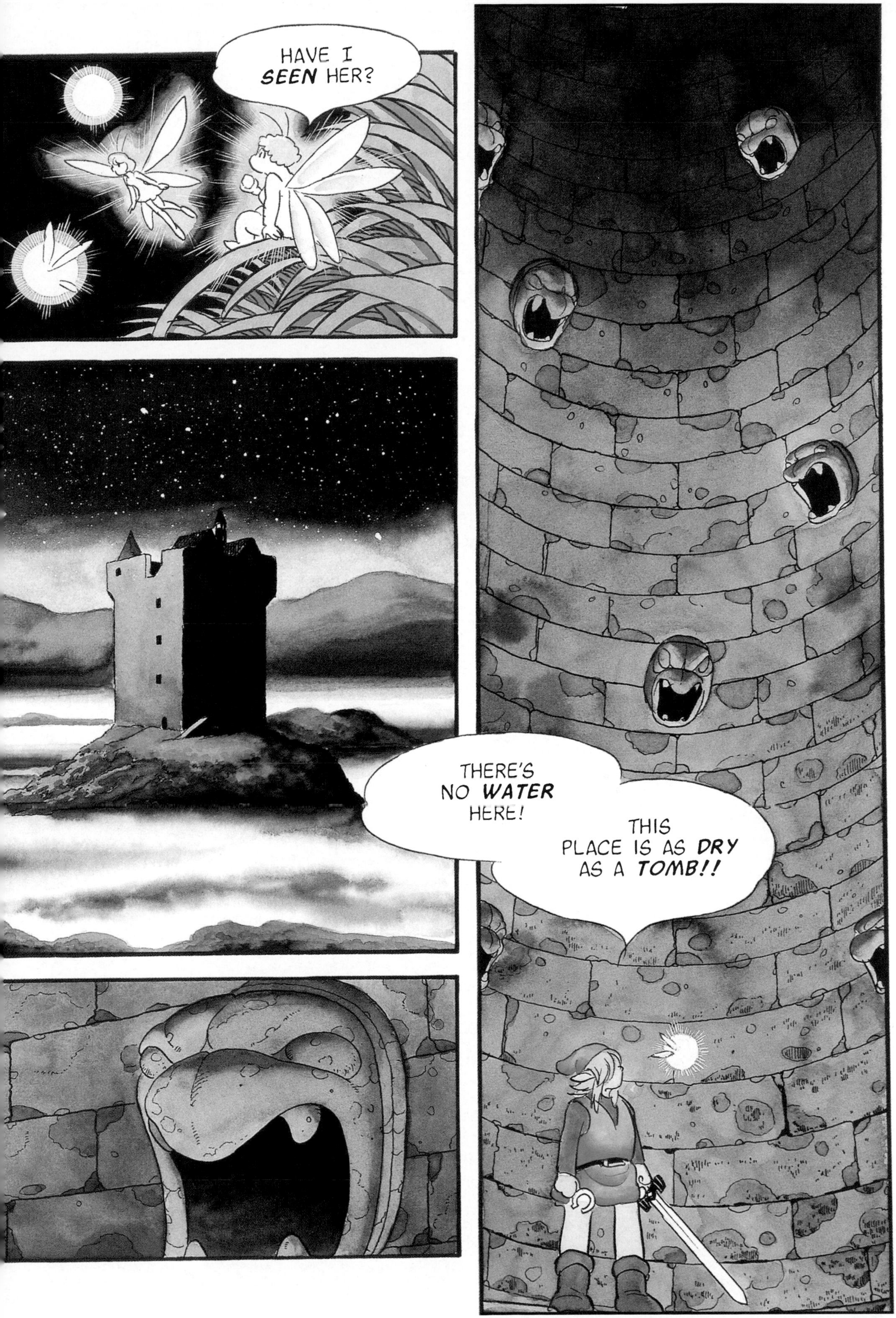
HAVE I *SEEN* HER?
THERE'S NO *WATER* HERE!
THIS PLACE IS AS *DRY* AS A *TOMB!!*

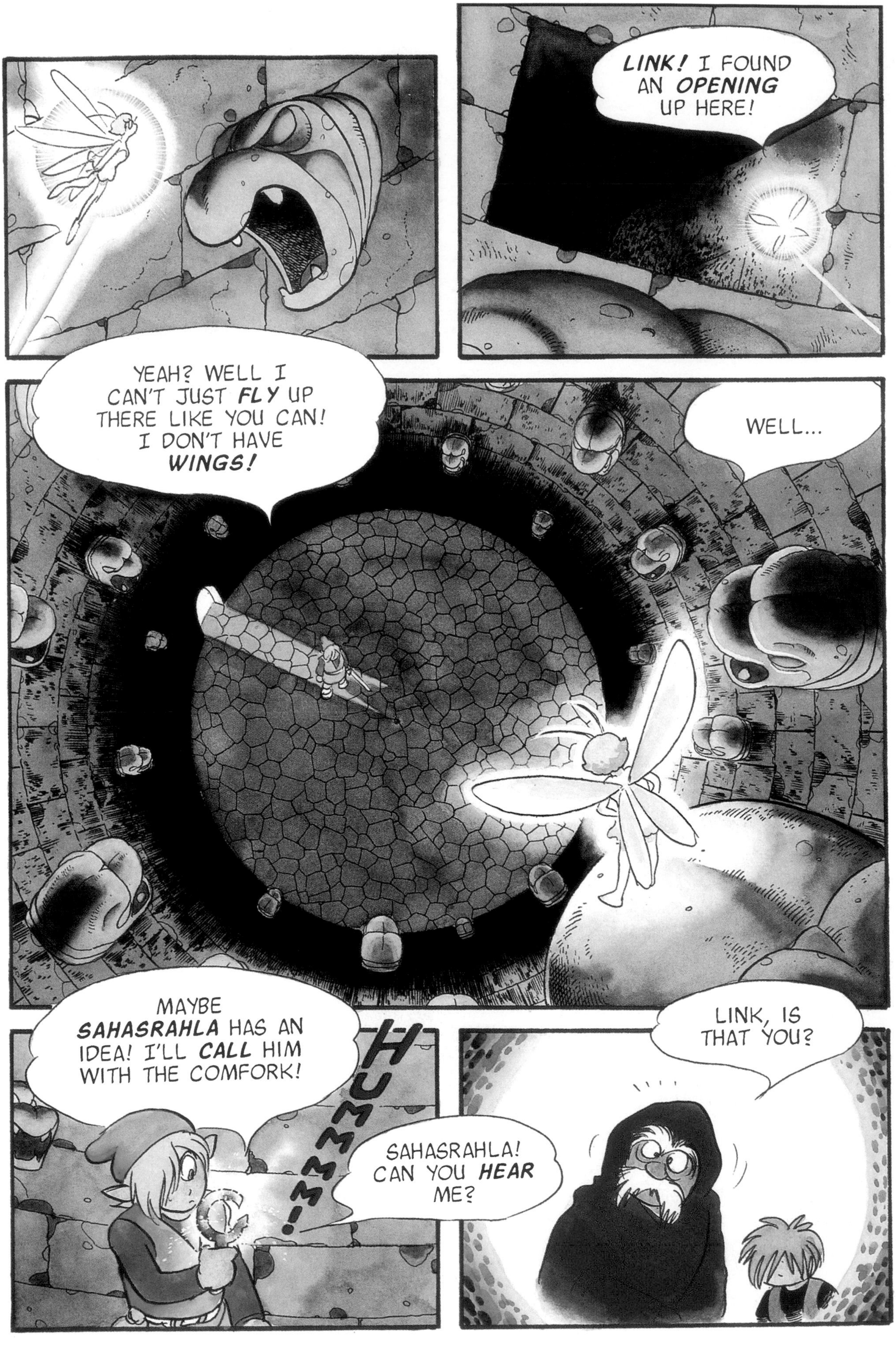
LINK! I FOUND AN OPENING UP HERE!
YEAH? WELL I CAN'T JUST FLY UP THERE LIKE YOU CAN! I DON'T HAVE WINGS!
WELL...
MAYBE SAHASRAHLA HAS AN IDEA! I'LL CALL HIM WITH THE COMFORK!
HUMMMM!
SAHASRAHLA! CAN YOU HEAR ME?
LINK, IS THAT YOU?

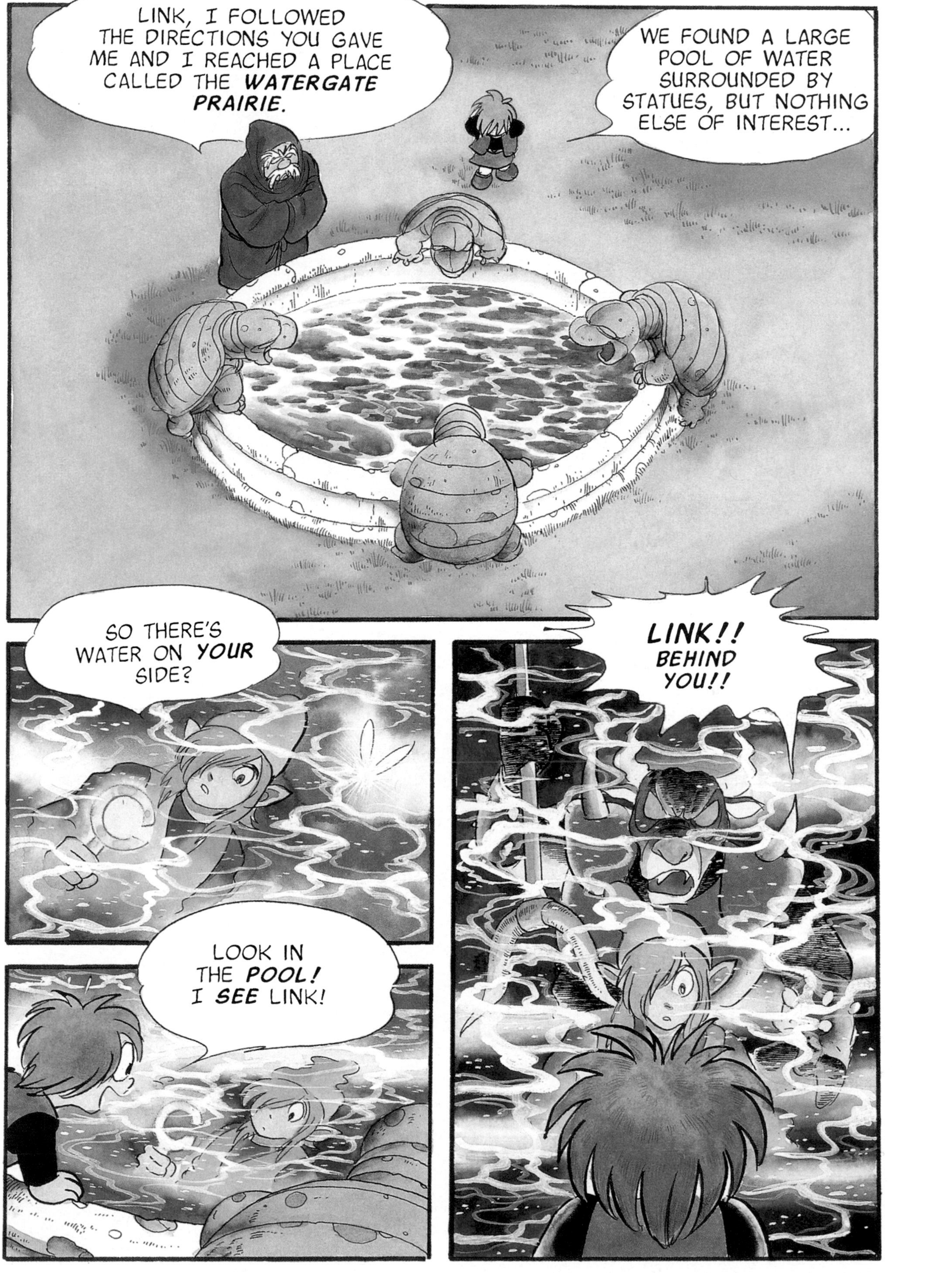
LINK, I FOLLOWED THE DIRECTIONS YOU GAVE ME AND I REACHED A PLACE CALLED THE **WATERGATE PRAIRIE**.
WE FOUND A LARGE POOL OF WATER SURROUNDED BY STATUES, BUT NOTHING ELSE OF INTEREST...
SO THERE'S WATER ON **YOUR** SIDE?
LOOK IN THE **POOL!** I **SEE** LINK!
LINK!! BEHIND YOU!!

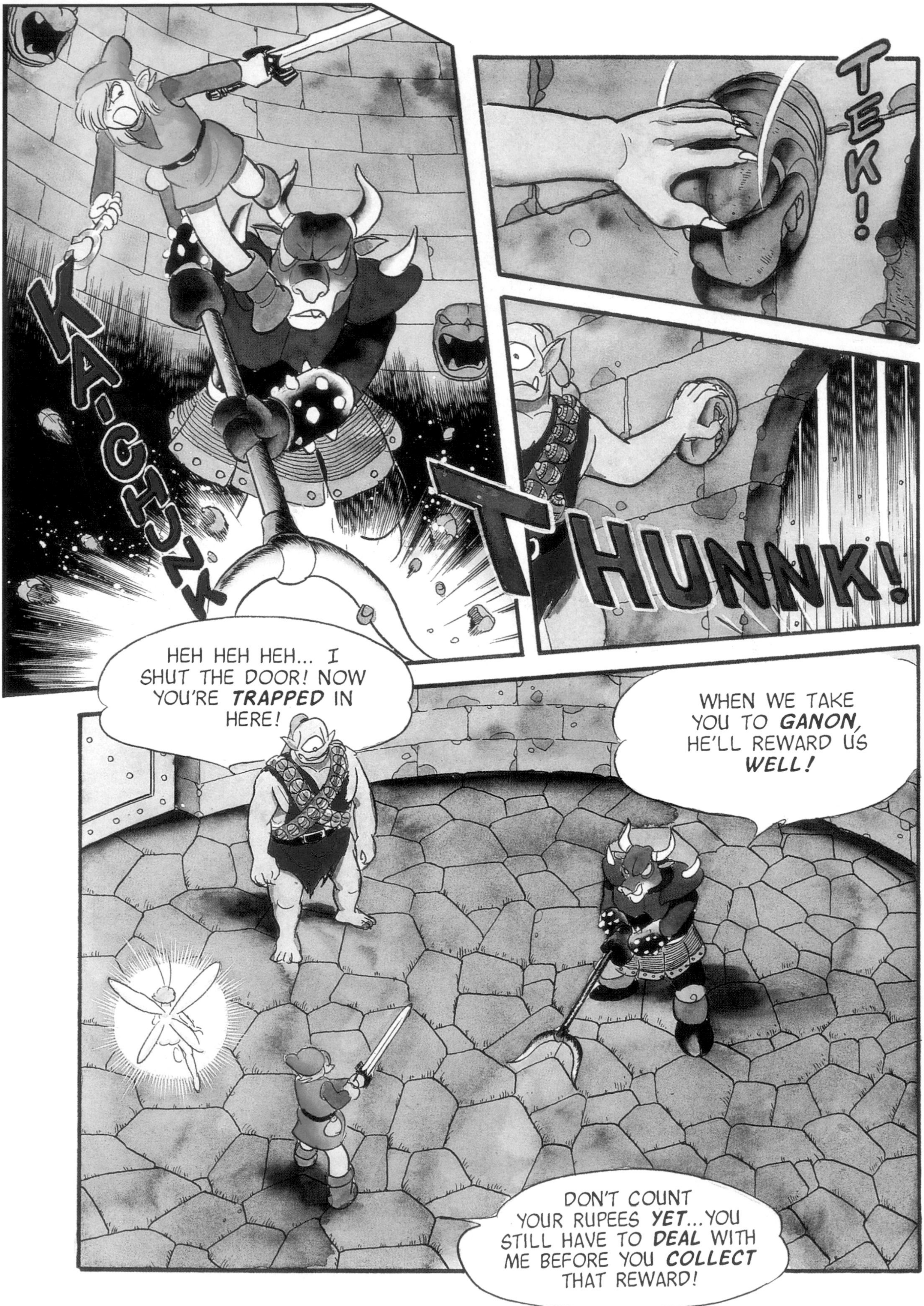
KA-CHUNK
TEK!
THUNNK!
HEH HEH HEH... I SHUT THE DOOR! NOW YOU'RE ***TRAPPED*** IN HERE!
WHEN WE TAKE YOU TO ***GANON,*** HE'LL REWARD US ***WELL!***
DON'T COUNT YOUR RUPEES ***YET***...YOU STILL HAVE TO ***DEAL*** WITH ME BEFORE YOU ***COLLECT*** THAT REWARD!

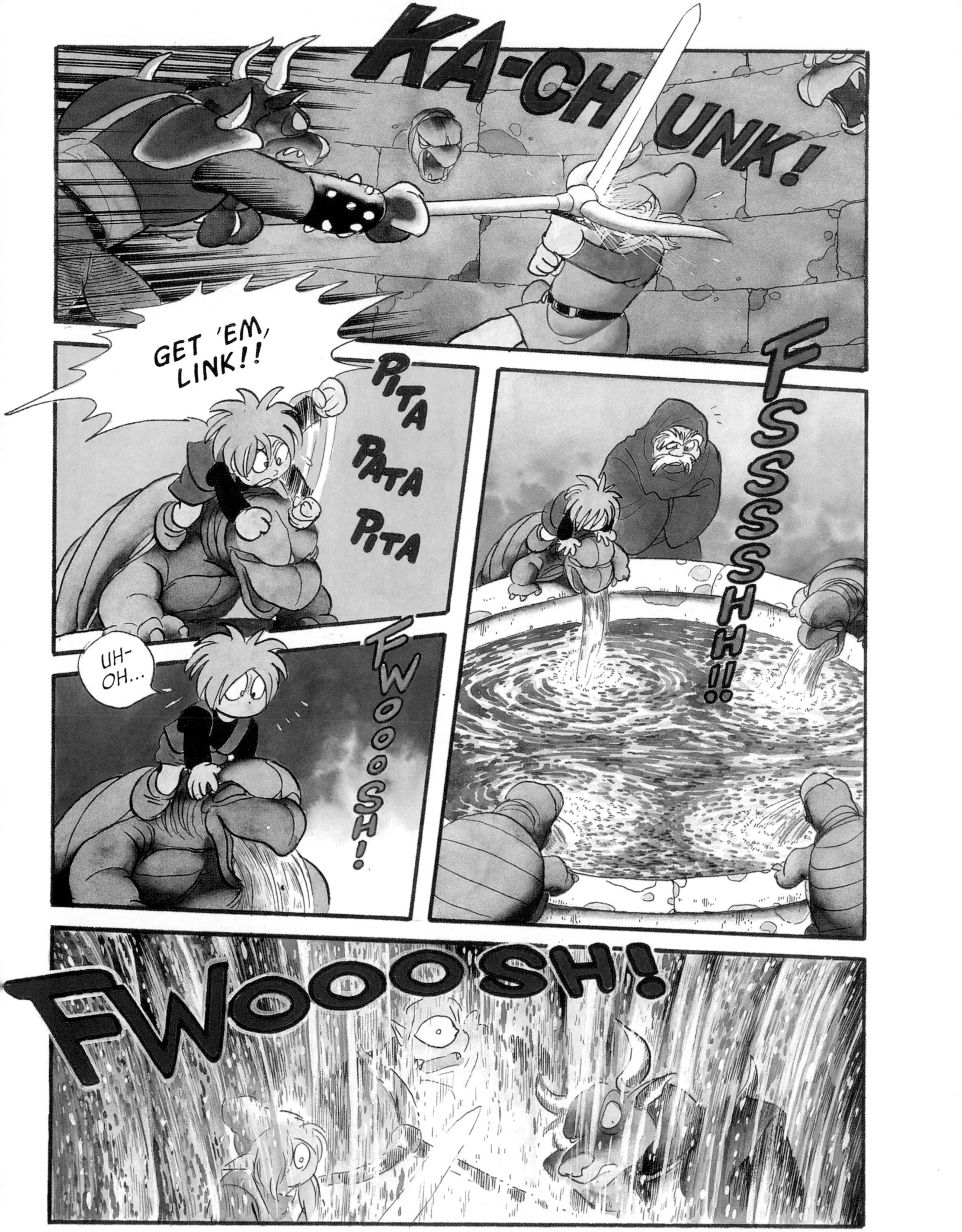
KA-CHUNK!
GET 'EM, LINK!!
PITA PATA PITA
UH-OH...
FWOOOSH!
FSSSSSHH!!
FWOOOSH!

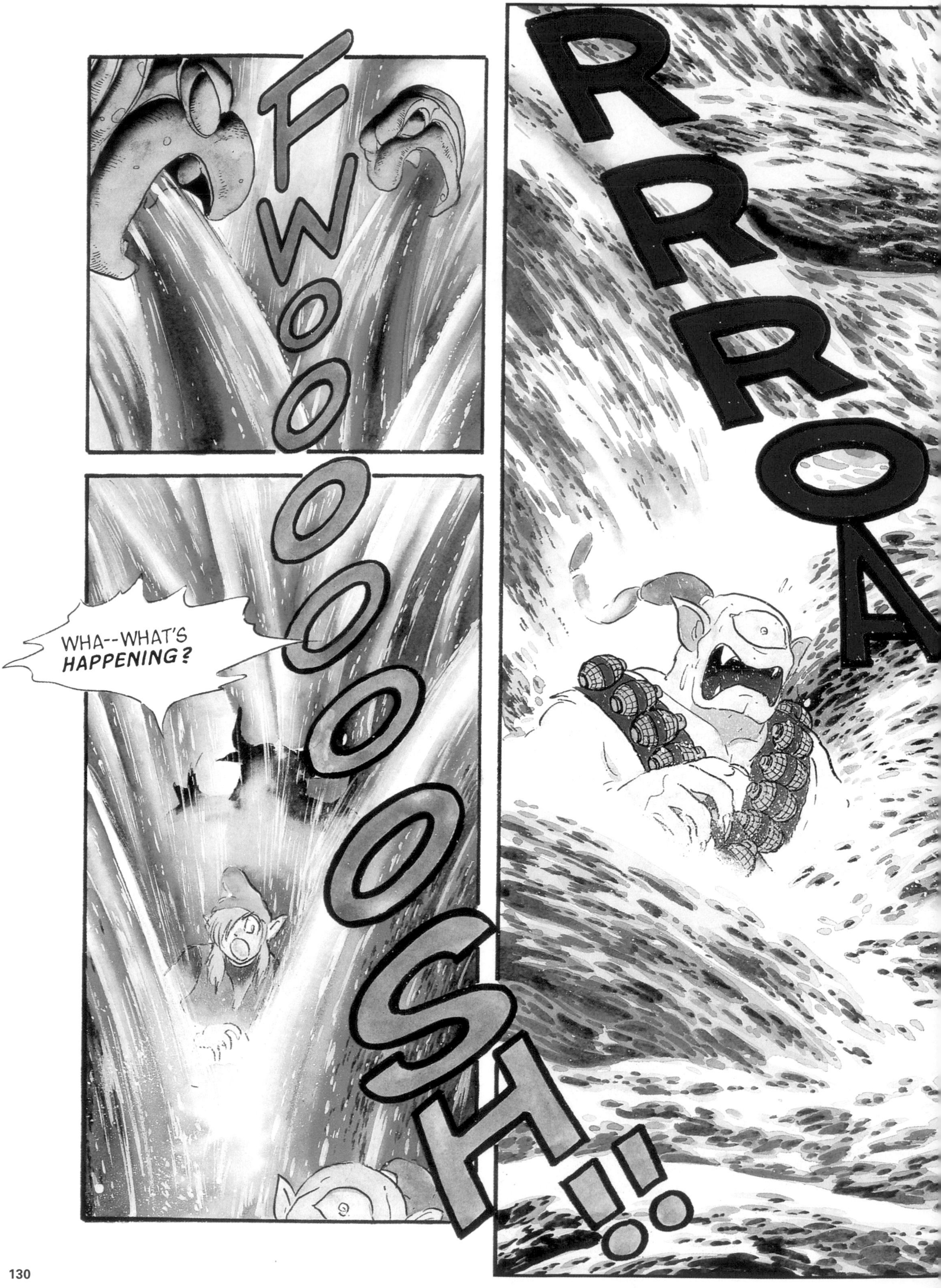
FWOOOOOOSH!!
WHA--WHAT'S *HAPPENING?*
RRROA

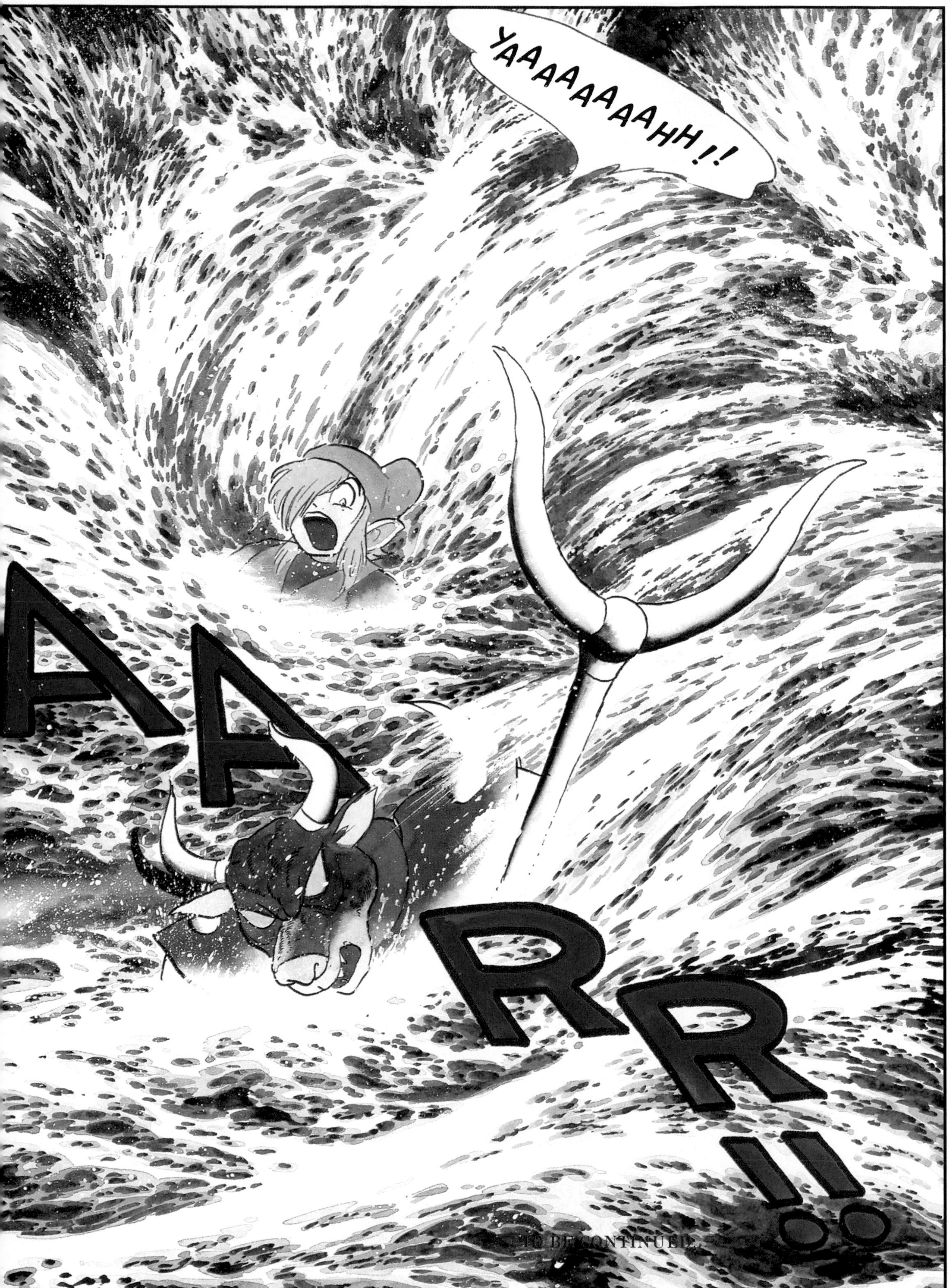
YAAAAAAAAHH!!
AAARR!!
TO BE CONTINUED...

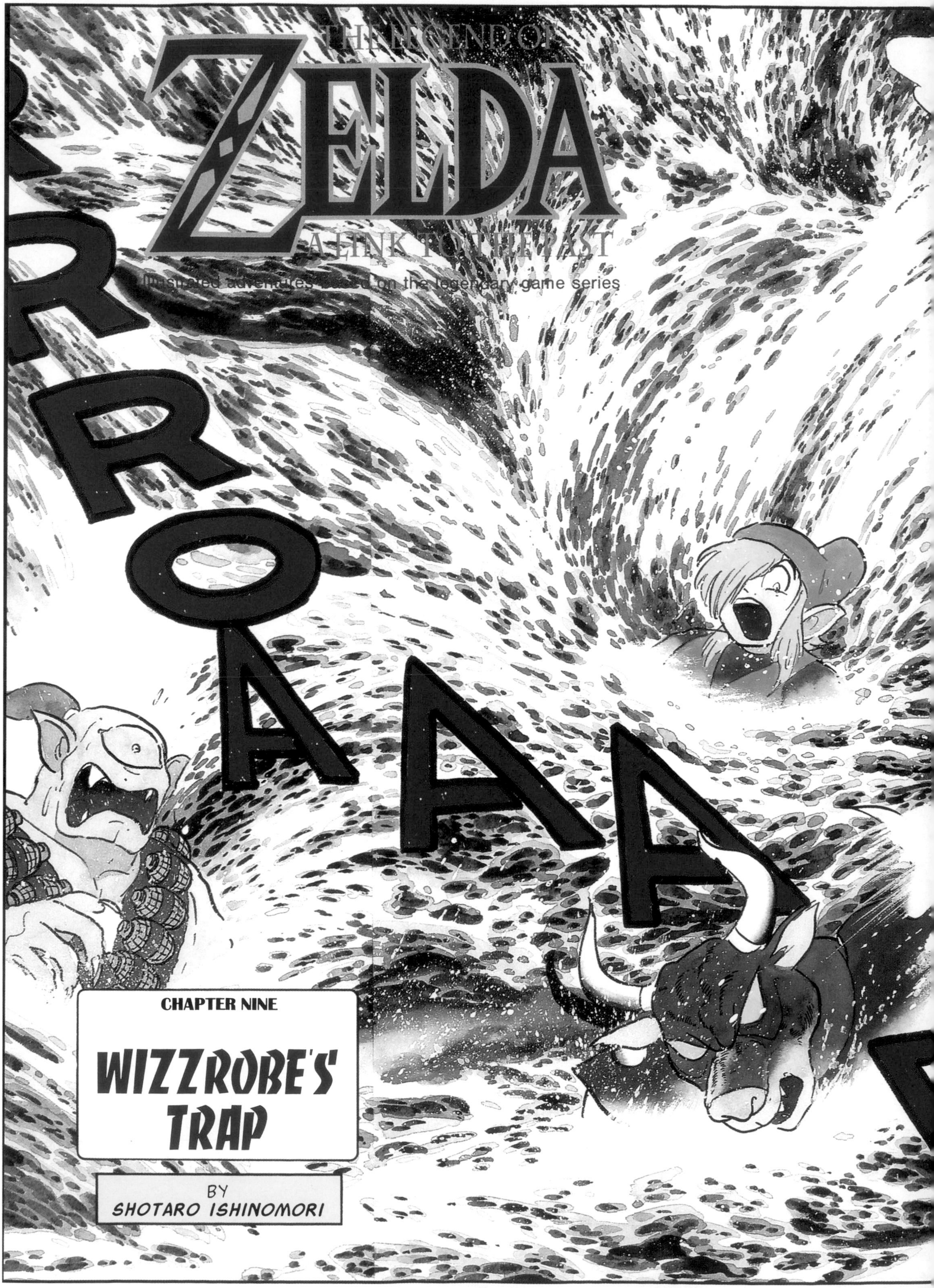

THE LEGEND OF
ZELDA
A LINK TO THE PAST
Illustrated adventures based on the legendary game series
RRROAAAA
CHAPTER NINE
WIZZROBE'S TRAP
BY
SHOTARO ISHINOMORI

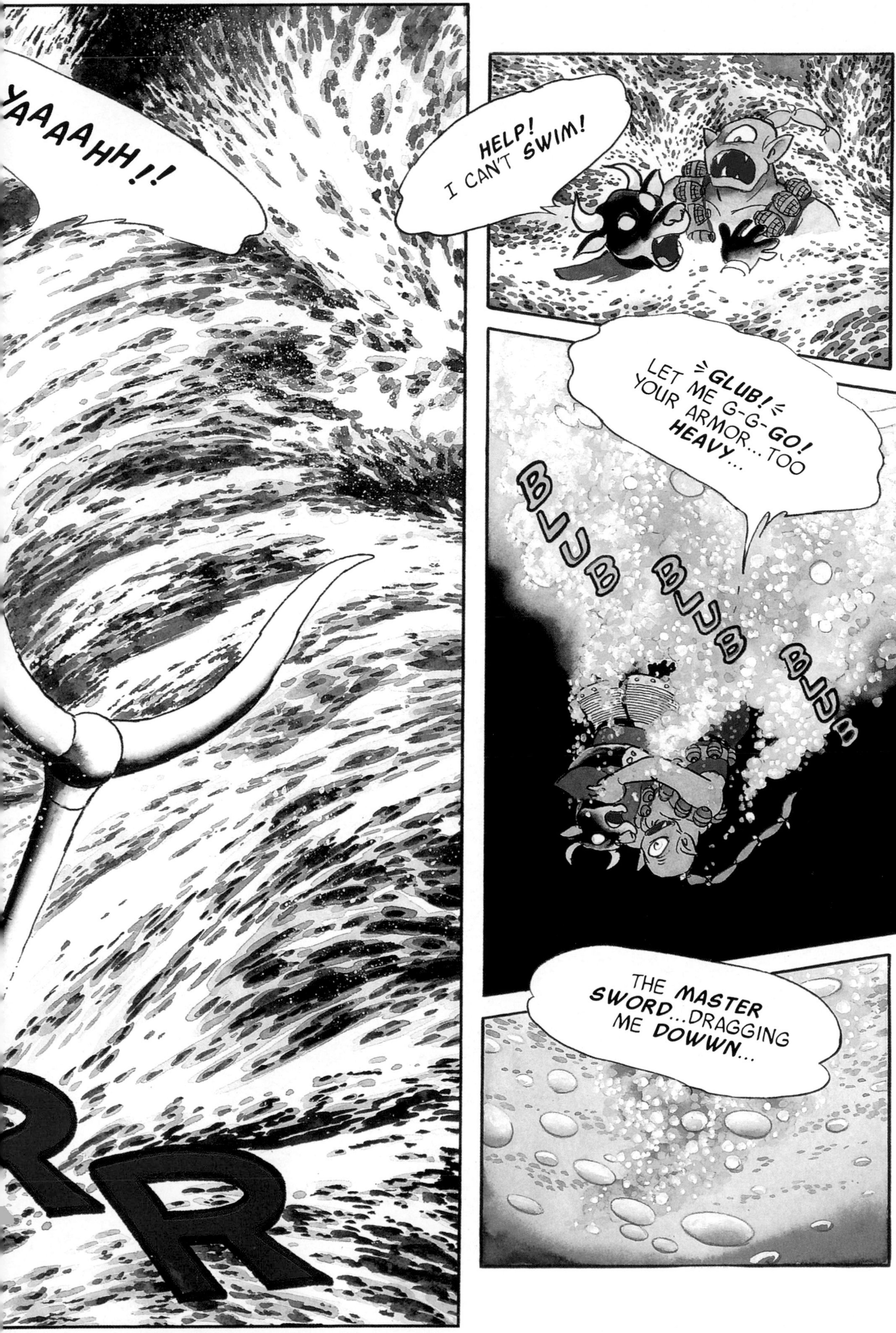
YAAAAHH!!
RR
HELP! I CAN'T SWIM!
GLUB! LET ME G-G-GO! YOUR ARMOR...TOO HEAVY...
BLUB BLUB BLUB
THE MASTER SWORD...DRAGGING ME DOWWN...

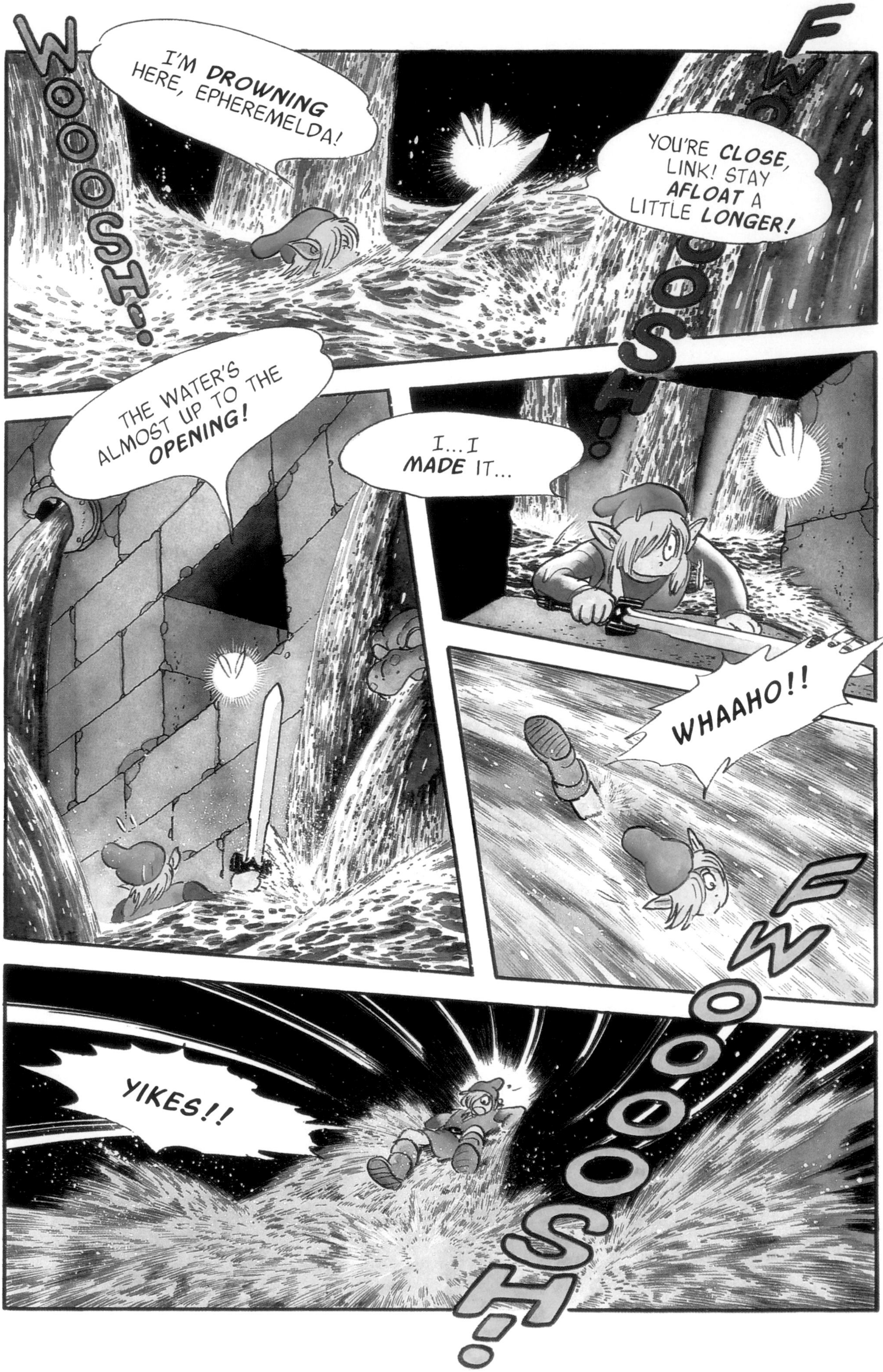
WOOOOSH!!
I'M DROWNING HERE, EPHEREMELDA!
YOU'RE CLOSE, LINK! STAY AFLOAT A LITTLE LONGER!
FWOOOOSH!
THE WATER'S ALMOST UP TO THE OPENING!
I...I MADE IT...
WHAAHO!!
YIKES!!
FWOOOOOOSH!

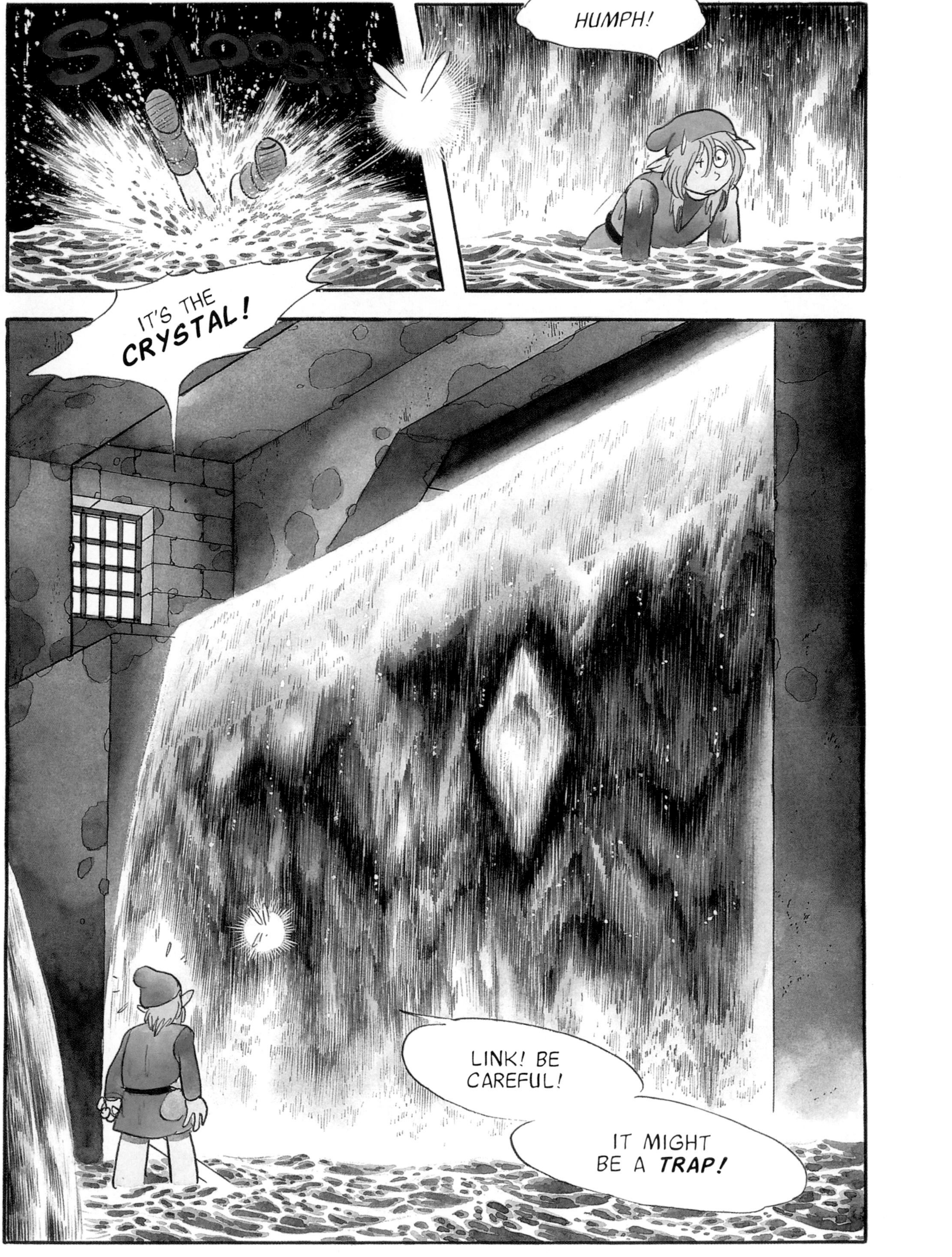
SPLOOSH!!
HUMPH!
IT'S THE CRYSTAL!
LINK! BE CAREFUL!
IT MIGHT BE A TRAP!

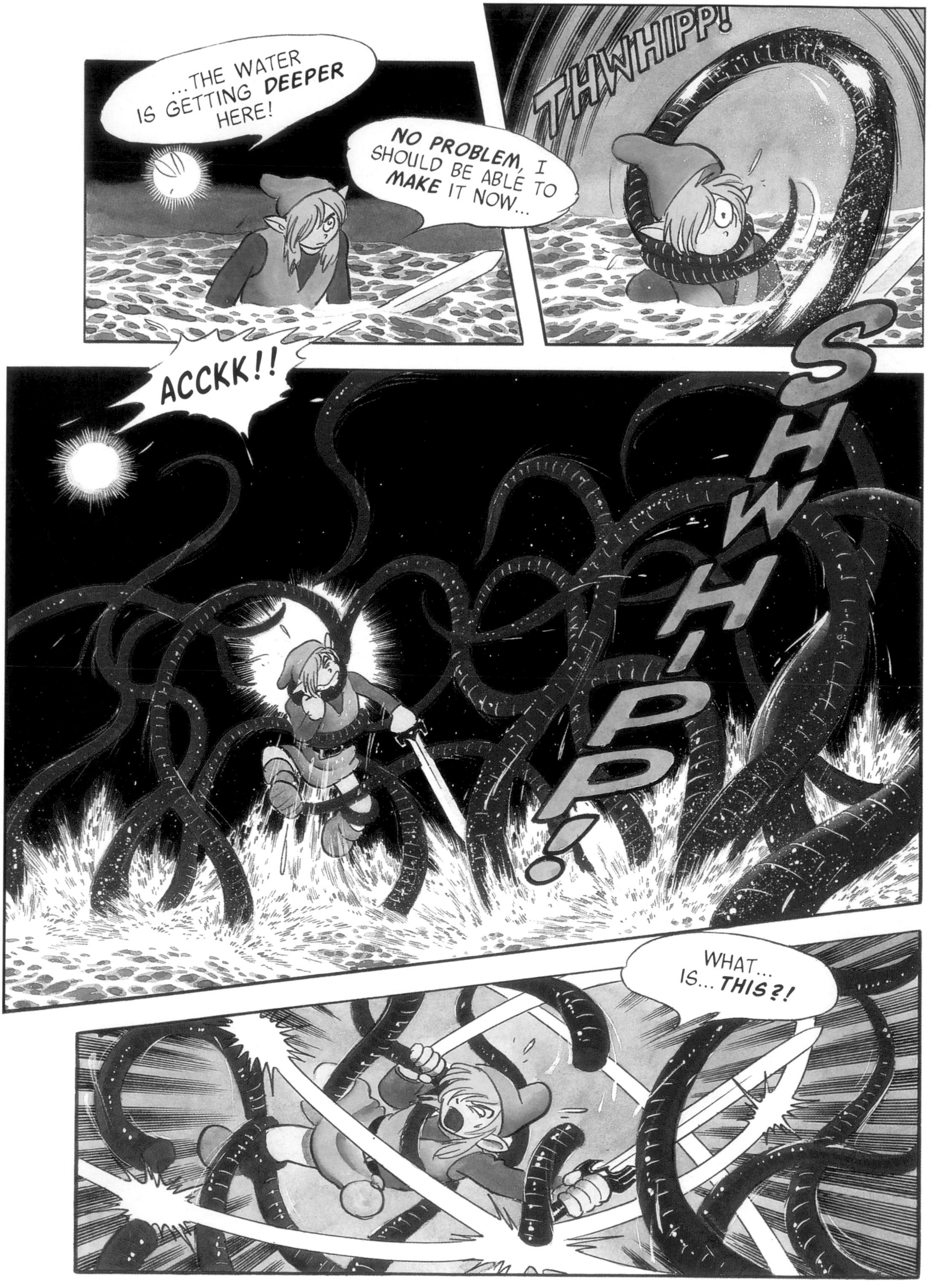
...THE WATER IS GETTING DEEPER HERE!
NO PROBLEM, I SHOULD BE ABLE TO MAKE IT NOW...
THWHIPP!
ACCKK!!
SHWHIPP!
WHAT... IS... THIS?!

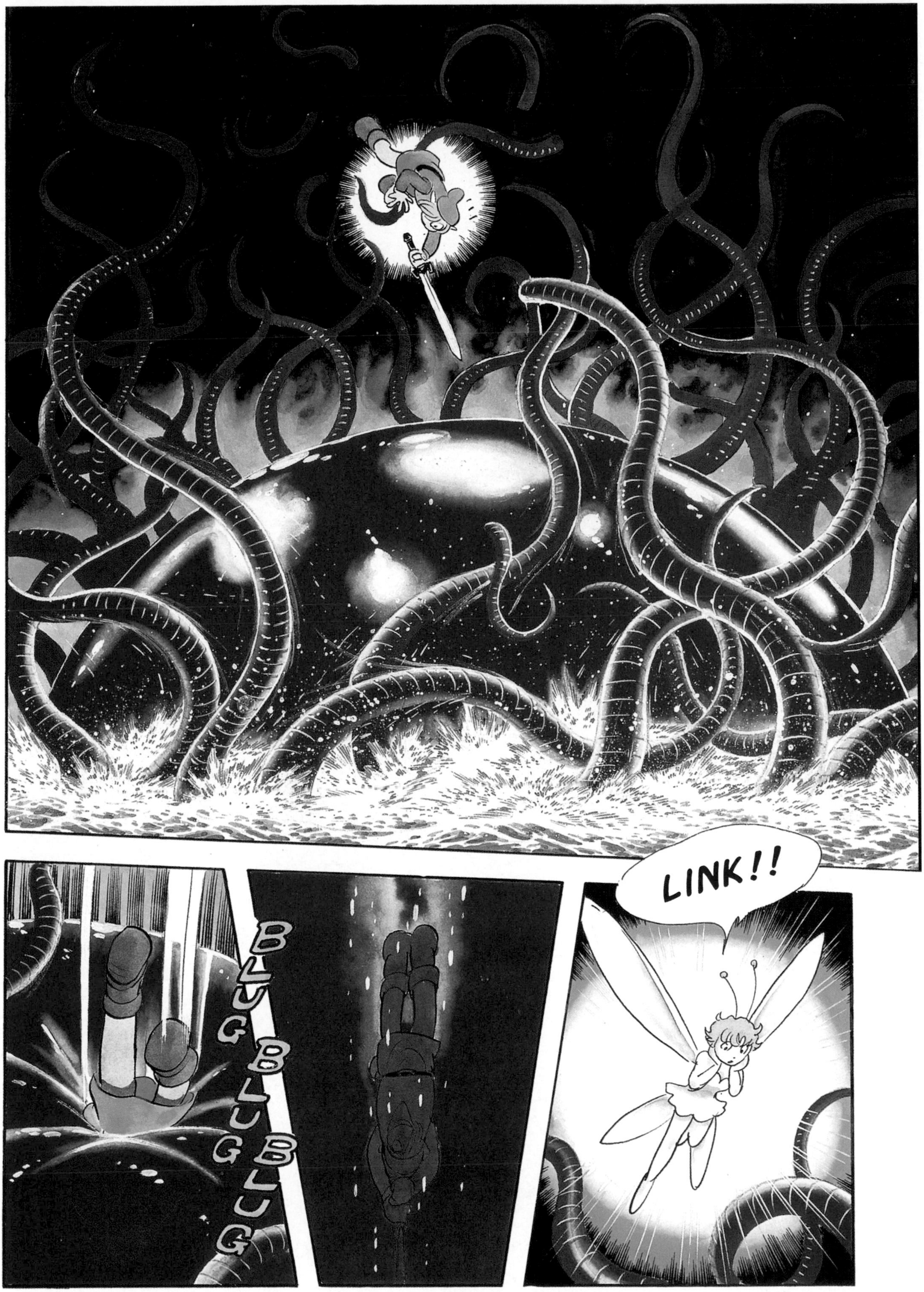
BLUG
BLUG
BLUG
LINK!!

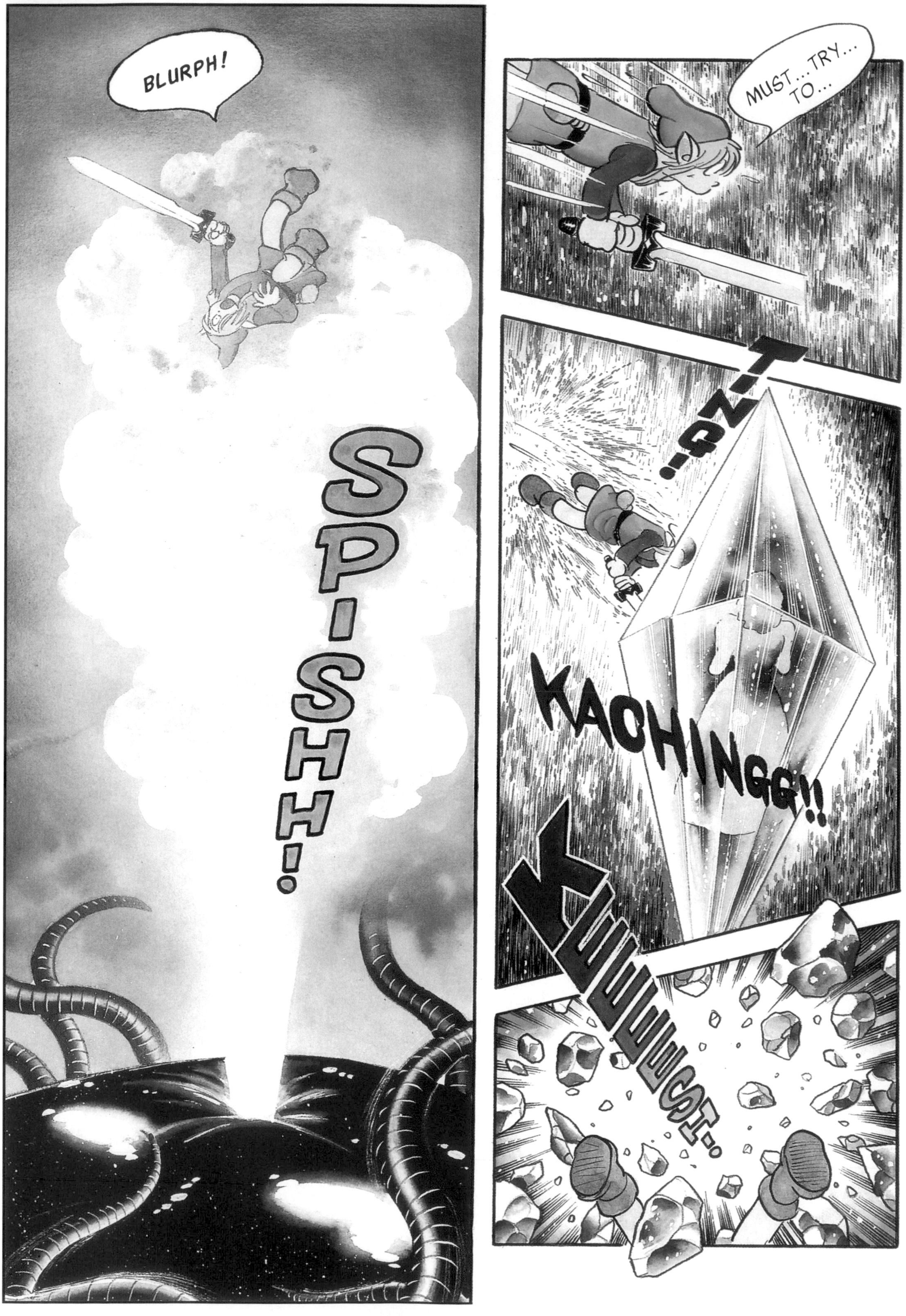
BLURPH!
SPISHH!
MUST...TRY... TO...
TINQ!!
KACHINGG!!
KWEEEESH!!

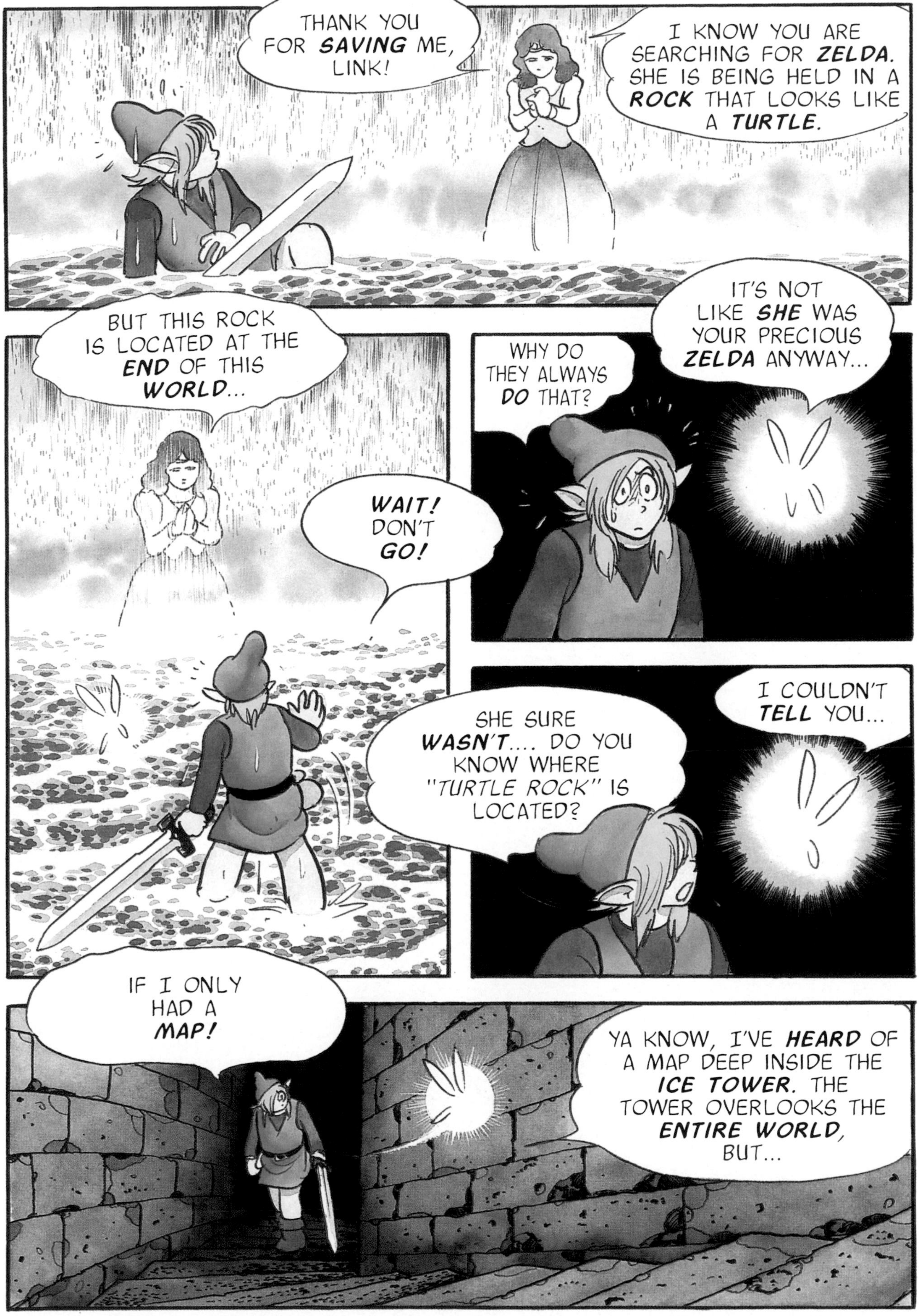
THANK YOU FOR SAVING ME, LINK!
I KNOW YOU ARE SEARCHING FOR ZELDA. SHE IS BEING HELD IN A ROCK THAT LOOKS LIKE A TURTLE.
BUT THIS ROCK IS LOCATED AT THE END OF THIS WORLD...
WAIT! DON'T GO!
WHY DO THEY ALWAYS DO THAT?
IT'S NOT LIKE SHE WAS YOUR PRECIOUS ZELDA ANYWAY...
SHE SURE WASN'T.... DO YOU KNOW WHERE "TURTLE ROCK" IS LOCATED?
I COULDN'T TELL YOU...
IF I ONLY HAD A MAP!
YA KNOW, I'VE HEARD OF A MAP DEEP INSIDE THE ICE TOWER. THE TOWER OVERLOOKS THE ENTIRE WORLD, BUT...

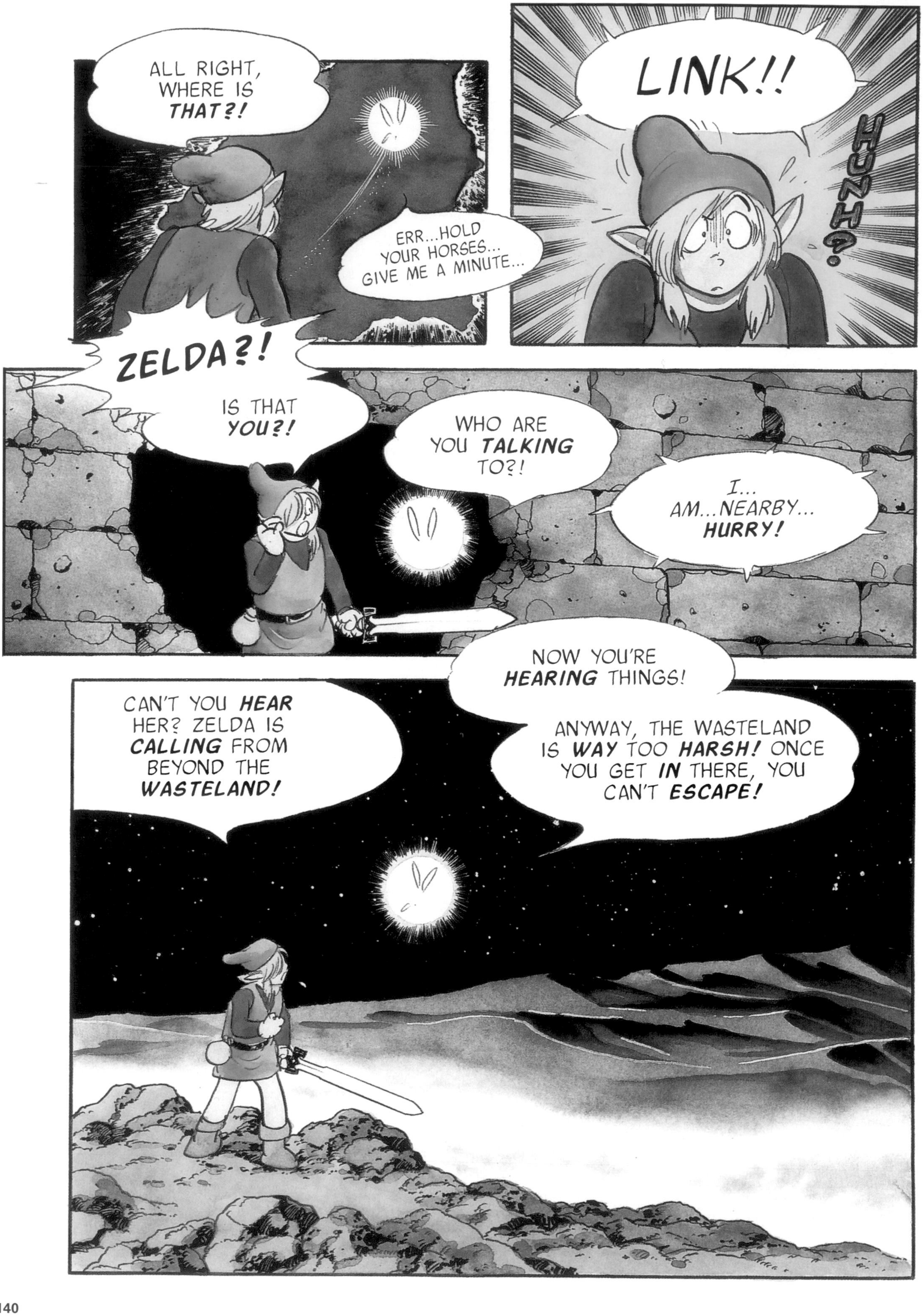
ALL RIGHT, WHERE IS THAT?!
ERR...HOLD YOUR HORSES... GIVE ME A MINUTE...
LINK!!
HUNH?!
ZELDA?!
IS THAT YOU?!
WHO ARE YOU TALKING TO?!
I... AM...NEARBY... HURRY!
CAN'T YOU HEAR HER? ZELDA IS CALLING FROM BEYOND THE WASTELAND!
NOW YOU'RE HEARING THINGS!
ANYWAY, THE WASTELAND IS WAY TOO HARSH! ONCE YOU GET IN THERE, YOU CAN'T ESCAPE!

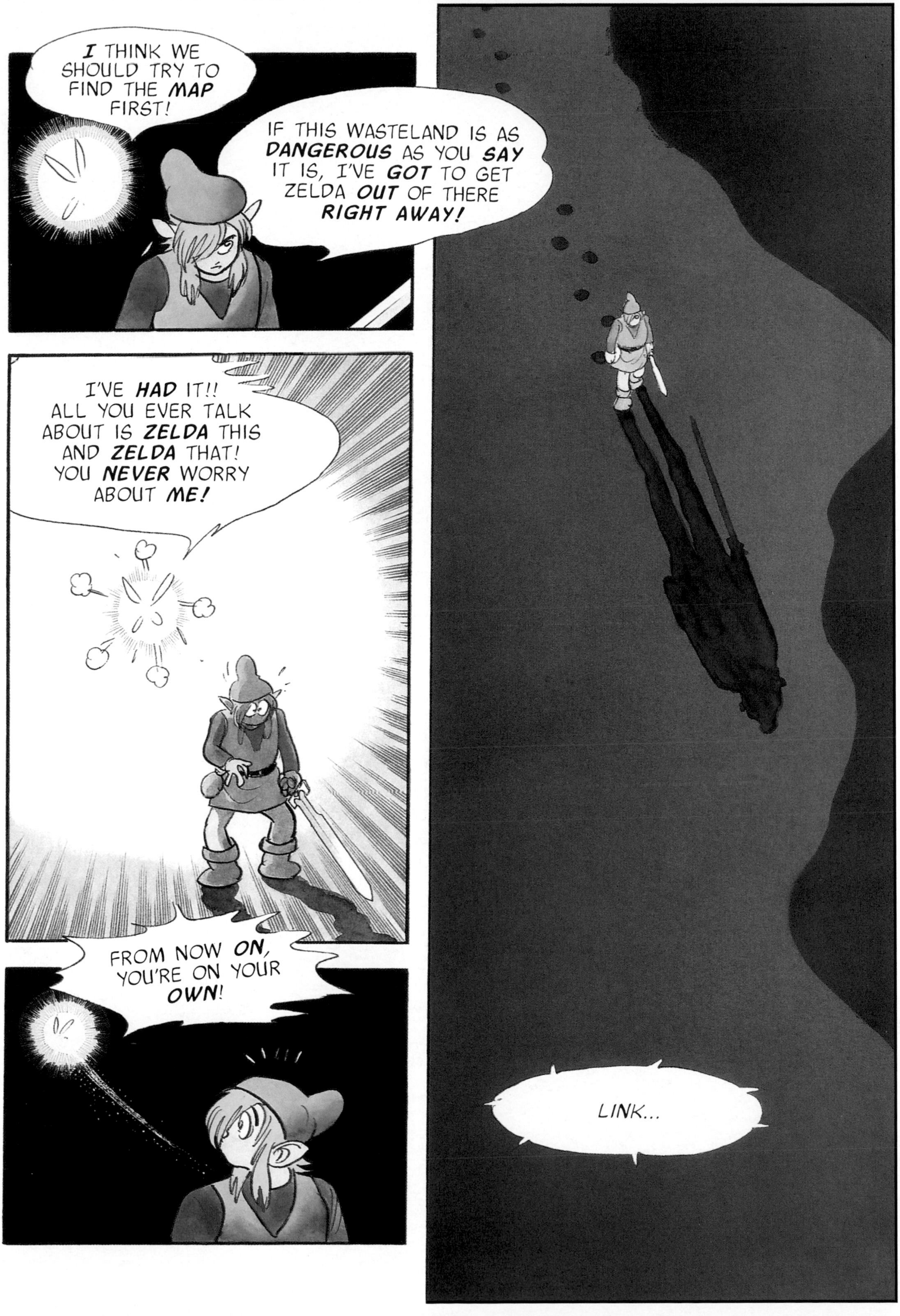

I THINK WE SHOULD TRY TO FIND THE MAP FIRST!
IF THIS WASTELAND IS AS DANGEROUS AS YOU SAY IT IS, I'VE GOT TO GET ZELDA OUT OF THERE RIGHT AWAY!
I'VE HAD IT!! ALL YOU EVER TALK ABOUT IS ZELDA THIS AND ZELDA THAT! YOU NEVER WORRY ABOUT ME!
FROM NOW ON, YOU'RE ON YOUR OWN!
LINK...

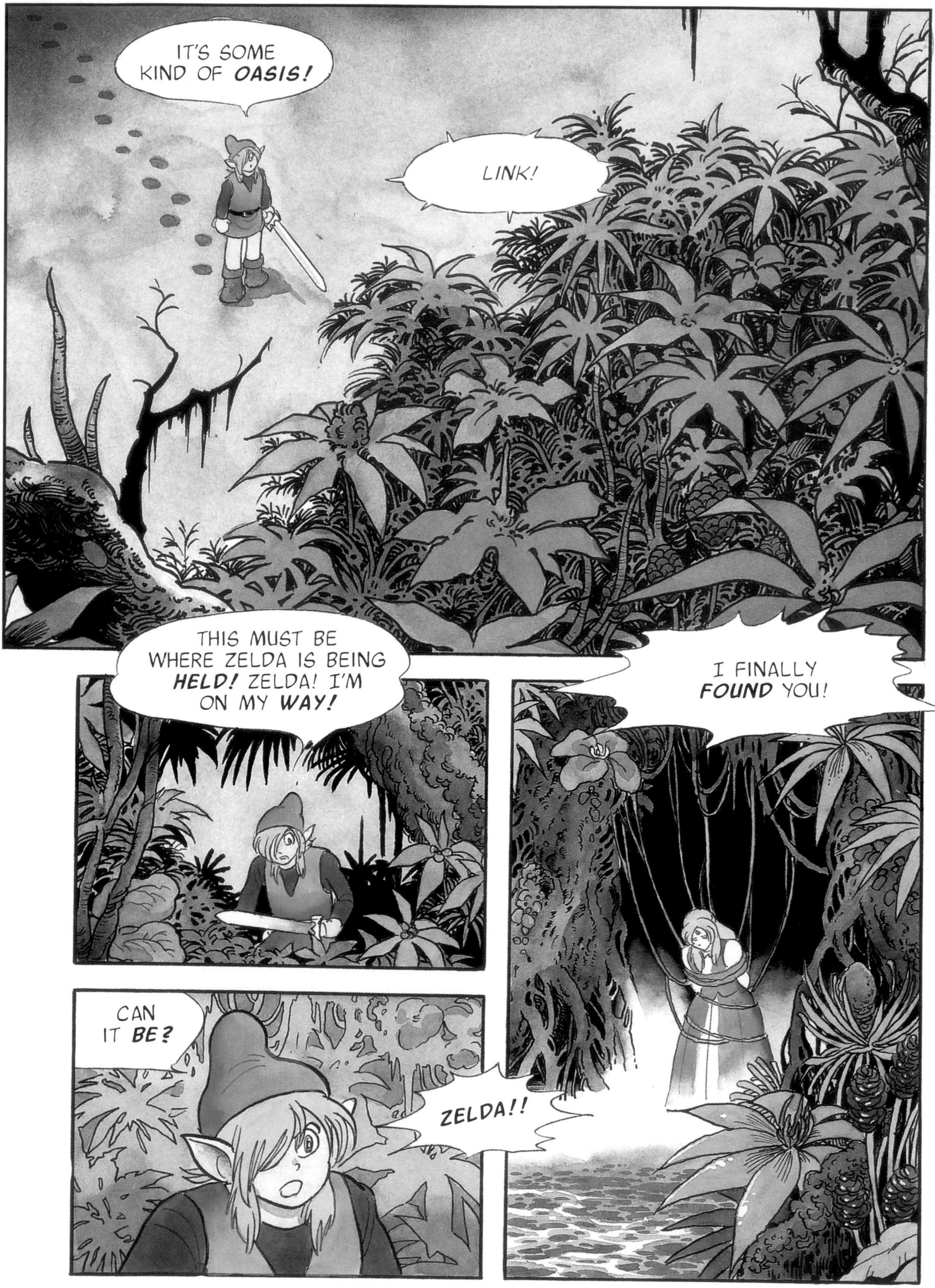
IT'S SOME KIND OF **OASIS!**
LINK!
THIS MUST BE WHERE ZELDA IS BEING **HELD!** ZELDA! I'M ON MY **WAY!**
CAN IT **BE?**
ZELDA!!
I FINALLY **FOUND** YOU!

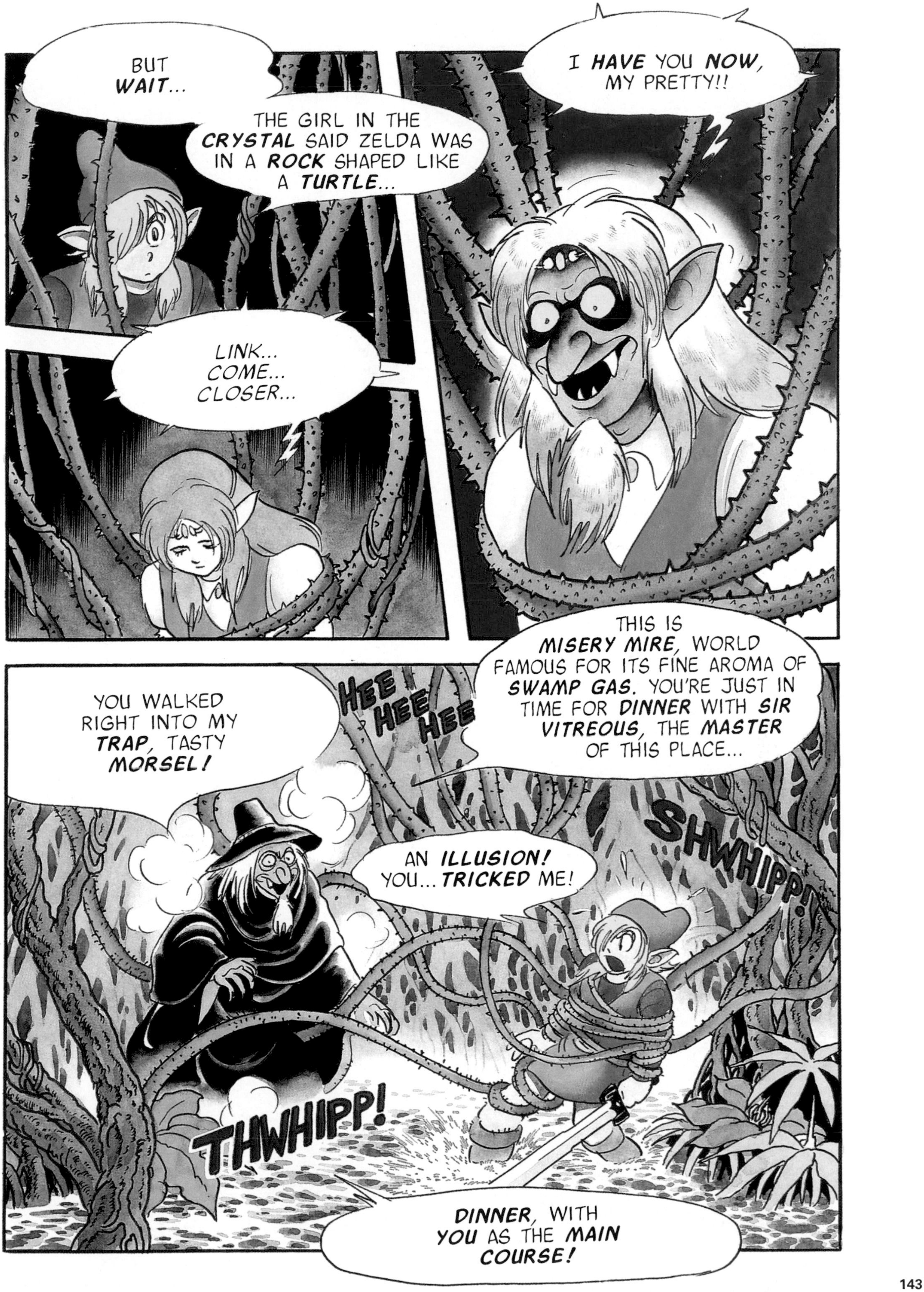
BUT WAIT...
THE GIRL IN THE CRYSTAL SAID ZELDA WAS IN A ROCK SHAPED LIKE A TURTLE...
LINK... COME... CLOSER...
I HAVE YOU NOW, MY PRETTY!!
YOU WALKED RIGHT INTO MY TRAP, TASTY MORSEL!
HEE HEE HEE
THIS IS MISERY MIRE, WORLD FAMOUS FOR ITS FINE AROMA OF SWAMP GAS. YOU'RE JUST IN TIME FOR DINNER WITH SIR VITREOUS, THE MASTER OF THIS PLACE...
SHWHIPP!
AN ILLUSION! YOU... TRICKED ME!
THWHIPP!
DINNER, WITH YOU AS THE MAIN COURSE!

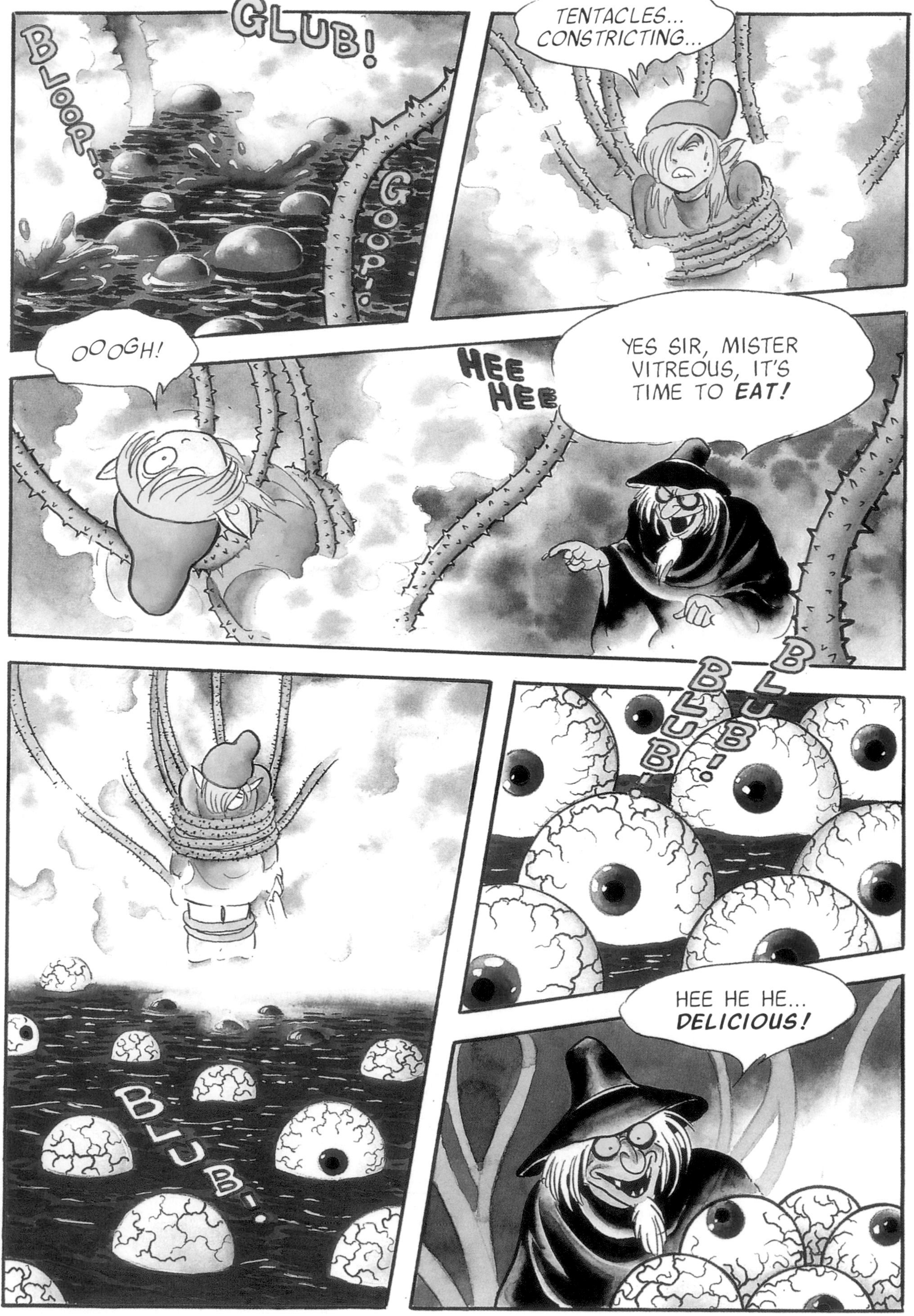
GLUB!
BLOOP!
GOOP!
TENTACLES... CONSTRICTING...
OOOGH!
HEE HEE
YES SIR, MISTER VITREOUS, IT'S TIME TO **EAT!**
BLUB!
BLUB!
BLUB!
HEE HE HE... **DELICIOUS!**

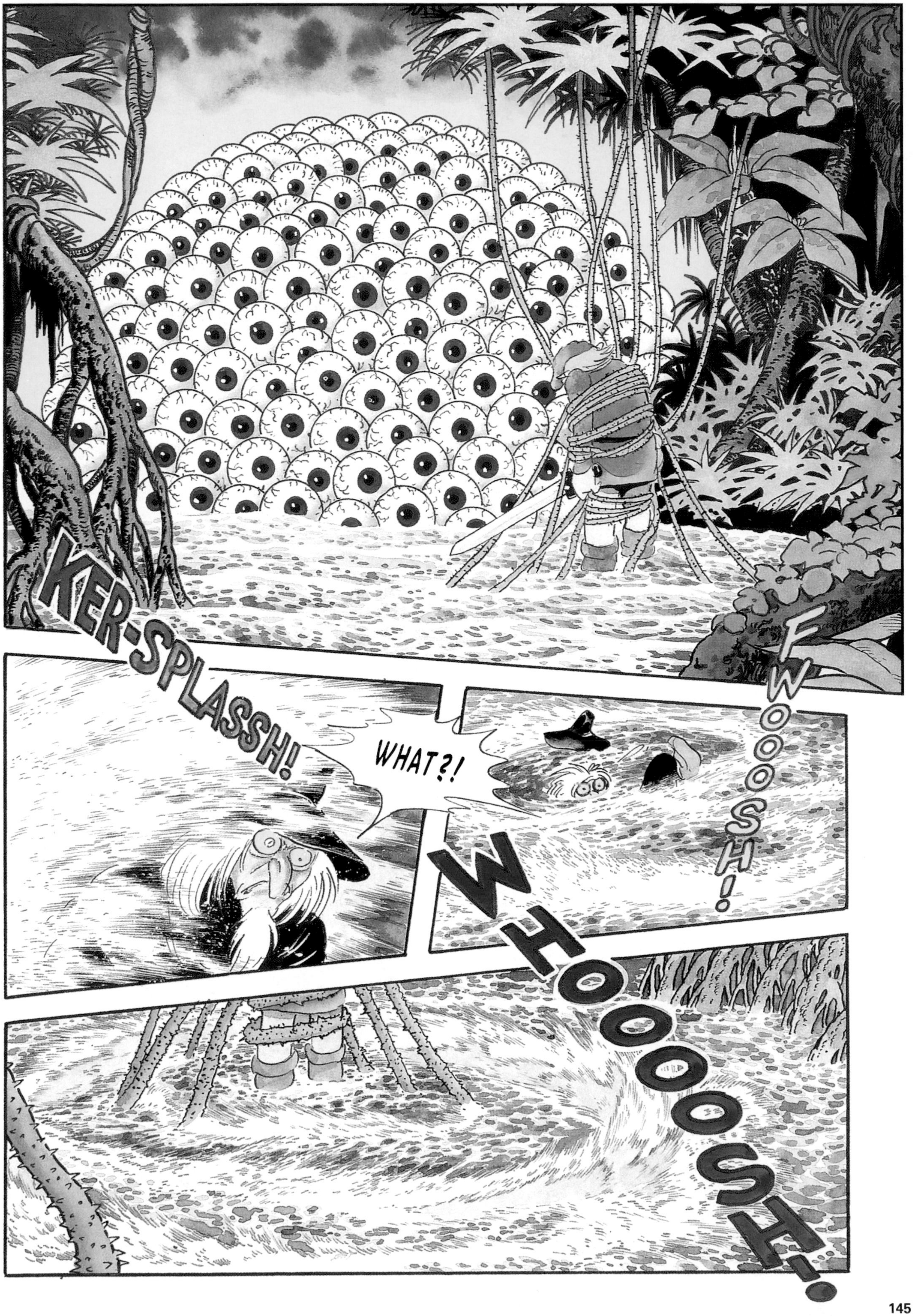
KER-SPLASSH!
WHAT?!
FWOOOSH!
WHOOOOOSH!

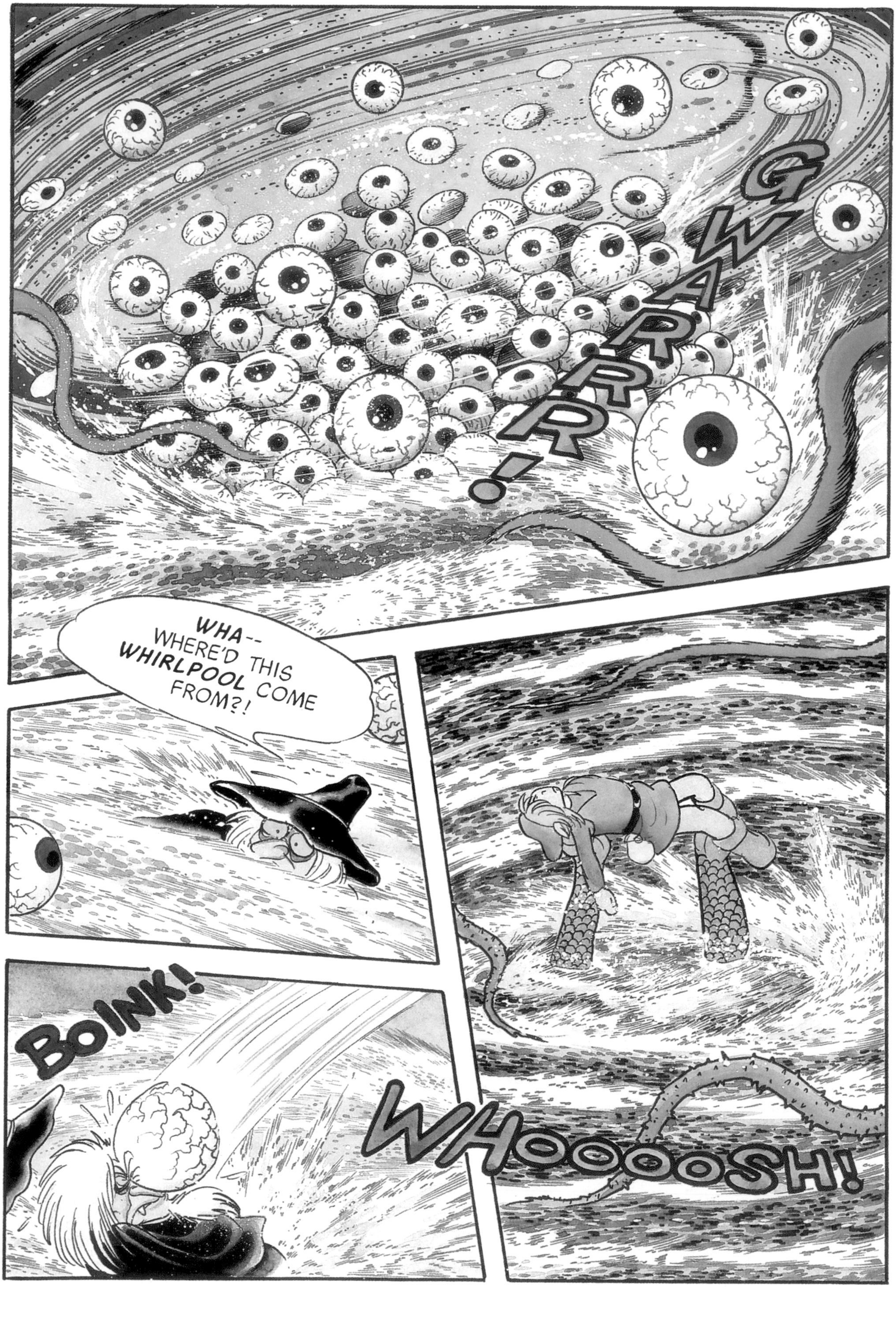
GWARRRR!
WHA-- WHERE'D THIS WHIRLPOOL COME FROM?!
BOINK!
WHOOOOSH!

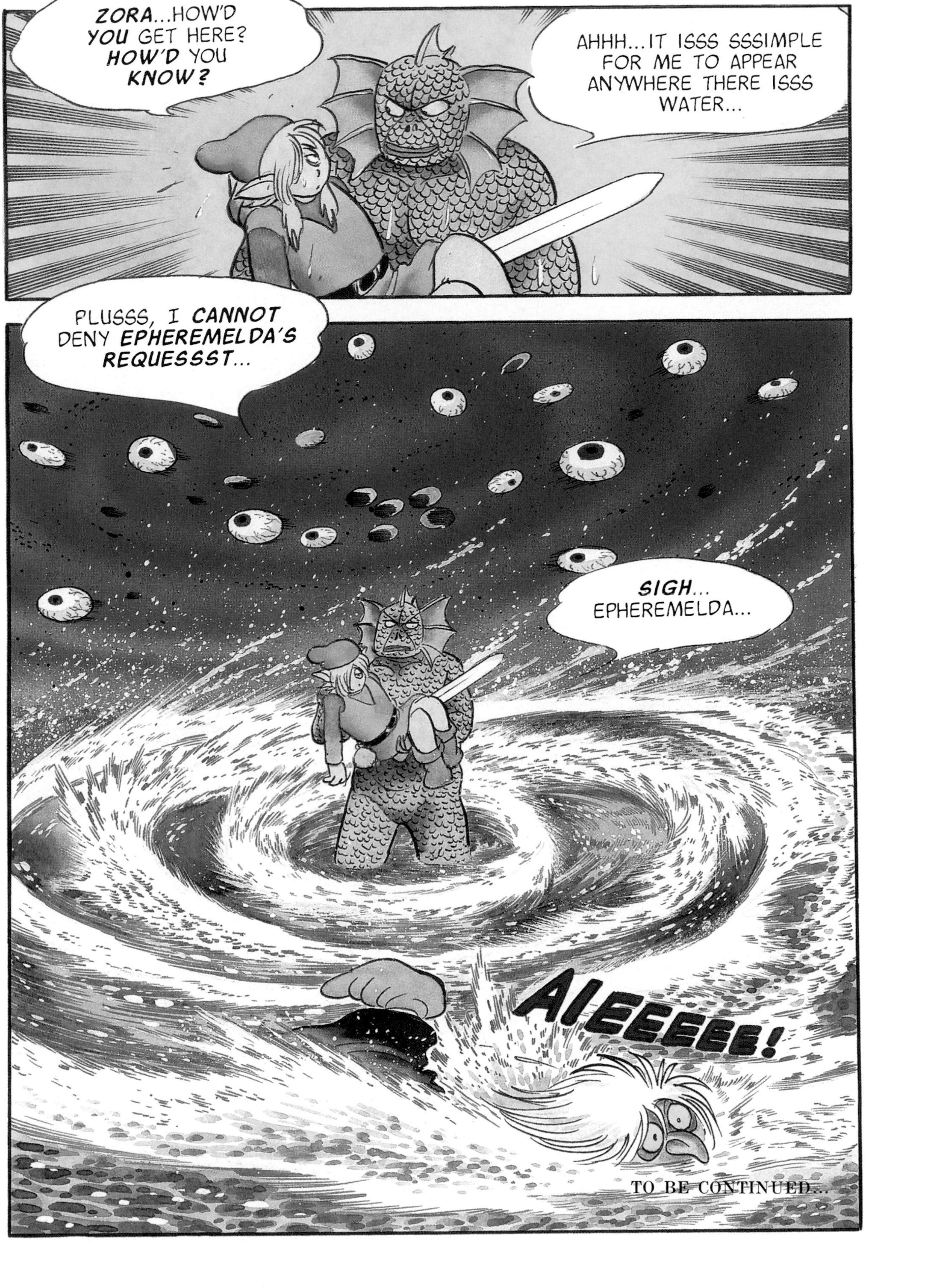
ZORA...HOW'D YOU GET HERE? HOW'D YOU KNOW?
AHHH...IT ISSS SSSIMPLE FOR ME TO APPEAR ANYWHERE THERE ISSS WATER...
PLUSSS, I CANNOT DENY EPHEREMELDA'S REQUESSST...
SIGH... EPHEREMELDA...
AIEEEEEE!
TO BE CONTINUED...

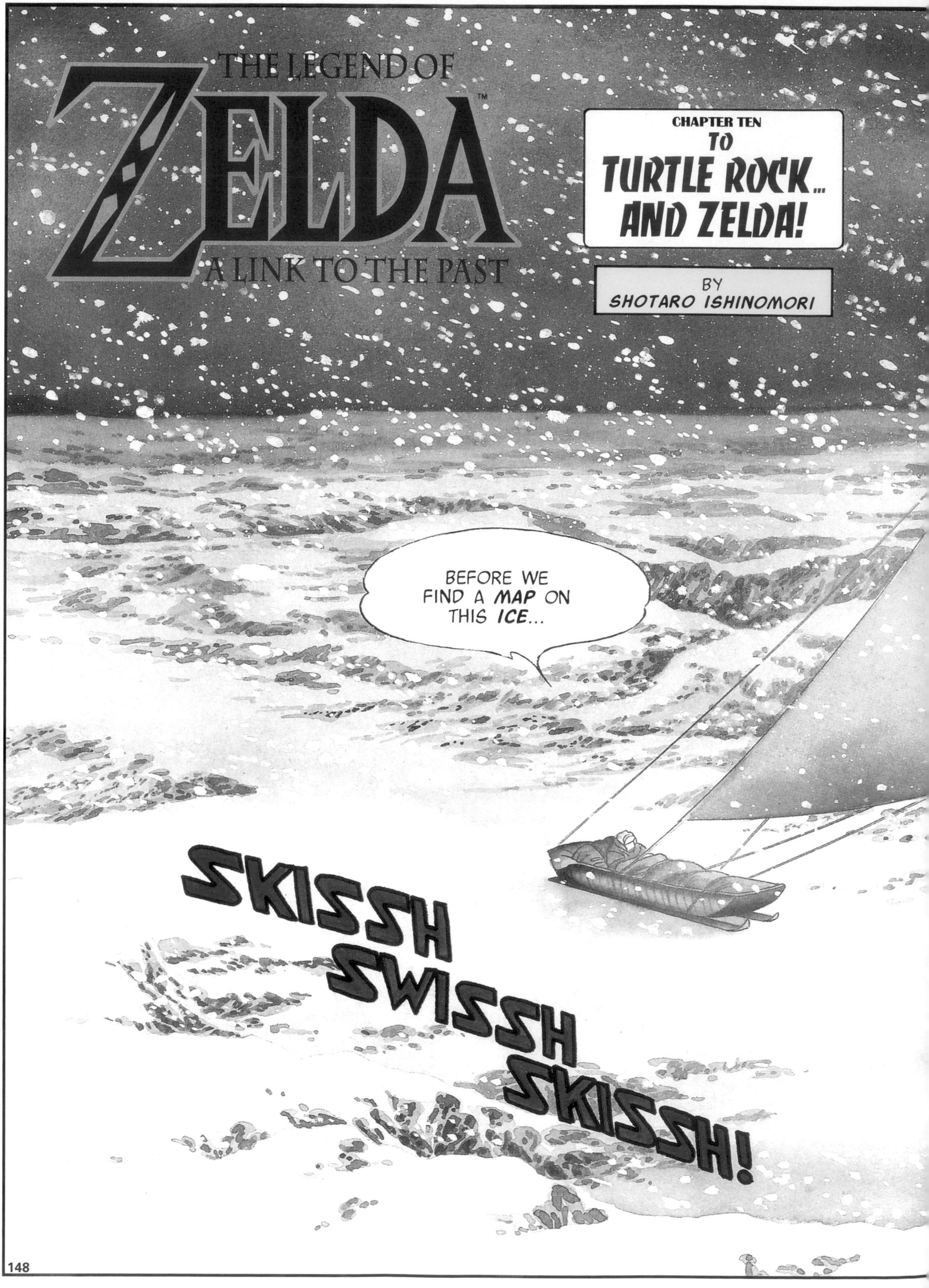
THE LEGEND OF
ZELDA™
A LINK TO THE PAST
CHAPTER TEN
TO
TURTLE ROCK...
AND ZELDA!
BY
SHOTARO ISHINOMORI
BEFORE WE FIND A MAP ON THIS ICE...
SKISSH
SWISSH
SKISSH!

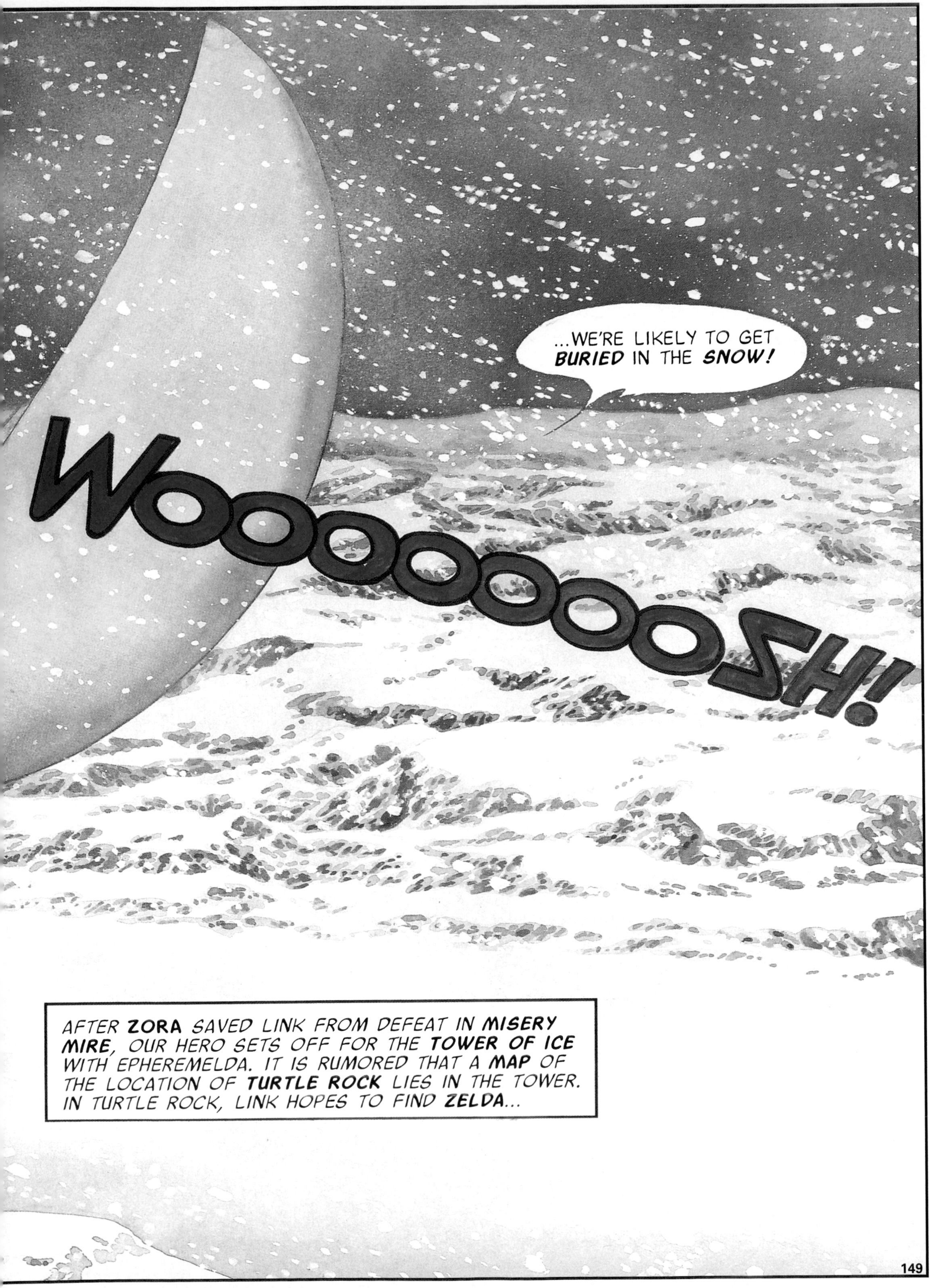
...WE'RE LIKELY TO GET **BURIED** IN THE **SNOW!**
WOOOOOOOOSH!
AFTER **ZORA** SAVED LINK FROM DEFEAT IN **MISERY MIRE**, OUR HERO SETS OFF FOR THE **TOWER OF ICE** WITH EPHEREMELDA. IT IS RUMORED THAT A **MAP** OF THE LOCATION OF **TURTLE ROCK** LIES IN THE TOWER. IN TURTLE ROCK, LINK HOPES TO FIND **ZELDA**...

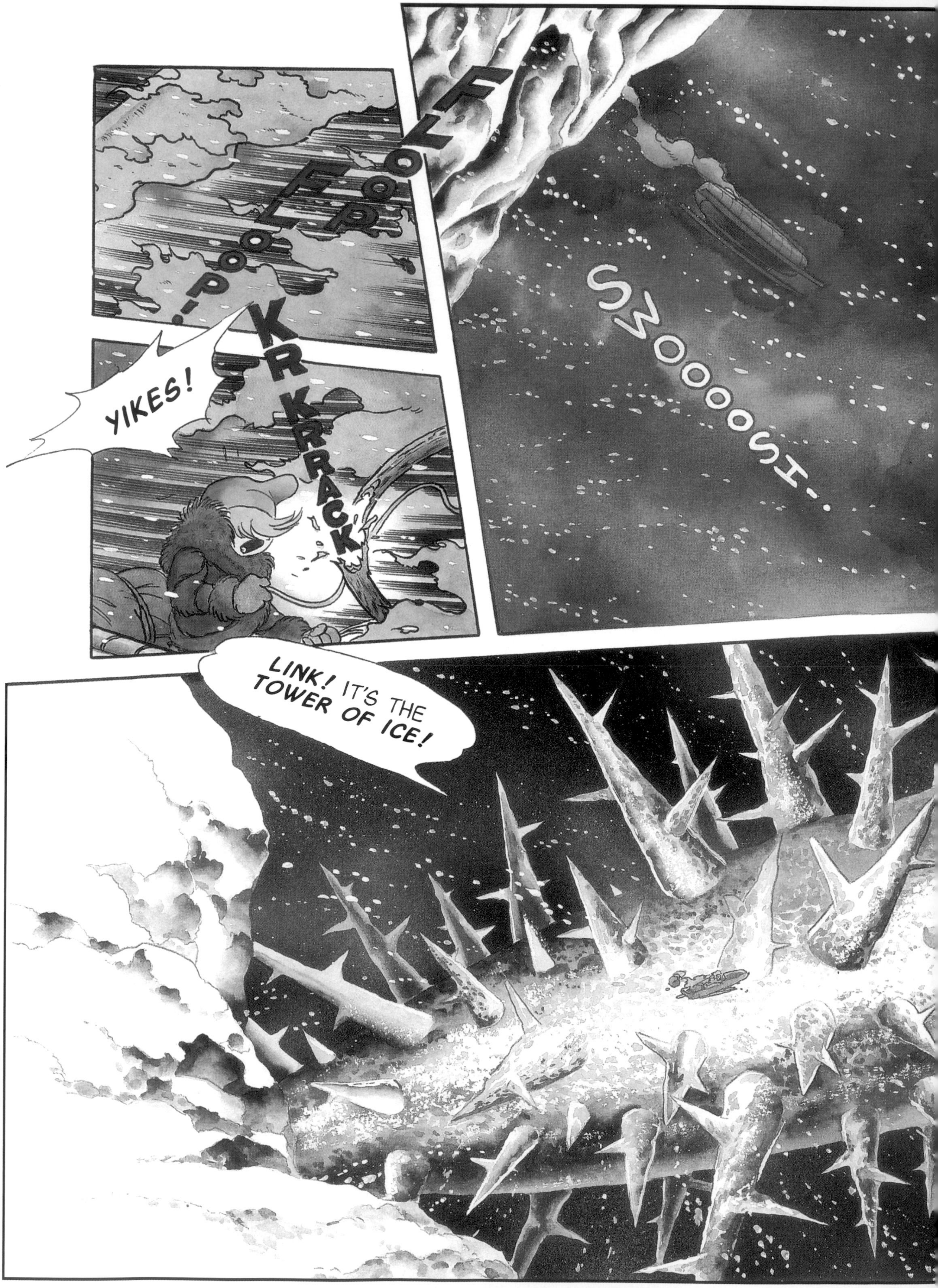
FLOOP
FLOOP!
KRKRRACK!
YIKES!
SWOOOOSH..
LINK! IT'S THE TOWER OF ICE!

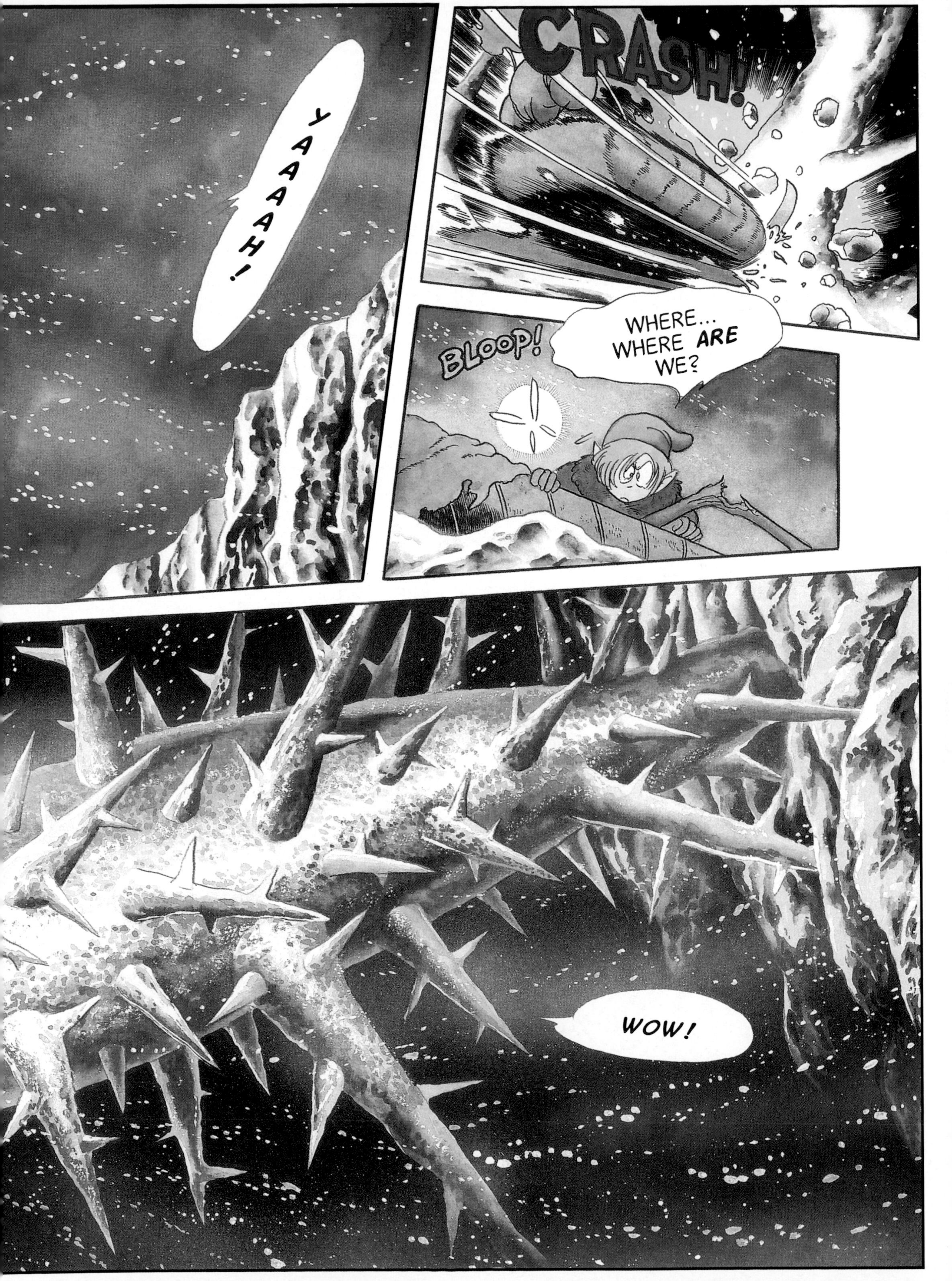
YAAAAAH!
CRASH!
BLOOP!
WHERE... WHERE ARE WE?
WOW!

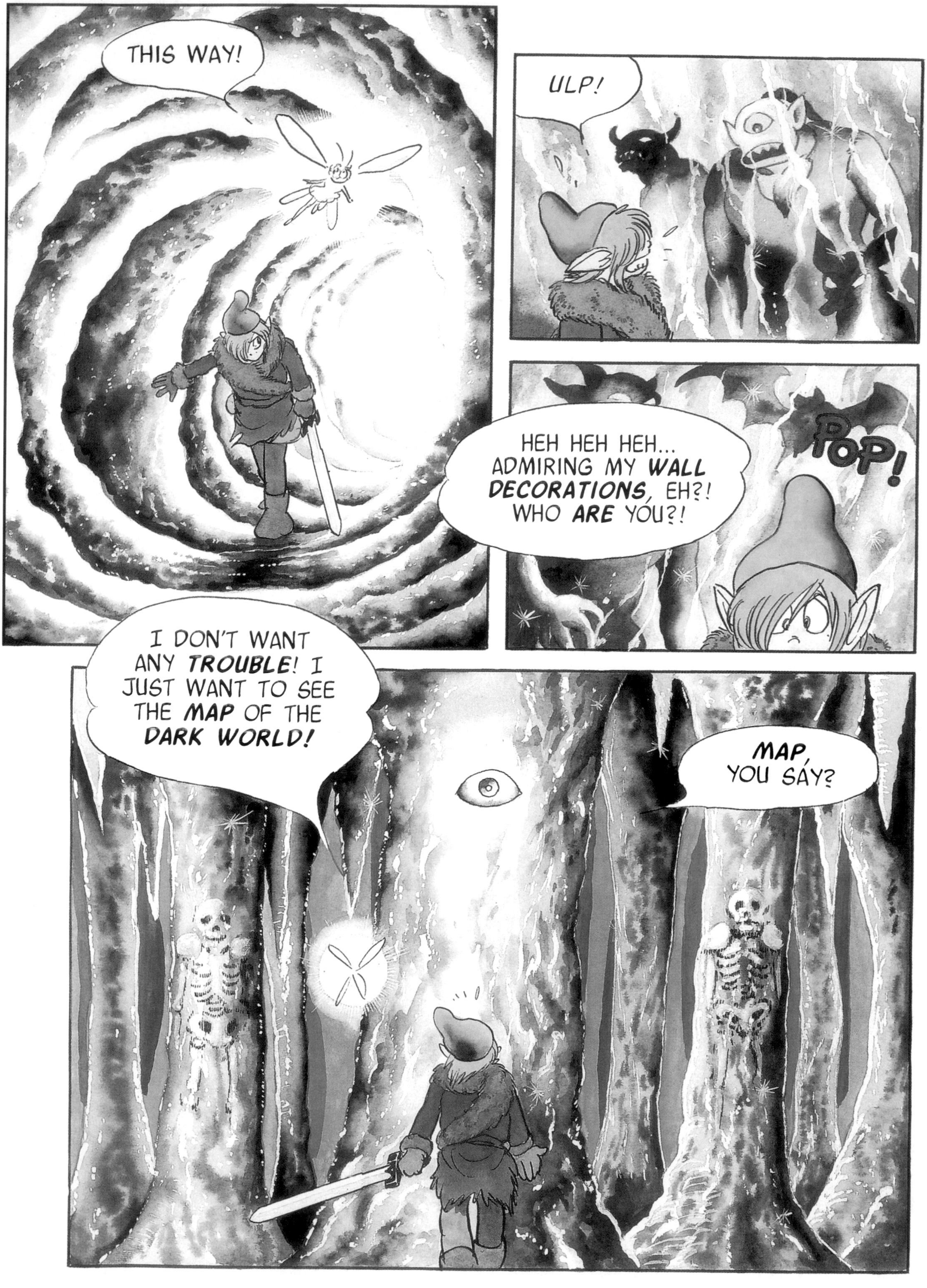
THIS WAY!
ULP!
HEH HEH HEH... ADMIRING MY **WALL DECORATIONS**, EH?! WHO **ARE** YOU?!
POP!
I DON'T WANT ANY **TROUBLE**! I JUST WANT TO SEE THE **MAP** OF THE **DARK WORLD!**
MAP, YOU SAY?

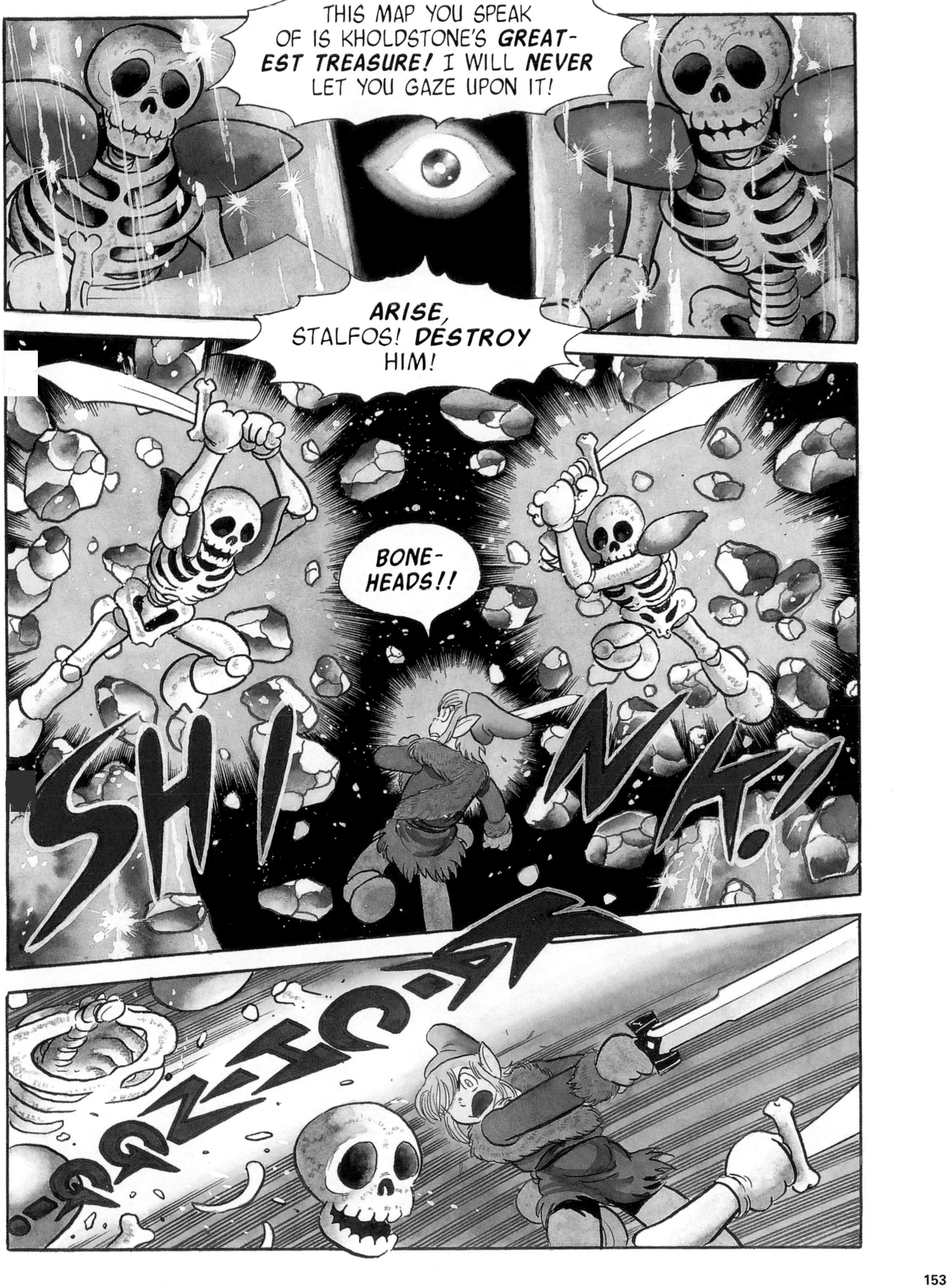
THIS MAP YOU SPEAK OF IS KHOLDSTONE'S **GREAT-EST TREASURE!** I WILL **NEVER** LET YOU GAZE UPON IT!
ARISE, STALFOS! **DESTROY** HIM!
BONE-HEADS!!
SHINK!!

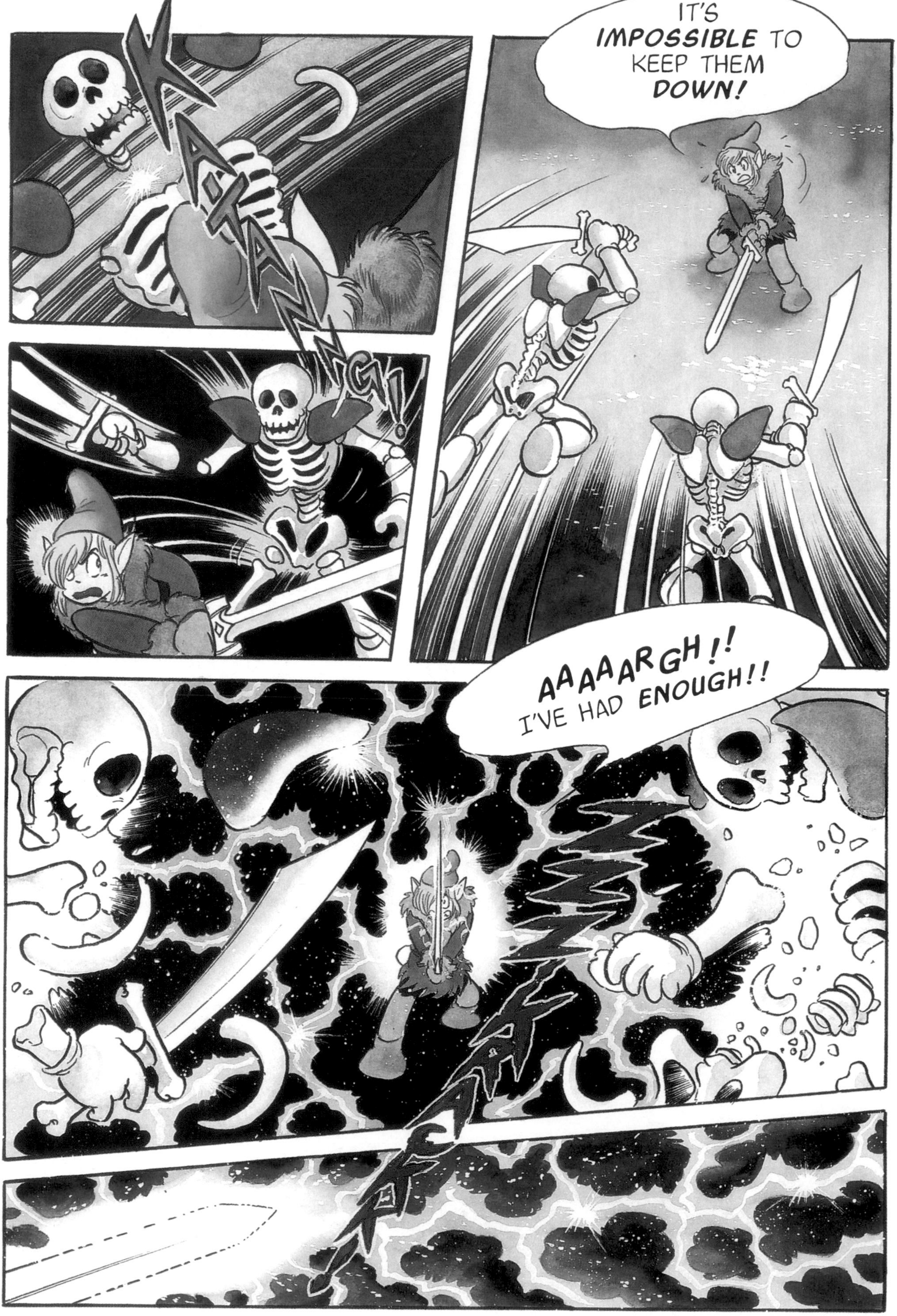
KAKANNGH!
IT'S IMPOSSIBLE TO KEEP THEM DOWN!
AAAAARGH!! I'VE HAD ENOUGH!!

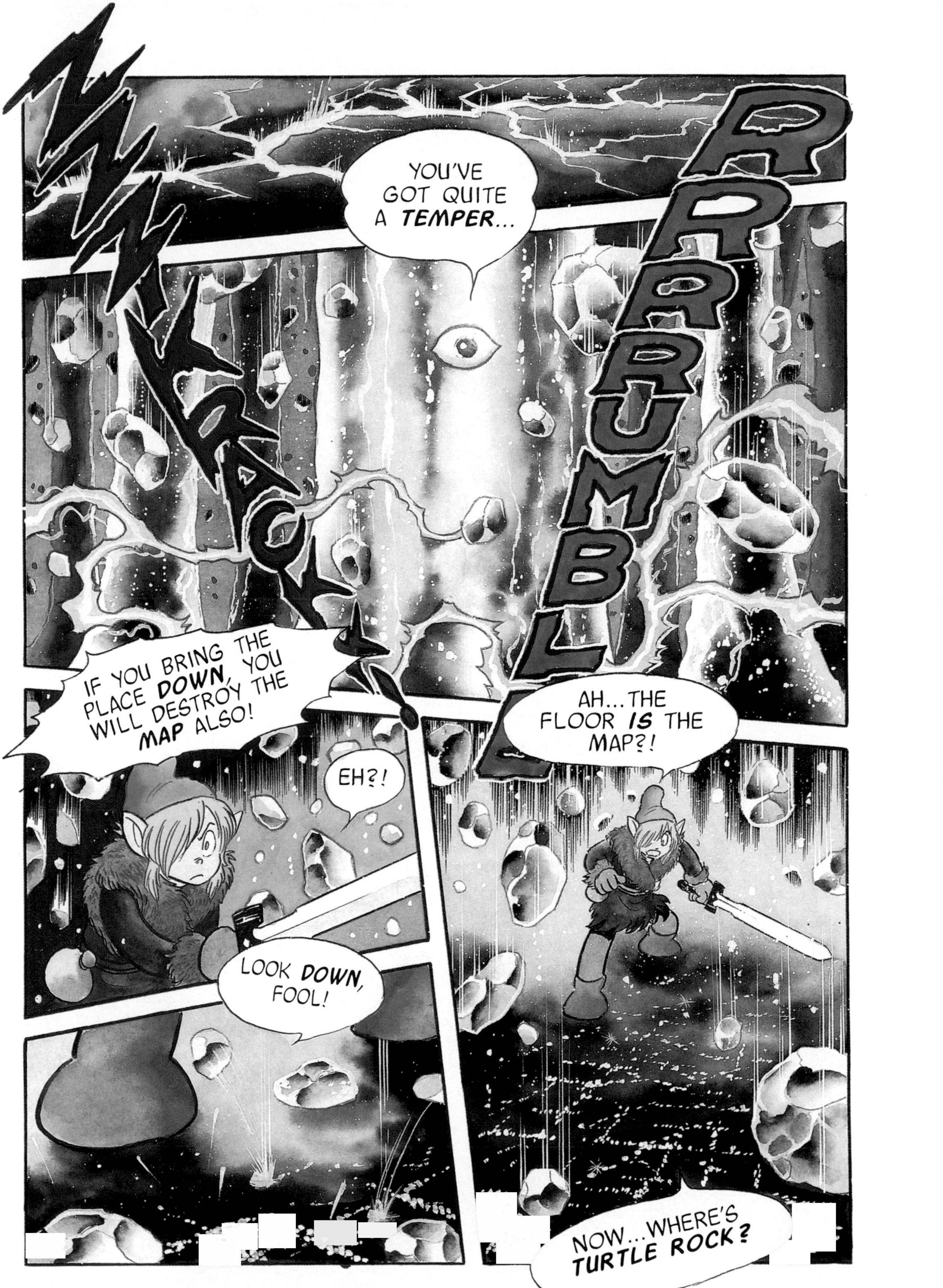
KRACK!
YOU'VE GOT QUITE A **TEMPER**...
RRRRUMBLL
IF YOU BRING THE PLACE **DOWN**, YOU WILL DESTROY THE **MAP** ALSO!
EH?!
LOOK **DOWN**, FOOL!
AH...THE FLOOR **IS** THE MAP?!
NOW...WHERE'S **TURTLE ROCK?**

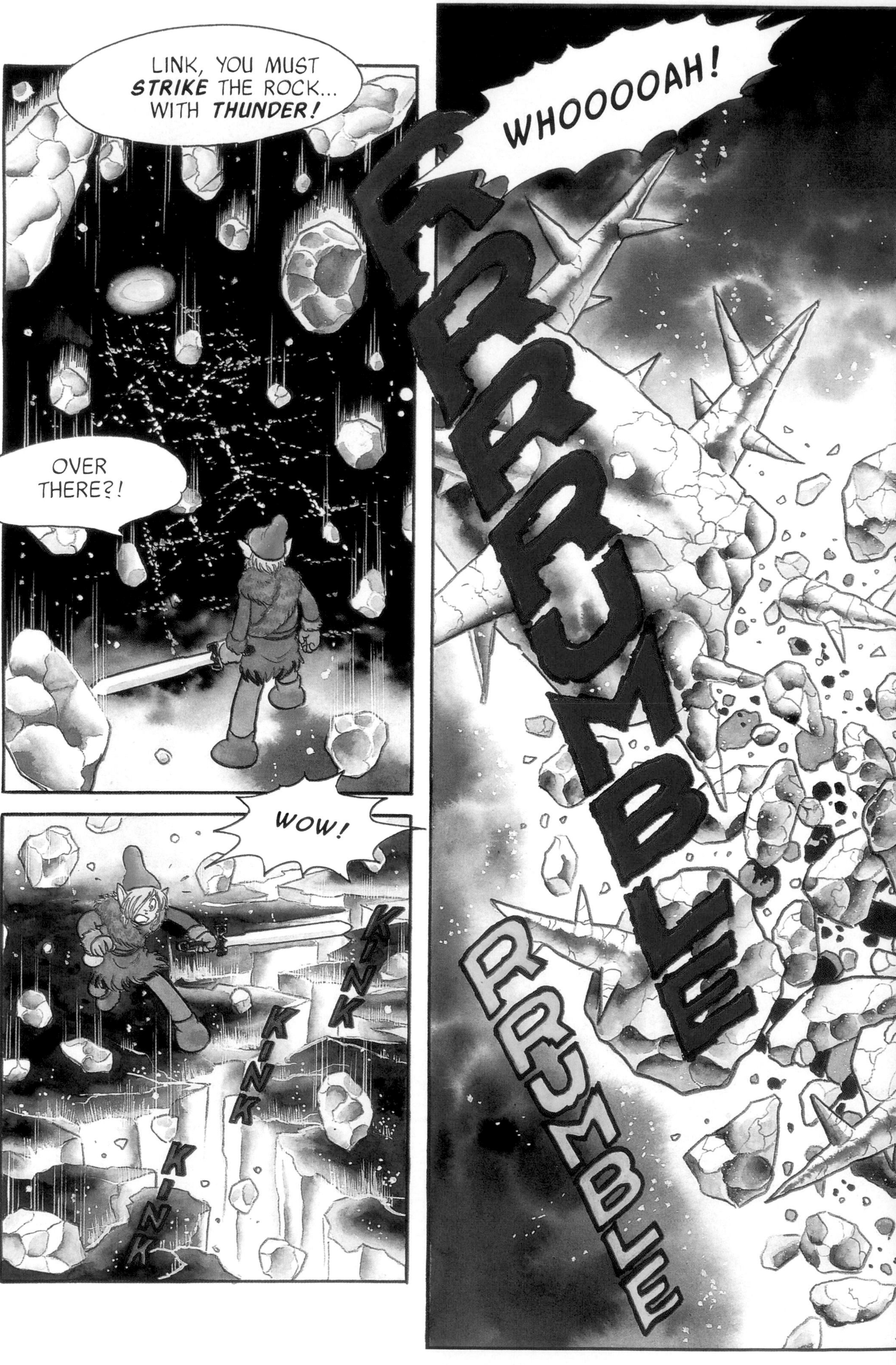
LINK, YOU MUST **STRIKE** THE ROCK... WITH **THUNDER!**
OVER THERE?!
WOW!
KINK
KINK
KINK
KINK
WHOOOOAH!
CRRRUMBLE
RRUMBLE

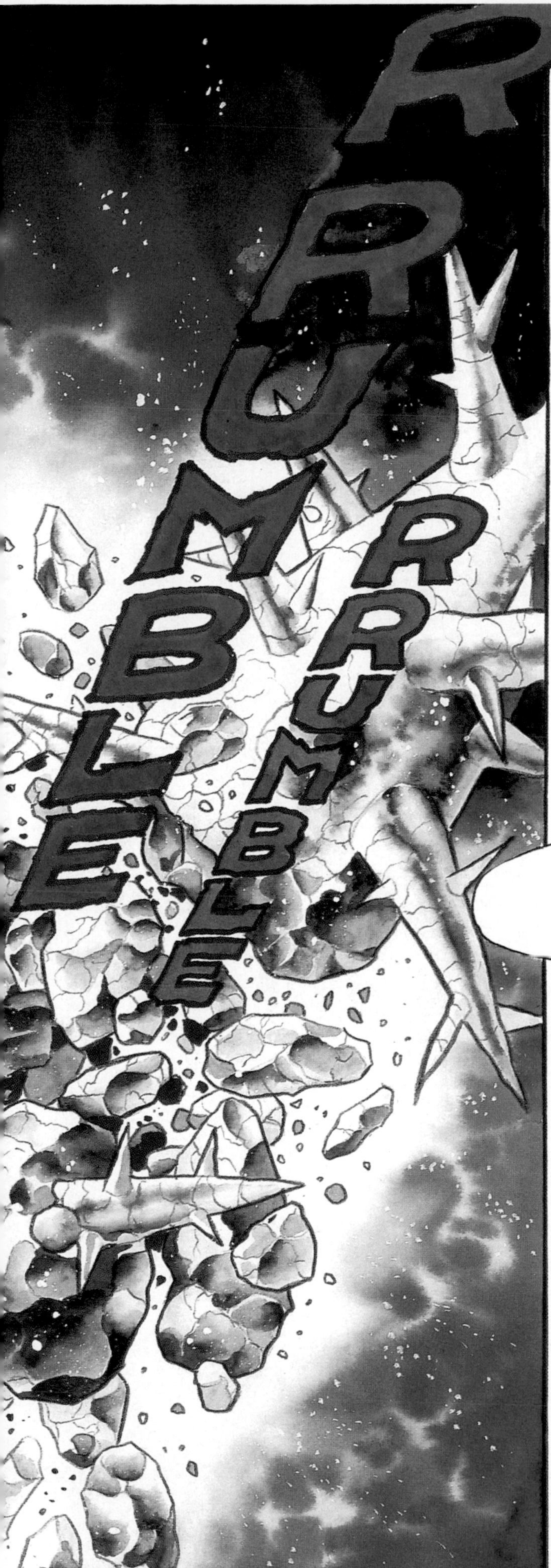
RRUMBLE
RRUMBLE

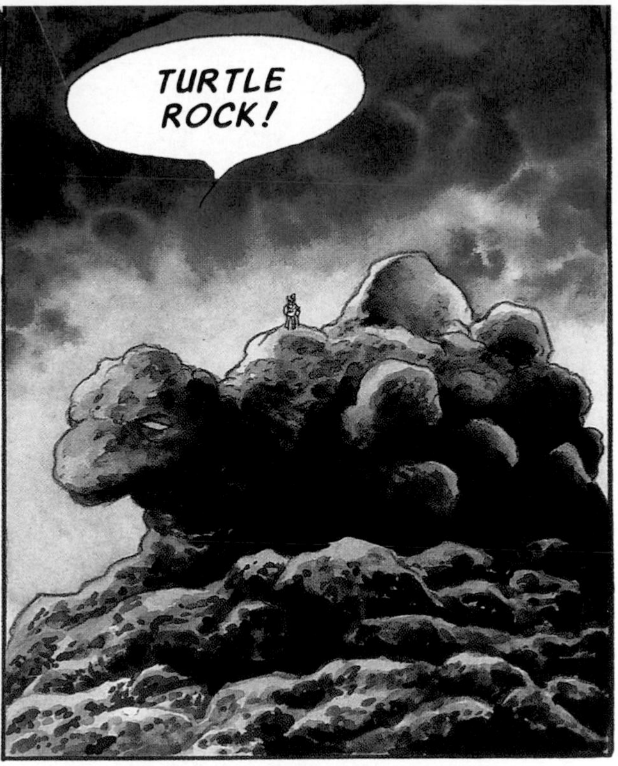
TURTLE ROCK!

FOLLOWING THE MAP HE GLIMPSED IN THE ICE TOWER, LINK FINALLY ARRIVED AT TURTLE ROCK WITH EPHEREMELDA, BUT...

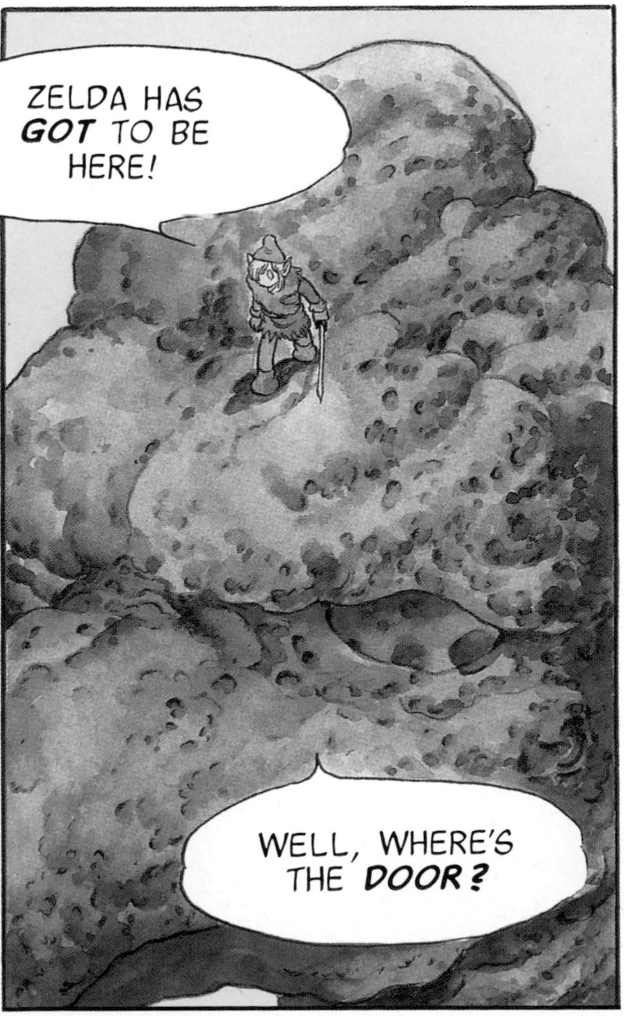
ZELDA HAS GOT TO BE HERE!
WELL, WHERE'S THE DOOR?

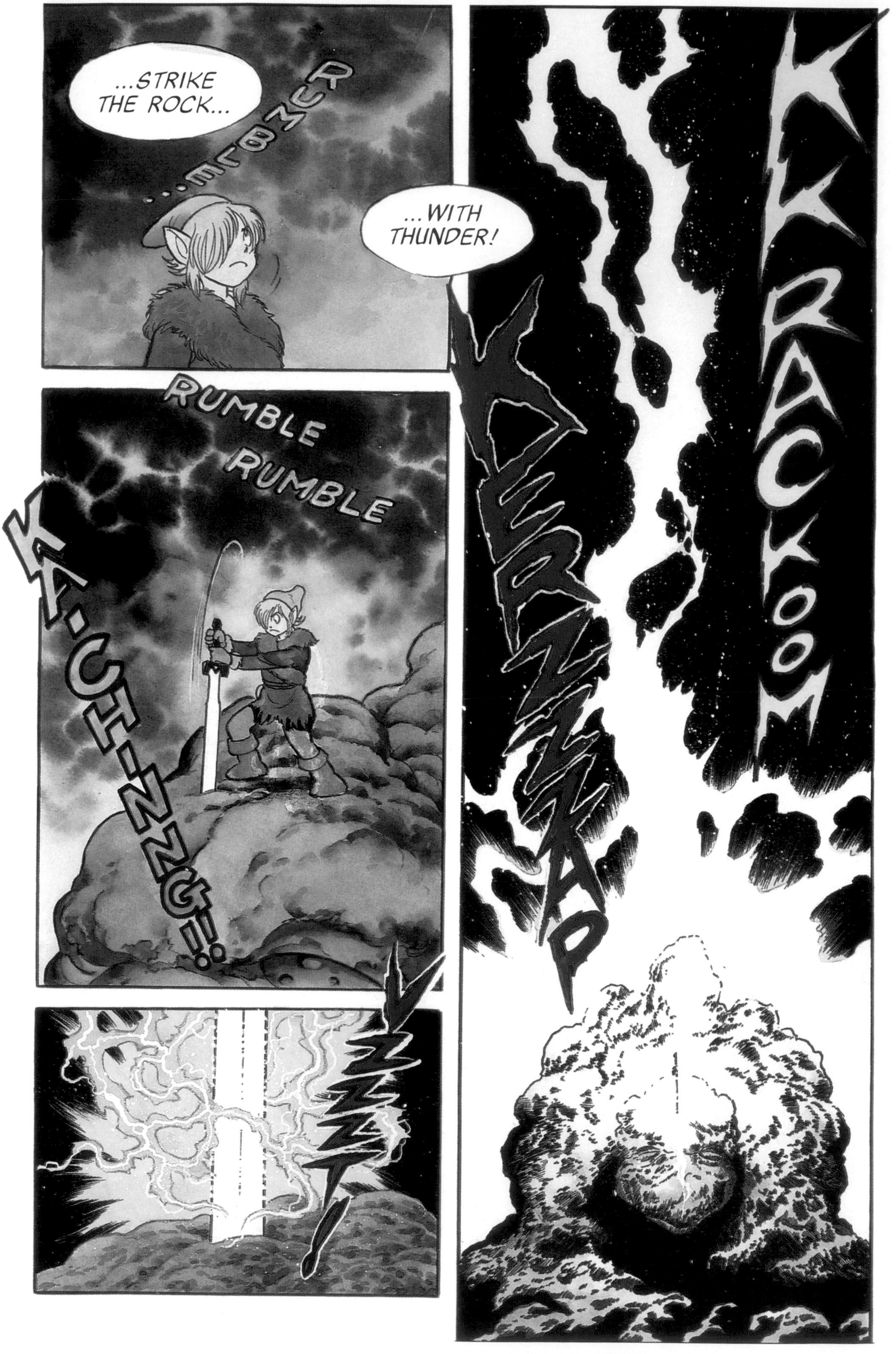
...STRIKE THE ROCK...
RUMBLE...
...WITH THUNDER!
RUMBLE
RUMBLE
KA-CHINNG!!
KRACKOOM

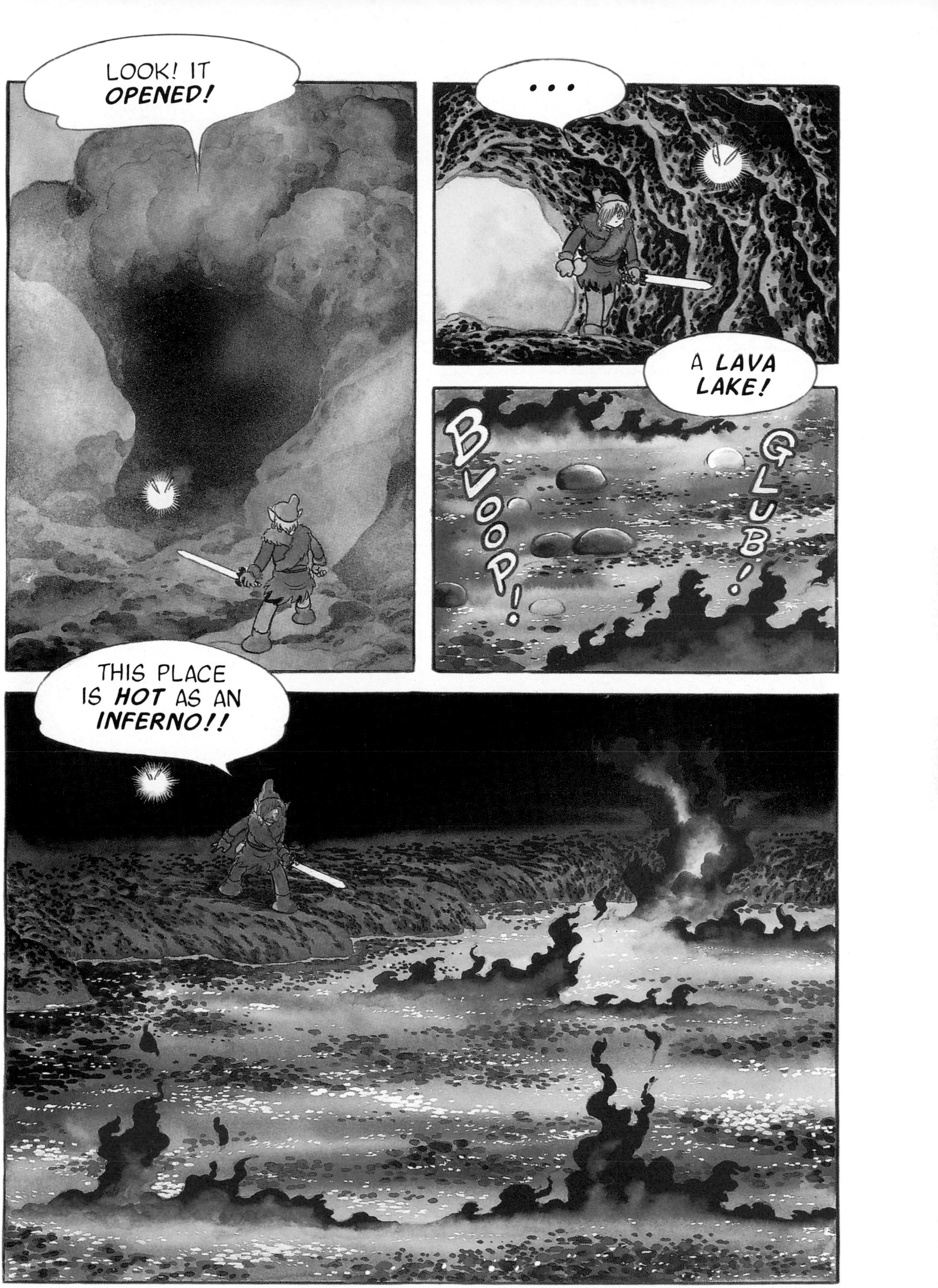
LOOK! IT OPENED!
...
A LAVA LAKE!
BLOOP!
GLUB!
THIS PLACE IS HOT AS AN INFERNO!!

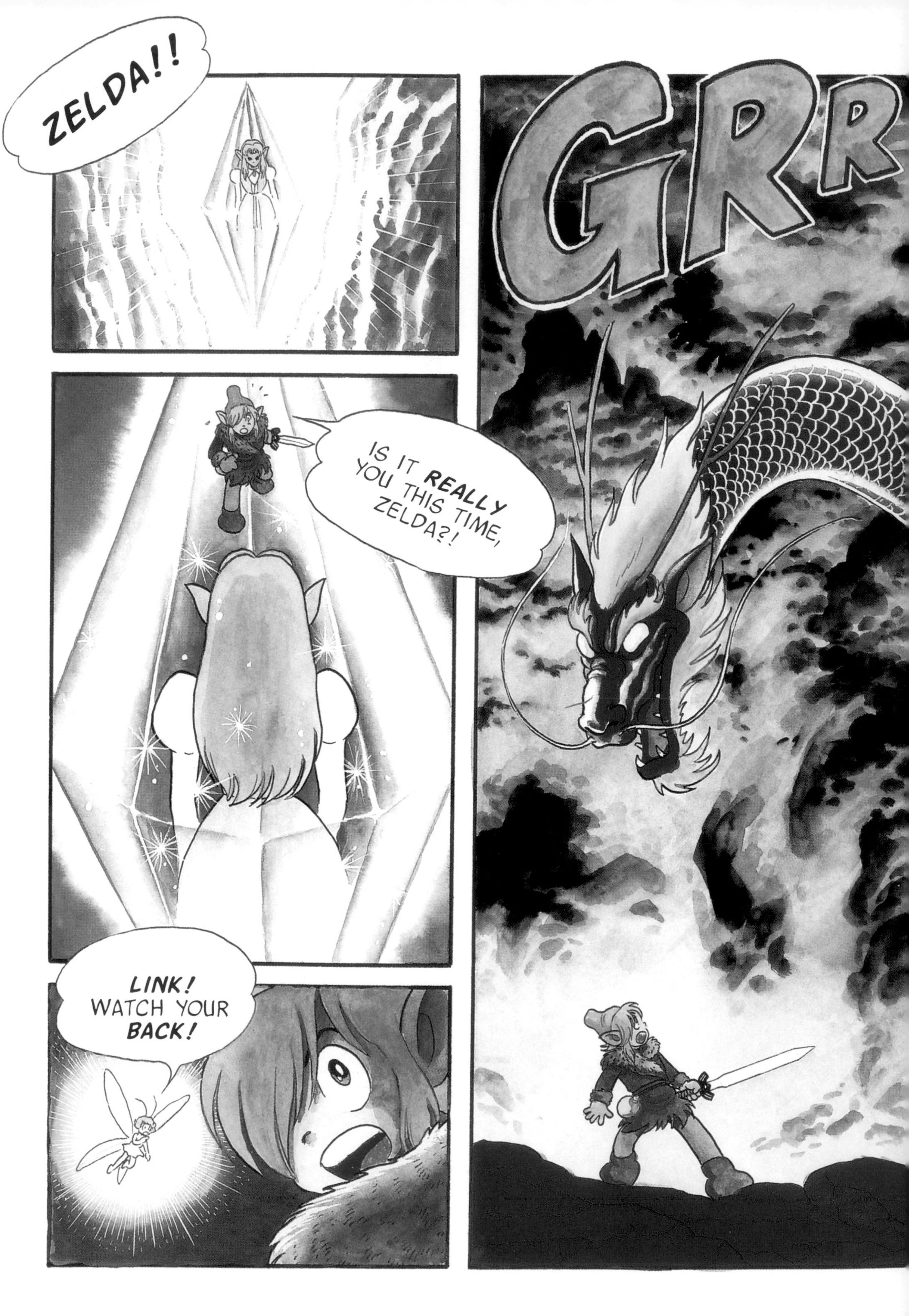
ZELDA!!
IS IT REALLY YOU THIS TIME, ZELDA?!
LINK! WATCH YOUR BACK!
GRR

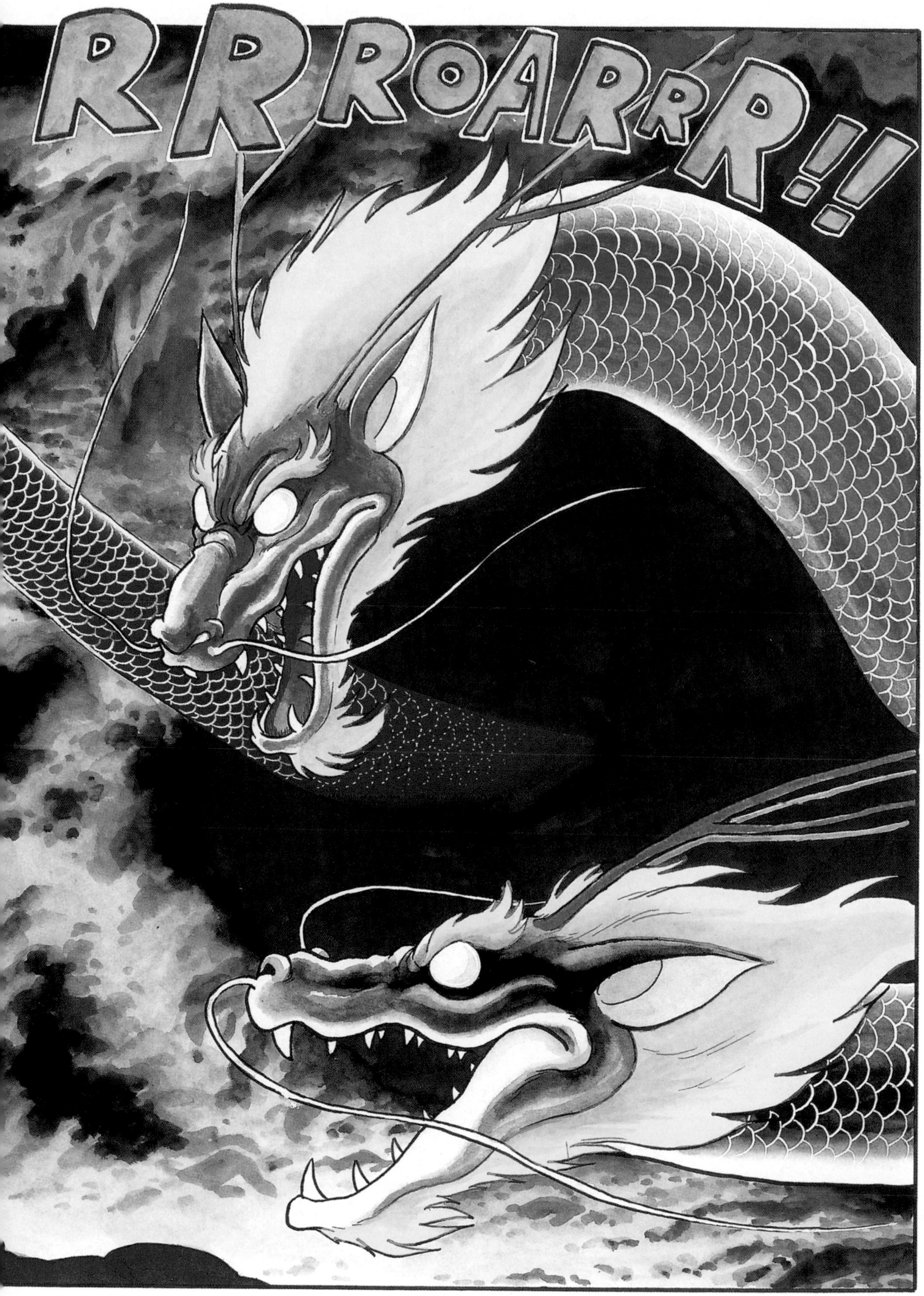
RRROARRRR!!

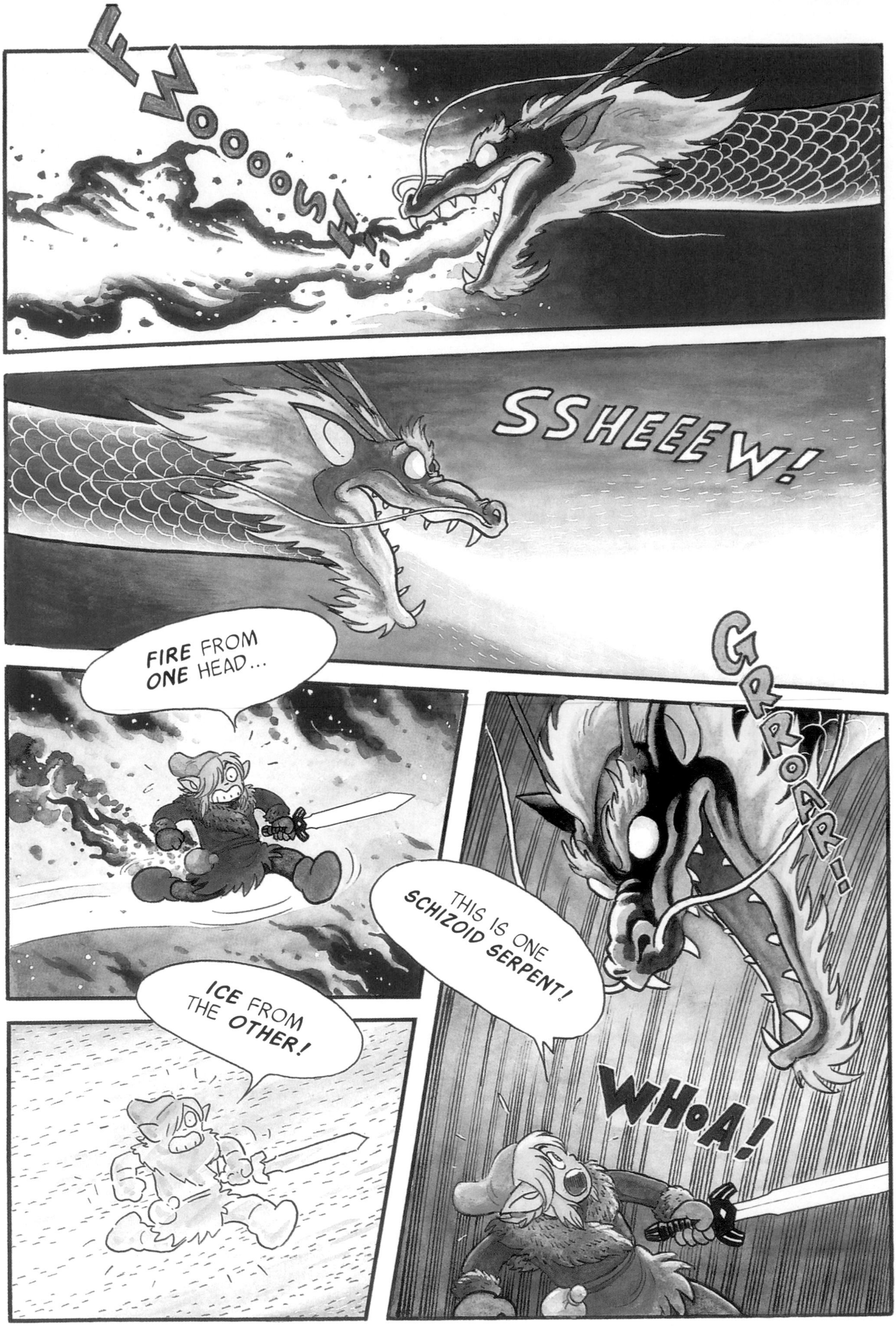
FWOOOOSH!!
SSHEEEW!
GRROAR!!
FIRE FROM ONE HEAD...
ICE FROM THE OTHER!
THIS IS ONE SCHIZOID SERPENT!
WHOA!

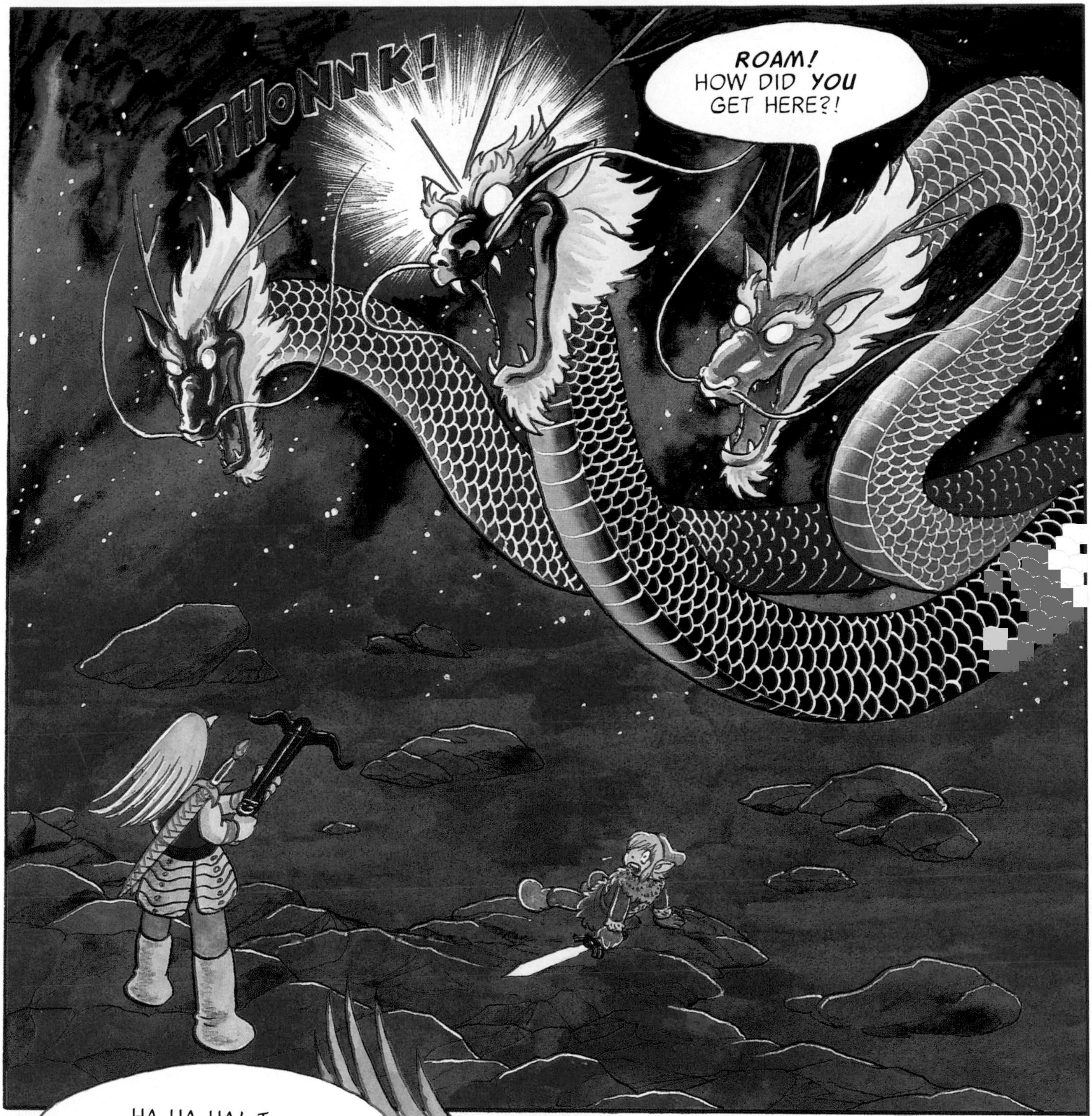
THONNK!
ROAM! HOW DID YOU GET HERE?!

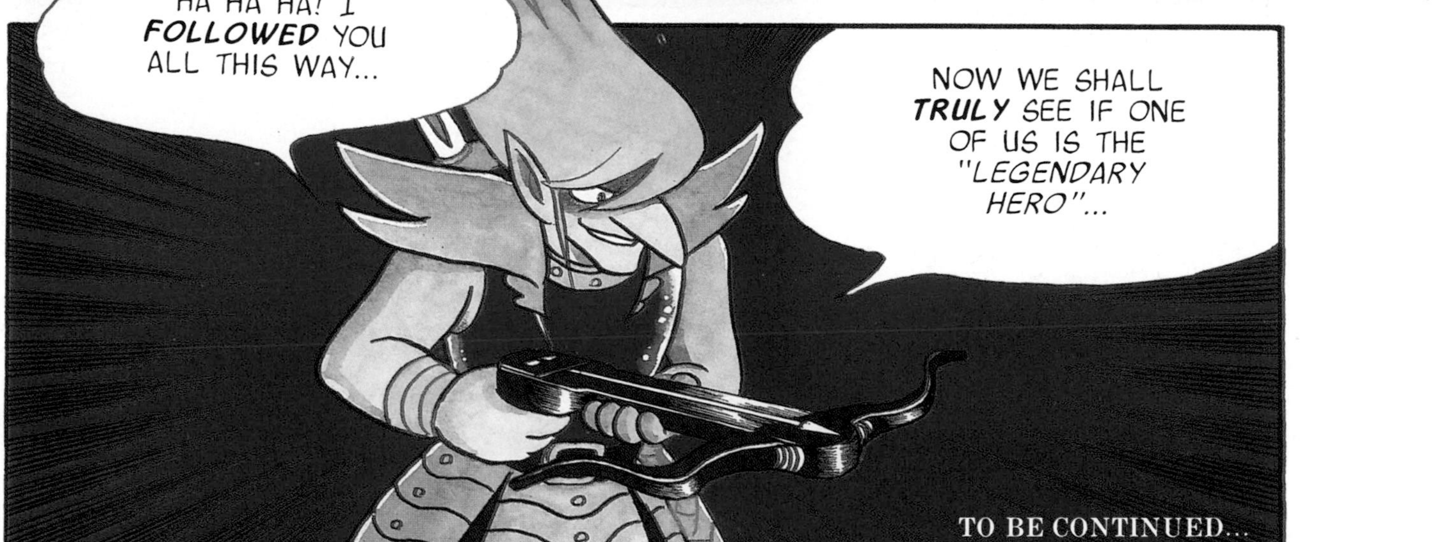
HA HA HA! I FOLLOWED YOU ALL THIS WAY...
NOW WE SHALL TRULY SEE IF ONE OF US IS THE "LEGENDARY HERO"...
TO BE CONTINUED...

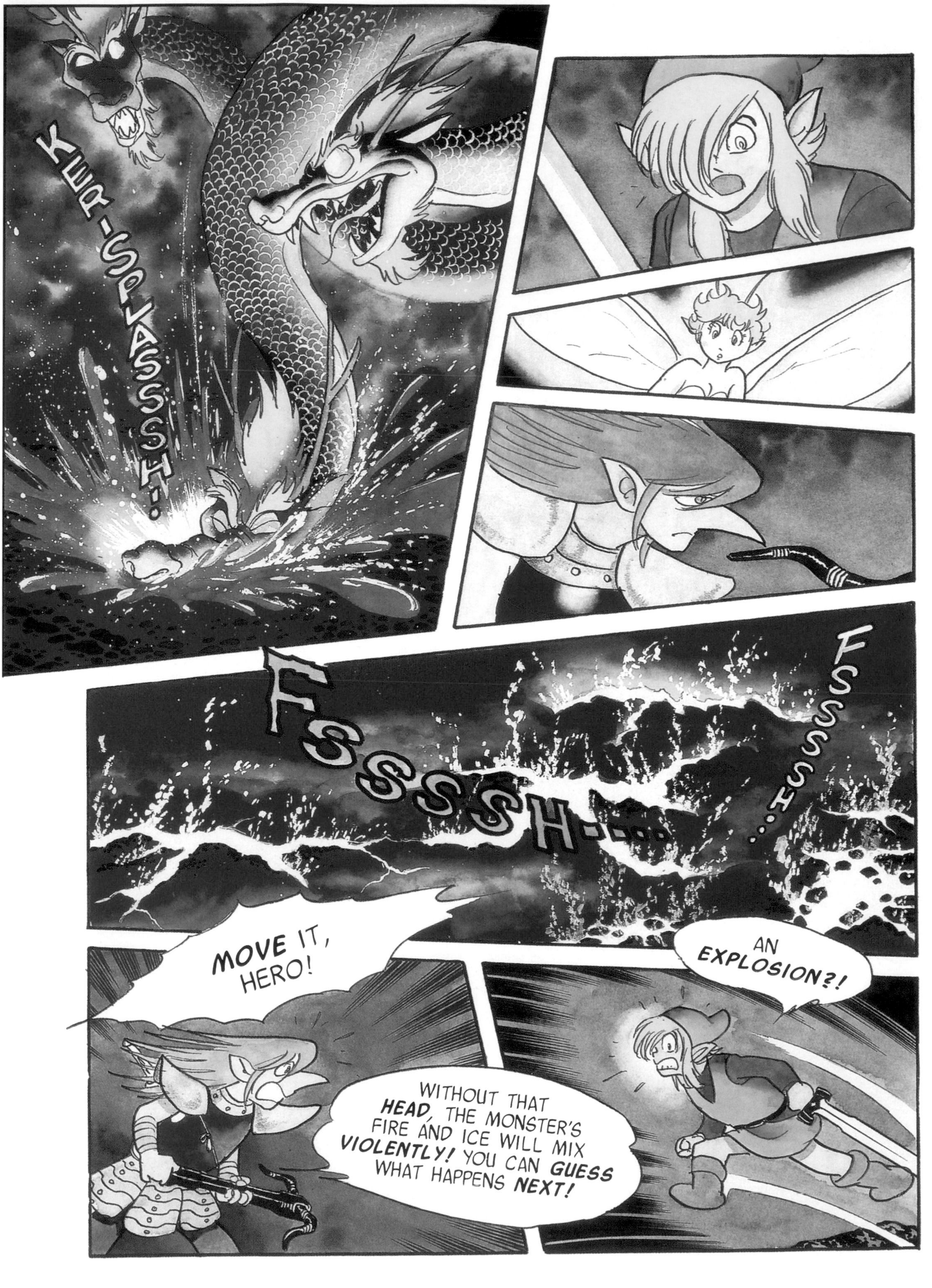
KER-SPLASSSH!
FSSSSH...
FSSSSSH...
MOVE IT, HERO!
WITHOUT THAT HEAD, THE MONSTER'S FIRE AND ICE WILL MIX VIOLENTLY! YOU CAN GUESS WHAT HAPPENS NEXT!
AN EXPLOSION?!

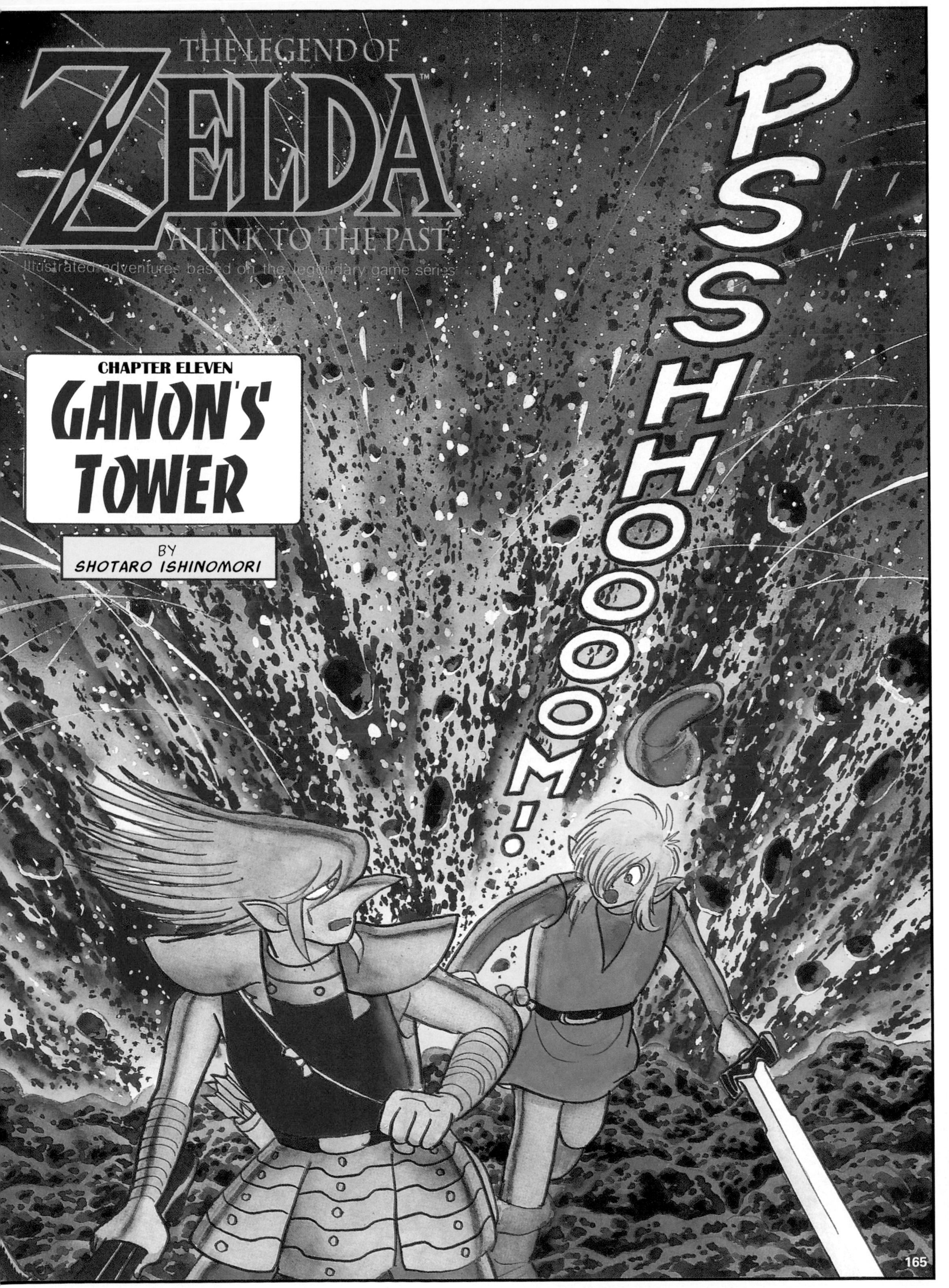
THE LEGEND OF
ZELDA
A LINK TO THE PAST
Illustrated adventures based on the legendary game series
CHAPTER ELEVEN
GANON'S TOWER
BY
SHOTARO ISHINOMORI
PSSHHOOOOOM!

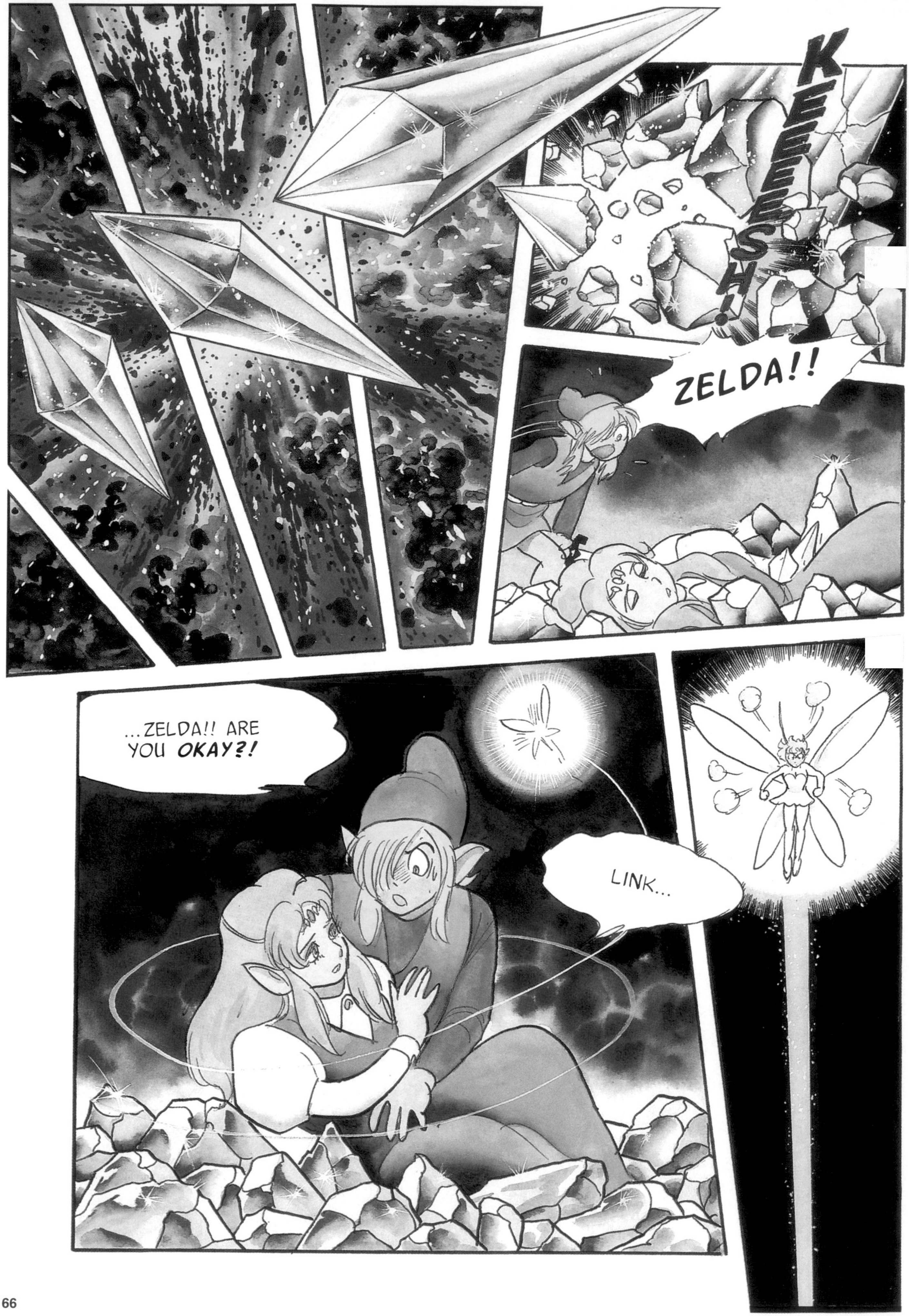
KEEEESH!
ZELDA!!
...ZELDA!! ARE YOU OKAY?!
LINK...

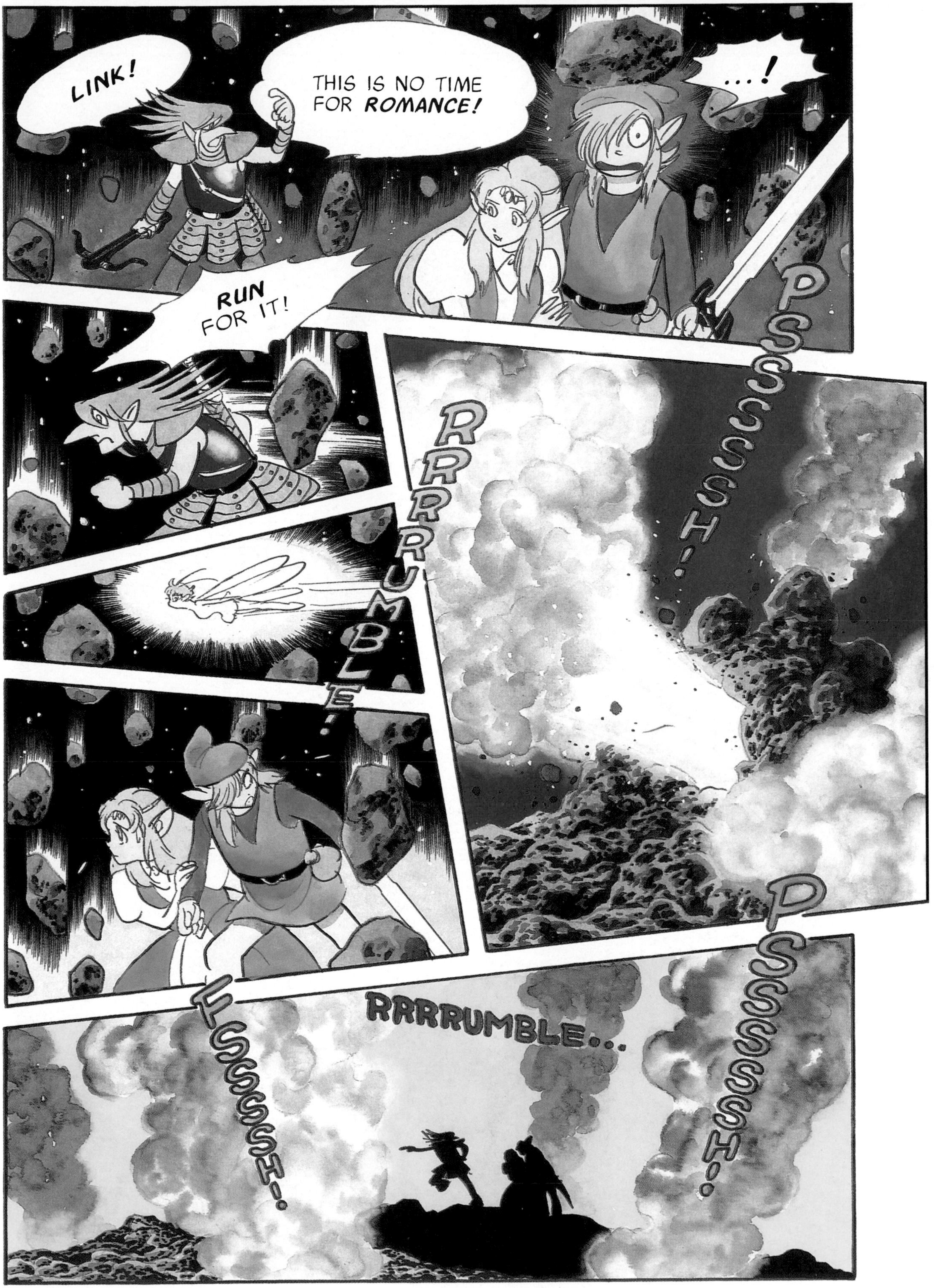
LINK!
THIS IS NO TIME FOR ROMANCE!
...!
RUN FOR IT!
PSSSSSSH!
RRRRRUMBLE!
PSSSSSSSSH!
FSSSSSH!
RRRRUMBLE...

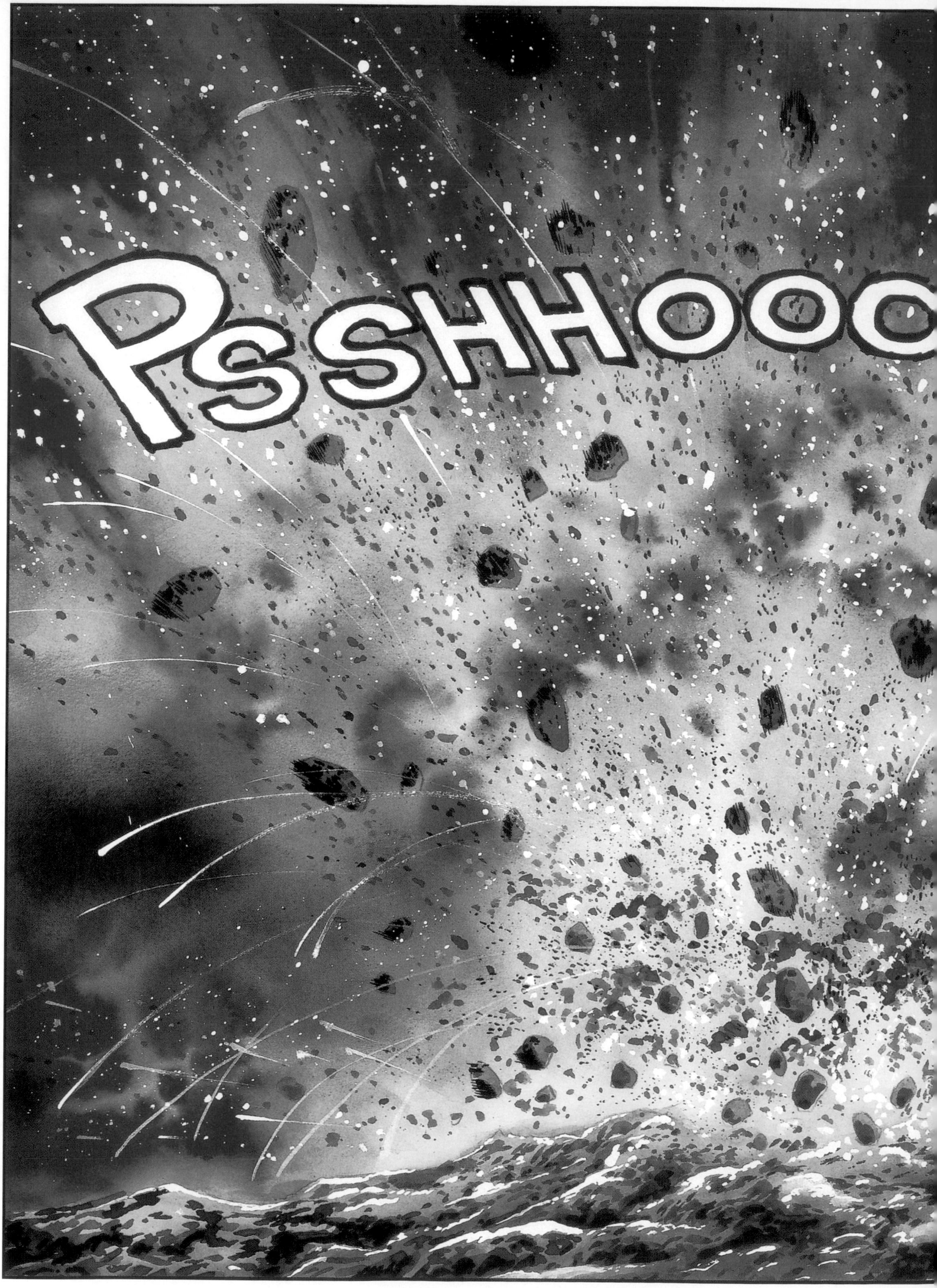
PSSHHOOO

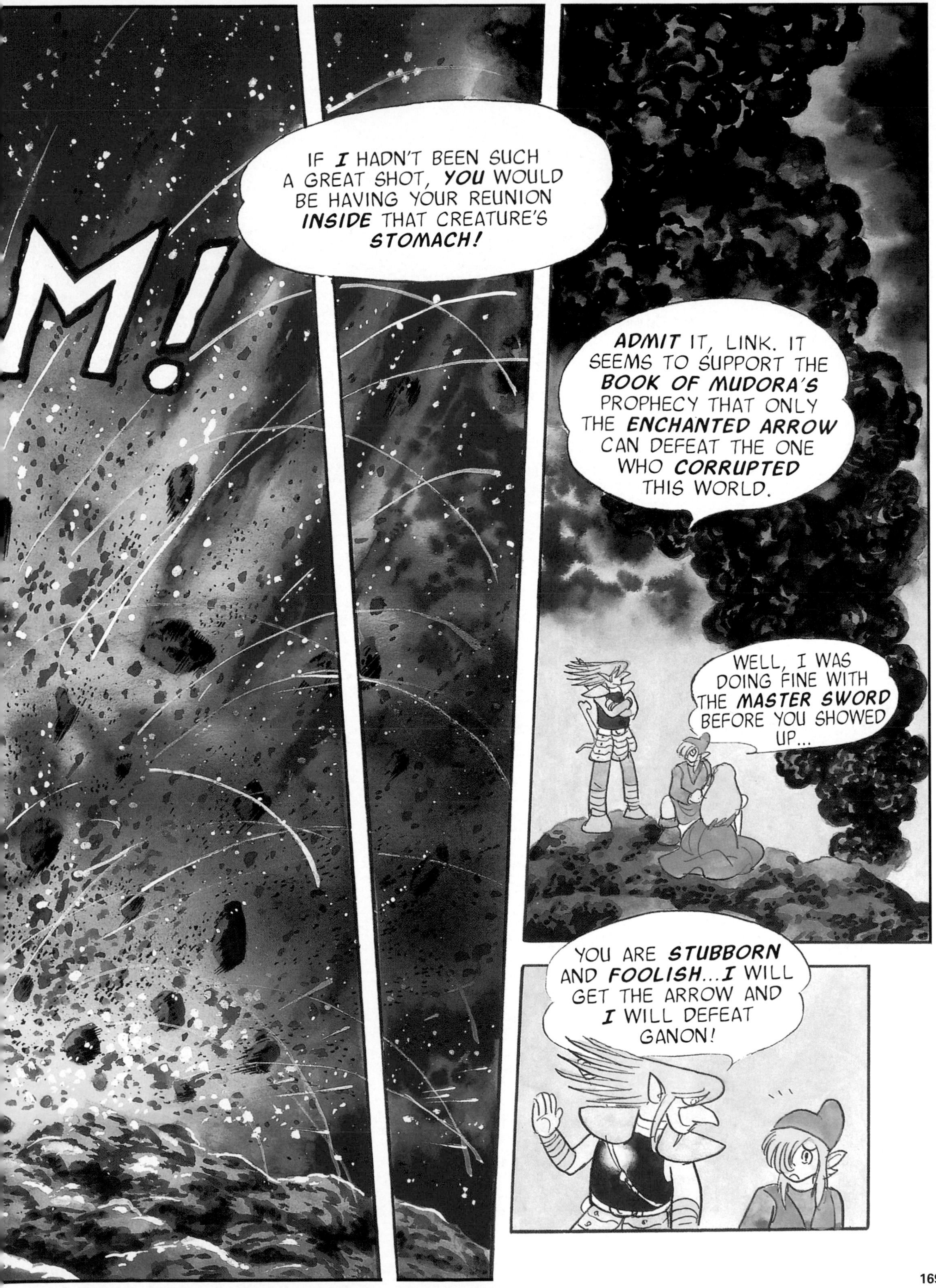
M!
IF I HADN'T BEEN SUCH A GREAT SHOT, YOU WOULD BE HAVING YOUR REUNION INSIDE THAT CREATURE'S STOMACH!
ADMIT IT, LINK. IT SEEMS TO SUPPORT THE BOOK OF MUDORA'S PROPHECY THAT ONLY THE ENCHANTED ARROW CAN DEFEAT THE ONE WHO CORRUPTED THIS WORLD.
WELL, I WAS DOING FINE WITH THE MASTER SWORD BEFORE YOU SHOWED UP...
YOU ARE STUBBORN AND FOOLISH...I WILL GET THE ARROW AND I WILL DEFEAT GANON!

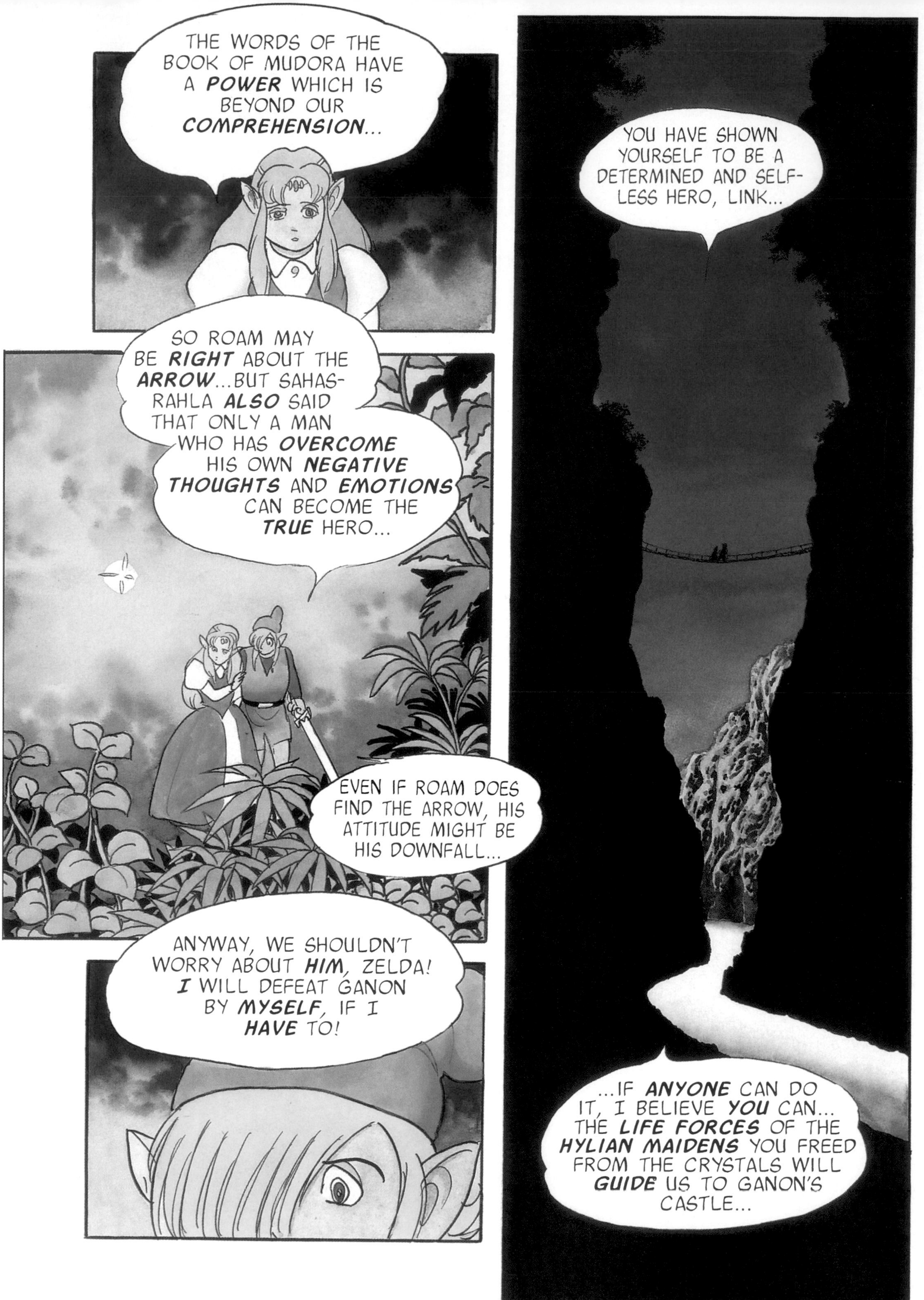
THE WORDS OF THE BOOK OF MUDORA HAVE A POWER WHICH IS BEYOND OUR COMPREHENSION...
SO ROAM MAY BE RIGHT ABOUT THE ARROW...BUT SAHASRAHLA ALSO SAID THAT ONLY A MAN WHO HAS OVERCOME HIS OWN NEGATIVE THOUGHTS AND EMOTIONS CAN BECOME THE TRUE HERO...
EVEN IF ROAM DOES FIND THE ARROW, HIS ATTITUDE MIGHT BE HIS DOWNFALL...
ANYWAY, WE SHOULDN'T WORRY ABOUT HIM, ZELDA! I WILL DEFEAT GANON BY MYSELF, IF I HAVE TO!
YOU HAVE SHOWN YOURSELF TO BE A DETERMINED AND SELF-LESS HERO, LINK...
...IF ANYONE CAN DO IT, I BELIEVE YOU CAN... THE LIFE FORCES OF THE HYLIAN MAIDENS YOU FREED FROM THE CRYSTALS WILL GUIDE US TO GANON'S CASTLE...

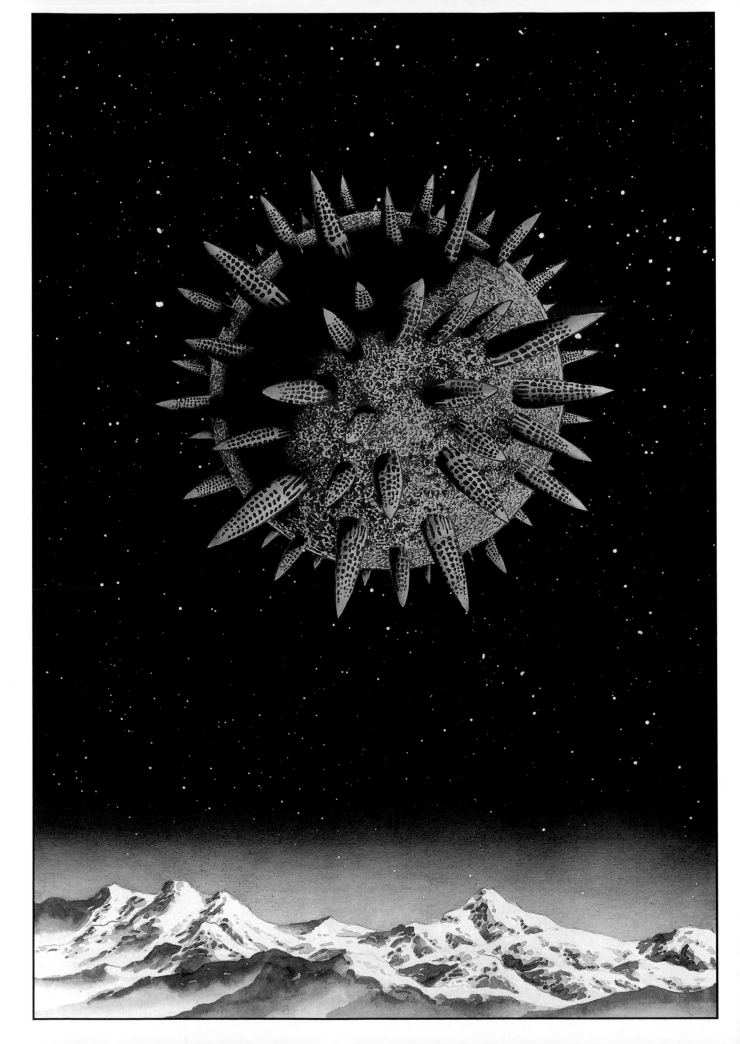

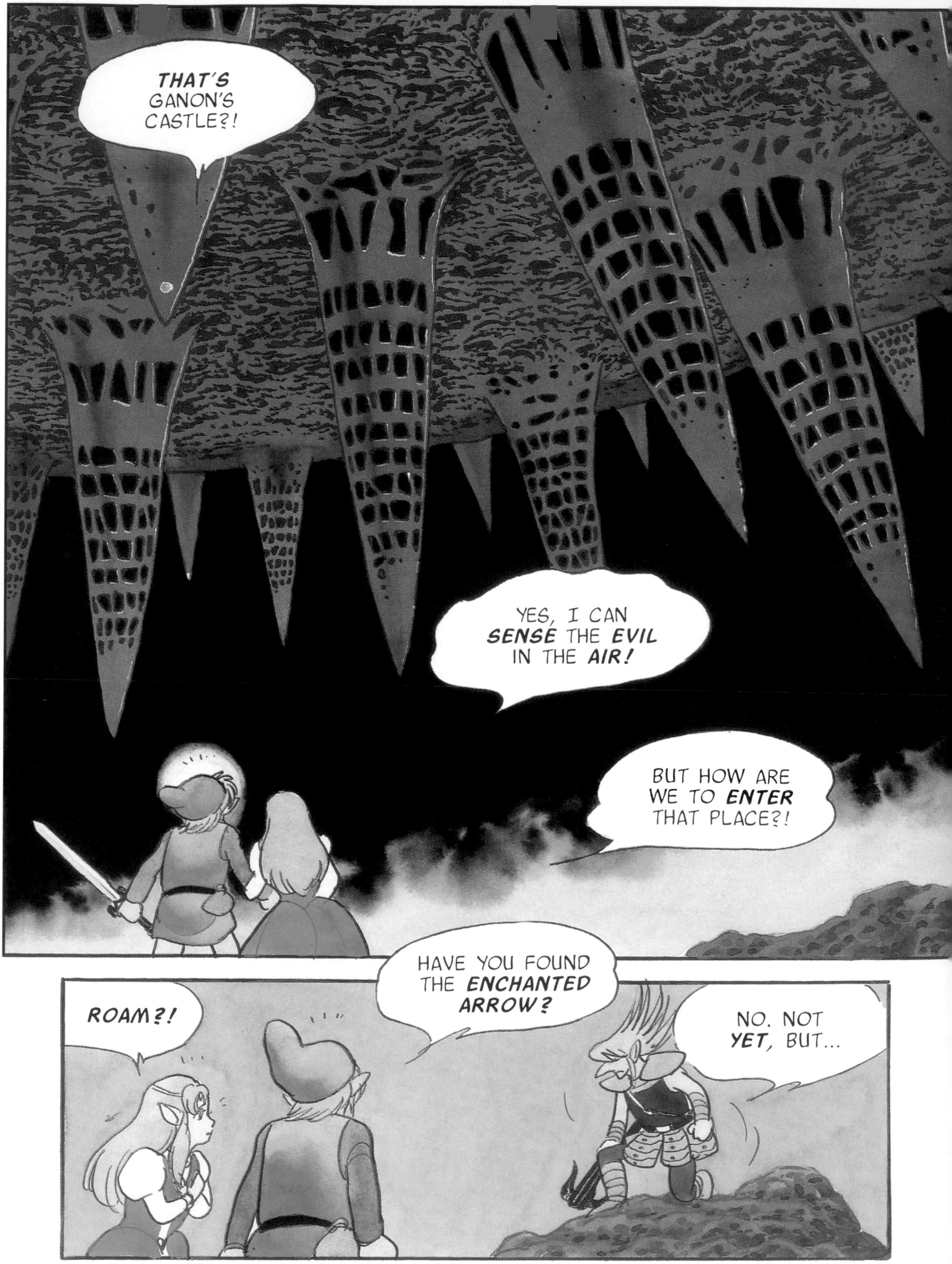
THAT'S GANON'S CASTLE?!
YES, I CAN SENSE THE EVIL IN THE AIR!
BUT HOW ARE WE TO ENTER THAT PLACE?!
ROAM?!
HAVE YOU FOUND THE ENCHANTED ARROW?
NO. NOT YET, BUT...

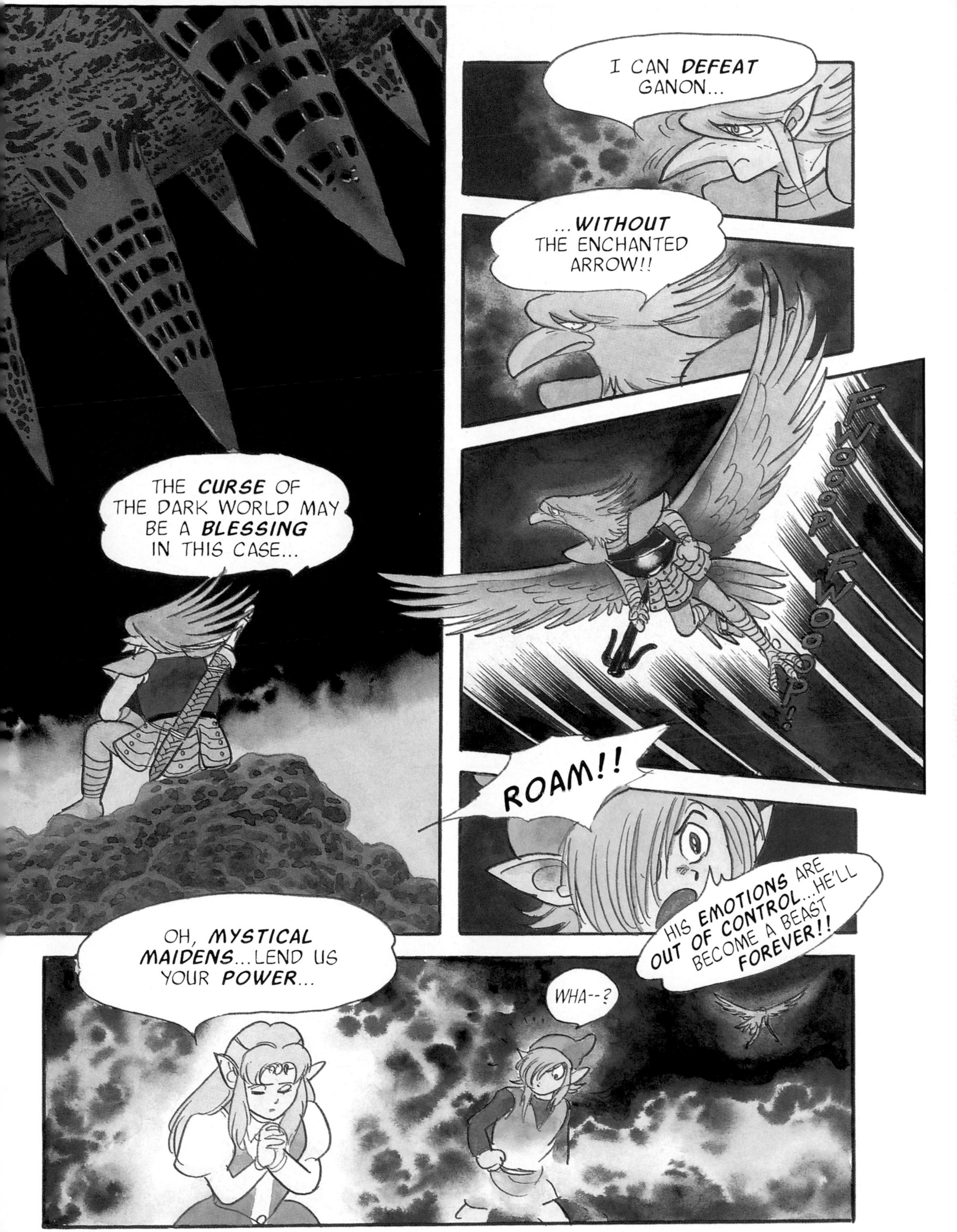
THE CURSE OF THE DARK WORLD MAY BE A BLESSING IN THIS CASE...
I CAN DEFEAT GANON...
...WITHOUT THE ENCHANTED ARROW!!
FWOOOP FWOOOOP!!
ROAM!!
HIS EMOTIONS ARE OUT OF CONTROL...HE'LL BECOME A BEAST FOREVER!!
OH, MYSTICAL MAIDENS...LEND US YOUR POWER...
WHA--?

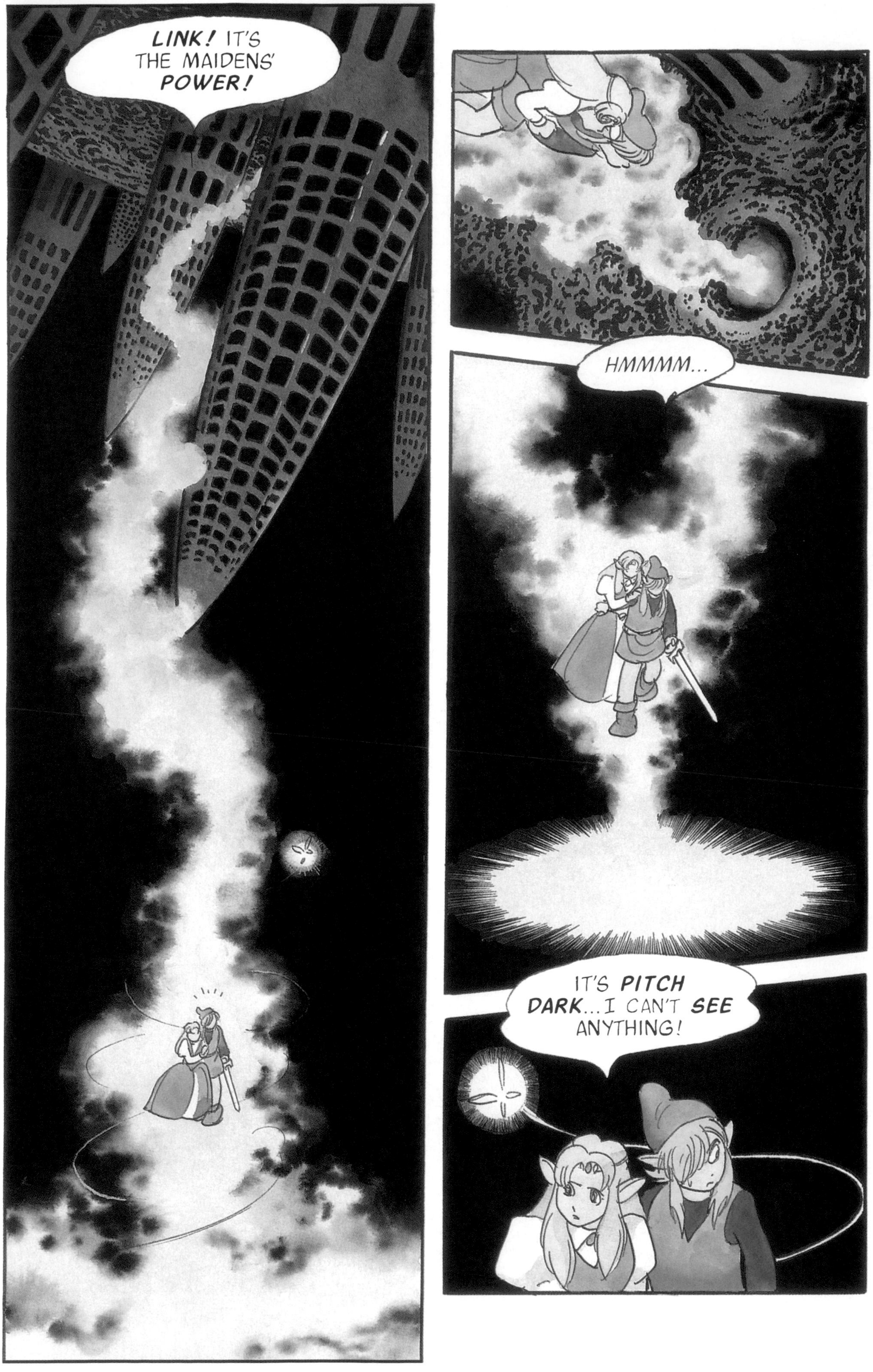
LINK! IT'S THE MAIDENS' POWER!
HMMMM...
IT'S PITCH DARK...I CAN'T SEE ANYTHING!

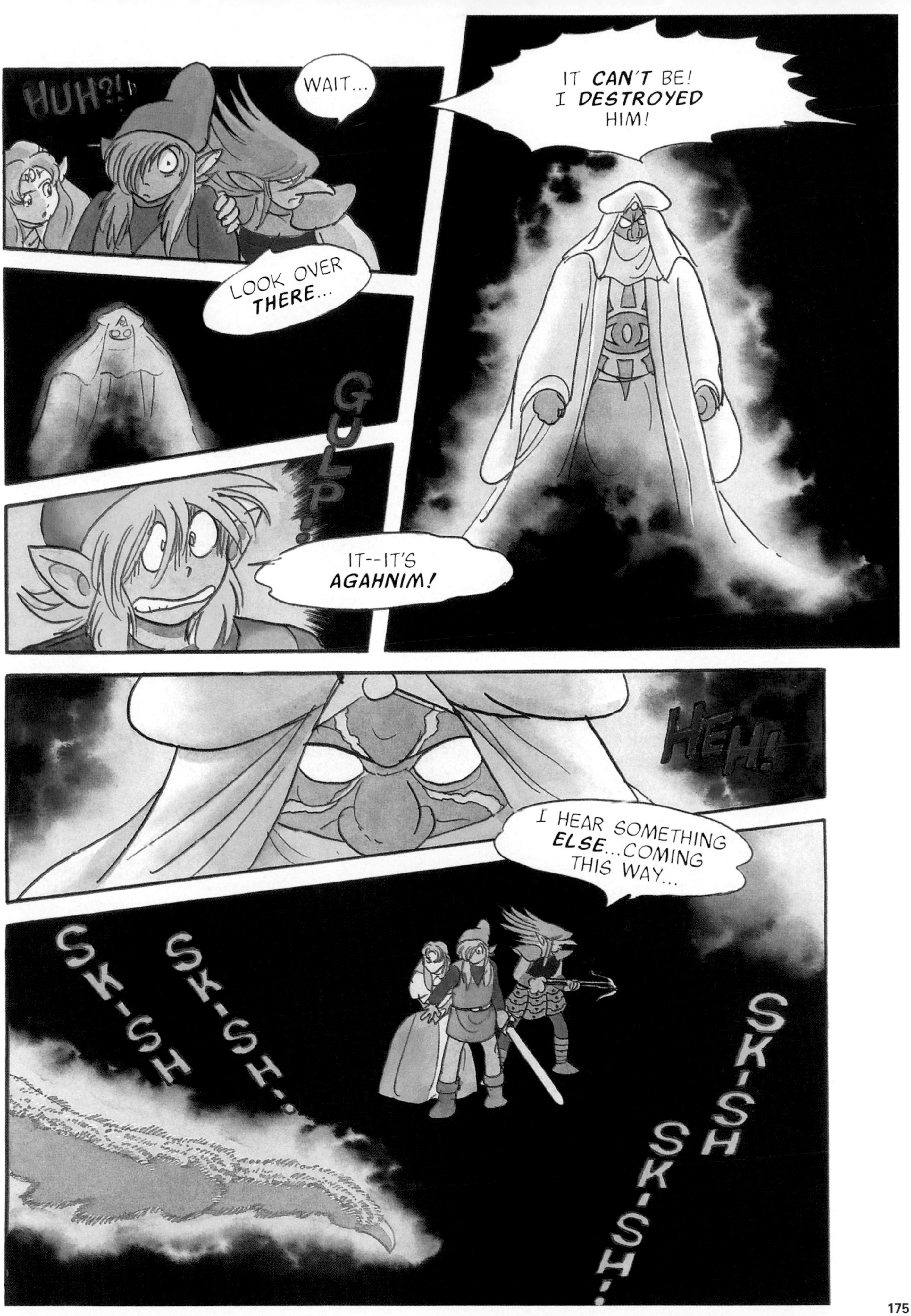
HUH?!
WAIT...
LOOK OVER THERE...
GULP!
IT--IT'S AGAHNIM!
IT CAN'T BE! I DESTROYED HIM!
HEH!
I HEAR SOMETHING ELSE...COMING THIS WAY...
SK-SH
SK-SH...
SK-SH
SK-SH-SH...

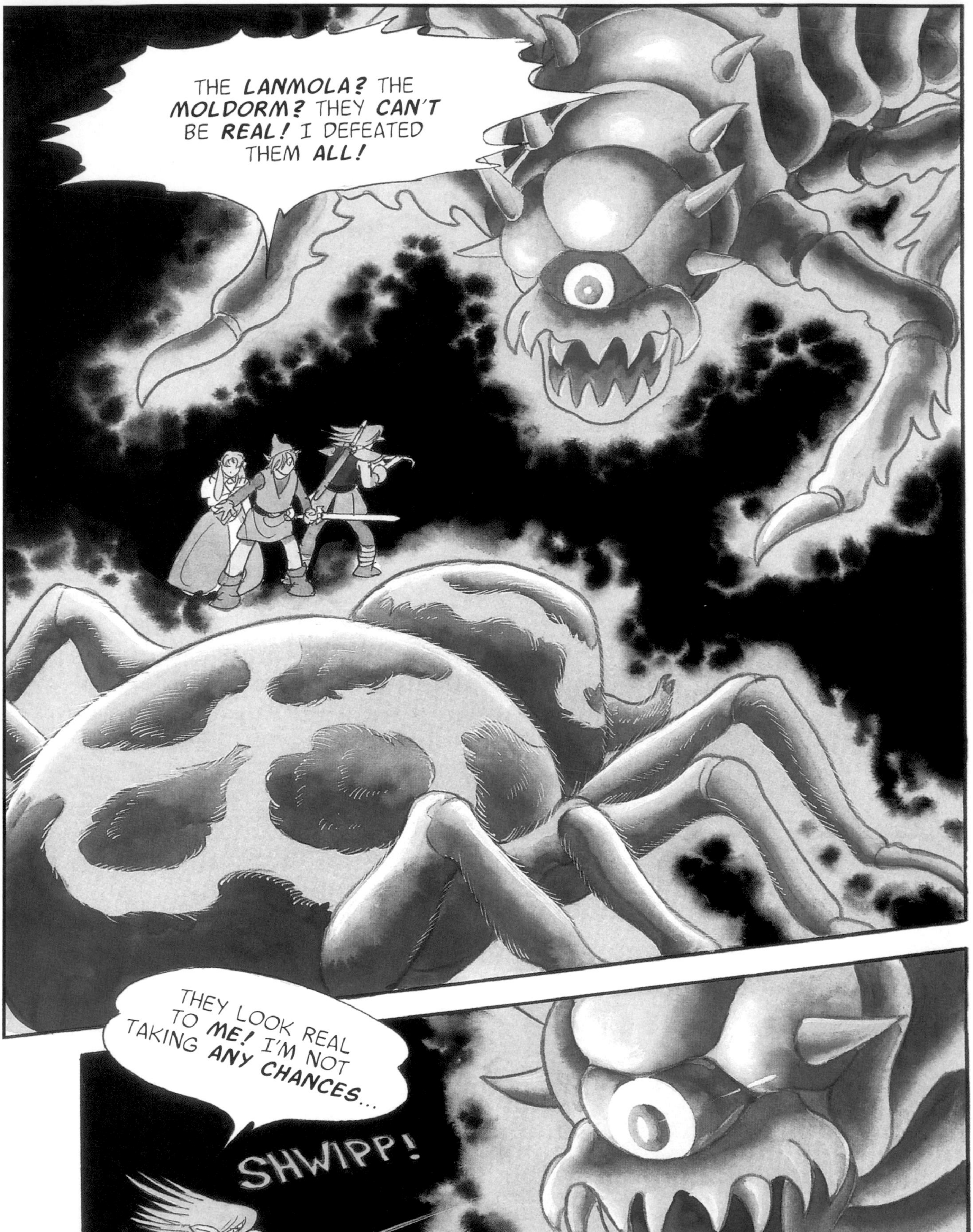
THE LANMOLA? THE MOLDORM? THEY CAN'T BE REAL! I DEFEATED THEM ALL!
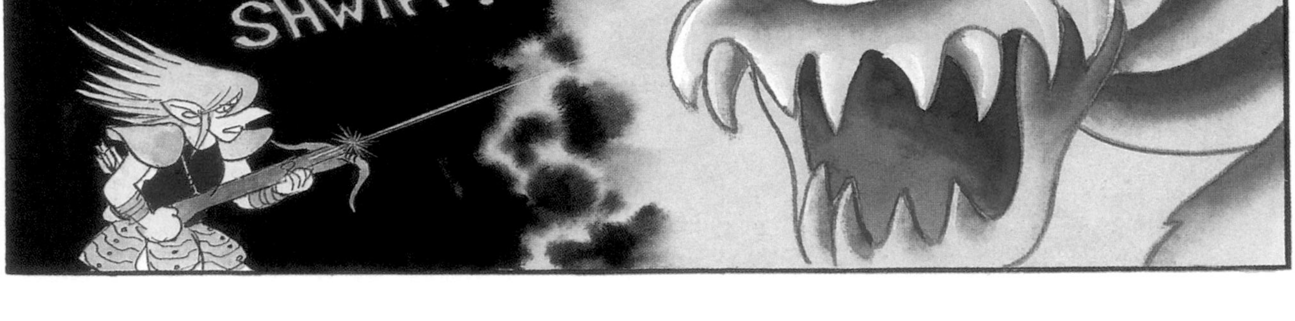
THEY LOOK REAL TO ME! I'M NOT TAKING ANY CHANCES...
SHWIPP!

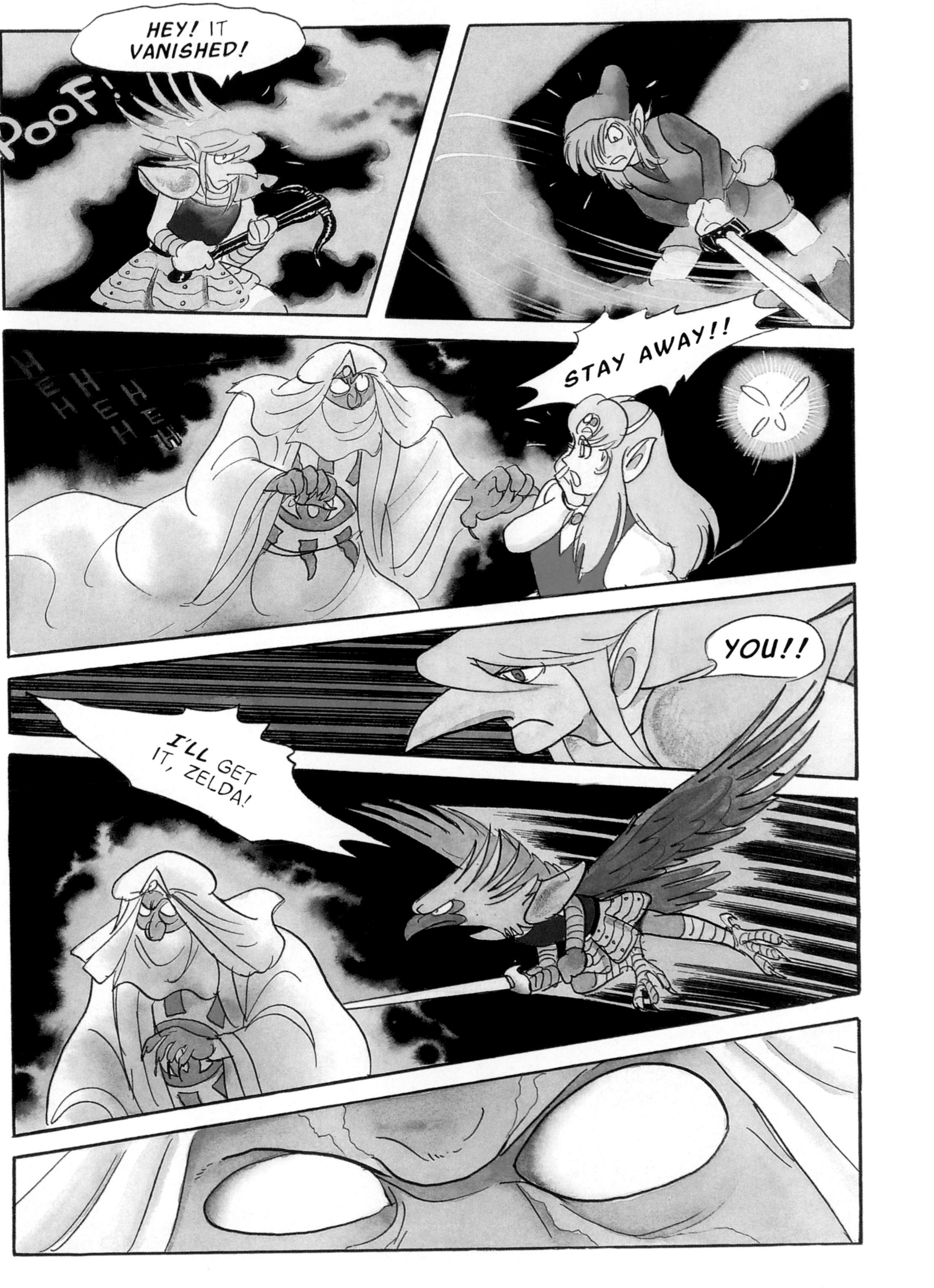
HEY! IT VANISHED!
POOF!
STAY AWAY!!
HEH HEH HEH HEH
YOU!!
I'LL GET IT, ZELDA!

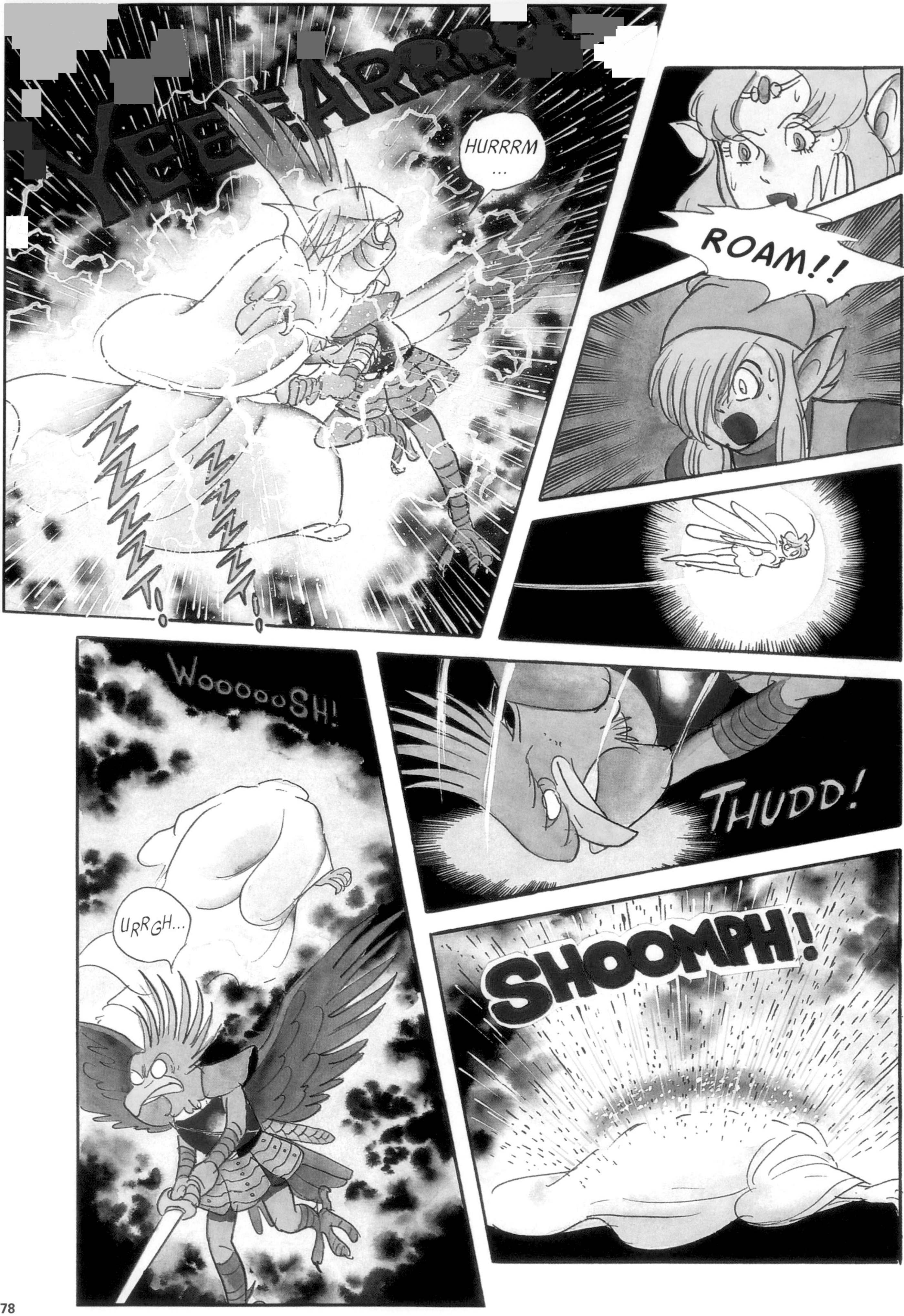
HURRRM ...
ZZZZZT!
ZZZZZT!
ROAM!!
WoooooSH!
URRGH...
THUDD!
SHOOMPH!

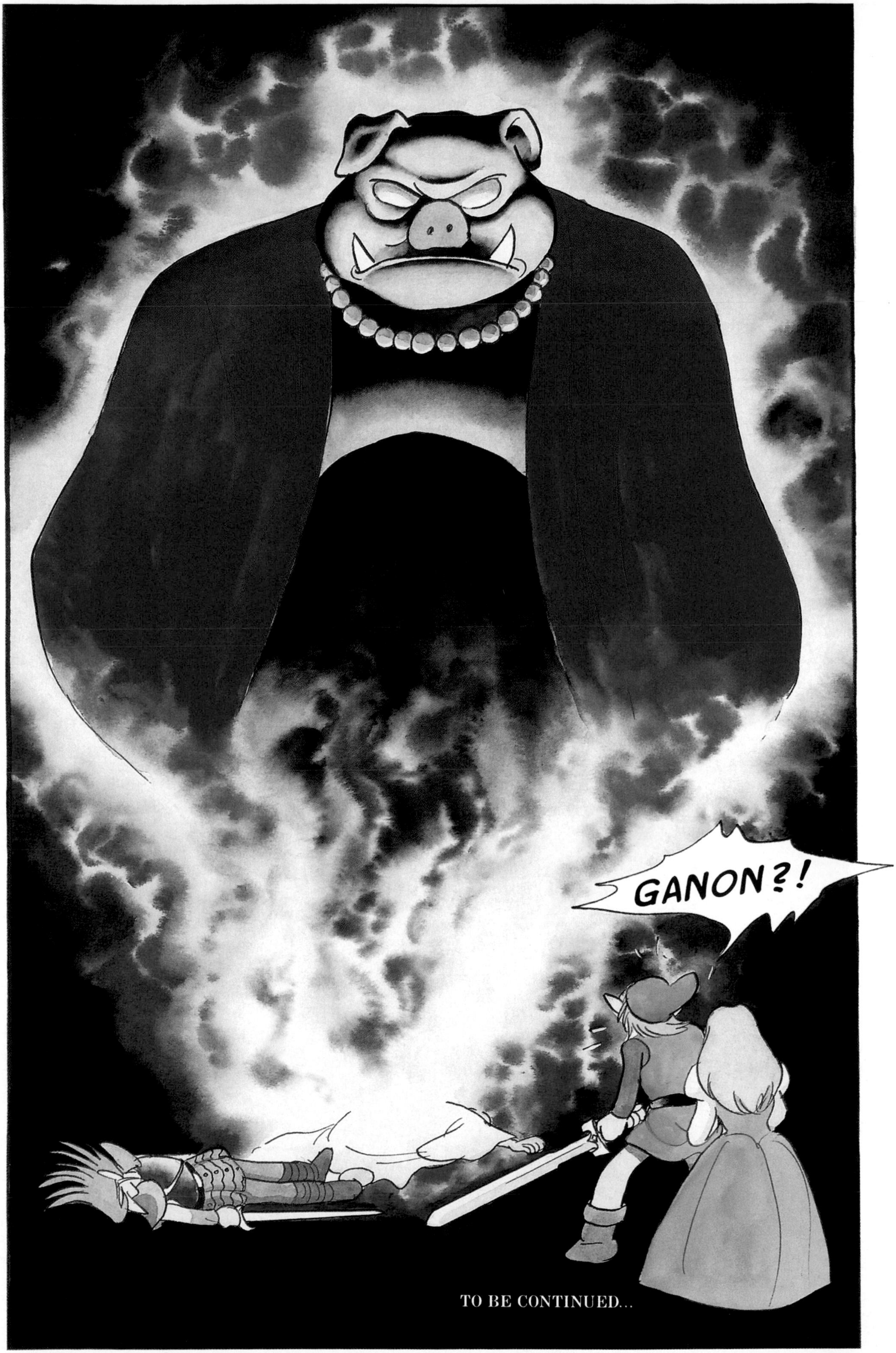
GANON?!
TO BE CONTINUED...

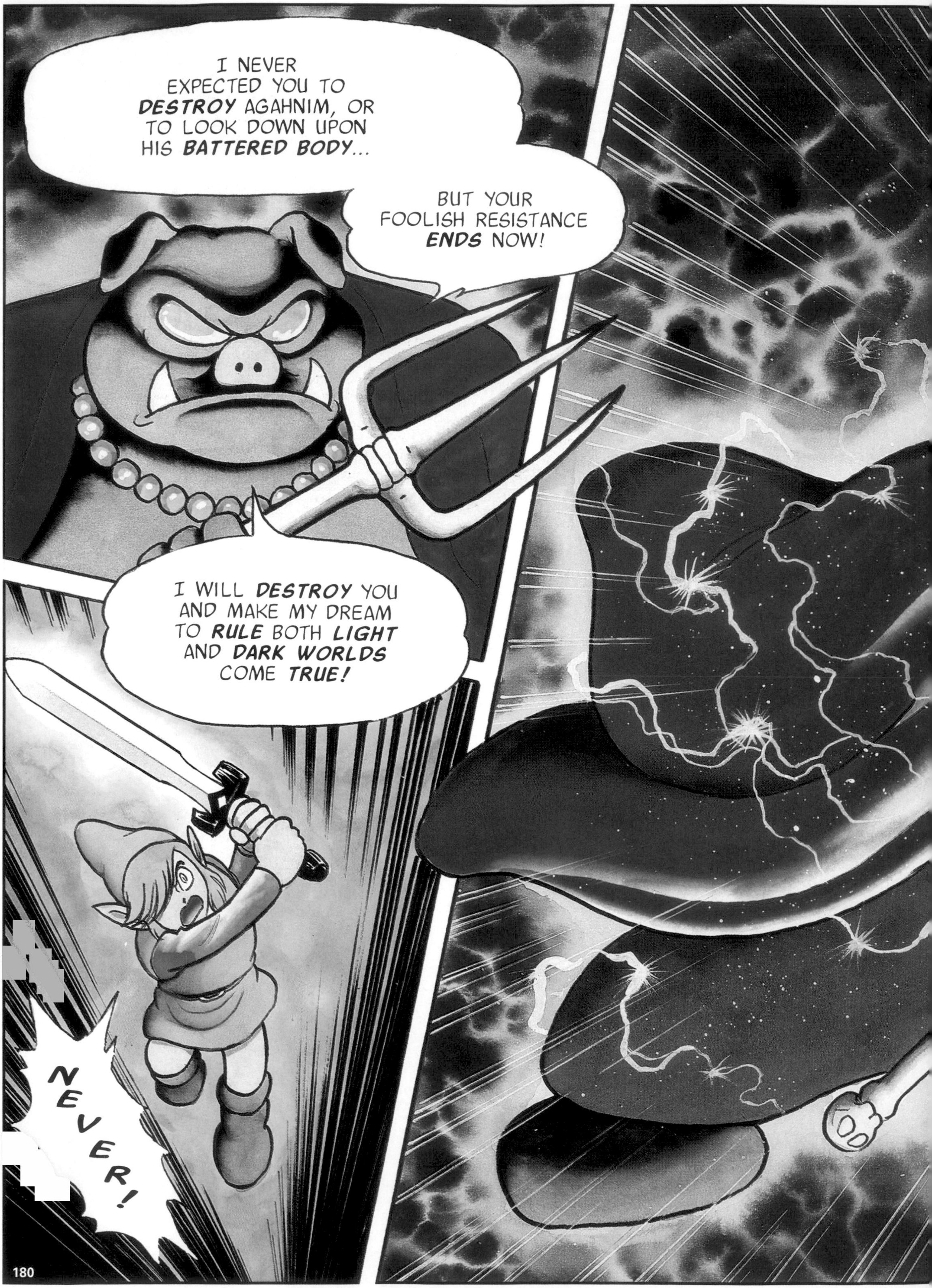
I NEVER EXPECTED YOU TO DESTROY AGAHNIM, OR TO LOOK DOWN UPON HIS BATTERED BODY...
BUT YOUR FOOLISH RESISTANCE ENDS NOW!
I WILL DESTROY YOU AND MAKE MY DREAM TO RULE BOTH LIGHT AND DARK WORLDS COME TRUE!
NEVER!

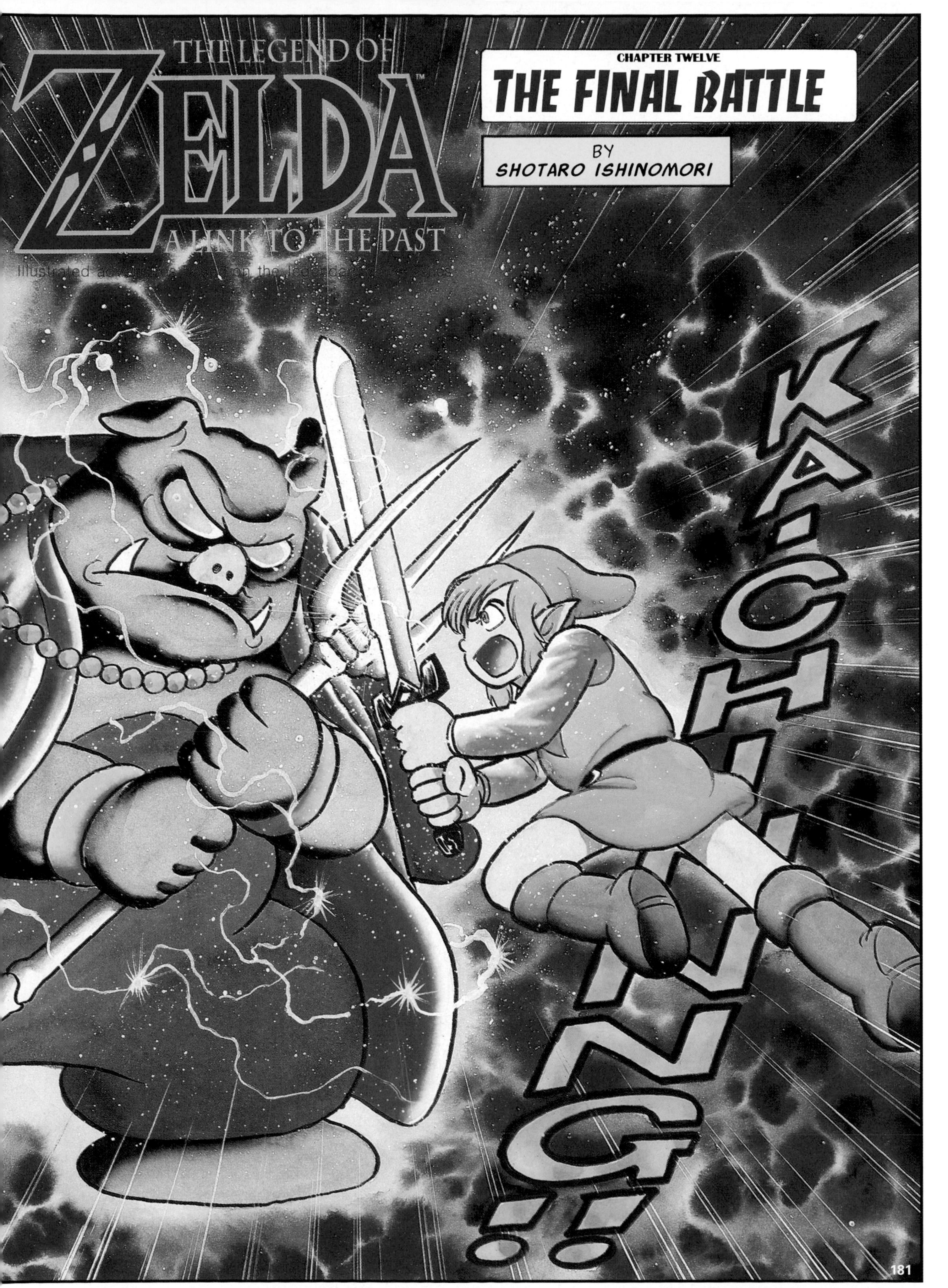
THE LEGEND OF
ZELDA
A LINK TO THE PAST
CHAPTER TWELVE
THE FINAL BATTLE
BY
SHOTARO ISHINOMORI
KA·CHIINNG!!

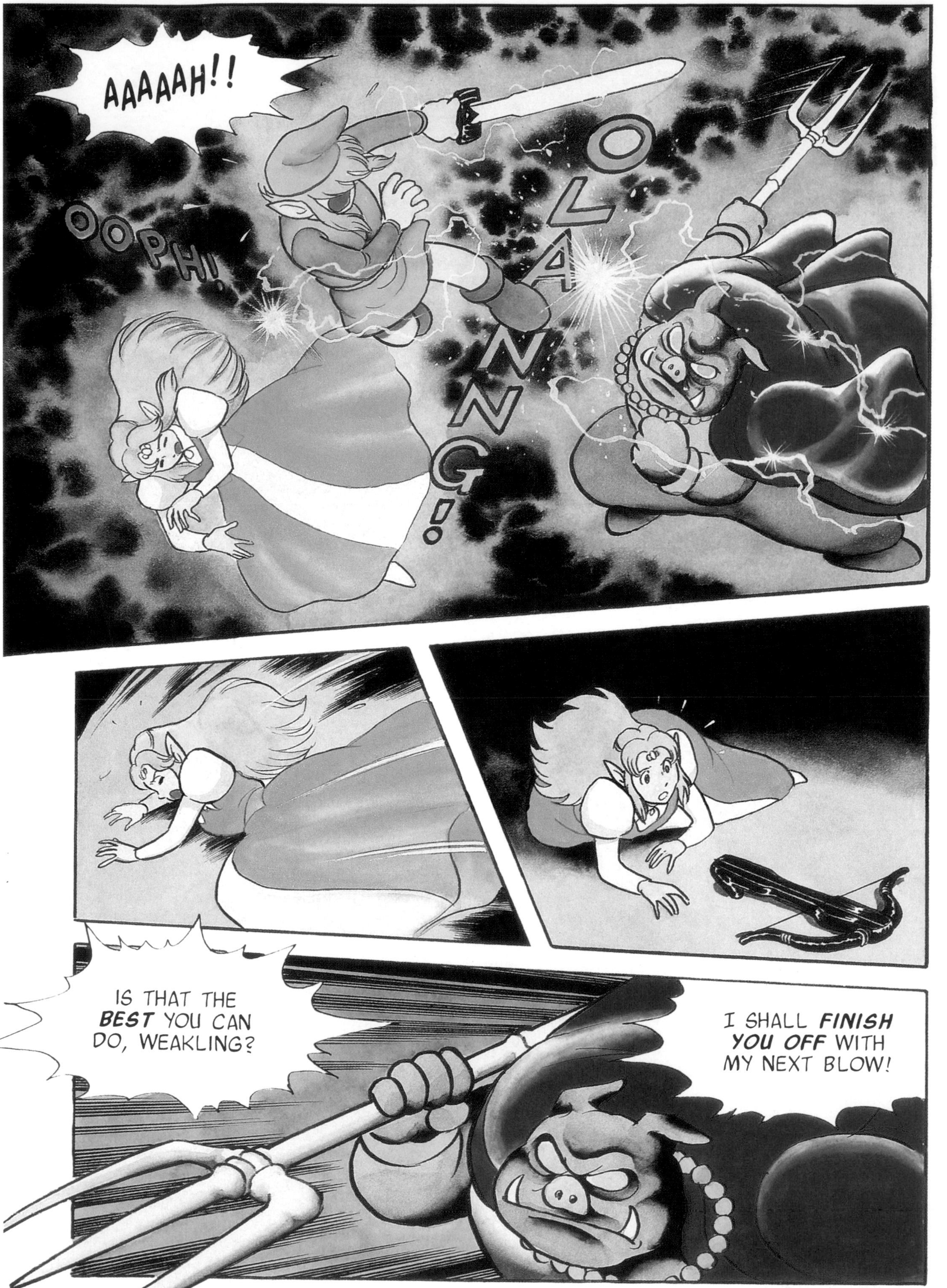
AAAAAH!!
OOPH!
CLAANNNG!
IS THAT THE BEST YOU CAN DO, WEAKLING?
I SHALL FINISH YOU OFF WITH MY NEXT BLOW!

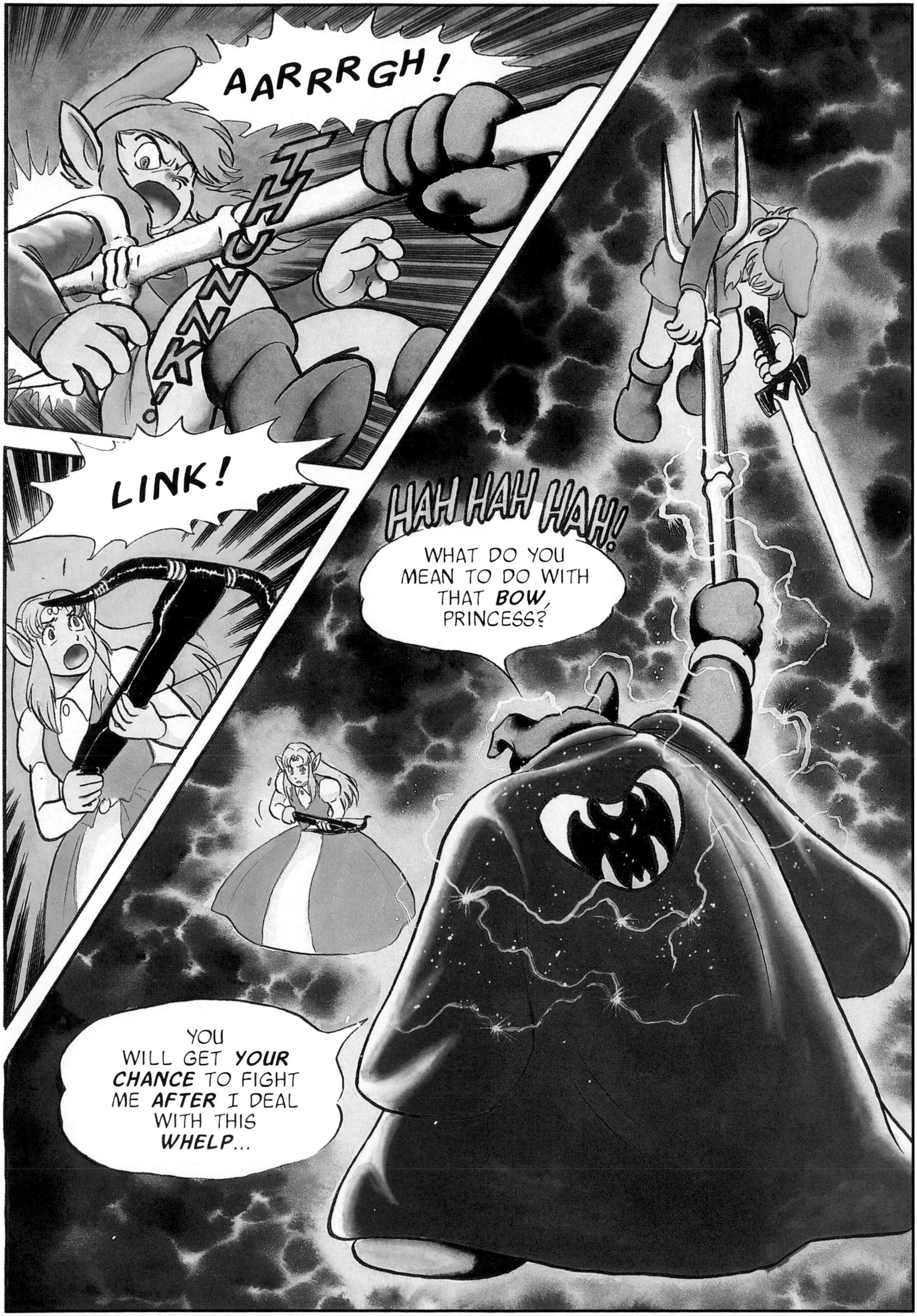
AARRRGH!
THUNK!
LINK!
HAH HAH HAH!
WHAT DO YOU MEAN TO DO WITH THAT BOW, PRINCESS?
YOU WILL GET YOUR CHANCE TO FIGHT ME AFTER I DEAL WITH THIS WHELP...

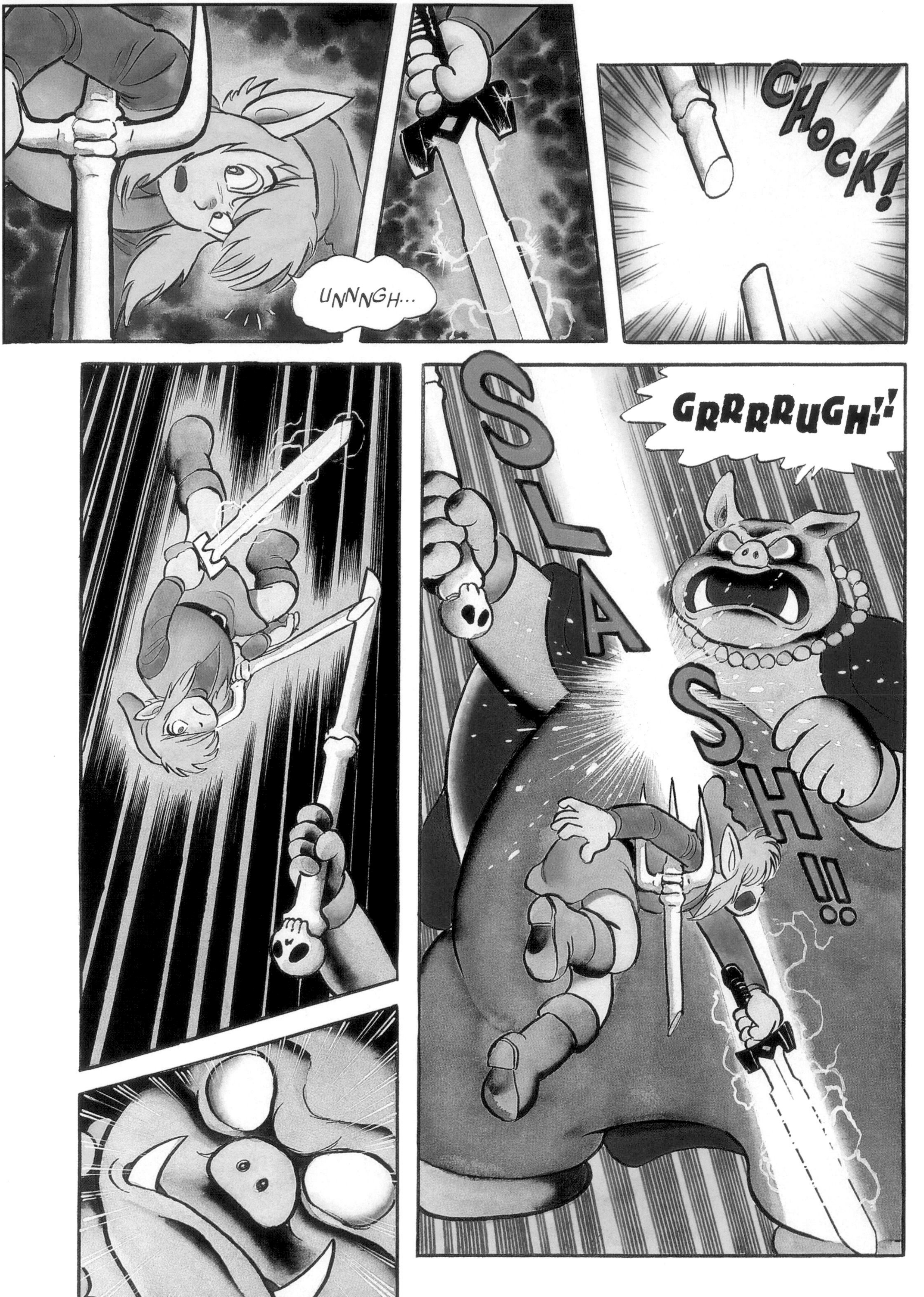
UNNNGH...
CHOCK!
SLASH!!
GRRRRUGH!!

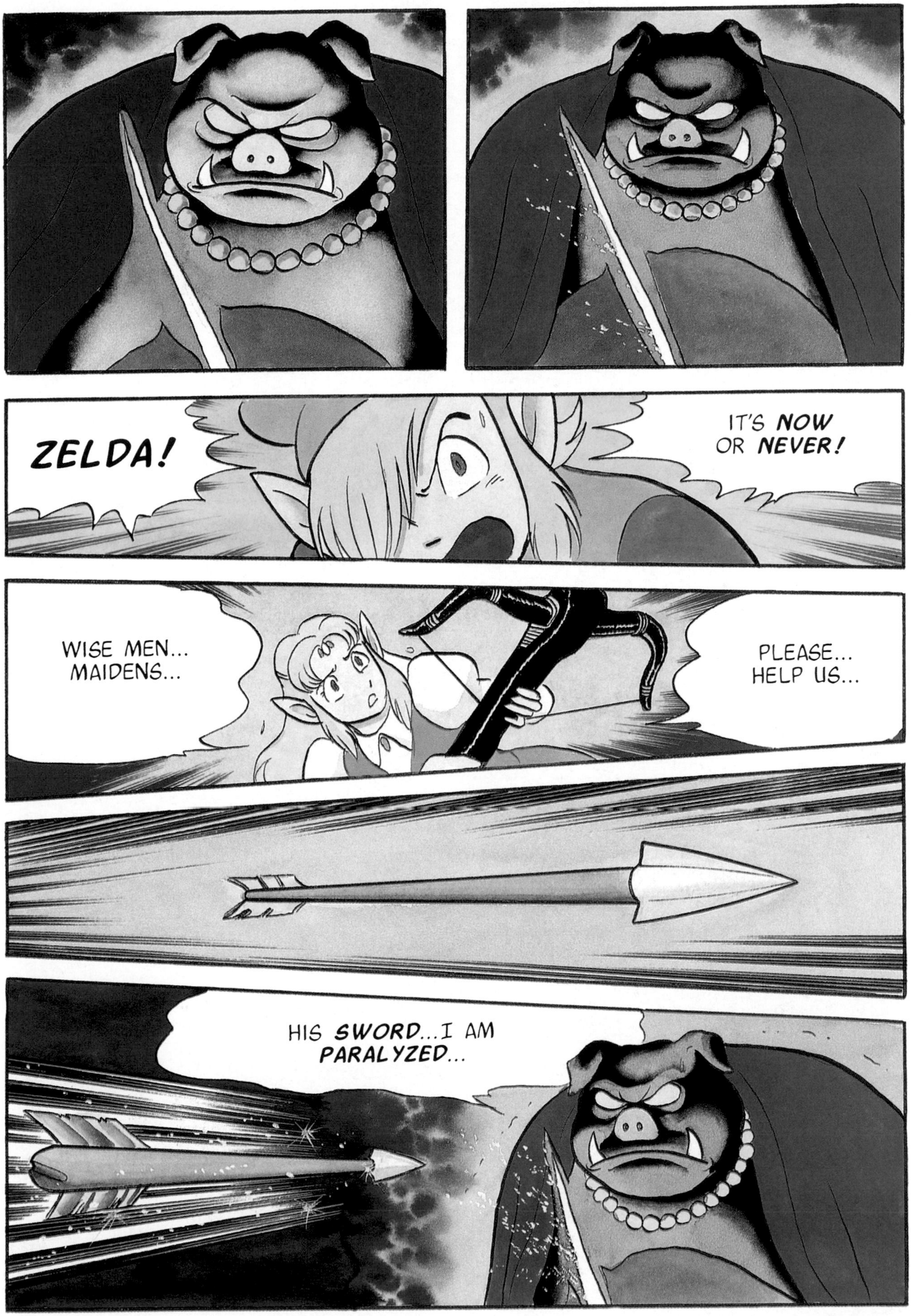
ZELDA!
IT'S NOW OR NEVER!
WISE MEN... MAIDENS...
PLEASE... HELP US...
HIS SWORD...I AM PARALYZED...

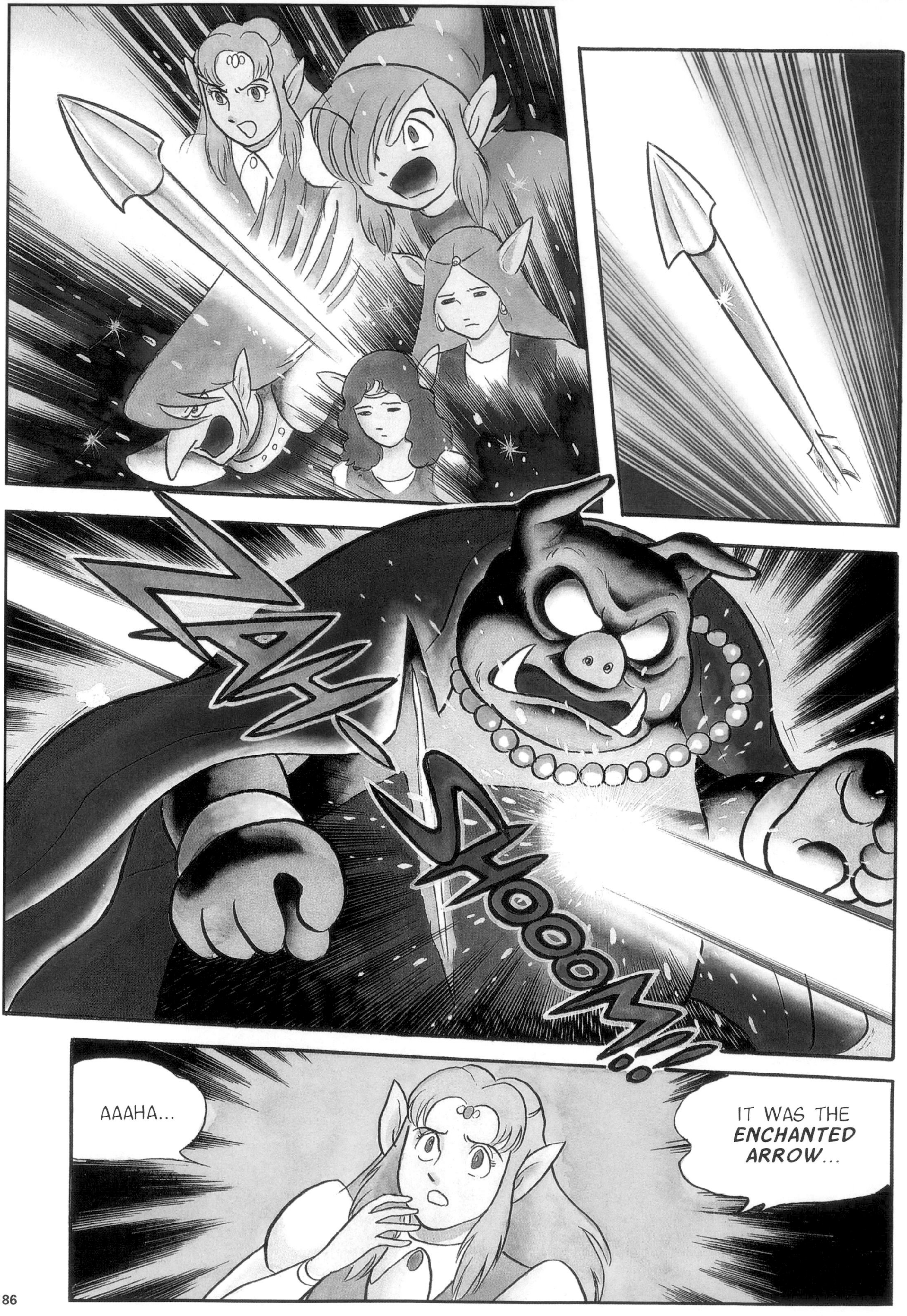
ZASH
SHOOOM!!
AAAHA...
IT WAS THE *ENCHANTED ARROW*...

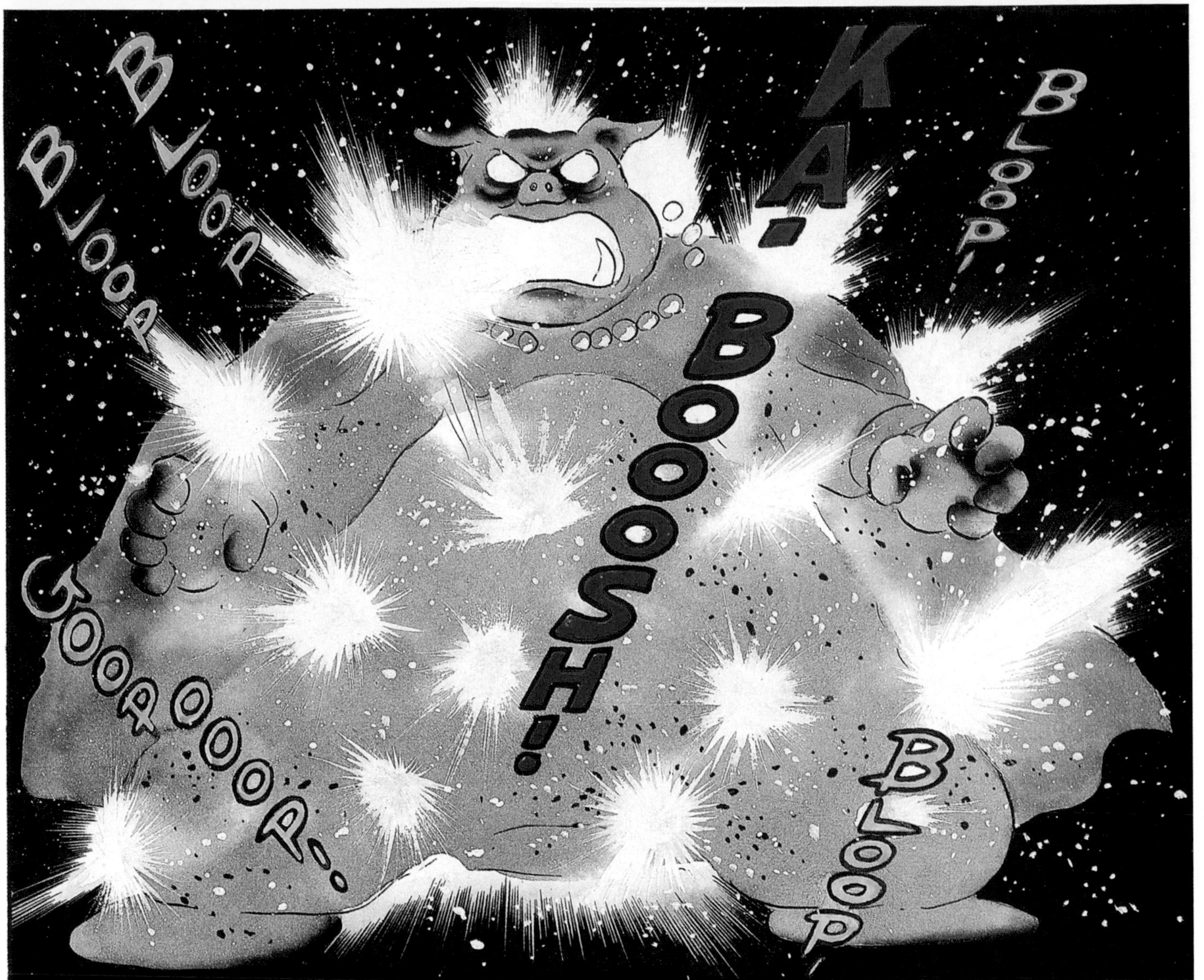
BLOOP
BLOOP
KA-BOOOOSH!
BLOOP!
GOOPOOOOP...
BLOOP!

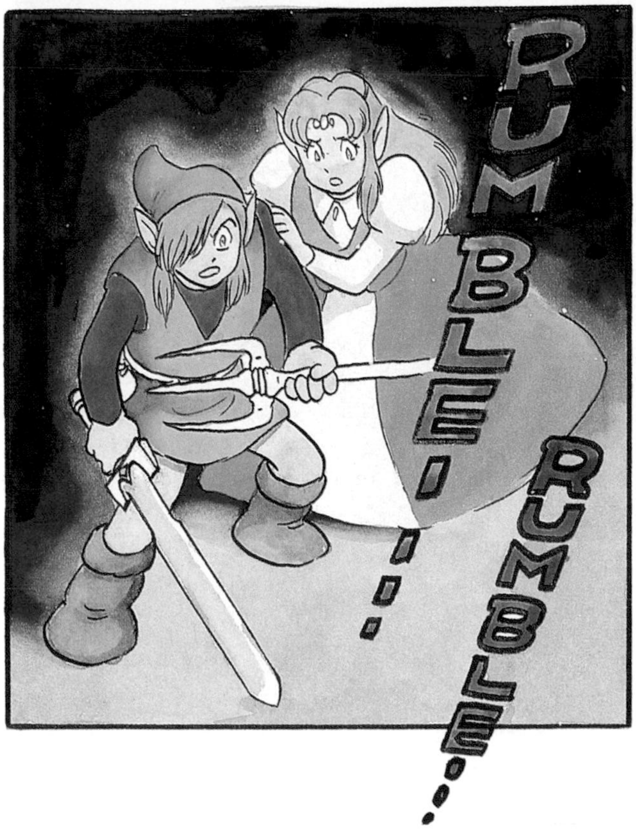
RUMBLE...
RUMBLE...

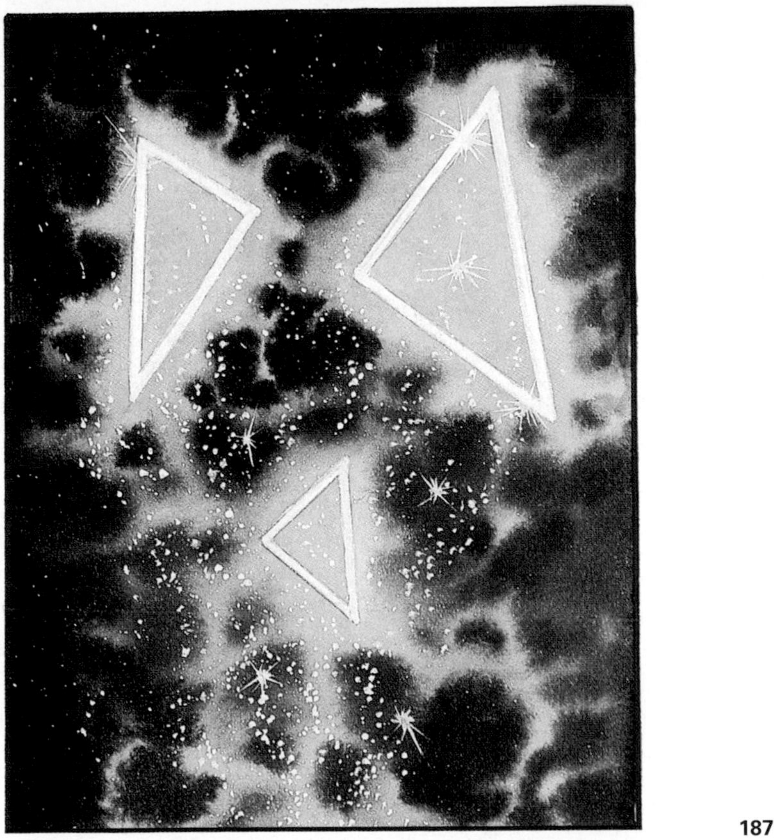

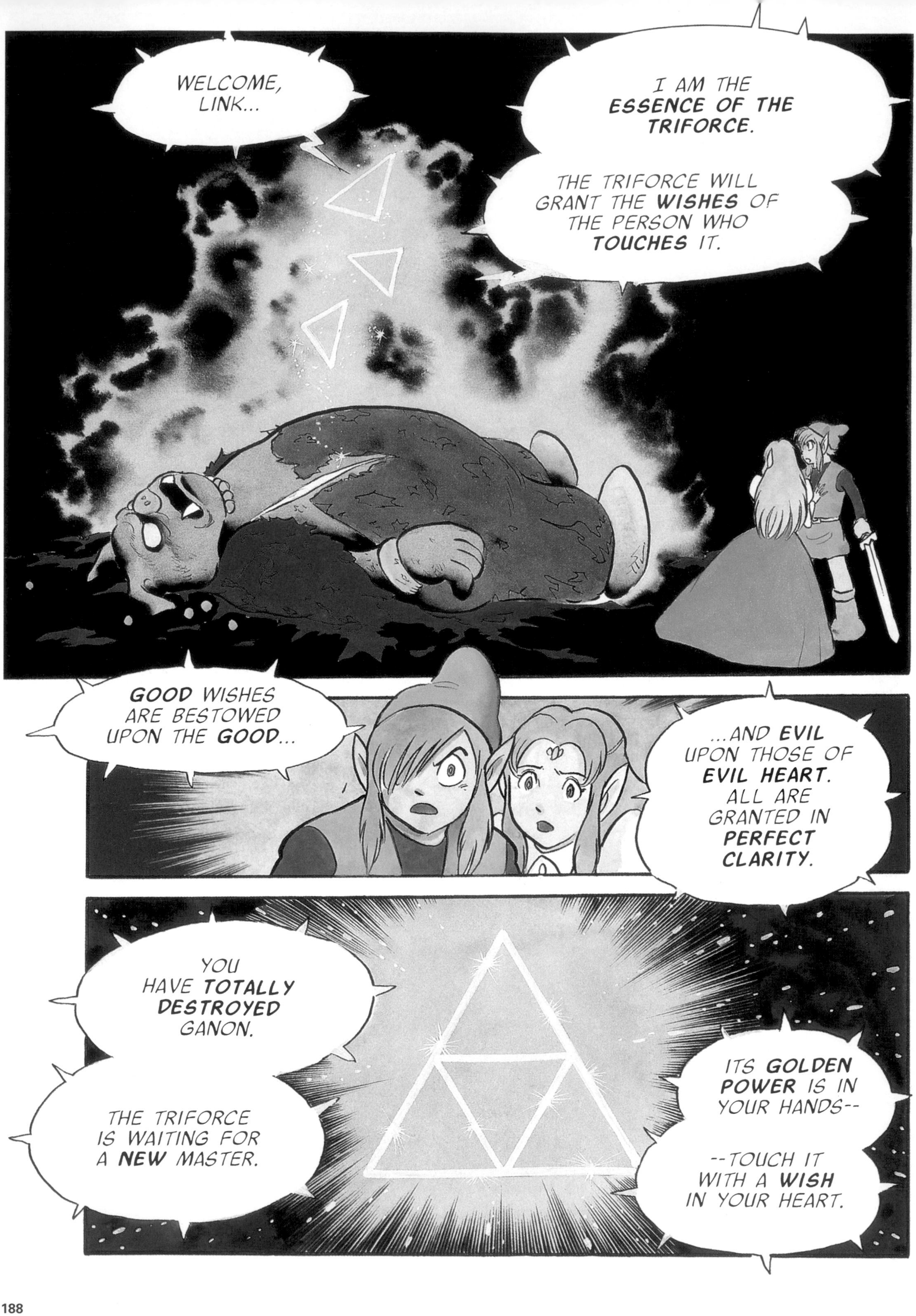

WELCOME, LINK...
I AM THE **ESSENCE OF THE TRIFORCE**.
THE TRIFORCE WILL GRANT THE **WISHES** OF THE PERSON WHO **TOUCHES** IT.
GOOD WISHES ARE BESTOWED UPON THE **GOOD**...
...AND **EVIL** UPON THOSE OF **EVIL HEART**. ALL ARE GRANTED IN **PERFECT CLARITY**.
YOU HAVE **TOTALLY DESTROYED** GANON.
THE TRIFORCE IS WAITING FOR A **NEW** MASTER.
ITS **GOLDEN POWER** IS IN YOUR HANDS--
--TOUCH IT WITH A **WISH** IN YOUR HEART.

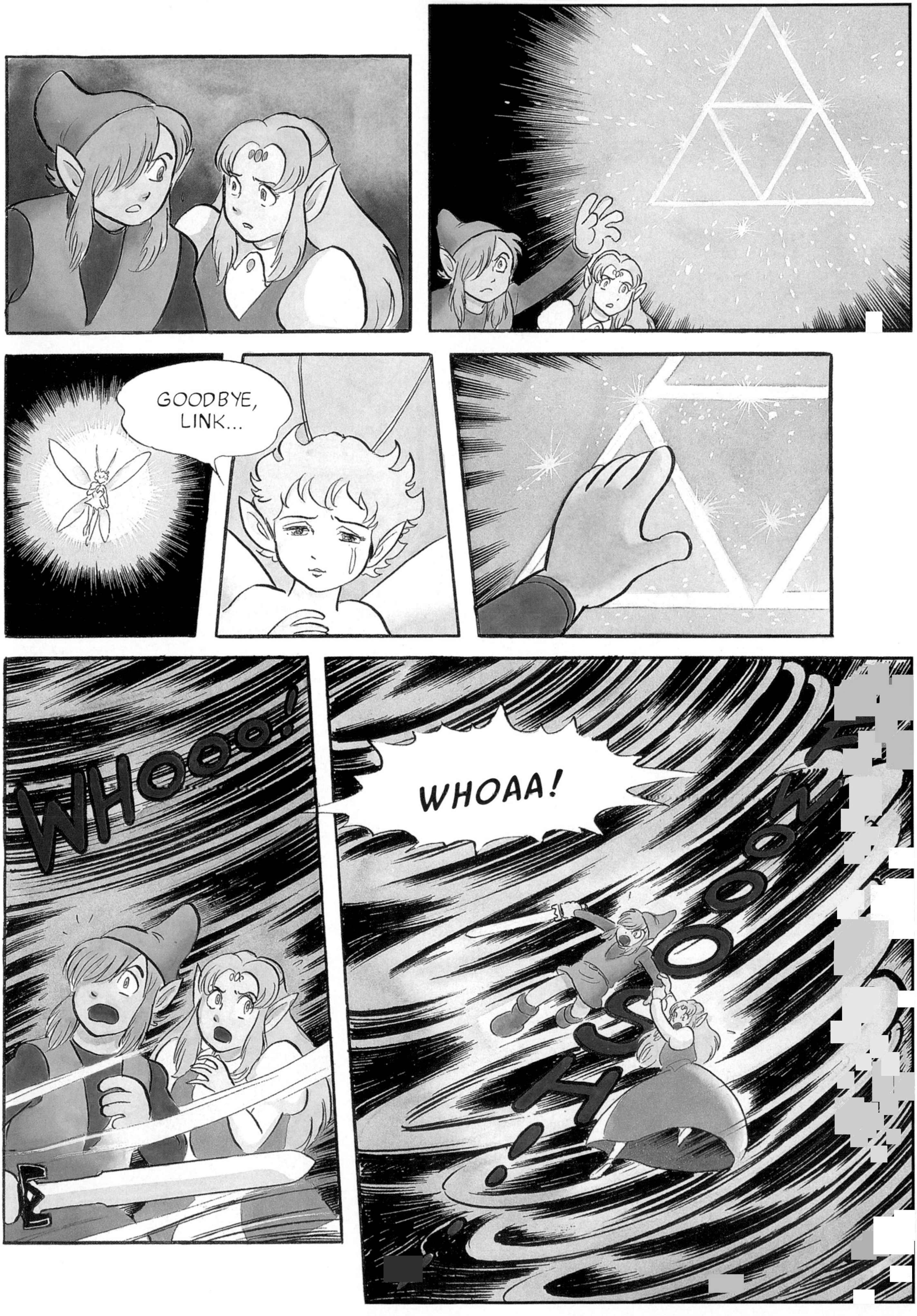
GOODBYE, LINK...
WHOOOO!
WHOAA!
FWOOOOSH!!

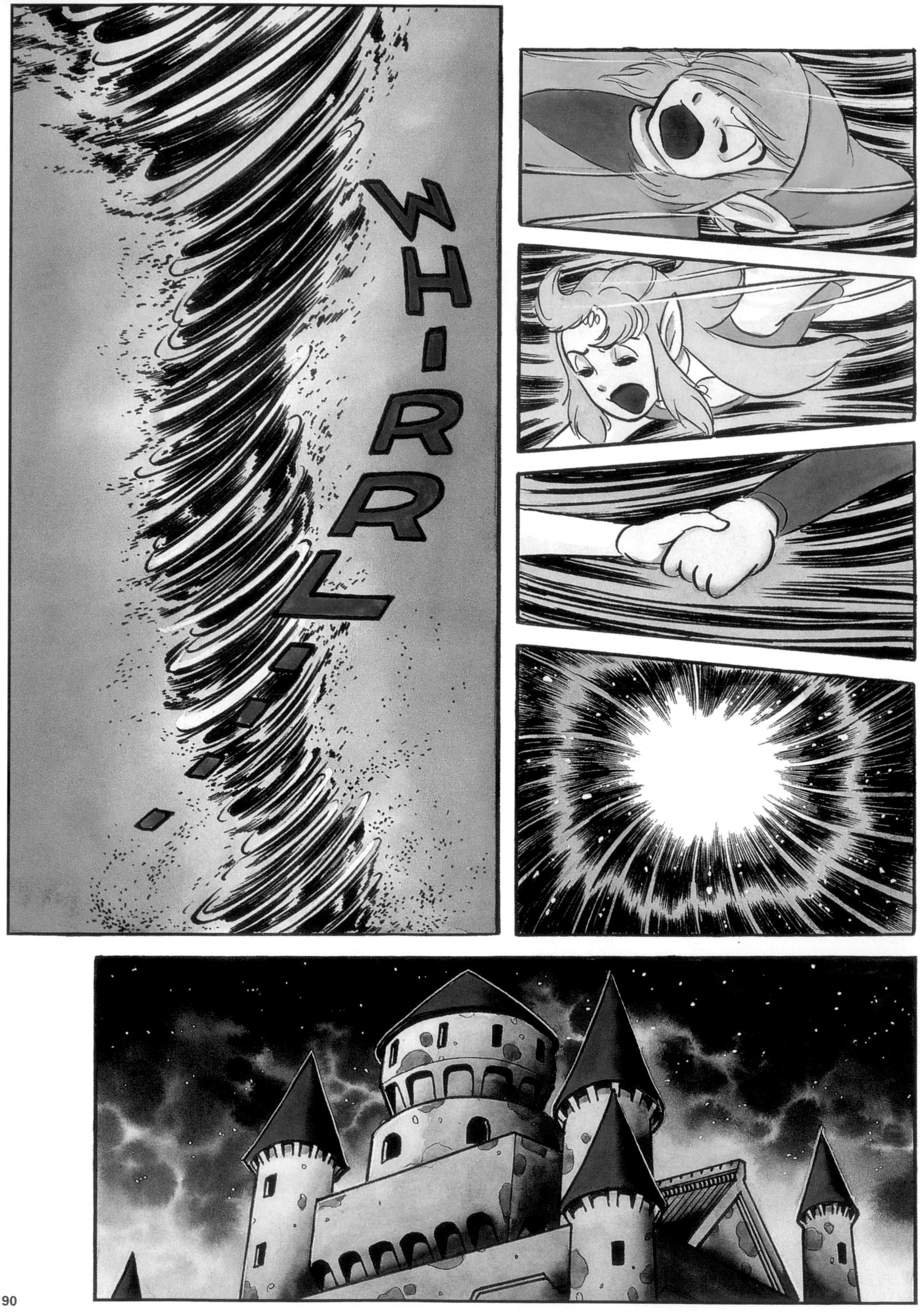
WHIRRL.....

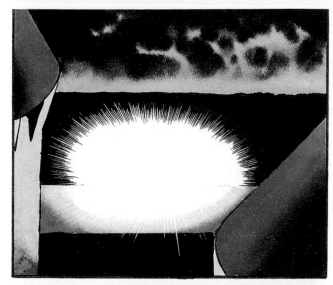

HYRULE, MY HOMELAND!

WE *MADE* IT! WE'RE *BACK!*

LINK...

UNCLE!

FATHER! MOTHER!

YOU HAVE DONE WELL, LINK...

IN THE IMPRISONING WAR OF YEARS PAST, GREAT ARMIES RISKED ALL TO SEAL GANON IN THE DARK WORLD.

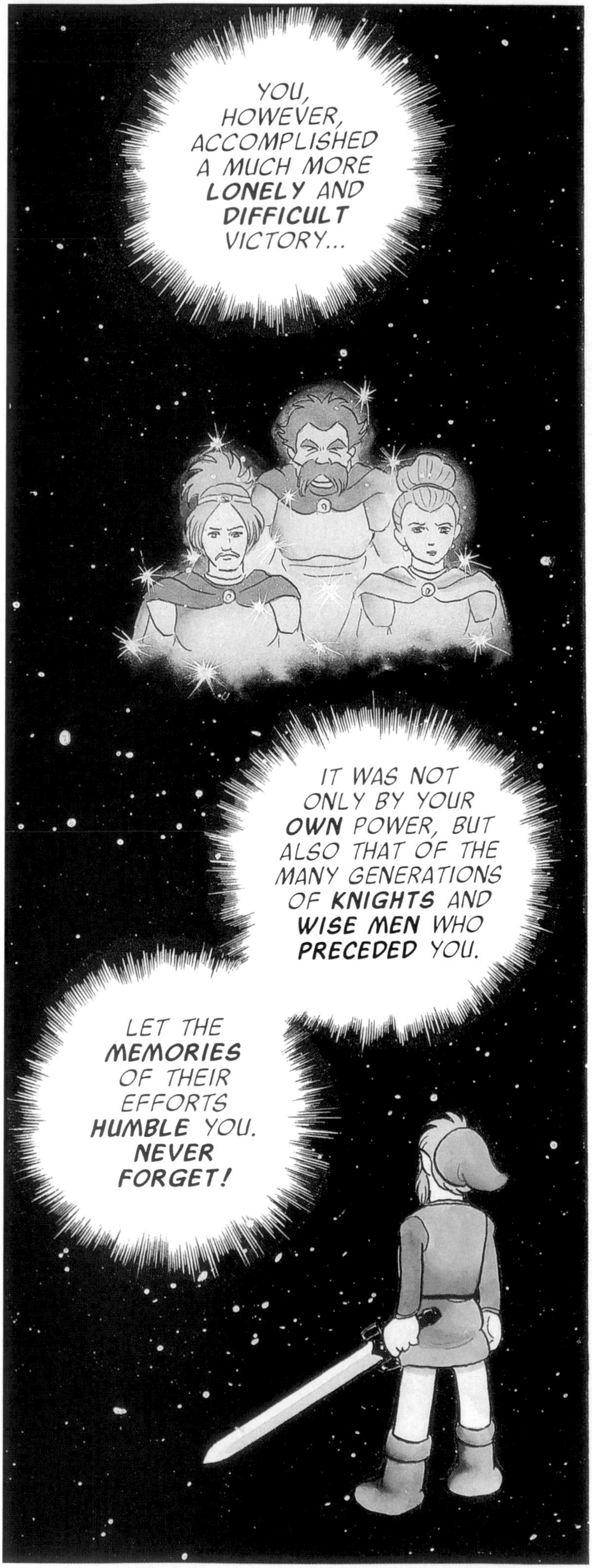
YOU, HOWEVER, ACCOMPLISHED A MUCH MORE **LONELY** AND **DIFFICULT** VICTORY...
IT WAS NOT ONLY BY YOUR **OWN** POWER, BUT ALSO THAT OF THE MANY GENERATIONS OF **KNIGHTS** AND **WISE MEN** WHO **PRECEDED** YOU.
LET THE **MEMORIES** OF THEIR EFFORTS **HUMBLE** YOU. **NEVER FORGET!**

FOLLOWING GANON'S DEFEAT, THE DARK WORLD **VANISHED**, RELEASING MANY WHO HAD BEEN **TRAPPED** THERE IN **MONSTROUS FORM**. THE LONGED-FOR **PEACE** ONCE AGAIN RETURNED TO HYRULE.

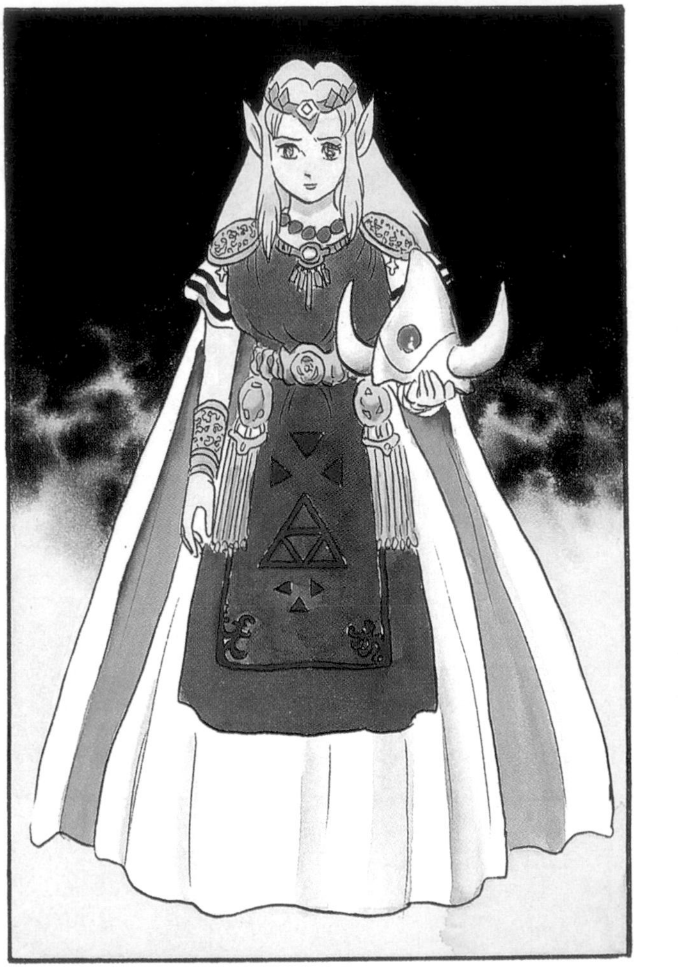

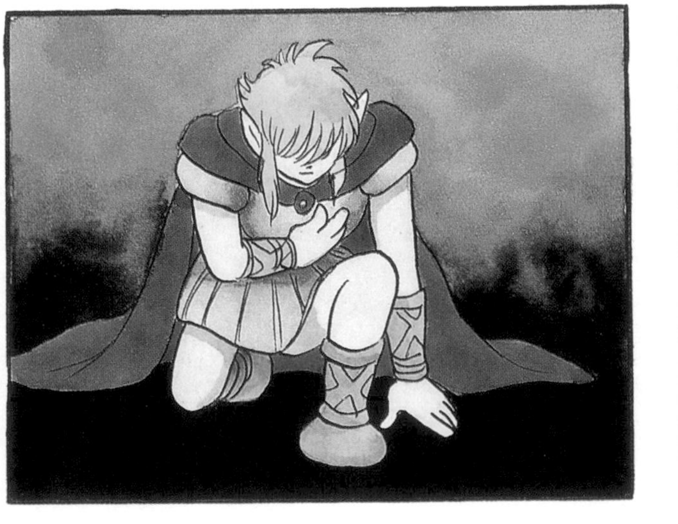

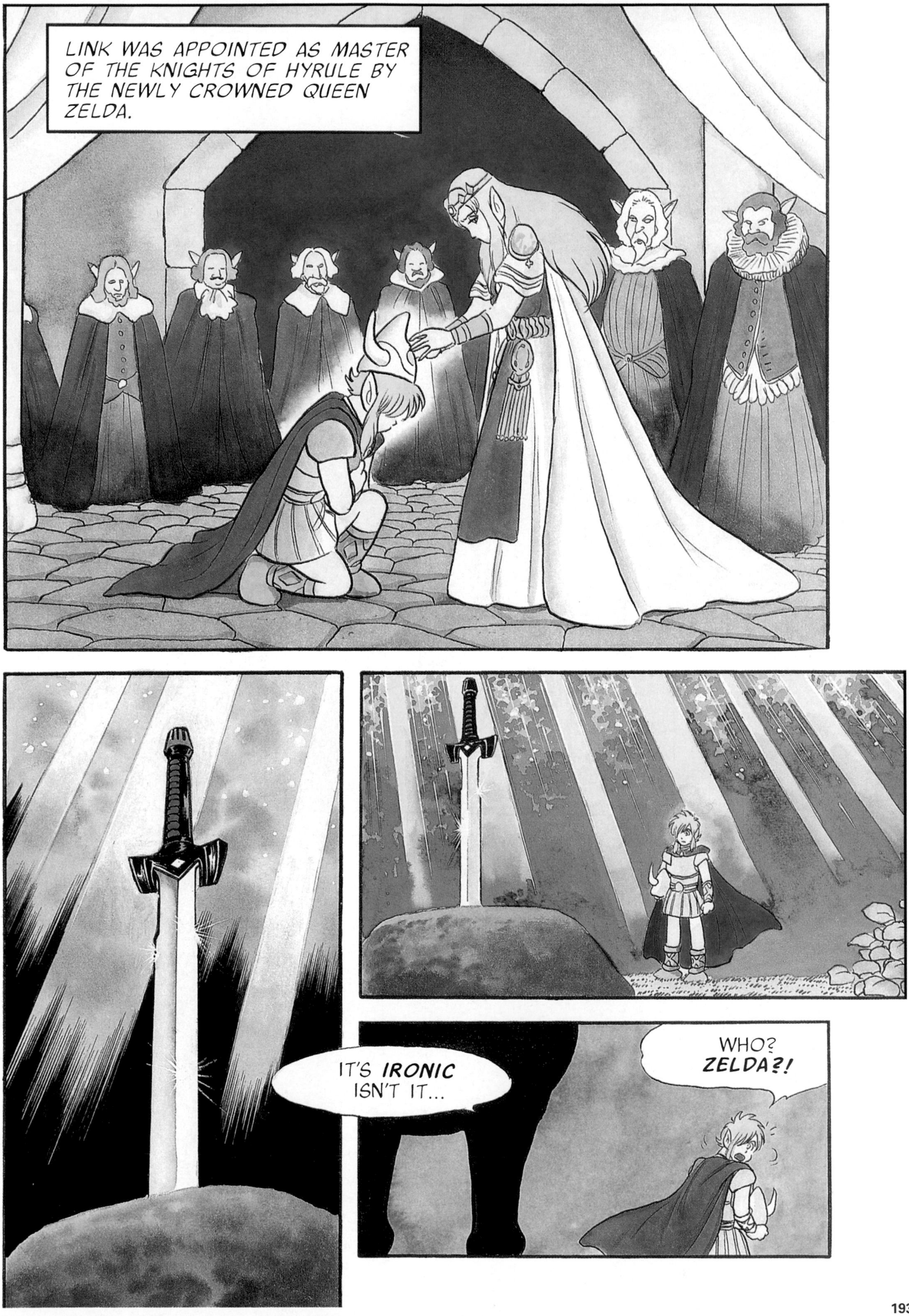
LINK WAS APPOINTED AS MASTER OF THE KNIGHTS OF HYRULE BY THE NEWLY CROWNED QUEEN ZELDA.
IT'S IRONIC ISN'T IT...
WHO? ZELDA?!

THE *PSYCHIC LINK* BETWEEN US WAS SO *STRONG* WHEN I WAS IN GANON'S CLUTCHES...

...BUT NOW THAT WE ARE BOTH *FREE*, AND AT *PEACE*...

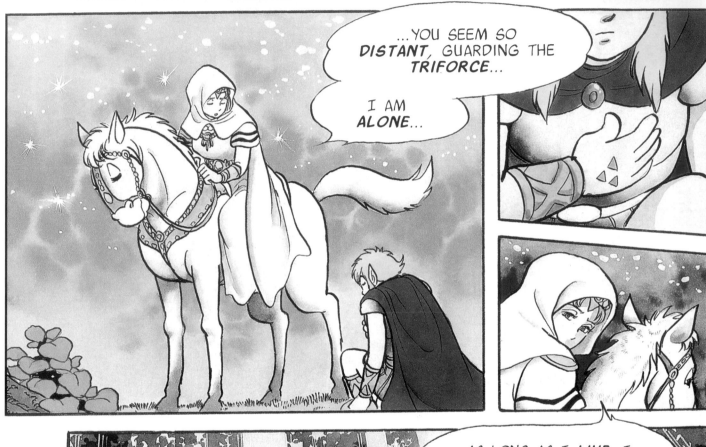

...YOU SEEM SO *DISTANT*, GUARDING THE *TRIFORCE*...

I AM *ALONE*...

AS LONG AS I *LIVE*, I SHALL NEVER *FORGET* THE TIME WHEN WE WERE *TOGETHER* IN OUR *DREAMS*...

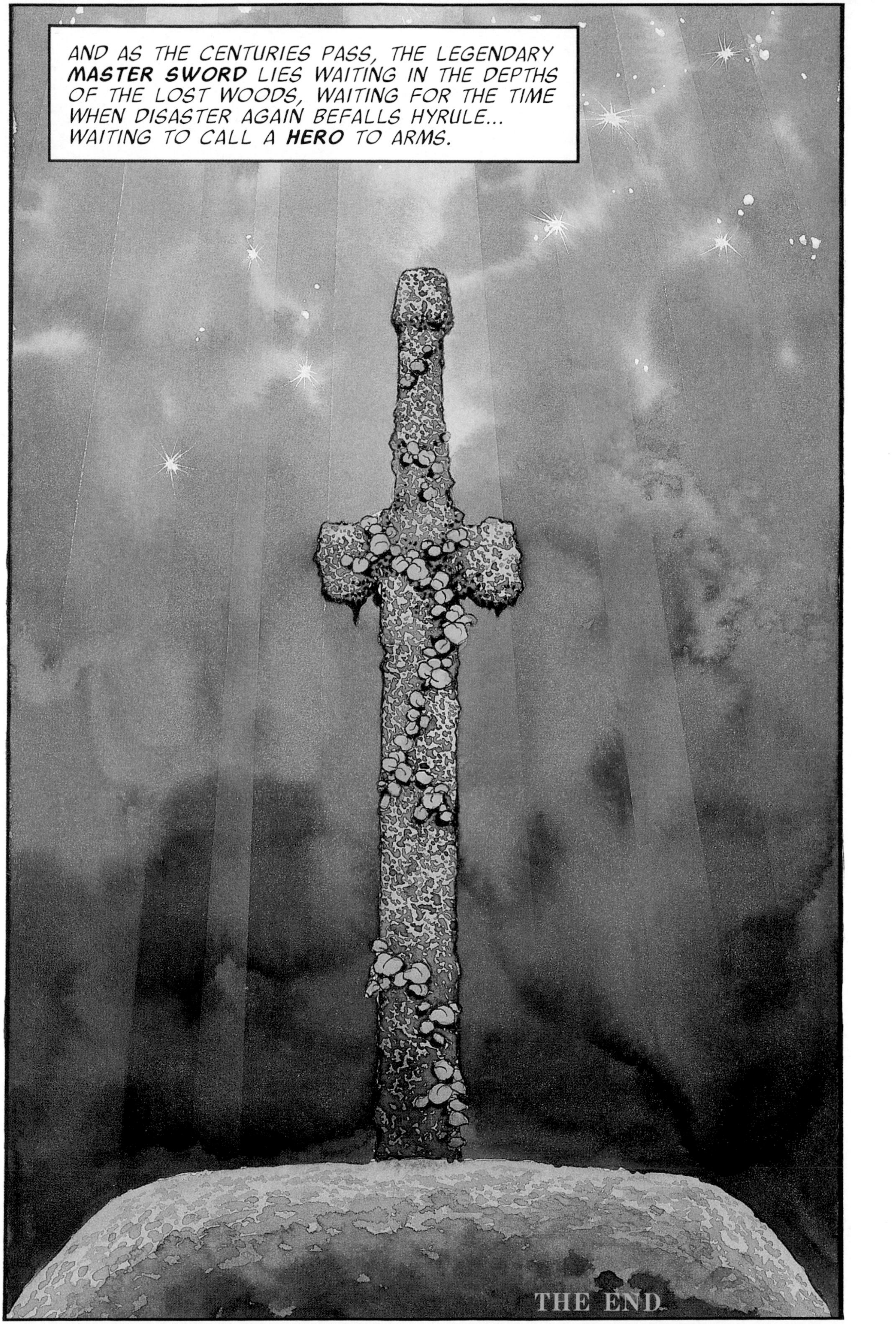
AND AS THE CENTURIES PASS, THE LEGENDARY **MASTER SWORD** LIES WAITING IN THE DEPTHS OF THE LOST WOODS, WAITING FOR THE TIME WHEN DISASTER AGAIN BEFALLS HYRULE... WAITING TO CALL A **HERO** TO ARMS.
THE END

About the Comics

The comics in this book were originally serialized in *Nintendo Power* magazine. The first of twelve parts appeared in January 1992 (Volume 32) and the series ran through December 1992 (Volume 43). Although the story loosely follows the plot of the Super Entertainment System game *The Legend of Zelda: A Link to the Past*, some new twists and characters were added to preserve the element of surprise and add to the dramatic flow.

About the Author

Shotaro Ishinomori is one of Japan's most famous and prolific comic book creators. Among his most popular works are *Cyborg 009, Masked Rider* and *Hotel*. In 2008, Guinness World Records named Ishinomori the world record holder for the "most comics published by one author" for creating more than 770 stories collected in a total of 500 volumes of manga. The Ishinomori Manga Museum in Japan is dedicated to Ishinomori's manga works.